CALIGULA

THE CORRUPTION OF POWER

Anthony A. Barrett

A TOUCHSTONE BOOK
Published by Simon & Schuster
New York   London   Toronto   Sydney   Tokyo   Singapore

Touchstone
Simon & Schuster Building
Rockefeller Center
1230 Avenue of the Americas
New York, New York 10020

1 3 5 7 9 10 8 6 4 2 Pbk.

Library of Congress Cataloging in Publication Data
Barrett, Anthony, date.
Caligula : the corruption of power / Anthony A. Barrett.—1st Touchstone ed.
p. cm.
"A Touchstone book."
Reprint. Originally published: New Haven : Yale University Press. 1990.
Includes bibliographical references and index.
1. Caligula, Emperor of Rome, 12–41. 2. Rome—History—Caligula, 37–41.
3. Roman emperors—Biography. I. Title.
DG283.B37 1991
937'.07'092—dc20
[B]   90-27220
CIP
ISBN 0-671-73849-6Pbk.

CONTENTS

List of Illustrations   vi

Outline of Significant Events   xii

Foreword   xv

1 Family Background   1

2 Struggle for the Succession   17

3 Private Pursuits   42

4 The New Emperor   50

5 Signs of Strain   73

6 Conspiracy   91

7 North Africa   115

8 Britain and Germany   125

9 Divine Honours   140

10 Assassination   154

11 Aftermath   172

12 Caligula and the Jews   182

13 Caligula the Builder   192

14 Fit to Rule?   213

    Appendix 1: Caligula's named victims   242

    Appendix 2: Coins, Inscriptions and Sculpture   244

Notes and References   255

Bibliography   316

Index   329

THE
ILLUSTRATIONS

Photographs between pages 166 and 167

1	The Grand Camée
2	Agrippina Major
3	Gemellus
4	Drusilla
5	Caligula
6	Caligula
7	Caligula
8	Caligula
9–13	Aureii and Denarii
14	Quinarius
15	Sestertius
16–19	Sestertii
20–21	Dupondii
22–24	Asses
25	Quadrans
26	Didrachm
27–28	Drachms
29	Coin of Miletus: unidentified temple
30	Coin of Apamea: Caligula's Sisters
31	Coin of Herod Agrippa: Caesonia

LINE ILLUSTRATIONS

Stemmata

1 The Julio-Claudians   viii–ix
2 The dynastic links of Antonia Minor   25
3 The family connections of Vinicius and Vinicianus   33
4 The family connections of Herod Agrippa   35
5 The family connections of M. Aemilius Lepidus, husband of Drusilla   83
6 The family of Cunobelinus   128

Maps and Plans

1 The Roman world during the lifetime of Caligula   x–xi
2 North Africa   114
3 The North West   124
4 The Eastern Mediterranean   181
5 Ager Vaticanus   197
6 The Palatine Hill   204
7 'Caligula's house'   208

The author wishes to thank Dr Miriam Griffin for permission to reproduce stemma no. 1 from her book *Nero: the End of a Dynasty* and Professor Anthony Birley for permission to adapt map no. 1 from *Marcus Aurelius: a Biography*.

vii

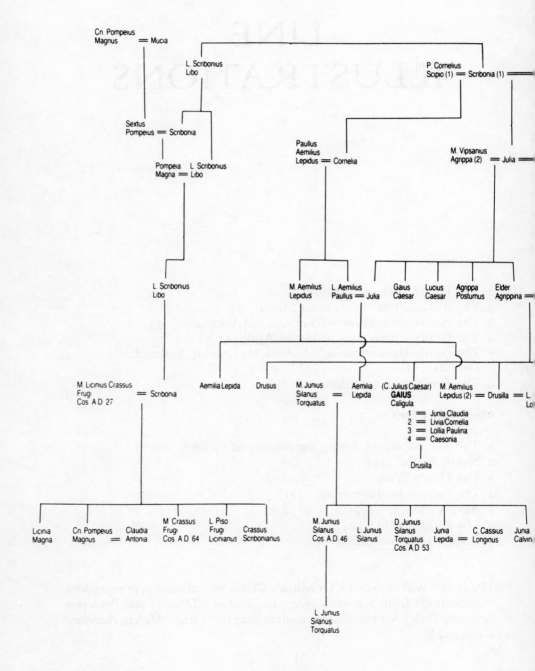

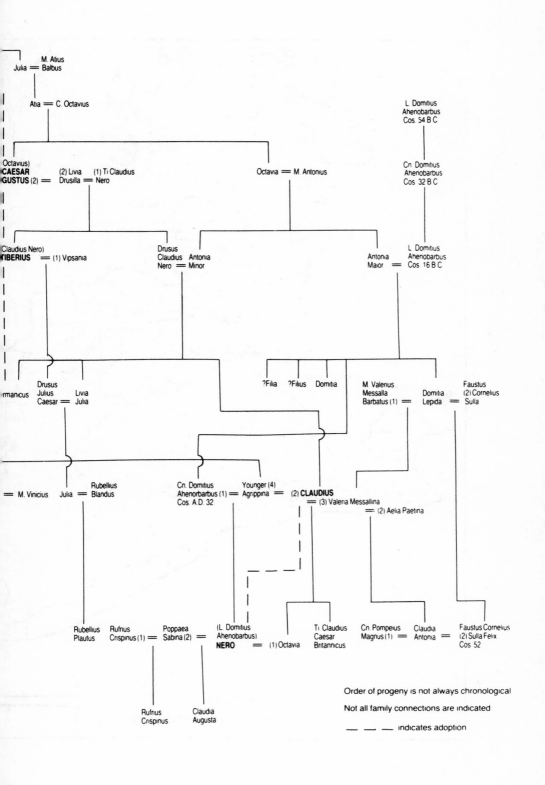

Order of progeny is not always chronological

Not all family connections are indicated

— — — indicates adoption

BRITANNIA

LOWER
GERMANY

Cologne
Bonn CHATTI

Elbe

BELGICA

LUGDUNENSIS

Rhine

Danube

UPPER
GERMANY

RAETIA

NORICUM

Lyon

ALPES

AQUITANIA

Po

Aquileia

PANNONIA

NARBONENSIS

DALMATIA

M

NARBONENSIS

TARRACONENSIS

LUSITANIA

CORSICA

Rome

MAC

BAETICA

SARDINIA

EP

TINGITANA

Iol-Caesarea

Carthage

SICILIA

ACHA

CAESARIENSIS

M   A   U   R   E   T   A   N   I   A

AFRICA

——— Frontier

0

- - - Provincial boundary

0

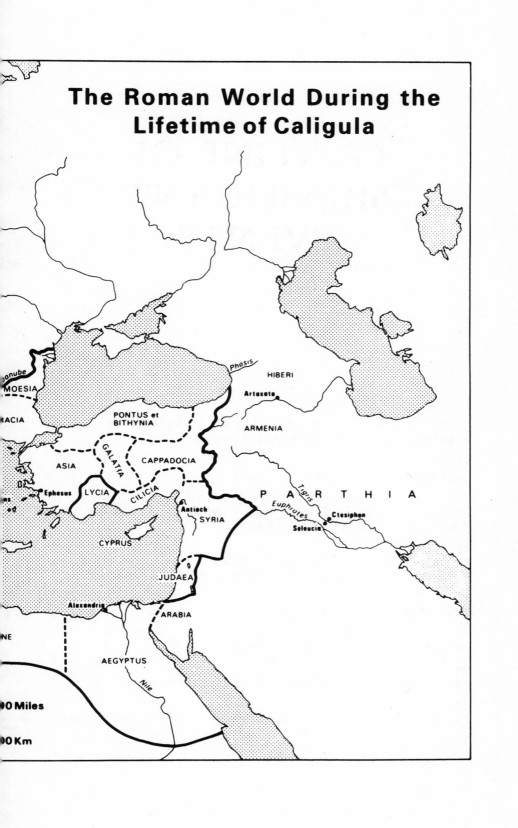

The Roman World During the Lifetime of Caligula

OUTLINE OF SIGNIFICANT EVENTS

Highly speculative dates are indicated by italics. The chronology of events in Judaea in 39 and 40 is particularly uncertain.

12
August 31   Birth of Caligula

14
May 18   Caligula sent to Gaul/Germany by Augustus
August 19   Death of Augustus

17
May 26   Caligula attends Germanicus' triumph in Rome
After summer   Caligula accompanies parents on eastern mission

18
Early in year   Caligula delivers speech in Assos

19
October 10   Death of Germanicus

20
Early in year   Caligula returns to Italy with mother

27
Late in year   Caligula moves to Livia's house on the Palatine

29
Before June   Livia dies

Caligula moves to house of Antonia

31

Before October	Death of Nero (brother)
After August 31	Caligula summoned to Capri
October 18	Sejanus falls

32   Flaccus appointed Prefect of Egypt

33   Caligula made quaestor
Caligula marries Junia Claudia
Deaths of mother and Drusus (brother)

35   Tiberius names Caligula joint heir with Gemellus

36   Arrival of Herod Agrippa in Capri

37

Early in year	Vitellius reaches a settlement with the Parthians
March 16	Death of Tiberius
March 18	Caligula hailed as Imperator by Senate
March 28	Caligula enters Rome
March 28 or 29	Caligula granted powers by senate
April	Caligula recovers remains of mother and Nero
April 21	Formal confirmation of Caligula's powers
May 1	Death of Antonia
July 1	Caligula enters first consulship (for two months)
August 30/31	Dedication of Temple Augustus
September 21	Title of Pater Patriae granted by senate
After September 21	Caligula falls ill
Late October	Caligula recovers
Near end of year	Deaths of Gemellus and Junius Silanus
	Caligula marries Livia/Cornelia

38

In course of year	Abolition of sales tax
	Restoration of elections to people
Early in year	Death of Macro and wife
June 10	Death of Drusilla
August	Arrival of Herod Agrippa in Alexandria
	Disturbances in Alexandria
September 23	Consecration of Drusilla
shortly later	Caligula marries Lollia Paulina
October	Flaccus arrested and banished
October 21	Fire in the Aemilian district

39

January 1	Caligula enters second consulship (30 days)
early in year?	Caligula denounces the senate
	Restoration of maiestas charge
Spring?	Marriage to Caesonia
One month later	Birth of Drusilla (daughter)

xiii

Summer	Bridge at Baiae
	Imperial control of Legio II (Africa)
After September 3	Consuls removed from office
Before October 27	Prosecution of Sabinus, governor of Pannonia
	Execution of Lepidus
	Departure of Caligula for Mevania
	Gaetulicus (and Lepidus) exposed
	and probably executed
	Galba appointed to Upper Germany
	Agrippina and Livilla (sisters) banished
	Caligula departs for the North
After October 27	Further maiestas trials in Rome
	Caligula meets first senatorial deputation in Lyons
Winter of 39/40	Alexandrian envoys leave for Rome
	Disturbances at Jamnia

40

January 1	Caligula enters third consulship (12 days)
Early in year	Caligula joins Rhine armies
	Caligula receives surrender of Adminius at Channel
Early in year	Ptolemy summoned to Rome
Spring?	Petronius ordered to place statue in Temple at
	Jerusalem
May	Caligula receives second senatorial delegation
End of May	Caligula in vicinity of Rome
	First meeting with Alexandrian deputation
Summer	Caligula in Campania
Summer	Meeting with Herod Antipas
	Return of Herod Aggrippa to Rome
	Ptolemy executed in Rome
	Rebellion in Mauretania
August 31	Entry into Rome, and ovation
After August 31	Second meeting with Alexandrian deputation
	Imposition of new taxes in Rome
Late in year	Execution of suspected conspirators

41

January 1	Caligula enters fourth consulship (6 days)
Late January	Assassination during Ludi Palatini

54

October 13	Death of Claudius

68

June 9	Death of Nero

FOREWORD

THE EMPEROR COMMODUS is said to have put a man to death simply
for reading Suetonius' *Life of Caligula*. The punishment may seem
excessive, but it is probably safe to say that of all the emperors of ancient
Rome none, with the possible exception of Nero, surpasses Caligula's
reputation for infamy, and Nero, it must be pointed out, had fourteen years
to perfect his image, against Caligula's modest four. The quintessential mad
despot, Caligula has inspired plays, films, several series for television. Yet
while the public at large seems to find him irresistible, academic
biographers have tended to give him a wide berth. Nor is this surprising.
The loss of the relevant books of the most important ancient commentator
on the Julio-Claudian period, the historian Tacitus, means that we have
to rely for our information on markedly inferior sources, in particular
the late historian Dio and the biographer Suetonius. Their evident bias
is not the main problem. Scattered references to Caligula made by Tacitus
in the context of other emperors make it clear that his account must have
been no less hostile than those that have survived, and in any case
allowance can always be made for prejudice. A much more serious
difficulty is that much of the surviving material is anecdotal and trivial,
often in the form of the emperor's intentions, rather than his actual deeds,
and generally presented with such little coherence that even a simple but
reliable reconstruction of chronological events still largely eludes us. As
a consequence, most surveys of Caligula's life, more popular on the
continent than in the English speaking world, have tended to avoid
critical analysis and to limit themselves essentially to paraphrased selections
of Suetonius and Dio.

The biographical format imposes undeniable limitations on the serious
study of any historical period, and it might well be asked why Caligula
of all emperors should merit one in any case. His reign was exceptionally
brief, shorter, for example, than those of Galerius (six years), or Crispus
(nine), or Licinius the First and the Second (twenty three between them),
emperors who have suffered general neglect and whose names remain
obscure. Moreover, he had no profound views on government, as far as
we can tell, and represents no major historical trend. There is, of course,

a simple, immediate response to the question. Whether perversely or not, the literate reading public finds the life of Caligula interesting, while it stubbornly persists in showing little or no interest in Probus, Galerius or the like. Since the interest exists, it should be met by a sober study that takes account of up to date research and the latest archaeological developments. The result might be no more than an approximation of the actual events, more so than most political biographies, but it should, at least, be motivated by a serious attempt at academic truth, rather than by mere commercial sensationalism.

Quite apart from the need to serve the lay public, however, it would be a mistake to dismiss Caligula's reign as historically insignificant. Events with far-reaching consequences occur in this period. Caligula formulated the plans for the conquest of Britain, put into effect by his successor two years later. His reign saw the first serious outbreak of anti-semitism in the Roman world. Most important of all, he was the first Roman emperor in the full sense of the word, handed by a complaisant senate almost unlimited powers over a vast section of the civilized world. The manner of his accession established a pattern that was to be repeated through the next four centuries. If Caligula teaches us any lesson, it is perhaps that history seems to teach us nothing. The Roman senate soon came to regret that they had so enthusiastically handed over supreme power to a personable but totally inexperienced young man. Less than fifteen years later they went through almost the same ritual, and endured under Nero an extended reprise of what they had already suffered.

A biography should perhaps answer one basic question. What sort of person is its subject? Unfortunately, in the case of Caligula this is not easy to answer. To the ancient sources he was a destructive monster. The opportunistic philosopher Seneca, seeking to curry favour with the emperor Claudius, assured him that his predecessor had 'wasted and utterly destroyed the empire'. This is patently untrue. Under Caligula the Roman provinces seem to have enjoyed stable and orderly govern-ment: the frontiers were secure, the Romans had worked out a *modus vivendi* with their arch-rival Parthia and the German incursions into Gaul had been stemmed. Also, it is clear that many individual senators did very well under Caligula, despite their desperate attempts to doctor the record afterwards. Even the most diehard critics of Caligula will admit that there are some things that do not add up about our picture of his reign. He supposedly cut a ridiculous figure in leading his troops personally into battle (no emperor had taken to the field in over fifty years). Yet two years after his death, Claudius repeated the gesture, and rode out at the head of his army in Britain. Caligula supposedly left Rome utterly bankrupt. But, again, his successor found the treasury so healthy that he could abolish taxes and engage in expensive building projects. Caligula is said to have the blood of his people on his hands.

Certainly, the inevitable repression that followed the series of plots against his life is presented with a vividness and gusto that creates the impression of a blood-bath. Yet the public reaction to his assassination was actually anger. Moreover, the list of his named victims is not a long one, and many of those on it do seem, on *prima facie* evidence, to have been involved in plotting against him.

Could the ancient writers have distorted the record so seriously? One passage of Seneca is particularly telling. He describes how Caligula would offer his foot to be kissed, an abominable practice that struck at the very heart of Roman *gravitas* and *dignitas*. On this one occasion, and only this once, Seneca plays fair, and admits that this may not actually be what happened — that there are some who say that the emperor was only showing off his new slippers! This illustrates the enormous task facing the historian, who must make sense from nonsense. If we were to throw out every anecdote about Caligula that looks suspect we would be left with virtually no biography. The great problem is that where the archaeological record is missing also, there are no historiographical tools to enable us to sort out the gems from the dross, beyond basic commonsense and a feeling for what is reasonable, rather arbitrary and personal criteria, which scholars rightly view with some suspicion.

Of course many figures of the past have been badly treated by a hostile historical tradition. But Caligula's case is rather special. It must always be borne in mind that his successor Claudius found himself in a very sensitive position when he came to power. He had become emperor as a result of the incumbent's murder. To avoid setting a precedent, it was important for him to promote the notion that Caligula had died, not because the imperial system was inherently evil, but because Caligula was an inherently evil emperor. Claudius, himself a historian, would have given other historians their lead. He would have been aided and abetted in this by the senatorial 'Quislings', men who had done very well under Caligula but who afterwards would have deemed it in their interest that the historical record should read how they had lived in constant peril of extermination, surviving only by their wits or by the luckiest twists of fate. It would be paranoid to suggest that there was a 'conspiracy' to suppress the truth about Caligula. But at the least there would have been little incentive to expand on the few merits that he did possess. Glimpses of these merits are discernible from time to time in the sources, but they are faint indeed.

The two serious analytical studies of his reign as a whole have sought to rectify the impression created by the sources, perhaps going too far the other way in the process. H. Willrich, whose work was published in a series of articles in 1903, saw in Caligula's actions a deliberate and coherent attempt to revert to the Caesarian concept of monarchy and a conscious decision to dismantle the artifical system evolved under

Augustus, and rendered largely inoperative under Tiberius. Caligula, as a descendant of Antony, was well suited for this role. His actions, as viewed by Willrich, are rational and, in their own context, logical, the expression of a consistent political philosophy. Balsdon's *The Emperor Gaius*, published some thirty years later, set out with a more modest and probably more acceptable thesis. To Balsdon, Caligula was intelligent, and consistent in his policies if not always wise in his decisions, and the picture of him as a mad sadist is the result of distortion by the sources. There is much that is attractive in Balsdon's readable study, but, as will soon become apparent, on many points the present work takes issue with him. In his zeal to be fair to his subject, Balsdon has perhaps been too charitable.

This book was undertaken without *parti pris*, and without preconceptions. Its primary aim has been to attempt a reconstruction of events. The historian's proper role, of course, is to look beyond the events themselves and to identify significant trends. But the opportunity for this is limited in Caligula's reign. Since any broad generalization will have to depend often on reconstructions that are hypothetical, the process becomes hazardous. It has been speculated, for instance, that the conspiracy of AD 39 might have been prompted by Caligula's marriage to Caesonia in the spring of that same year. This provokes speculation about the dynastic plans of some of the participants, perfectly valid, except it may well be that the marriage took place in the autumn, well after the conspiracy had been exposed, in which case, no matter how brilliant the insights, they will have been totally misdirected. This is a constant and frustrating difficulty of the period, which is not likely to disappear except with the discovery of the lost books of Tacitus' *Annals*. In reconstructing events, I have attempted to resist excessive speculation. Where I have yielded is on some of the key points where the evidence is ambiguous and an author is obliged to take some stand, and where the currently received wisdom is itself based essentially on speculation. In particular I have little in detail to say about Caligula's mental state. Since experts admit the immense difficulty even of person-to-person psychoanalysis it seem to me a self-indulgence to attempt it over a gulf of some two thousand years, and in any case the subject will be systematically treated in Professor A. Ferrill's projected psychological study of Caligula. I have also tried to resist the temptation, to which many have succumbed in the past, of building elaborate theories on the foundations of very casual allusions in the sources.

The conclusions I have reached will surely be dismissed by some (the inevitable fate of any biography of Caligula), but they are where the sources, both primary and secondary, seem to me most reasonably to lead. This is certainly not a revisionist study, and it does not attempt to rehabilitate Caligula. As an individual he was intelligent, as Balsdon suggests, but he was also insufferably arrogant and totally wrapped up in his own sense of importance. He also seems to have lacked any basic sense of moral responsibility. He was quite unsuited either by temperament or training to rule an empire, and probably any one of the 600 or so senators would have done no worse. Unlike Balsdon and Willrich, I see no consistency or coherence in his policies, and little administrative talent beyond an ability to chose subordinates who served him ably and, while he was alive, loyally. The traditional problem of Caligula's reign has been to explain why he descended into autocracy. In my view the great mystery is not why things went wrong, but how any intelligent Roman could possibly have imagined that they could go otherwise. To make an inexperienced and almost unknown young man, brought up under a series of aged and repressive guardians, master of the world, almost literally overnight, on the sole recommendation that his father had been a thoroughly decent fellow, was to court disaster in a quite irresponsible fashion. The Romans may have resented the subsequent burden of autocracy, but it was an autocracy largely of their own making.

In keeping with the tradition of the series of which it is a part, this book is intended to appeal to readers with a general interest in Roman imperial history, as well as to give the specialist some food for thought. To this end Latin and Greek passages have generally been translated in the text, except where context or linguistic similarities make it unnecessary, and technical terms are explained except, again, where ignorance of them should not seriously hamper understanding of the narrative. For the benefit of the general reader it must be emphasized that the illustrated sculpture has been identified by scholars in the past essentially on the basis of subjective judgement, and the attributions must be treated with some caution. Issues likely to be of interest only to the specialist are assigned to appendices at the ends of the chapters. Roman praenomina are given in their full forms in the text (not normally in the footnotes). For the sake of clarity, the technically incorrect name 'Herod' Agrippa is often used of the colourful Jewish ruler. Moreover, the distinctive 'Caligula', rather than 'Gaius', has been deliberately used, on the grounds that in general, as opposed to narrowly academic, practice, that is how perfectly sensible people refer to him, and that is how some of the ancient, albeit less familiar, sources, like Eutropius and Aurelius Victor, refer to him also. Balsdon refrained from using 'Caligula', on the grounds that the emperor found the name 'undignified and insulting'. He thereby manifested an old world courtesy which I feel his subject had hardly merited, and which I do not try to emulate. For what it is worth, the same emperor, according to Seneca, was insulted to be called Gaius. He was clearly not an easy man to please.

The attempt to meet a fairly wide readership presents a number of inevitable drawbacks. Some of the information that is provided will seem elementary and superficial to the specialist. The first two chapters, in particular, contain some very basic information, meant to offer a summary of events from the rise of Augustus to the accession of Caligula. This kind of background material is essential for the non-specialist, but unfortunately must summarize in brief paragraphs, without lengthy comment, issues that are highly complex and often very controversial, and may seem like a potted history of the period, at times with little direct reference to Caligula. For this, and for what might seem an almost Plautine habit of repeatedly identifying my characters (who at times all seem to the lay reader to have the same name), I plead the specialist's indulgence.

The usual inconsistencies abound. Large, imprecise, distances are expressed in 'miles', since that is what the idiom of the language dictates. But in accordance with modern practice the metric system is used to define precise archaeological descriptions. It is also one of the curiosities of our language that we speak of Marc Antony but Marcus Agrippa, use the modern terms for, say, Naples and Mainz, but prefer the ancient ones of Bononia (Bologna) and Puteoli (Pozzuoli), and tend to flip back and forth between Lugdunum and Lyons, Tibur and Tivoli. This book follows no rules beyond the author's own perception of current use.

At the heart of any study of Caligula's reign is the problem of the literary sources. While the subject may not appeal to the general reader, it simply can not be ignored, and a brief outline of the issues is essential. Moreover, many of the events of Caligula's reign were shaped over fifty years earlier, when Augustus transformed the way Rome was governed, and at least an elementary acquaintance with the settlement he established is essential for an understanding of the Julio-Claudian period. The paragraphs that follow are the briefest possible introduction to the two subjects, and may safely be skipped by anyone claiming even an nodding acquaintance with Roman history and historiography.

The Literary Sources

There are two major surviving contemporary sources for the Caligulan period. Seneca the Younger (before AD 1–65) was a witness to the events of the reign and would have known Caligula personally. He was a philosopher (in the broadest sense) rather than historian, but often drew his *exempla* from recent events and can potentially be a useful source of information. In fact, though he refers to Caligula frequently he provides little of political significance and his allusions to this particular emperor are generally of relatively little positive value, as he was clearly obsessed by personal antipathy. Seneca made a career from obsequious flattery of the living emperors and unfettered vilification of their dead predecessors. He would have good personal reasons for hostility towards Caligula, at both the personal and the political level. He was exiled because of his adultery with one of the emperor's sisters, an affair that may well have had political overtones; moreover, Caligula ridiculed his literary style.

Another contemporary was Philo (about 30 BC–AD 45), a native of Alexandria, who led the Jewish delegation to Rome in 39/40. He has left us two works in Greek which refer to this period, the *In Flaccum* and a work of uncertain title conventionally referred to as the *Legatio*. In both he is preoccupied with Jewish problems and Roman history enters only to the extent that it impinges on Jewish events. Philo is an apologetic writer whose aim is to show his people in the best possible light. He makes no attempt to conceal his hostility towards Caligula and the Alexandrian Greeks, who together share the blame for the troubles of the Jews. Another important, though later, Jewish source, is Josephus (born 37/8), pro-Roman with little sympathy for the extremes of Jewish nationalism, but clearly in complete sympathy with Jewish religious sentiment. His *Jewish War*, the history of the Jewish uprising against Rome in 66-70, with an extensive introduction, was written originally in Aramaic, and Josephus provided an amplified Greek translation, which appeared 75-79. His *Jewish Antiquities* was apparently written from the outset in Greek, dealing with the history of the Jewish people down to the outbreak of the war. It appeared in 93-4. Josephus provides the most detailed account of any phase of Caligula's reign — the events surrounding his assassination. He wrote at some length on the event because it served an important moral purpose, bringing happiness to the world and saving the Jews from destruction. Unfortunately, for all his moral earnestness, Josephus' version is in places hopelessly confused and riddled with mistakes, some of them the result of his uncritical methods, but many apparently the consequence of his own creativity, since it seems to have been distorted to underscore the moral lesson that it sought to teach. The corrupt state of the manuscripts further compounds the confusion. Balsdon described Josephus as 'in historical judgement the most worthless of our authorities'. It is only fair to add that on more purely Jewish affairs his account is much more valuable.

The most important sources for the reign are, of course, Suetonius and Dio. Gaius Suetonius Tranquillus was born about AD 70, possibly in North Africa. He held a number of appointments under Trajan and Hadrian. The *Lives of the Caesars* is his most famous work, one only of a wide range of topics composed during a prolific career. Suetonius does not claim to write history, and there is no evidence of a broad grasp of major issues in his works. He shows little interest in great public or political matters, unless they reflect on the behaviour of the emperor. One great disadvantage for the modern historical researcher is that he did not adopt a chronological approach and probably took it for granted that the basic outline of events would already be familar to his reader. Although he is capable of serious historical research, making use of original sources such as letters or public records, he is often unreliable. His main failing is not, apparently, that he fabricates material, but rather that he has a tendency to believe, or at least to record, the worst, and is unable to resist colourful anecdotes, expecially if they reflect badly on his subject. He does not seem to have considered it part of his role to assess the validity of rumours but merely to record them, and is too keen to accept absurd or scandalous accounts, even where his sources offer reasonable ones. The Elder Seneca's account of Tiberius' death, which seems convincing, is given in the *Life of Tiberius* along with others that are unconvincing, and is not even mentioned in the *Caligula*. In the *Life of Galba* events in Germany are presented as a brilliant feat of arms, while in the *Life of Caligula* they are part of an absurd farce.

Cassius Dio was a provincial aristocrat of Nicaea in Bithynia, the son of a consular, who held the consulship himself in 222 and 229. His history, written in Greek, seems to have covered the period from the early kings down to Severus Alexander. It displays little interest in deep analysis and is essentially a compilation of facts, with little scope for theorizing or judgement. Where he expresses an opinion it tends to be relevant only for the specific issue at hand, and he provides no coherent body of political ideas. He rarely cites his literary sources, and never does so in the Caligula chapters. Like Suetonius he makes little effort to distinguish between hostile and favourable sources, between the plausible and the absurd. His account of Caligula takes up Book 59 of his history. Unfortunately there is a gap in the middle and a quaternion of the MS from the end of Book 59 to the beginning of Book 60 is lost. For most of AD 40 we have to depend on the epitomes made by Johannes Xiphilinus in the eleventh century and of Johannes Zonaras in the early twelfth. The epitomators (especially Xiphilinus) have a tendency to select rather than summarize, so that some of the important narrative is lost entirely, such as the incorporation of the provinces of Mauretania in AD 40, mentioned only in the index.

Dio's great value is that he is the only source to treat Caligula's reign in an annalistic form, although his scheme is far from rigid. He will sometimes treat issues thematically, out of chronological context. Thus Caligula's leanings towards self- deification are treated under the year 40, but include incidents that must belong to an earlier part of the reign. It might be expected that Dio as an annalistic historian rather than biographer would be less prone to gossip and distortion than was Suetonius. In fact, this is not so. By contrast with Suetonius, who lists a number of worthy achievements of Caligula 'the princeps', as opposed to his excesses as 'monster', Dio is grudging when it comes to giving the emperor any credit for his achievements, and even condemns some that Suetonius classifies as statesmanlike. In his general desire to exaggerate his cruelty, Dio seems to take liberties with the facts. Under 37, for instance, he says that Caligula punished those who had plotted against his mother and brothers. Then he places in 38 the convictions of the same people, on the basis of documents assumed destroyed earlier. But under 39 we are told that in that year Caligula presented the evidence on the cases before the senate and the persecutions began.

Both Dio and Suetonius embellish and exaggerate. Suetonius tells us, for example, that when the cost of providing cattle to feed the wild beasts became prohibitive Caligula used criminals to feed them, without discriminating according to the charge. In its bare essentials this is probably the true story. It reappears in a different form in Dio, who likes to emphasize the theme of indiscriminate cruelty. He claims that when there was a shortage of criminals to be given to the wild beats Caligula ordered that the unfortunate spectators standing near the benches be seized and be thrown to them. To make sure that there would be no complaint he ordered that their tongues be cut out. The story is recycled in yet another form by Suetonius, who was particularly sensitive to mistreatment of equestrians. He asserts that when a Roman knight was about to be thrown to the beasts he protested, and so had his tongue cut out before he was sent to the arena. Underlying these stories is the brutal but traditional Roman penalty of *damnatio ad bestias*, for which there were precedents going as far back as Scipio Africanus, who after his victory over Carthage threw deserters and runaway slaves to the beasts. The practice was continued until at least Constantine, who disposed of his German prisoners in this way. Caligula probably behaved no better or worse than his successors. Claudius made use of this form of punishment, as did Nero in the famous persecution of the Christians after the fire of Rome. The story thus indicates how unreliable in their details such anccedotes are, and also how the events distorted in them have to be seen within the framework of Roman traditions.

The Augustan Settlement

The second topic requiring some preliminary consideration is the Augustan settlement. The battle of Actium in 31 BC left Octavian (later, Augustus), the adopted son of Julius Caesar, in effective control of the political and military affairs of Rome. For ambitious Romans the traditional career structure of the old republic still, however, existed, even if it no longer led to the excercise of real political power. The chief legislative and deliberative body continued to be the senate, which in this period consisted essentially of some 600 former magistrates of the rank of quaestor or higher. A man could become quaestor in his twenty-fifth year. Twenty were elected annually, concerned generally with financial matters. The quaestorship could be followed by one of two offices, that of aedile, concerned with certain aspects of municipal administration, or tribune, appointed originally to protect the interest of the plebeians, but in the imperial period concerned mainly with minor judicial matters. The quaestorship would often, however, be followed directly by the next office in the strict hierarchy, and the first of major importance, the praetorship (twelve elected annually, at least five years after the quaestorship), which brought responsibility for the administration of justice, and also for the organization of the public games. Eventually, at the legal age of forty-three a man could enter one of the two consulships. Many of the consuls' old functions had been taken over by imperial officials, but they did retain certain important responsibilities, such as the presidency of the senate. The post remained prestigious, and no more than half who embarked on a senatorial career could hope to attain it.

Consuls and praetors excercised a special power — *imperium*, and after their term of office they would often be granted a 'province', which by the Augustan age generally meant a specific territory organized as an administrative unit. In their provinces they continued to exercise their *imperium* 'in the capacity of' their earlier offices, that is *proconsule* or *propraetore*. In early 27 BC Octavian gave up the powers he had assumed, and he placed his provinces at the disposal of the senate to dispense, theoretically, as they thought fit. They in turn granted him an enormous province, embracing, as its core, Gaul, Syria and most of Spain, known for convenience as the 'imperial provinces', for a period of ten years, with provision for renewal. It was in these areas that, with some exceptions, the Roman legions were stationed, and since Augustus, as he was known from then on, personally appointed the commanders (*legati*), he was in effect the commander in chief of the Roman army. The privilege of the 'Triumph', the great military parade through Rome that followed a victory of a commander in the field gradually became the prerogative of the emperor and his family. In very general terms, although the division was not rigid, the senate looked to the administration of the remaining 'senatorial' provinces, strategically of less significance and governed by ex-praetors and ex-consuls chosen by lot. Egypt had a special status, ruled as a sort of private imperial domain by Augustus in his capacity as successor of the Ptolemies.

Augustus held a consulship continually from 31 BC on. This, as he recognized, blocked the career prospects of ambitious contemporaries, and also reduced the number of potential administrators of consular rank. Accordingly, he resigned the office after 23 BC, to hold it again on only two occasions. Moreover, from 5 BC it became routine for the consuls to resign at least half way through the year, to make way for replacements 'suffects', thus further increasing the supply of men of proconsular rank.

In compensation for giving up the consulship in 23 BC, Augustus was granted proconsular *imperium maius* for life, which, being *maius* ('greater'), prevailed in the senatorial as well as in the imperial provinces; moreover it was valid not only in the provinces but within the city of

Rome also. In the same year, he assumed the traditional authority of the tribunes, the *tribunicia potestas*. This gave him certain legal rights, to convene the senate and assemblies of the people, to initiate legislation and to exercise a veto. Even more importantly, it conferred on him *sacrosanctitas*, a significant element in the evolving notion of the princeps as one meriting exceptional awe and reverence.

While the Roman noble families, previously the dominant force in Roman political life, might resent the changes wrought by Augustus, and look back with nostalgia at the old republic, for many Romans the imperial period was the opening of opportunities. This applied in particular to the equestrian class. They occupied the second rank of the Roman social and economic hierarchy (not the nobility, which required a higher (curule) magistracy, if not a consulship, in one's family background), and constituted essentially the financial and mercantile class. They had, with minor exceptions, been largely barred from service to the state and were now given new opportunities for administrative duties. At the apex of their career stood the four major Prefectures of Egypt, the Praetorian Guard, the Annona (corn supply) or the Vigiles (city police).

The structure was, with some modifications, still in force in the Caligulan period, when the careful balances put in place under Augustus were to be subjected to their severest test. History records that despite Caligula's best efforts, the system would long survive him!

The most pleasant task in a project of this type is to record the generous assistance of friends and colleagues. Like many others, I find myself particularly indebted to Graham Webster, who has provided steadfast help and guidance from the outset. Henry Hurst has kept me regularly informed on his excavations in the Roman forum and kindly shared his tentative thoughts prior to the final overall interpretation of the site. A number of scholars have offered guidance on specific issues, eiher in corespondence or in discussions, and I thank in particular John Casey, Paul Gallivan, Roger Ling, Peter Wiseman, Brooks Levy and Ian Carradice. Duncan Fishwick has been extremely helpful on a number of points in the text, particularly the problems of emperor worship. My colleagues in Vancouver, James Russell and Hector Williams, have kept me informed of recent archaeological thinking, and I have also much benefited from the lively comments of our graduate students, especially Sandra Duane, Lindsay Martin and Kathy Sherwood. On the technical side I am grateful to Margaret Milne for drawing the maps, and to Olga Betts for help with the more complicated aspects of moving the material about on computers. My family has been a constant source of support and encouragement. Doreen and Jacky read the proofs and offered very frank criticism; Sarah, in addition, helped me in the preparation of the Index. As the manuscript moved slowly to its closing stage Peter Kemmis

Betty displayed an admirable combination of patience, amiability and persistence in getting it to Press.

Much of the research for *Caligula* was undertaken during the tenure of a Visiting Fellowship at Clare Hall in the University of Cambridge, and my task was considerably lightened by the intellectual stimulation and warm collegiality that I experience there.

· 1 ·

FAMILY
BACKGROUND

WHEN THE FUTURE emperor Gaius Caligula was born, in AD 12, he came
into a Roman world that had been dominated by a single individual for
some forty years. The Battle of Actium in 31 BC and the defeat of the combined forces of Marc Antony and Cleopatra brought an end to almost a
century of unrest and political violence. The victor, Octavian (Gaius Julius
Caesar Octavianus), adopted son of the murdered Julius Caesar, emerged
from it as the most powerful figure in the state. In 27 BC he began the process by which the traditional form of the Roman republic could be theoretically restored while he, in practical terms, remained firmly in power. Thus
he resigned the extraordinary powers he had accumulated, receiving
certain others in return, nominally bestowed by the senate and the
Roman people. Augustus, as he henceforth was known, sought to present
his role as that of *princeps* 'first citizen', one magistrate among many
others, with greater powers than they but not inherently superior or different. By holding significant offices concurrently, however, with extensions
of the powers that he held, he effectively controlled political and military
life in Rome and the provinces.

The last century of the republic had seen a succession of powerful military commanders who exploited the loyalty of their troops to further their
own political ambitions. The impossibility of a return to the old republic
had been symbolized by the constitutional appointment in 43 BC of the
'second' triumvirate which handed over effective control of the state to a
partnership of three powerful military figures, Marcus Lepidus, Marc
Antony and Octavian. The eventual emergence of a form of monarchy, no
matter how well disguised to avoid offending Roman sensibilities, was the
inevitable next stage. The change was not necessarily for the worse, since
as compensation for the loss of real political independence, Augustus was
able to offer Rome a period of peace and relative stability.

When he came to power Caligula fell heir to the political and military
order first established by Augustus and nurtured by his successor Tiberius.
Caligula also enjoyed the more personal advantage of a distinguished family background. He was the first of the Roman emperors who could claim
a link by blood-line, rather than simply by marriage or adoption, with
both of the two great families, the Julian and the Claudian, that have given

I

their name to Rome's first dynasty. Through his mother, Agrippina (fig. 2), he could trace a direct link to Augustus. In 21 BC that emperor approved the marriage between his only child, his daughter Julia, and his old comrade-in-arms Agrippa (64/3–12 BC, fig. 24). Although of obscure family origins, Agrippa had proved himself a man of considerable talent and energy, and a loyal supporter of Octavian/Augustus after the murder of Julius Caesar in 44 BC. He was largely responsible for the defeat of Antony at Actium, and had followed this with a number of important military and diplomatic missions, playing a key role also in the great building programme in the city of Rome. Julia, at the time of their marriage, was only eighteen, but already a widow, having previously been married to her cousin Marcellus. This second marriage seems, on the whole, to have proved successful, and she bore Agrippa five children, including Caligula's mother. It was only later in life that Julia began to show a streak of wilful independence, combined with a sharp and cutting tongue, that both her daughter Agrippina and her grandson Caligula appear to have inherited.

Caligula's family history on his father's side was also impressive. His paternal grandfather, Nero Claudius Drusus, came from an ancient and distinguished Roman family, through both Drusus' father and his mother, Tiberius Claudius Nero and the notorious Livia. Both parents belonged to branches of the Claudian family (Livia's name derived from an adoption). Tiberius Claudius Nero, the father, was for a time an opponent of Octavian and was obliged eventually to leave Italy, but made use of a general amnesty to return in 39 BC with his wife Livia and their infant son, the future emperor Tiberius (born 42 BC).

The return was to prove dramatically significant for later history. Octavian became infatuated with Livia and pressured her husband to divorce her, even though she was pregnant. Octavian likewise divorced his own similarly pregnant wife, Scribonia. On 17 January 38 BC, only three days after the birth of her second son, Drusus (Nero Claudius Drusus, the grandfather of Caligula), Livia married Octavian. Her former husband died in relative obscurity in 33 BC, giving over his two sons, Drusus and Tiberius, to the tutorship of Octavian, who took appropriate steps to introduce them to public life, allowing them to enter office before the legal minimum age. Drusus strengthened his bond with Augustus when in about 16 BC he married Antonia, the daughter of Marc Antony and Augustus' sister, Octavia. Antonia was a strong willed and independent woman, widely respected and admired. She bore her husband three children, the promising and highly popular Germanicus (Caligula's father, born 16 or 15 BC), Claudius (born 10 BC), who was lame and sickly, but had common sense and a sharp mind, and would himself go on to become emperor, and a daughter Livilla (born 13 BC), destined to become the mistress of the notorious Sejanus. Through Antonia Caligula could thus trace a second, less direct link with Augustus, and was the first emperor descended from Augustus' arch-enemy, Marc Antony.

When Caligula came to power he saw as one of his priorities the military defeat of the rebellious Germans along the Rhine frontier. He had, in a sense, inherited this task from his grandfather, Drusus, who in a series of brilliant campaigns between 12 and 9, carried Roman arms as far as the Elbe. His death in 11, from a riding accident, plunged Rome into deepest mourning. Drusus' tremendous popularity had been enhanced by his personal affability and charm, as well as the widely held belief that he was determined to push for the return of the old republican system. He was honoured by the posthumous title of Germanicus, which passed also to his descendants. More importantly, he was also to bequeath to his descendants, including Caligula, the belief that the northern frontier was for their family the field of honour, where their place in military history was to be established.

After Drusus' death other commanders continued operations in Germany, which came to an abrupt and disastrous end when the Roman army suffered one of the greatest military defeats of her history. In AD 9 three legions were massacred in the Teutoburg forest and their commander, Varus, committed suicide. The Roman dream of expansion beyond the Rhine had now to be abandoned. Tiberius rushed to the area to organize the Rhine defences and to forestall any invasion of Gaul.[1] Eight legions in all were deployed to defend the frontier, equally divided between the two command districts of Lower and Upper Germany, not strictly speaking provinces but under the overall jurisdiction of the governor of the Three Gauls. Tiberius did his work with great vigour. He returned to Rome in AD 11, and his place in Germany was taken by Drusus' son Germanicus, whose charm far exceeded his talents, and whose popularity would outstrip even his father's.

Germanicus, father of Caligula, was born May 24, 16 or 15 BC.[2] Despite his later fame, virtually nothing is known of his early life before his adoption by Tiberius in AD 4. This adoption represents one of several attempts by Augustus to deal with perhaps the most intractable difficulty of his principate, the succession question, and to this we must briefly turn, since it is an issue that must be understood, at least in outline, as a background to the events that would lead eventually to Caligula's accession. The problem was made especially complex by the fact that Augustus' real position in the Roman state was a personal one and there was no theoretical mechanism by which authority could be handed on to a successor. When in the years immediately following the Battle of Actium special powers were conferred on him he went to great pains to emphasize that they had been granted by the senate, and, in theory, for a limited period of time. On his death the senate could, again in theory, act as it thought fit and bestow the appropriate powers on the most qualified successor. The reality was, of

3

course, quite different. Augustus had based his claim to power on the principle that he was Caesar's son, and the basic drive of human nature would have impelled him to keep the succession in his own line and within the Julian family. It could even be argued that he had almost a responsibility to ensure that one of his own line would succeed, to prevent the clash of rival factions and a renewal of the chaos of the civil wars. His strategy was to associate his designated choice with him as partner in the chief powers of the principate, the proconsular imperium and tribunician power. In this way he could place all of his prestige and position behind his own candidate while in theory leaving the actual decision on whether to confirm and renew these powers to the senate. By 21 BC he had found a solution to the twin demands of responsibility to orderly government and of instinctive familial ambitions. Agrippa divorced his own wife to marry the emperor's daughter Julia, presumably with the idea that while he might control affairs in the event of Augustus' death, power would at least eventually pass to one of emperor's line. The birth of two sons Gaius (20) and Lucius (17) boded well for the plan, and Augustus confirmed their place in the succession by adopting both in 17. By the time of his death in 12 BC, Agrippa had fathered, in addition to Gaius and Lucius, daughters Julia (born about 19) and Agrippina, the mother of Caligula (born about 14), and a third son, AgrippaPostumus, born, as his name indicates, after his father's death, and whose wild behaviour would apparently rule him out as a factor in the Augustan plans. In part to provide a proper upbringing for Gaius and Lucius, Augustus sought another husband for his daughter. His stepson Tiberius was called upon to fill the role, and accordingly divorced his wife, Agrippa's daughter Vipsania, whom he had married in 20/19 BC. He seems to have been genuinely fond of Vipsania, and would come to regret bitterly his marriage (in 11) to the headstrong Julia.

Tiberius had enjoyed a successful military career on the northern frontiers. He held the consulship first in 13 BC, and in 8 assumed the office for a second time, and two years later, a clear sign of Augustus' favour, was granted *tribunicia potestas* and an important mission to the East with proconsular *imperium maius*. But his success was overshadowed by the popular attention now being paid to the emperor's grandson (and adopted son) the young Gaius Caesar. Tiberius was by nature sober and austere, in his true element on campaign with his soldiers, and uncomfortable amidst the intrigue and politics of Rome. He felt, correctly, that Augustus had little affection for him and that at best he would be the successor of last resort. He also knew that Gaius enjoyed a popularity that he could not hope to match. For his own peace of mind, he decided that his best course was to remove himself from the political arena, and he persuaded a reluctant Augustus to allow him to retire to Rhodes. As it turned out he found his life there to be very much that of an exile and he was obliged to humble himself by making repeated requests to be allowed to return.

Permission was finally granted in 2 AD, shortly before Augustus suffered a major blow, when Lucius Caesar died on his way to Spain. Yet another serious setback to his dynastic plans befell him less than two years later, when Gaius died from a wound suffered while on a mission to the East.

At long last, Tiberius was given formal and unequivocal recognition as Augustus' successor. On June 26, AD 4, at the age of 45, he was finally adopted (with Agrippa Postumus) as Augustus' son, and granted *tribunicia potestas*, probably for a term of ten years, as well as a command in Germany.[3] But any pleasure that Tiberius might have felt over this development would have been tinged with humiliation, since he was in turn obliged to adopt his nephew Germanicus, even though he had a natural son, Drusus, probably only two years younger. It is noteworthy that Agrippa Postumus played no part in Augustus' dynastic schemes. He received the *toga virilis* (the token of manhood) in AD 5, but by the following year, it seems, had started to fall into disgrace. His ties with his family were severed and he was eventually sent into permanent exile on the island of Planasia near Corsica. The official reason was his *ferocia* ('beastly nature'), and it is possible that he suffered from some form of mental derangement.[4]

The attitude of the ancient sources towards Germanicus is one of unfettered admiration. Suetonius, who devotes to him a large section of the *Life of Caligula*, claims that he surpassed his contemporaries both in physical and moral qualities, and was a gifted man of letters into the bargain. But despite his supposed achievements he remained modest and considerate, and was immensely popular, partly because it was felt that he had inherited his father's republican leanings. Tacitus compares him to Alexander the Great, saying that if he had ruled he would have outdone him in military achievements just as he surpassed him in personal qualities.[6] These impressions clearly represent a romanticised view of Caligula's father, one that was no doubt fostered among the Roman people by anti-Tiberian elements after his early death. Although a closer inspection of his career reveals serious errors of judgement and even a degree of emotional instability, the reality would prove far less important than the image in fostering the prospects of his son for the principate.

As a clear indication of Augustus' determination to be succeeded by someone from his own line, Germanicus, shortly after his adoption by Tiberius, was married to the emperor's granddaughter Agrippina. Germanicus' new wife possessed the streak of powerful independence that seems to run though many of the women of the Imperial family. Her mother Julia would be controlled neither by her father nor by Tiberius and her behaviour was eventually to lead to her banishment to the island of Pandateria. Agrippina's sister, the younger Julia, who matched her mother's reputation for waywardness, was also condemned to permanent banishment from Rome. Agrippina differed from her mother and sister in that her private life appears to have been beyond reproach. But she showed the same determination to control events rather than to be controlled, the same reluctance to yield to forces far more powerful than herself. Tacitus is well disposed towards her, yet even his sympathetic portrait is marked by phrases like 'excitable', 'arrogant', 'proud', 'fierce', 'obstinate', 'ambitious'. His observations are reinforced by other sources. Suetonius records that her grandfather, Augustus, who had fixed views on moderation and propriety in speech, cautioned his granddaughter not to speak *moleste* ('offensively').[6] This streak of ruthless arrogance contributed very largely to her eventual destruction.

Agrippina was aware that in Imperial Rome a woman could not excercise power in her own right, but she could see in Livia a precedent for the central role that the wife of the emperor could play. While it would be wrong to deny her the normal familial affections, it is hard not to believe that behind her almost fanatical devotion to her family there lurked definite political ambitions. She was to bear Germanicus nine children, six of whom survived infancy. Apart from Caligula there were two other, older, sons, Nero (born about AD 6, and to be distinguished from the notorious emperor), Drusus (about 7/8) and three daughters Agrippina Minor (15), Drusilla (16, Fig 4) and Livilla (17 or 18).[7] The children thus included not only a future emperor, but also, in Agrippina Minor, the mother of yet another, Nero.

Germanicus first achieved distinction serving under Tiberius during the Pannonian revolt, where he showed courage and military skill. In AD 11 he went to Germany to join Tiberius once again. No important successes were recorded in this year, no doubt reflecting Tiberius' cautious policy of consolidating a defensive position rather than engaging in reckless military adventures, and Germanicus returned to Rome no later than the autumn of 11, celebrating his first consulship in the following year.[8] We know little of his term of office, except that he slaughtered 200 lions during the Ludi Martiales.

It was thus during his father's consular year, AD 12, that Gaius (Caligula) was born. The date of August 31 is fixed precisely by both Suetonius and the Fasti.[9] There is less certainty about the place of birth, and Suetonius' discussion of the question is one of the most detailed of its kind in any ancient historian.[10] Suetonius admits that there is conflicting testimony on the question, and lists the suggestions. Gaetulicus, military commander in Upper Germany in Caligula's reign and poet (and destined to be executed by Caligula as a conspirator), wrote that the birth-place was Tibur (Tivoli), Pliny the Elder placed it in Germany, at Ambitarvium among the Treveri, while an anonymous epigram that circulated when Caligula was emperor claimed: 'a baby in the camp, a son in the line, he was sure to be next emperor, it's a very clear sign' (*castris natus, patriis nutritus in armis/ iam designati principis omen erat*).[11] Suetonius is not impressed. He dismisses

Gaetulicus as a flattering liar, then goes on to refute Pliny's evidence. An inscription seen at Ambitarvium referring to Agrippina's delivery, and taken by Pliny to refer to Caligula's birth, could refer to the birth of one of Agrippina's daughters. Unspecified historians of Augustus, Suetonius says, were in agreement that Germanicus did not return to Germany until the close of his consulship (when Caligula was already born). Suetonius provides his own candidate, Antium, and claims that he saw the birth there recorded *in actis*, presumably the Acta Diurna, or record of important public events.[12] Antium (Anzio) had long been a favourite resort of the wealthy Romans, and was much favoured by the Julio-Claudians. Augustus enjoyed living there, and it was the birthplace of the emperor Nero, and of his daughter Claudia Augusta. Suetonius' further argument that Caligula preferred Antium before all other places, and planned to move the seat of empire there, is hardly conclusive, and somewhat anti-climactic. In any case, the latter story was told also of Alexandria. One may wonder why, if the evidence for Antium was so explicit, Suetonius should have been so defensive, and his purpose may have been to show up other historians with a display of his scholarship. It is worth noting that Tacitus, not mentioned by Suetonius (perhaps intentionally), accepts that Caligula was born in the legionary camp (*in castris genitus*).[13]

By at least the end of 12, Germanicus returned to the north, as governor of the Three Gauls, which would have given him overall authority over the eight legions posted on the Rhine. Caligula seems to have stayed in Rome, with his great-grandfather Augustus, in the imperial residence on the Palatine. On 18 May 14, when not quite two, he was sent to join his mother in an unspecified location. Germanicus was at this time engaged in carrying out a census among the Gauls, and because of her pregnancy Agrippina had perhaps remained in Cologne (Oppidum Ubiorum). It is only by assuming that she and her husband were in different locations that we can make sense of the letter that Augustus wrote to her on that occasion, part of which is quoted by Suetonius.[14] In it the emperor expresses his worry about his great-grandson's health and reports that he is sending him in the company of a physician, whom they are welcome to keep. He also expresses the hope that Agrippina will reach her husband in good health (his concern may allude specifically to her pregnancy). On joining his mother in Germany, Caligula seems to have become the favourite of the troops, displaying a precocious sense of self-importance, dressed up in a little soldier's uniform and earning the nickname of Caligula ('little boots') from the *caliga* or hob-nailed boots worn by soldiers of the rank of centurion down. In later life, according to Seneca, he was to find the name distasteful.[15] The idea for his costume could well have been his mother's. Certainly, one of the rumours later fed by the sinister praetorian prefect Sejanus to Tiberius was that Agrippina was responsible for parading him in an ordinary soldier's garb, and that she had asked that he be called 'Caesar Caligula'.[16]

Hardened soldiers throughout history have always been prone to sentimentality, and this game did seem to create a strong bond between them and the infant Caligula, and may perhaps explain in part why the legend grew that he was born on campaign.

On 19 August AD 14, Augustus died, to be succeeded by his adopted son, the fifty-five year old Tiberius.[17] There was no precedent to show how the succession should be effected, and in a sense none was needed. In his will Augustus named Tiberius heir to most of his estate and bequeathed to him the title of Augustus. But of more constitutional significance, in the previous year the emperor had granted him proconsular *imperium* equal to his own, as well as a renewal of his tribunician power. By virtue of these powers Tiberius was able to handle immediate administrative problems, and his position was strengthened when the consuls swore an oath of loyalty, and administered the same oath to the senate, knights and people. Tiberius behaved from the outset as if he were emperor, giving the watchword to the praetorian guard in his capacity as *imperator* and despatching letters to the armies. In Rome at least the Augustan scheme had worked well.

For the modern historian the situation is complicated by the senate's role in Tiberius' elevation. He was rigidly conservative in his adherence to constitutional niceties, and would have been greatly concerned to ensure that the ancient body play its proper legal part in confirming the accession. Unfortunately neither the procedure, nor even the precise chronology of events, comes through clearly in the sources. There was a key meeting of the senate on September 17, shortly after the funeral. Augustus was declared a god, and exceptional honours voted for Livia. Then the senate entreated Tiberius, though whether to accept or continue the principate is not made clear (there is no specific report of the substance of their motion). Tiberius for his part expressed great reluctance, pointing out that the burden of rule was too great for a single person. The purpose of these proceedings has been much discussed. It has been argued that Tiberius was seeking the moral authority of the senate, or that he relinquished his powers to have them re-confirmed by that body, or that the senate confirmed not Augustus' powers (which Tiberius already had) but his *provincia*, or that he asked the senate to devalue the enormous *provincia* that had befallen him.[18] Whatever the true sequence of events, Tiberius in the end yielded. As will be made clear, his successor Caligula would assume the principate under quite different circumstances.

Outside of Rome Augustus' death had an unsettling effect on the northern legions, where harsh conditions of service and unfulfilled commitments had already created a serious problem of morale. Drusus, the son of the new emperor, was despatched to Pannonia, where violent riots had flared up among the troops, and by a shrewd combination of diplomatic tact and firmness, aided by a timely lunar eclipse, suppressed an incipient

8

mutiny. The troubles on the Rhine were concentrated in Lower Germany, and resulted basically from the same grievances as in Pannonia, but they are given a political colour in the ancient sources, who all assert that the soldiers wanted Germanicus to seize supreme power, a claim of affection that is not easy to reconcile with his subsequent difficulties in securing their obedience.[19]

On hearing in Gaul of Augustus' death Germanicus administered the oath of allegiance to the Sequani and Belgae, then hastened to the legions of Lower Germany, where riots had broken out and discipline had collapsed, with centurions being attacked and murdered. The officers seemed afraid to assert their authority, but history does record that a youthful Cassius Chaerea cut his way through a mob of mutineers. He would return to the historical stage some years later as tribune in the praetorian guard, to play a pivotal role in the murder of Caligula. When he reached the camp Germanicus tried to appeal to the mens' loyalty, promising to see that their grievances would be dealt with. His efforts failed, and making a histrionic threat to commit suicide he was jokingly encouraged to see it through. In the end he was reduced to producing a forged letter of Tiberius supposedly offering concessions, and to dipping in to the money that he carried with him for official expenses, which seems, for the moment, to have worked. The arrangement was thrown into some jeopardy by the arrival of an embassy of the Senate, as the soldiers mistakenly believed that they had come to invalidate Germanicus' agreements. Both Germanicus and the senators were subjected to various indignities, and even Germanicus' own officers criticized him for his weakness in dealing with the mutineers. The precise sequence of events that followed is unclear. At this stage Agrippina, along with Caligula, was with her husband in Cologne. By the time of the mutinies she was pregnant again (she seems to have lost the child), and for her and Caligula's safety Germanicus arranged for them to leave to seek protection among the Treveri. As the procession moved out of the camp, Agrippina clasped her son to her, comforted by the tearful wives of Germanicus' officials. According to Dio the soldiers (of Legions I and XX) seized Agrippina and the child. When they realized that she was pregnant they let her go, but kept Caligula. Finally they saw that they would achieve little by holding the infant hostage, and released him also. Suetonius reflects this version of events in the report that during his German campaign of 39/40 Caligula, now emperor, planned to punish the troops because they had seized him during the revolt.[20] Another version reported by Tacitus and followed by Suetonius in a different context was that the soldiers were moved to remorse and shame that the commander's wife, granddaughter of Augustus and a lady of outstanding chastity, should, along with her little son, the child of the legions, be forced to seek the protection of the despised Treveri. The pitiful sight, it is claimed, was enough in itself to persuade them to lay down their weapons. It is possible that the first, rather sordid, account is the true one and that the second represents a pro-Germanicus version, perhaps circulated by Agrippina.[21] Whatever the truth, the soldiers do seem to have relented, and this at last produced decisive action from Germanicus, although he went to great lengths to avoid any ill feeling towards himself, and left it to the soldiers to deal with the ringleaders, which they did with striking severity.[22]

Germanicus rightly appreciated that the best way of stifling any remaining thoughts of mutiny lay in action, and that same autumn launched a raid into the territory of the Marsi over the Rhine from Vetera, and defeated them, prudently withdrawing, however, when neighbouring tribes came to their assistance.[23] It was probably Tiberius' hope that Germanicus would limit himself to this single action, arranging in early 15 that a triumph be granted for his success, a gesture clearly out of proportion to the modest military successes gained.[24] But Germanicus clearly had visions of emulating his father and of pushing the Roman frontier east to the Elbe, and pursued a more vigorous and far-reaching campaign in 15. The season started off well. The Romans advanced north east, eventually reaching the Teutoburg forest. Moving ceremonies were held in honour of the legionaries who had died under Varus and a funeral mound was raised. The troops now set off in pursuit of the Germans under Arminius, the leader who had inflicted the great defeat on them in AD 9, but Germanicus made the mistake of penetrating too deeply into their territory, and almost fell into the same trap as had Varus. He extricated himself with difficulty. In full retreat, the exhausted Romans poured over the Rhine bridge at Vetera, where they were met by Agrippina who shouted words of encouragement as they crossed over, distributing clothing and bandages to those who needed them. They discovered later that her contribution had been more than merely a boost to morale. When the bad news from Germany had filtered through, no doubt in exaggerated form, there had been some who had feared that the way was open for a German invasion and had wanted to destroy the bridge. It had been saved only by Agrippina's personal intervention.

Further campaigns were conducted in AD 16. Germanicus transported his eight legions down the Weser and inflicted two major defeats on the enemy. But Arminius remained free, and on the return voyage a disaster struck the Romans when the fleet was hit by a storm. The survivors were cast along the shoreline of the north sea, some as far afield as Britain. Fresh incursions were made into Germany later in the same year to discourage the hostile tribes from taking advantage of this setback and to prevent morale from suffering.

As Tacitus describes the situation, AD 16 supposedly ended with the Romans in a state of elation, and Germanicus believing that with one more year he could complete the conquest as far as the Elbe. Tiberius thought otherwise. It was clear to him that further armed intervention would in fact achieve little, since the defeated enemy had an amazing capacity to regroup and to return as vigorous as before. Germanicus, he decided, would have to be recalled. This need not mean that Tiberius was jealous of his stepson's achievements, as Tacitus suggests.[25] From the onset a cautious strategist like Tiberius must have understood that Germanicus' policy was doomed to fail. He rightly appreciated that the conquest of Germany would require a steady policy of 'pacification' with military settlements established in relative proximity, and an extensive network of communications. This was the strategy that would work so well during the initial conquest of Britain. In Germany it would have required an enormous outlay of men and material, more than he was willing to countenance. It is, admittedly, difficult to understand why Tiberius allowed two full years of campaigning. But it must be remembered that Germanicus had been appointed to his German command not by Tiberius but by Augustus. The emperor was thus caught between due deference to the wishes of Augustus, and the practical policy that his soldier's instinct demanded.

Tiberius would have felt obliged, of course, to make every effort to ensure that the withdrawal would not be taken as a slight, and the most diplomatic way to achieve this was to adopt the posture that the war had been won, and that Germanicus had achieved signal successes. The emperor wrote to him at the end of 16 suggesting that the best course of action would be to wait until the Germans fell out amongst themselves, as they inevitably would. He also suggested that if any further glory was to be won in Germany, Germanicus' stepbrother Drusus should be given his opportunity. There is no reason to think that Germanicus would have taken any offence at this last suggestion. His steadfast loyalty toward Tiberius throughout his career had no doubt been made easier by the complete impartiality that the emperor seems to have maintained in his treatment of the two young men, *cum... integrum inter duos iudicium tenuisset*, ('although he had kept his judgement impartial between the pair') as Tacitus remarks. The situation was helped by the abiding and apparently genuine friendship between the two step-brothers, a friendship that matched the earlier closeness between Tiberius and his brother Drusus. To Tacitus, Germanicus and the younger Drusus were *egregie concordes* (in splendid harmony'), and these close feelings would be strengthened by the fact that Drusus was married to Germanicus' sister Livilla.[26] We should accordingly treat with great caution the old claim that two rival parties organized themselves around the two young men.[27]

Germanicus returned to Rome a conquering hero. On 26 May 17, he celebrated a splendid triumph for his victories over the Cherusci, Chatti and Angrivarii and the other tribes west of the Elbe.[28] There was a great procession of spoils and captives, with reconstructions of mountains, rivers and battles, and Tiberius distributed a largesse of 300 sesterces each to the people. What moved the specators most, however, was the noble impression made by Germanicus, who rode in a chariot with his five children. Caligula was now almost five years old. This triumph, with himself at the centre of an adoring populace, must have remained as one of his earliest and most vivid childhood impressions.

Germanicus was kept busy for much of the remainder of the year in various functions. He dedicated the restoration of the ancient temple of Spes, entered a chariot in the Olympic games, and was an active patron in Rome for private individuals and communities. Yet none of this, even combined with the promise of a consulship in the following year as Tiberius' colleague, would have seemed adequate compensation for his loss of command in Germany. But Tiberius had a plum to offer — the leadership of an important mission to the East. A number of serious problems had arisen there, in particular the threat of a clash with Parthia. Through much of her recent history Rome had found herself at constant loggerheads with this great kingdom located between the Euphrates and the Indus. The main area of contention was Armenia, a mountainous country east of the Euphrates, bordering on the NW of Parthia (the area west of the Euphrates was defined by the Romans as Armenia Minor). The Parthians had a long-standing claim on Armenia, which ran counter to Rome's desire to maintain the area as a protectorate. By 17 Armenia was without a king, and both Rome and Parthia would be anxious to secure a ruler well-disposed to them. Apart from this thorny issue, there were other problems to be dealt with. Archelaus, King of Cappadocia in Asia Minor, had been summoned to Rome by Tiberius and accused of treason. He was not convicted — there may not even have been a trial — but he died before he could return to his kingdom, perhaps in 17. The status of his former domain was in a kind of limbo.[29] At about the same time two other rulers in Asia Minor died, Antiochus III of Commagene, and Philopator II, who ruled the Amanus in Cilicia.[30] Commagene posed particular problems, as a major section of the nobility desired annexation by Rome while the general population remained loyal to the old dynasty, and both sides sent deputations to Rome.

Tiberius argued in the senate that the problems needed the presence of a figure like Germanicus, since he was himself too old and his son Drusus was too young. These comments were not misplaced, since whatever his deficiencies as a military commander, Germanicus possessed real talents as a diplomat. He set off on his mission in the autumn of AD 17, accompanied by Agrippina, Caligula and a large retinue. It is possible that the occasion is recorded on the famous gem, the Grand Camée, now in the Bibliothèque Nationale in Paris. This splendid piece has been much discussed for well over a century, and there is no clear consensus on what it depicts.[31] Many scholars believe, however, that the gem represents the departure of Germanicus on his mission to the East. According to this view the central figure is the enthroned Tiberius, who bestows the task on Germanicus, who faces him, accoutred in battle armour. Behind Germanicus stand Agrippina and the young Caligula (fig. 1). Final certainty on the scene is of course impossible, and even if it does represent the departure of Germanicus, the cameo may well have been engraved some years after the event.

Germanicus' journey resembled a splendid triumphal procession, as cities competed to outdo each other in the richness of their welcome. He first visited his step-brother Drusus in Dalmatia, then proceeded to Nicopolis, the city founded by Augustus near Actium. He spent some days there, and visited the bay where the great battle had taken place. He was in Nicopolis when he entered his second consulship, in 18.[32] He then went to Athens where he displayed his full talents as a diplomat. Entering the city with only one lictor, in deference to its status as a *civitas libera*, he dressed in Greek clothes and sandals and lavished compliments on the citizens, who in turn heaped honours upon him. From Athens he sailed to Euboea, then Lesbos, where Agrippina gave birth to the last of her children, Julia Livilla. Agrippina no doubt stayed in Lesbos when Germanicus, accompanied by Caligula, set off on a grand tour of north-west Asia minor. They visited Perinthus and Byzantium, then passed through the Bosphorus to the mouth of the Black sea. A planned visit to Samothrace on the return journey was prevented by unfavourable winds. Instead they went to the Troad, visiting the site of Troy and the city of Assos. Later, on Caligula's accession, the people of Assos were keen to remind him of his visit with his father, and sent the new emperor a decree of loyalty. It seems that Caligula, yielding nothing to his father in diplomatic charm, had made some sort of address to them, although hardly six years old. The Assos decree, preserved in an inscription, asks him to 'care for the city, as he had promised when he first came with his father Germanicus'.[33] This is the first recorded demonstration of Caligula's considerable oratorical skill. To what extent he owed his precocious ability to his father is uncertain, as Germanicus was dead before the boy entered his truly formative years, but this early incident, even allowing for the inevitable rhetorical exaggeration, does suggest that Germanicus might have fostered his son's talents in this area (see p. 48). From Assos father and son continued along the coast of Asia, visiting the oracle of Apollo at Colophon. At some point they rejoined Agrippina and the new daughter, and the whole family continued the journey east, for we next hear of them in Rhodes, where they encountered Gnaeus Calpurnius Piso, on his way to Syria. Piso had been appointed, with the approval of the senate, to replace Caecilius Criticus Silanus as the new governor of the province.[34] Piso was a man of rough tongue and bloody-minded independence, reluctant, if we are to believe Tacitus, to yield first place even to Tiberius. It is very likely that Tiberius had at the back of his mind the idea that he would impose some restraint on Germanicus, but it seems unlikely that Piso had been given more sinister instructions from the emperor deliberately to embarrass the mission, as Tacitus seems to imply.

Piso had travelled first to Athens. He lacked Germanicus' tact, and chose to insult the inhabitants as dregs, a quite different nation from the great Athenians of old, and criticized Germanicus for lavishing praise on what was little more than a rabble. Once settled in Syria, according to Tacitus, he sought to ingratiate himself with the legions by distributing bribes and relaxing discipline. His wife Munatia Plancina was also active; she lost no opportunity to insult Agrippina, while at the same time apparently trying to emulate her, riding in the cavalry exercises and taking part in the manoeuvres of the cohorts.[35]

If Germanicus was aware of what was happening behind his back, he did not allow it to interfere with his mission. He proceeded straight to Armenia, where he established, as king, Zeno, the son of Polemo the late king of Pontus. Zeno, who adopted the Armenian name Artaxias, proved highly popular among his new subjects and ruled for 16 years, with the apparent acquiescence of Parthia. Other problems in Asia Minor were also dealt with. Quintus Veranius was sent to organize Cappadocia, which was turned into a province under an equestrian governor. Archelaus' son was allowed to retain a small part of the original kingdom in Rough Cilicia. The revenues that accrued to Rome from Cappadocia proved so lucrative that Tiberius was able to reduce the 1 per cent sales tax imposed throughout the empire by Augustus after the civil wars to ·5 per cent. Commagene was organized by Quintus Servaeus, who remained for a time as propraetor. It was later incorporated into Syria. There is no information on the fate of Philopator's kingdom in Cilicia, which may similarly have been swallowed up by Syria.[36] Once these adminstrative problems had been settled, Germanicus, in late 18, made for Syria, where he had his first formal meeting with Piso, at Cyrrhus, in the camp of Legio X. It was a cool encounter, as earlier in the year Germanicus had instructed Piso that he (or his son) should take a detachment of troops to Armenia, and Piso had simply ignored the order. From now on, whenever they met there was friction. One anecdote illustrates the strain between the two men. When Aretas, the king of the Nabataeans, gave a banquet, heavy gold crowns were presented to Germanicus and Agrippina, lesser ones to Piso and others. In a fit of pique Piso threw the one offered to him to the floor, declaring that the banquet was supposedly intended for the son of a Roman princeps, not a king of Parthia. He then launched into an attack on luxurious living, listened to by a furiously silent Germanicus.[37]

In the winter of 18/19 Germanicus visited Egypt, partly for administrative purposes, partly to see the antiquities, presumably taking his son with him. He was received rapturously in Alexandria, and from there took a trip up the Nile, first visiting Thebes, where he took a keen interest in the extant inscriptions, then the great Colossus of Memnon, the pyramids, Lake Moeris, and finally Syene, the southern limit of the Roman empire. When he returned to Alexandria, he was to find a rebuke from Tiberius awaiting him.[38] The emperor had written to remind him that Augustus had prohibited senators from visiting Egypt without permission. The prohibition arose from Egypt's enormous importance as grain supplier, but in Germanicus' case was little more than a breach of protocol rather than any fear that he had designs on the province. Tiberius clearly felt that his stepson was perhaps beginning to forget his place, and needed to be curbed, if only for his own good.

On his return to Syria Germanicus and Piso found that disagreement over their respective mandates made effective collaboration impossible. They clashed violently, and Piso decided that it would be prudent for him to leave. His preparations were cut short, however, by news that Germanicus had fallen seriously ill. He bided his time in Seleucia to await events. Germanicus was convinced that Piso had poisoned him, in collusion with his wife, and the discovery of spells and curses and evidence of witchcraft strengthened this conviction. Piso was finally ordered out of the province completely. He set sail and had reached the island of Cos when news arrived that Germanicus had succumbed to the illness.

Germanicus died in Antioch on 10 October 19, at the age of 33.[39] It is quite possible there was nothing sinister about his death. Syria was a notoriously unhealthy spot, and about a century later Trajan was to die from a disease contracted there. Agrippina herself was ill before she left and even Martina, the suspected poisoner, died at Brundisium on her way back.[40] But Germanicus had been convinced that he was being murdered, and before his death asked his entourage to ensure that Piso and his wife's villainy be brought to account. He also left telling instructions for Agrippina — that she was to put aside her pride and to avoid provoking those more powerful than herself in her own drive for power. His funeral was held at Antioch, the body being exposed before cremation to show proof of poisoning.[41] Finally Agrippina, worn out and ill, but determined on revenge, set sail for Italy.

The lingering death of Germanicus had caused tensions to rise in Rome. The first reports caused an outbreak of hatred against Tiberius and Livia, and supicions that they had plotted the murder along with Piso and his wife — the reported motive being their supposed fear that if Germanicus had come to power he would have restored the republican constitution. The temporary jubilation caused by a false report that he had survived only deepened the grief when it was shown to be untrue, and intensified popular sympathy for Agrippina and hostility towards Tiberius and Piso. Numerous honours were voted Germanicus, recorded by Tacitus and in inscriptions found in Etruria and Spain.[42] Suetonius gives an even more vivid picture of the reaction to his death outside of Rome, perhaps of limited historical importance in itself but useful in showing the kind of legend that grew around Germanicus, one which Caligula was able later to exploit. Barbarian nations, we are told, at war with Rome or with one another, sought truces, foreign kings removed their beards and shaved their wives' heads, and even the King of Parthia interrupted his hunting and banquets. Meanwhile Agrippina, sailing through the winter season, had by early 20 reached Corcyra. She lingered there to regain her spirits and presumably to ensure that news of her imminent arrival would precede her to Italy and ensure a lively reception. Finally she reached Brundisium, and as she entered the harbour every spot that commanded a view of the sea was occupied. The crowds watched as she disembarked, carrying the urn with Germanicus' ashes, and clutching little Caligula and his sister. Two cohorts of the praetorian guard escorted the urn on its journey to Rome, carried on the shoulders of tribunes and centurions. The magistrates of Calabria, Apulia and Campania were ordered to honour the ashes as they passed through their districts, and in every town they passed through the people donned mourning and burned incense. Germanicus' brother Claudius, along with his stepbrother Drusus, together with the rest of his children, met the cortege at Tarracina, and as it made its way into the city the consuls and members of the senate, as well as ordinary people, went out to meet it. In a great public ceremony the ashes were laid in the mausoleum of Augustus. That the general population might have lamented that 'the republic had now perished and all hope was dead' would have been troubling enough for Tiberius, but what must have rankled most was the outburst of popular feeling for Agrippina, who was called the *decus patriae, solum Augusti sanguinem, unicum antiquitatis specimen* ('the glory of her country, the last of Augustus' line, an unmatched example of ancient virtues').[43]

Tiberius, Livia and Antonia did not attend the funeral — we are not told the reason. Tiberius, in character, sought to keep the tragedy in perspective and issued a declaration that many illustrious Romans had died for their country, though none had been so deeply mourned. He reminded the people of the other losses that the Imperial family had suffered over the years, observing that men were mortal, only the state was immortal. Tiberius' observations may have been well founded, but they were not likely to win him friends. Nor did the subsequent trial and suicide of Piso change feelings. Tiberius' desire to keep the proceedings impartial was bound to be misconstrued. Nor did his intervention on behalf of Plancina (at the request of his mother), help matters, since it simply confirmed a popular suspicion that he and Livia had been involved in Germanicus' death, and it aggravated the fear of *optimus quisque* ('all decent people') that the same poisons would now be turned against Agrippina and her children.[44]

Germanicus had been a man of worthy but not outstanding achievements. He was, in fact, much more important in death than in life. His untimely end provided a focus for the ill-feelings towards Tiberius and created a legend of superhuman qualities which, no doubt with some external manoeuvring, were to be transferred in the popular mind to Caligula. Germanicus' death in Syria in AD 19 marked the first stage in the process that would bring his son to the throne some 18 years later.

· 2 ·

THE STRUGGLE FOR
THE SUCCESSION

WITH THE DEATH of Germanicus in AD 19, it might be expected that the succession would pass automatically to Tiberius' own son, Drusus, and the continuation of Tiberius' line must have seemed assured when Drusus' wife, Livilla, gave birth in the same year to twin sons, Tiberius Gemellus (fig. 3) and Germanicus (who died in 23).[1] All the same, Tiberius remained conscious of Augustus' intentions and dutifully promoted the sons of Germanicus, and the situation was helped by Drusus' apparently genuine affection for his late step-brother's children, a feeling that originated in his close friendship with Germanicus. The boys were placed in his charge and he treated them with extreme kindness.[2] We might suspect, of course, that Tiberius was motivated at least in part by the desire to remove the children from what he considered the baleful influence of their mother. In 20 he began to advance the career of Germanicus' eldest son Nero, commending him in the senate on his coming to manhood at the age of fourteen. Nero was given the privilege of seeking the quaestorship five years before the legal age and was also granted a priesthood, the occasion being marked by a donative to the people, and the popular delight at the turn of events was heightened by his betrothal to Drusus' daughter, Julia.[3] Tiberius' own son also received appropriate recognition, when, in 21, Drusus was appointed consul for a second time with his father as colleague, and in 22 was granted *tribunicia potestas* by the senate, which he apparently took up on April 23.[4]

None of this seems to have created tensions between the young men of the imperial family, and any potential rivalry would in any case have been completely overshadowed by the rise of the sinister Lucius Aelius Sejanus, Prefect of the Praetorian guard. Son of the Prefect Lucius Seius Strabo, Sejanus first comes to notice in some unspecified capacity in the retinue of Augustus' grandson Gaius Caesar. For all his evil reputation, he was clearly a man of considerable charm. By the time Tiberius came to power, Sejanus had managed to work his way into his affections, and succeeded in having himself appointed first as joint Praetorian Prefect with his own father (in AD 14), and then as sole Prefect (16/17). By 23 he had strengthened his position by concentrating the guard in a single set of permanent barracks just outside the city, near the Porta Viminalis.[5] Apart from his personal links with the emperor and his position in the Guard, Sejanus also built up support in the senate, and managed to arrange appointments for his cronies. The strength of his position was realized by AD 20. He was granted the *ornamenta praetoria*, the insignia of the praetor, with no power but much prestige, and both Dio and Tacitus speak of Tiberius at this time publicly describing the Prefect as the partner of his labours.[6] His achievement was symbolically capped by the betrothal of his daughter Junilla to the son of Claudius. It was a short-lived union. A few days later the young man, perhaps anxious to prove that he had not inherited his father's clumsiness, threw a pear into the air, deftly caught it in mouth, then choked to death.[7]

The precise nature of Sejanus' ambition has been much debated, and falls outside the scope of this book. In practical terms there could probably have been little prospect of his securing the principate for himself. There was a good stock of claimants in the Imperial house, and his equestrian rank would have been an impediment. He may well have seen his role rather as that of a power behind the throne, acting as a kind of regent for a young prince, an arrangement that he might have hoped to cement by a marriage into the Imperial family. What is certain, however, is that in furthering his ambitions Sejanus would face two major obstacles — Tiberius' son, Drusus and Germanicus' widow, Agrippina. Drusus' hostility would have been the more immediately apparent, since he must have felt that his natural role was being usurped, and that he was being set aside while his father relied on an outsider. As a result, the antagonism between the two men grew increasingly tense, until they even came to blows. Clearly, if Drusus should eventually succeed his father, Sejanus' own future would be bleak.

The Prefect made his attack indirectly through Drusus' wife. Turning his charms on Livilla he lured her into his bed, and, perhaps by playing on her ambitions for her own children, persuaded her to join him in a plot to eliminate her husband. In September, 23, to the great grief of Tiberius, Drusus died, almost certainly poisoned by his wife and her lover.[8] His death would mean that Germanicus' two elder sons, now aged 16 and 17, would be seen as the obvious candidates for the succession, since the other possible claimants were still too young to be considered seriously.[9] The two were described by Tiberius (after his own son's death) as the *unica praesentium malorum levamenta* ('the sole solace for my present woes') and he presented them to the senate in a moving speech, calling upon the senators to be their father and mother, to nurture them as grandsons of Augustus, offspring of splendid ancestors. Their futures looked promising indeed. In 23, when the cities of Asia were given permission to build a temple to Tiberius, Livia and the Senate, Nero gave a speech of thanks on behalf of the communities involved. He very much pleased the audience, who were captivated by his charm and modesty, made all the more attractive by Sejanus' patent hostility.[10]

Clearly, Tiberius was more than willing to show goodwill towards Agrippina's children, and if she had handled the situation with any degree of tact she might have survived Sejanus' inevitable attack. As it was, she played right into the Prefect's hands. The conviction that she had maintained since Antioch that her family was marked for destruction brought her into such opposition to Tiberius that her behaviour seemed to verge on treason. She appears to have been motivated partly by her vitriolic hostility towards the emperor, whom she never forgave for the death of Germanicus, and partly by her obsessive determination to promote the interests of her own children.

Agrippina's ill-concealed ambitions for her sons would doubtless have offended Livia and Livilla, who must have had hopes for Livilla's son Gemellus, a situation that Sejanus lost no time in exploiting. Egged on by him, they grumbled to Tiberius that Agrippina was casting greedy eyes on the throne. Early in 24 there occurred a diplomatic blunder that revealed clearly that Tiberius had begun to find Agrippina's attitude unbearably irksome. As the priests were taking the traditional vows for the safety of the emperor they included Nero and Drusus in the prayers. Ironically, Tacitus suggests that they did this to please Tiberius. He, however, was furious that the two young men should be placed at his level, and demanded to know from the priests if they had acted under pressure from Agrippina (which they denied). He then proceeded to instruct the senators on the dangerous effect of excessive distinctions on the impressionable minds of the young. According to Tacitus, Tiberius' extreme reaction to this incident was aggravated by Sejanus, who now fed to the emperor the idea of a split in the state and the formation of an 'Agrippina faction' (*qui se partium Agrippinae vocent*).[11]

Sejanus at first avoided a direct assault; his tactic was to strike at Agrippina through her prominent supporters. Throughout 24 and 25 there followed a series of prosecutions for treason, some of which, at least, were almost certainly due to Sejanus' machinations. By 25 Sejanus felt that his position was strong enough to seek permission to marry Drusus' widow Livilla, and in his written request to Tiberius presented as one of his arguments the claim that Livilla's children had to be protected against Agrippina's animosity. In the event, Tiberius withheld his permission, and in his refusal noted shrewdly that the union would simply inflame Agrippina and open the family rift even wider.[12] The refusal was a setback for Sejanus, but by no means a fatal one, especially since in his reply Tiberius suggested that at the appropriate time in the future he would receive his due reward. It seems hard, however, to believe that the emperor could not have realized from this incident the extent of the Prefect's ambitions. Sejanus continued his campaign against Agrippina.

In 26 a charge of adultery and of treason, by poison and spells, against the person of Tiberius was brought by the distinguished orator Gnaeus Domitius Afer against Claudia Pulchra, Agrippina's second cousin and close friend. Agrippina attempted to intercede with Tiberius, but with her usual lack of tact burst in on him while he was making a sacrifice to Augustus. Her choice of words on the occasion illustrates how offensive her behaviour could be. She rebuked Tiberius for sacrificing to Augustus while persecuting his descendants, and pointedly asserted that a blood relative (*caelesti sanguine ortam*) was the true object of the attack, clearly contrasting herself with Tiberius, linked to Augustus only by adoption. He was angered by the outburst, which he felt was provoked by Agrippina's personal ambition, and threw back at her the famous tag (in Greek) 'Just because you're not queen, my little daughter, do you think you've been wronged?'[13] In any case, her efforts failed to save her cousin, who, along with her lover, was condemned on the charge of adultery, although we do not know the sentence they received.

The prosecution of Claudia Pulchra, and Agrippina's own conduct during its course, no doubt paved the way for her own destruction. The residual anger from the incident may well account for Tiberius' refusal shortly afterwards to grant her request to remarry. The name of the intended husband is not revealed, but the later association of her name with that of Asinius Gallus certainly makes him a prime candidate. He would hardly, however, have recommended himself to the emperor, since he had earlier married Vipsania, for whom Tiberius had continued to feel affection even after their divorce. Agrippina's request was, it seems, not generally known, and Tacitus mentions that he read it in the memoirs of her daughter, Agrippina Minor. Sejanus could have got wind of her intentions, however, and may well have felt the need to press his campaign even more vigorously. He now tried a new tack. He persuaded Agrippina's supposed friends to convince her that Tiberius was attempting to poison her, and in turn alerted the emperor to her apparent paranoid suspicion. This led to an awkward incident at dinner, when Tiberius tested her by offering her some choice fruit that he had not tasted. When she, perhaps understandably, declined, he obliquely observed to his mother Livia that he could hardly be blamed for dealing sternly with a woman who accused him of trying to murder her.[14]

By 26, no doubt much disheartened by the feuding factions around him, Tiberius left Rome for Campania, and from there to Capri.[15] He would return to the city only for his funeral. Tacitus claims that it was Sejanus who urged the idea of leaving on Tiberius. The departure certainly suited the Prefect well, since he would now be able to launch a more open attack on Agrippina and her family. His first target was Caligula's brother Nero, who would be next in line for the succession, as Sejanus would have been reminded when the young man received the quaestorship in 5 December of that year. Although generally modest and reasonable, Nero had a habit of speaking his mind rather bluntly, and the example set by his mother would not have helped. Sejanus bribed Nero's freedmen and clients to urge him on. His ill-considered statements were routinely taken down and reported, with due exaggeration, to Tiberius. Sejanus even worked on Nero's brother Drusus, exploiting what Tacitus for the first time reveals as a savage jealousy against Nero, resented by Drusus as mothers's favourite.[16] Caligula was in a sense protected by his youth. In August of 26 he would only have turned fourteen, still too young to feel that his own ambitions were being thwarted by his older brothers.

The attacks on friends and supporters of Agrippina continued into 27. In that year an indictment was brought against Quintilius Varus. We do not know the charges, but it is probably significant that he was the son of Claudia Pulchra, and at one time betrothed to Germanicus' daughter Livilla.[17] Moreover, the prosecutor once again was Sejanus' tool, Domitius Afer. It is likely that he was accused of conspiracy; in the event the trial was postponed pending Tiberius' return to Rome, and nothing more is known of it. The chronology of the final stage of Sejanus' attack is very confused, and the evidence of the various literary sources difficult to reconcile.[18] According to Tacitus the final move was not made against Agrippina and Nero until after the aged Livia's death, which occurred in 29. This, however, is contradicted by Suetonius, who says that Caligula actually came under the care of Livia *after* his mother's banishment, and by Pliny, who asserts that the trial of one of Agrippina's supporters, Titus Sabinus, which belongs to 28, arose *ex causa Neronis* ('from the case of Nero'). Velleius, moreover, implies very strongly that Livia's death occurred *after* Nero and Agrippina had fallen into disgrace.[19] This conflicting testimony has been much discussed, and perhaps the most satisfactory resolution of the problem is along the lines proposed by E. Meise, that the final attack came in two phases, the first phase belonging to before 29, and the second, more serious, one following Livia's death in that year. Final certainty is, however, impossible.

Tacitus reveals that in 27 Sejanus made his emnity of Nero and Agrippina public, and that soldiers were set to keep watch on them and make detailed reports. What might this have involved? The use of soldiers implies that they were under some sort of house arrest. In a different context Seneca reports that Agrippina had a luxurious villa at Herculaneum where for a time she was held under guard.[20] It is just possible that the forced stay at Herculaneum belongs to 27, and that Nero's movements were similarly restrained, perhaps in Rome. If this was the case, Caligula and his sisters could well have been sent at that time to their great-grandmother Livia. Suetonius does, admittedly, say that their stay with Livia occurred after Agrippina had been *banished (ea relegata)* which would not strictly be the case if she were simply confined to her Campanian villa. But this is not a fatal objection. Suetonius' narrative is very summary at this point and information on Agrippina has been much telescoped.

The detailed reports of the soldiers on Nero apparently produced enough evidence to justify some sort of investigation, and to judge from the comment of Pliny, while the case was being prepared sufficient evidence came to light to begin action, probably in late 27, against the equestrian Titus Sabinus, on the charge of treason.[21] Sabinus had been devoted to Germanicus, and after the latter's death had remained a constant companion of his widow and children in public, and a frequent visitor to their home. The case against him had been planned originally in 24 but held in abeyance since then, perhaps to wait until the time was right for an attack on Agrippina and Nero. A certain Lucanius Latiaris acted as *agent provocateur*. He lured Sabinus to his house, and by pretending sympathy for Agrippina induced him to make injudicious remarks about Tiberius. Sabinus did not realize that Sejanus had agents concealed in the attic, keeping a record of his every word. He was immediately imprisoned, and a report was sent to the emperor, who wrote back on 1 January of the next year (AD 28) a strong letter denouncing him. The senate did not hestitate to act on it, and Sabinus was tried and executed forthwith. His body was hurled down the Gemonian stairs and flung into the Tiber. In a second letter that Tiberius wrote on the case, he thanked the senate for punishing a man *infensum reipublicae* ('hostile to the state'), and added that his life was in constant danger of plots from enemies. Although he mentioned no names there was no doubt in the minds of the senators, according to Tacitus, that Agrippina and Nero were meant.

According to this reconstruction, Caligula would have gone to live with his formidable great-grandmother Livia in her home on the Palatine in 27. She had, of course, ceased to exercise any serious influence on events, and, indeed, Tiberius reputedly spoke to her only once after his retirement to Capri. Nevertheless, she knew better than any other the intrigues of the court. Caligula, at an impressionable age, found himself under the wing of someone who would teach him that guile and cunning could achieve more in Imperial Rome than the kind of head-on attack his mother had employed. It was probably this craftiness that provoked him to liken Livia to the arch-trickster of legend, calling her 'a Ulysses in petticoats'. But there seems to have been some affection between them; at any rate on his accession Caligula finally honoured her legacies, left unpaid by Tiberius.[22]

Agrippina seems to have remained under some sort of house arrest for over a year. At any rate, following the trial of Sabinus, Tiberius apparently took no further action against her for the time being. The reason for this, according to Tacitus, was that she enjoyed the protection of Livia. This line of defence was lost when Livia died, in the early part of 29, at the ripe old age of 86, a longevity that she attributed to her regular exclusive intake of Pucinum wine.[23] The safeguard provided by Livia would not have stemmed from any affection for Agrippina, whom she seems to have hated. But while she was alive Sejanus would have been reluctant to make the naked bid for power that the elimination of Agrippina and Nero would have exposed. Her death, of course, changed the situation, and although the details are unknown to us, Sejanus must have pressed his case with Tiberius. His success was marked by the arrival of a letter from the emperor to the senate, denouncing Agrippina and her son (Tacitus reports a popular belief that the letter had been sent much earlier but suppressed by Livia). It studiously avoided charging treason, merely accusing Nero of sexual perversions and Agrippina of arrogant language and vexatious pride. The indictment placed the senate in a dilemma. Clearly there would have been those who were sympathetic towards Agrippina, as opposed to the Tiberian 'loyalists', who called for a trial. Then Julius Rusticus, appointed by Tiberius as a keeper of the record, who might have had some insight into the emperor's thinking, strongly urged the consuls not to introduce the question, in order to avoid taking any action that one day the emperor might regret. Accordingly, nothing was done. Meanwhile, as they dithered, a demonstration took place outside the senate-house. The people paraded images of Agrippina and Nero and claimed that the supposed letter of Tiberius was a forgery. Pamphlets under the names of consular senators were spread about, denouncing Sejanus.[24]

For his part Sejanus reported to Tiberius the senate's refusal to act and the public displays of disloyalty. While his report provoked yet another letter from Tiberius to the senate, the content of this last missive seems to have been ambiguous. The emperor repeated the allegations against Agrippina and Nero and rebuked the senators for their inactivity, but did not demand action, insisting that the matter be turned over to him. Unfortunately, Tacitus' account breaks off at this point, picking up again in late 31, and there are extensive gaps in Dio's account, thus making it extremely difficult to reconstruct events. A prosecution was instituted *in camera* before the emperor, and the main accuser was said to be Avillius Flaccus, who was in 32 appointed Prefect of Egypt. Apart from this information, we have no details of the proceedings.[25] That Agrippina might have been charged with planning to incite rebellion is suggested by the report of Tacitus that some urged her to 'seek refuge' with the Rhine armies, or to appear at the statue of Augustus in the forum, when it was most crowded, and appeal for the support of the senate and the people. It is indeed possible that Tiberius' suspicions were well grounded, and that Agrippina was actively involved in some plot to remove him from power.[26] Both she and her son Nero, who was declared a *hostis* ('public enemy'), were banished to small islands lying to the west of Naples, Nero to Pontia and Agrippina to Pandateria. According to Suetonius she was force-fed there to prevent suicide.

There is no way of telling how Caligula might have been affected by this turn of events. Being only the third son of Germanicus, as it turned out, worked to his advantage, since his career had not been advanced, and even though it would have been appropriate for him to have received the toga of manhood by 26, he still had not received it by 29, when he gave a further demonstration of his precocious rhetorical skills by delivering the funeral oration in honour of Livia.[27] After Livia's death in early 29, he passed into the care of yet another great woman of the Imperial house, his grandmother Antonia. His sister Drusilla was also at Antonia's house at this time, and the company probably also included his other sister Livilla (the eldest, Agrippina, had married in 28). Only one event is recorded during this period; Suetonius reports the gossip that Antonia caught her grandson *in flagrantibus* with Drusilla, a story that need not be taken seriously (p. 85). Antonia may, however, have been an important influence on Caligula in these years. As the daughter of Marc Antony she would no doubt have made Caligula aware of his ancestor's qualities and achievements, especially in the east, where she had very close contacts. She was friendly with the family of Herod, especially Berenice, and had dealings with Lysimachus, brother of the Philo who later headed a deputation of Alexandrian Jews to Caligula and wrote a first hand account of his experiences. Through her father she was half-sister of Cleopatra Selene, wife of Juba II of Mauretania, and step-aunt of Pythodoris, wife of Polemo I of Pontus, mother and grandmother of several eastern kings. Caligula always felt some degree of respect for Rome's client kings and the attitude may have first developed in Antonia's house. It seems that at the time Antonia was playing ward to some of her distant relatives, the sons of the murdered King Cotys of Thrace. On their father's death shortly before 19, Rhoemetalces, Polemo and Cotys (II) were sent to Rome to be brought up and they apparently spent time with Caligula. In a decree issued at Cyzicus on his accession they take pride in describing themselves as *syntrophous kai hetairous heautoi gegonotas* ('brought up together with him as comrades'). This early friendship was to bear fruit later when all three brothers were given kingdoms of their own. Among the Roman visitors to her house were Valerius Asiaticus and Lucius Vitellius.[28] Asiaticus became a friend of Caligula despite an obvious disparity in years (he held his first consulship in 35), and Vitellius' son, the future emperor, would later race chariots with him.

After the fall of Agrippina, Sejanus continued to consolidate his position. Lower Germany was governed by Lucius Apronius, the father

Stemma 2
The dynastic links of Antonia Minor

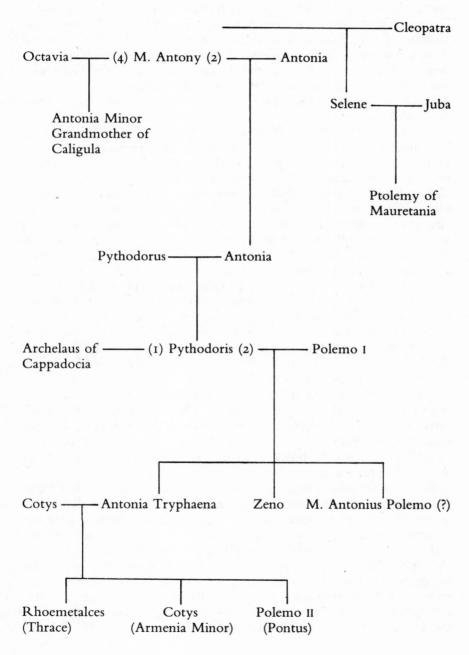

of Lucius Apronius Caesianus, one of Sejanus' friends. In 29 Upper Germany fell to Gnaeus Cornelius Lentulus Gaetulicus, whose daughter was betrothed to Sejanus' son Aelius Gallus.[29] Also, the treason trials continued. Of all the victims during this final phase of Sejanus' attack, the most prominent was Asinius Gallus (possibly the intended new husband of Agrippina). He had long been the object of Tiberius' irrational hatred, because of his marriage to Vipsania. The account of his case is derived mainly from the epitomes of Dio and is very sketchy. It does seem that he was charged in 30 (the nature of the charges is unclear), and held incommunicado pending the hearing of his case, which had still not taken place by 33.[30]

Sejanus' next target was Caligula's older brother Drusus. Foolishly, he had allowed himself to be used as a dupe in the campaigns against his mother and Nero, and had perhaps deluded himself into believing that he enjoyed the support and friendship of the Prefect. He was apparently on Capri with Tiberius when his mother and brother were condemned.[31] His wife Aemilia Lepida was suborned by Sejanus to bring a number of false charges (not identified) against him, and some time in 30 Drusus was sent back to Rome, where a certain Cassius was set up by Sejanus to press charges. Dio is the only source to say anything about the accusation, and he provides no specific details. Drusus was arrested and imprisoned in a cell beneath the imperial residence on the Palatine Hill.[32]

Sejanus' power now seemed unassailable, and the measure of his success is provided by the honours that befell him in 30 and 31. He was at last betrothed to Livilla.[33] Finally, he was chosen by Tiberius as colleague in the emperor's consulship in 31, despite his equestrian status. This was clearly a mark of enormous distinction, and in addition to it he received proconsular *imperium*, presumably in May 31, when he would have had to follow Tiberius' lead and resign his consulship.[34] It is impossible to determine what Tiberius was hoping to achieve in advancing Sejanus' career in this way. Perhaps he naively believed that in the event of his own death the Prefect would keep control over affairs until Caligula or Gemellus, who would become Sejanus' step-son, was old enough to assume the principate.

By about the middle of the year Sejanus' fortunes began to wane. The precise details of his fall from grace are unknown to us. It is difficult to know why he might have wanted to plot against Tiberius, since the emperor's death at this time would hardly have been in his interest. But such a tradition is found in Josephus and Suetonius and hinted at elsewhere.[35] According to Josephus it was Antonia who first gave Tiberius an indication of the danger posed by him, by smuggling a letter to the emperor in Capri through her freedman Pallas. Dio adds that the letter was written out by Caenis, Antonia's servant, who went on later to be the much-loved mistress of Vespasian.[36] If the story is true it could represent Antonia's natural desire to protect her grandson's interests. While it seems implausible that Sejanus would have planned any coup against Tiberius, it is not unlikely that he was plotting some move against Caligula. That there was some sort of campaign planned against him is suggested by the fate of a Sextius Paconianus, who was brought to trial later as one of those who had joined the conspiracy of Sejanus against Caligula.[37] The later, official, version of events seems to have been to explain Sejanus' downfall as the result of involvement in such a plot. In the brief autobiography written by Tiberius before his death, and seen by Suetonius, the emperor said that he had punished Sejanus for venting his hatred on the children of Germanicus.[37] Since Tiberius was an interested party we should perhaps pay little attention to this claim. If there is any truth to it, his concern could have been limited only to Nero (and perhaps Caligula), since after Sejanus' death neither the order for Drusus' arrest, nor for his mother's banishment, was revoked. In fact, it was about this time that Nero finally lost his battle against Sejanus. He died, in circumstances that were arranged afterwards to suggest suicide (Suetonius claims that he was tricked into suicide by a pretended sentence of death). This may have confirmed suspicions about Sejanus that Tiberius already felt, since the death was said to have occurred when he was already under a cloud.[39]

At some point after Caligula's nineteenth birthday (August 30, 31), Tiberius seems to have felt that it was time to bring the young man under his guidance, and summoned him to Capri. The future emperor's career began now to make its first advances. He was granted the *toga virilis* soon after his arrival, in a ceremony that seems perfunctory and without the elaboration or the donative that marked his brother's ceremony.[40] Willrich plausibly argued that both the delay and the modest arrangements were deliberate on Tiberius' part, and quite in character, since he wanted to avoid the danger of Caligula's head being turned, as seemed to have happened in the case of his brothers.[41] Moreover, according to Dio, Tiberius asked the senate not to make him conceited by numerous or premature honours.[42] Caligula was marked for the augurate (a relatively minor priestly office), in place of his brother Drusus according to Suetonius, but was elevated directly to a priesthood.[43] On that occasion Tiberius spoke well of him, praising his *pietas* and *indoles* (sense of duty and good character'). Dio adds the note that with his kind words Tiberius gave an indication that Caligula was to be his successor, and that this prospect was enormously popular among the Romans. If so, the popularity must have been because of the memory of Germanicus rather than any perceived merits of Caligula, who at this point must have been almost unknown.[44]

Tiberius finally struck against Sejanus on 18 October 31. To engineer the operation he called on the services of Quintus Naevius Cordus

Sutorius Macro, who was to play a prominent role in Caligula's early years. Macro was a 'self made' man of simple provincial origins, from the town of Alba Fucens. His rise from obscurity before the fall of Sejanus is unrecorded, except that he had been a Prefect of the Vigiles, whose fourteen cohorts were used in Rome essentially as a combination fire brigade and police force.[45] It appears that Macro entered Rome on the night of 17 October 31, having been secretly appointed to replace Sejanus as Prefect of the Praetorians. He made his arrangements with the consul Memmius Regulus and the current Prefect of the Vigiles, Graecinus Laco. The Vigiles played a key role in these events, and we can assume that Macro would earlier have ensured that the command remained with successors on whose loyalty he could rely. He fooled Sejanus into entering the Temple of Apollo on the Palatine, where a senate meeting was to be held, in the belief that he would hear that the emperor was to grant him *tribunicia potestas*. The Praetorians guarding the senate were ordered back to their barracks by Macro, and their place was taken by the Vigiles. When the letter from Tiberius was read, it turned out, in fact, to be a bitter denunciation of his former friend. Macro had in the meantime gone to the Praetorian barracks to confine the troops to their quarters, and the senate, bold now in the absence of the Praetorians, condemned Sejanus, who was then arrested by Laco. He was strangled in prison. The precautions taken by Macro were highly elaborate, and had apparently even included a plan to release Drusus from his cell and put him at the head of the rebellion, should Sejanus show any resistance. Macro's use of the Vigiles in this incident was a brilliant stroke, and although there was a breakdown of discipline among the Praetorians afterwards (they rioted because their loyalty had been called into question and because the Vigiles had preempted their role), it was clear that by the end of the day the new Praetorian Prefect had taken complete control. The enormous confidence that Tiberius placed in him is shown by the fact that he remained as sole prefect, without a partner. The senate showered honours on him, including the offer of *ornamenta praetoria*, which he declined, since he doubtless preferred to exercise real power.[46] Macro up to this point behaved like the archetype of a loyal soldier, prepared to do his master's bidding. But he soon showed that, like Sejanus, he was determined to exercise authority behind the throne. The whole incident must have convinced him of the vital role of military force in settling political questions, and it was to provide a compelling precedent when Tiberius died, leaving the succession issue open.

There remained one final blow for Tiberius. Before committing suicide, Sejanus' divorced wife Apicata revealed in a letter that her husband Sejanus had conspired with his mistress Livilla to kill the latter's husband Drusus. Tiberius' worst suspicions about the nature of his son's death were confirmed after he launched a thorough investigation. Livilla paid for her part in the plot with her life, starved to death by Antonia, her mother, according to some accounts.[47] Perhaps most significantly, the ouster of Sejanus did not bring about the release of Agrippina or of her son Drusus. This seems to confirm that Tiberius must have been convinced by overwhelming evidence of their guilt. Yet whatever his feelings towards other members of the family he certainly showed no hostility towards Caligula; when he referred to the youth's *pietas* on his elevation to the priesthood he may well have meant to emphasize that he was innocent of any involvement in conspiracies.[48] If Caligula's mind had been fed by his mother's denunciations of Tiberius and bitter complaints that her husband, his father, had been cheated by Tiberius of the principate, he did not show it, but kept whatever feelings he had to himself. It appears that from this point on Caligula began a campaign to consolidate his position as the likely successor, and that he was abetted in these efforts by Macro. This need not indicate any special bond of affection between the two. The new Prefect clearly recognized that Caligula's popularity as the son of Germanicus would in the end almost assure him of the principate, and Caligula in turn courted the favour of Macro as being the man whose military support was essential. According to Philo Macro assiduously worked on Tiberius to promote his protegé.[49] Philo claims that he represented Caligula as friendly and obedient, so devoted to Gemellus that he would be willing to give up his claim to the succession in the latter's favour. Much of this may well be the product of Philo's own imagination, but it is certainly not implausible. At any rate a number of *maiestas* trials occurred during this period, some of them clearly resulting from the efforts of Macro to get rid of the opposition by playing on the widely felt desire for vengeance against Sejanus and his supporters. Sextius Paconianus, who, as noted before, had helped Sejanus in plotting against Caligula, was brought to trial, and saved himself only by turning informer against Latinius Latiaris, who had played a key role in the prosecution of Titus Sabinus. Marcus Cotta Messalinus was accused in 32 of placing doubts on Caligula's masculinity and was saved only by the personal intervention of the emperor, his old friend. Sextus Vistilius, who made similar charges, was informed that he was no longer welcome with Tiberius. No trial was held, but he killed himself by opening his veins.[50] These were not the only ones to suffer. Tacitus speaks of charges of treason brought against five senators of high rank, Gaius Annius Pollio (suff. 21–2) and his son Lucius Annius Vinicianus, Gaius Appius Silanus (cos. 28), Mamercus Aemilius Scaurus (suff. 21?) and Calvisius Sabinus (cos. 26), all of whom were probably the targets of Macro's attacks. There may well have been lingering hints that they had plotted with Sejanus against Caligula; it is at any rate strongly implied by Tacitus that Scaurus was a friend of Sejanus. These last cases caused much consternation among the senators, but in the event the trials came to nothing. Celsus, one of the prosecutors, removed Appius and Calvisius from the charge. The three other cases were adjourned pending Tiberius' attendance in the senate (in the event he never came back to Rome). Celsus committed suicide later in the year, charged with conspiracy, and Scaurus was driven to suicide by Macro in 34, but the remaining three survived.[51] Among other individuals who survived was Lentulus Gaetulicus, the commander in Upper Germany and son in law of Lucius Apronius, commander in Lower Germany. Accused in AD 34 because he had betrothed his daughter to Sejanus' son he escaped conviction, saved, it would seem, by his control of powerful legions (p. 130).

It is clear that whatever Tiberius' feelings of antagonism towards Agrippina, he bore no grudge against Caligula. Indeed, there seems to have been some curious bond between the two, which may have been based on their shared scholarly interests. Tiberius took up responsibility for the young man's education, and Josephus observes that Caligula was inspired by Tiberius' intellectual achievements to apply himself to his own studies, gaining an outstanding eduction as a result.[52] Caligula may well have found in Tiberius a kindred spirit, and there is no reason to assume that their mutual affection was not genuine. There is, curiously enough, no hint that he felt any bitterness towards Tiberius over the fact that his mother and brother were languishing in exile or prison. Caligula's first instinct, of course, would have been to survive, and this would have required him to suppress any possible sense of moral responsibility, and have encouraged him to subordinate all other considerations to his own protection. He needed constantly to be on his guard, and the sources portray him as someone skilled at concealing his true feelings. We are told by Suetonius that while he was in Capri there had been some who tried to persuade him to complain but he did not, and ignored the destruction of his own family *incredibili dissimulatione* ('with remarkable pretence'). Presumably the troublemakers were agents of Sejanus, although it is difficult to identify them among the men known to have been on the island. Tiberius took with him to Capri Cocceius Nerva, a senator whose expertise lay in the knowledge of the law, Curtius Rufus, an equestrian with literary leanings, and a number of Greek scholars, the most famous being Thrasyllus, his astrologer.[53] In addition, Asinius Gallus, probably now in his seventies, the future emperor Galba, and an unnamed man of consular rank who wrote *Annales*, visited the island. The only person recorded there about the same age as Caligula was Aulus Vitellius, the future emperor. They were probably friends at the time (Vitellius' father was a visitor to Antonia's house), since they are later recorded as enjoying chariot races together in Rome.[54] None of the above seem likely to have been plotting against Caligula. Since on other occasions Sejanus worked through bribed freedmen, it is possible that he had arranged a network among the household staff on the island.

Tacitus tells us that Caligula learned his deceit at the knees of his grandfather Tiberius, *nihil abnuentem, dum dominationis aspiceretur* ('refusing nothing, in the hope of attaining power'), and aped his mood and words, concealing his monstrous character beneath a spurious modesty: *immanem animum regens subdola modestia*, giving rise to Passienus Crispus' *bon mot* that the world never knew a better slave or a worse master.[55] Passienus' observation is especially valuable. Twice consul, and married twice to wives from the imperial family (the second time to Caligula's sister Agrippina Minor), he clearly had a good insight into what was happening in court circles. Moreover, his witticism would have had little point among his contemporaries if it did not have a ring of truth. Later, it would suit Caligula's purpose to present himself in quite a different light, as one tormented by rage over the treatment of his family. He was probably responsible for the story which, according to Suetonius, made its way into some accounts (*quidam auctores*). In this version his family's fate drove Caligula to plot Tiberius' murder. He entered his bedroom with dagger in hand, but was overwhelmed with pity and threw the weapon down. Most implausibly Tiberius was supposed to have been aware of what happened, but did nothing.[56]

During this period, according to Suetonius, Caligula was indulged by Tiberius in his chosen excesses, in the hope that it would soothe his savage nature. He supposedly enjoyed watching torture, was given to sexual excesses and gluttony, and was obsessed by theatrical shows. This seems most unlikely, and Philo insists that while Tiberius was alive Caligula lived a moderate and restrained life.[57] Moreover, the fates of Cotta Messalinus and Sextus Vistilius, combined with his expulsion of the pervert *sphintriae* at the beginning of his reign, seem to indicate that Caligula adopted an almost prudish attitude towards sex. In any case Tiberius felt highly enough of him in 33 to appoint him to the quaestorship.[58] He also promised to advance him to the other offices five years earlier than was customary, although he wisely asked the senate not to make him conceited by numerous or premature honours. Various distinctions and minor offices were voted for him in Italy and the provinces.[59] The mints of some Roman colonies in Spain produced coins with the first identifiable representations of Caligula. Unfortunately, as is often the case on colonial issues, there is no attempt at realism, and they are of little value as portraits.

Ironically these marks of distinction were conferred in 33, the very year that Caligula's mother and brother died. Just as rumours were circulating that Drusus was about to be reconciled to Tiberius he was deliberately allowed to starve to death in his dungeon in the palace. The process stretched out over several days, the last spent in agony, as he even ate the stuffing from his mattress. Tiberius provided the horrified senate a verbatim account of his words and actions, along with his final delirious abuse of the emperor. Drusus was denounced in the strongest terms and described as *infestum reipublicae* ('hostile to the state'), and also, perhaps with reference to his disloyalty towards Nero, as *exitialis in suos* ('pernicious to his own family').[60]

Tiberius' intention in presenting this grisly record to the senate is unclear, but he may have wanted to provide a categorical demonstration that Drusus really was dead. Two years earlier, an imposter had appeared in Achaea and Asia, claiming to be Drusus, and had gained a number of adherents. He was eventually tracked down by Poppaeus Sabinus, governor of Achaea and Macedonia, and the fraud exposed.[61] Scarcely had the memory of the real Drusus' death faded, when news arrived that Agrippina had died on 18 October of the same year. She had starved herself to death. In informing the senate, Tiberius claimed that the suicide was due to her grief over the fate of her lover Asinius Gallus. Certainly, the sources seem to concede that the emperor had no direct role in her actual death, and there even seems to have been an attempt to force-feed her.[62] As it happened, she died on 18 October, the anniversary of Sejanus' death two years earlier, and in his report to the senators Tiberius dwelt on the coincidence. He also drew their attention to his clemency, in that Agrippina had not been strangled or thrown down the Gemonian stairs, the fate considered appropriate for traitors. Tacitus reports this as a piece of grim irony, but if taken at its face value it once again suggests that there might have been evidence available to Tiberius that Agrippina had been involved in some kind of plot. The senate responded by voting an expression of thanks for the emperor's Clementia, and for annual rites on the anniversary of the two deaths. In the same year, 33, Tiberius crossed over to the mainland to be present in Antium for the marriage of Caligula and his first wife Junia Claudia, daughter of Marcus Junius Silanus.[63] Caligula's father-in-law belonged to a family that rose to prominence under the Julio-Claudians. He was suffect consul in 15, and five years later interceded quite successfully with Tiberius on behalf of his brother Decimus, who had been banished because of an affair with Julia the Younger. Two years later he sought to strengthen his position with the emperor even further by proposing that the Roman year be dated from the emperor's accession, instead of by the consuls. There is no further mention of him for ten years, when he is grouped with others castigated by Tacitus for their servile behaviour towards Tiberius. Because of his rank in the senate he had, by the time of the emperor's death, acquired the privilege of casting his vote first, and Tiberius held him in such high regard that he refused to try any case on appeal from his decision; Syme has suggested that Silanus might even have been a Claudian on his mother's side, with some kinship to the emperor.[64]

The relative distinction of Caligula's bride seems to indicate that he

Stemma 3
The family connections of Vinicius and Vinicianus

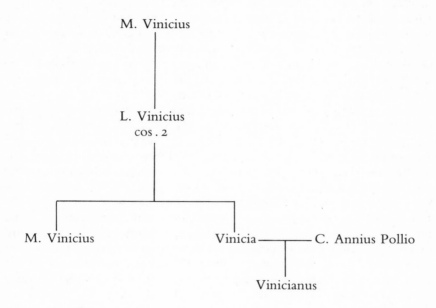

M. Vinicius

L. Vinicius
COS . 2

M. Vinicius   Vinicia —————— C. Annius Pollio

Vinicianus

enjoyed Tiberius' favour, and this stands in contrast to the unimpressive matches of his two unmarried sisters, announced in the same year. Agrippina had already been betrothed, in 28, to Gnaeus Domitius Ahenobarbus, a man described by Suetonius as detestable in every aspect of his life, but who, all the same, enjoyed a distinguished lineage (he was grandson of Marc Antony and Octavia). Drusilla was now married to Lucius Cassius Longinus, who belonged to an old plebeian noble family. He had not achieved any distinction, and was a man known more for his affability than his energy. Livilla was given to Marcus Vinicius. Since he is to play an important role in Caligula's later career, some information on his background might be appropriate. His grandfather Marcus had belonged to an equestrian family from Cales in Campania, and went on to become a personal friend of Augustus. He acquired a reputation as a fine soldier, winning the *ornamenta triumphalia* and holding the suffect consulship in 19 BC (the first of his family to do so). His descendants did not, however, achieve the same distinction. His son Lucius (consul AD 2) made no mark in the military sphere, although he did acquire a reputation as an orator and connoisseur of literature (he was an admirer of Ovid). Lucius' son, Marcus Vinicius, husband of Livilla, seems to have been of a rather quiet and retiring disposition, and to have inherited his father's

33

interest in literature, since he was the patron of the historian Velleius
Paterculus, who dedicated his work to him. He was consul in 30, and
survived the fall of Sejanus unscathed. Like Cassius Longinus he was a
safe, but far from brilliant, match. Also, in the same year, Julia, daughter
of Drusus (son of Tiberius) was married to Rubellius Blandus, grandson
of a knight from Tibur, a marriage so undistinguished that it caused the
household much distress. All of this leaves open the possibility that
Tiberius was taking measures to ensure that there would be no serious
rivals to complicate his plans for the succession.[65]

Caligula's wife Junia probably joined him when he returned to Capri,
to an atmosphere of increasing intrigue. Macro had by now decided that
Caligula's star was in the ascendant, and sought to ingratiate himself with
the young man and to press his case with Tiberius. To this end he did
not hesitate to exploit even personal tragedy. At some point Junia became
pregnant; neither she nor the infant survived the birth.[66] It would not
have been surprising for Caligula to turn to another woman for comfort,
and Macro's wife Ennia Thrasylla, was on hand to provide it.[67] The
precise circumstances of the affair are obscure. Tacitus, followed essentially
by Dio, probably comes closest in his claim that after Junia's death Macro
induced his wife to have a liaison with Caligula, in order to curry favour
with him, while Caligula was happy to go along with the scheme, since
he realized that Macro's support would benefit him. Suetonius even
claims that he undertook to marry her if he became emperor, swearing
to it on oath, and confirming the promise with a written contract.[68] In
any case, when Caligula later decided to get rid of Macro, he would use
the charge of pandering.

While on Capri Caligula made the acquaintance of one individual who
was to remain a close and trusted friend throughout his reign. Julius
Agrippa (often referred to incorrectly, but conveniently, as 'Herod'
Agrippa), grandson of Herod the Great of Judea, was a man whose
personality in many respects mirrored Caligula's own.[69] Agrippa was
brilliant, unpredictable, much given to reckless extravagance. In this he
resembled Caligula, but he also possessed both a highly developed sense
of self preservation and fine talents as a diplomat. Most importantly, he
was energetic in the defence of his own people, at a point in their history
when such defence would prove most invaluable. His family background
was hardly less tragic and dramatic than Caligula's had been. His father
Aristobulus was executed (along with Aristobulus' brother, Alexander)
by his grandfather Herod in 7 BC, when the hostility between Herod
and his sons, and suspicions of treason, reached their final vicious climax.

Agrippa was born in 10 BC, and not long after his father's death was
taken to Rome by his mother Berenice (neice of Herod), to stay at the
home of Antonia, Caligula's grandmother. Antonia was on close terms
with Berenice, and these close personal ties were strengthened even

Stemma 4
The family connections of Herod Agrippa

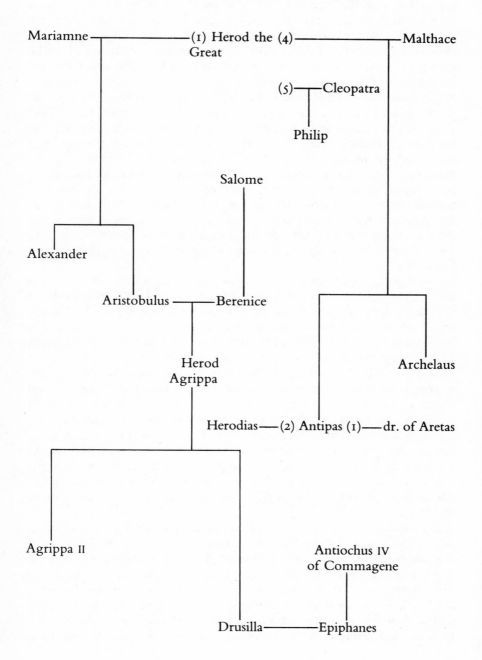

further by the friendship between Berenice's mother, the famous Salome, and Augustus' wife Livia. Agrippa thus had the opportunity to mix with the children of the imperial family at an early age and to establish a rapport that would serve him well throughout his colourful life. He made early contact with the future emperor Claudius, and was especially close to Drusus, Tiberius' son. As he grew to manhood Agrippa became increasingly extravagant. He was unable to meet his debts in Rome, and his problems reached a climax on the death of Drusus in the autumn of AD 23, when he suddenly found himself cut off from the imperial circle. At this point he judged it prudent to abandon the scene both of his youth and of his bad debts, and returned to his homeland, avoiding his relatives by burying himself away in a remote part of Idumea, the semi-desert area south of Judaea. The wilds of Idumea were considerably less to Agrippa's tastes than had been the cosmpolitan attractions of Rome. He grew highly despondent, to the extent of considering suicide, but was rescued from this drastic step by his brother-in-law (and half-uncle) Antipas, who had been appointed by Augustus as tetrarch of Galilee and Peraea, on his father Herod's death. Antipas founded a new capital city, on Hellenistic lines, at Tiberias, where he placed Agrippa in charge of its financial affairs.

For Agrippa the circumscribed life of a municipal civil servant seems to have proved distinctly unexciting, and he resented his brother-in-law's unpleasant habit of casting his poverty in his teeth. We do not know how long he stayed in Tiberias, but by AD 32/3 he had moved to Syria, now governed by an old friend from his Roman days, Lucius Pomponius Flaccus. Agrippa had Flaccus' ear, but indiscreetly accepted a bribe to use his influence in promoting the interests of Damascus in a boundary dispute with Sidon. Flaccus discovered the corruption, and Agrippa fell out of favour. He now seems to have felt it an opportune time to return to Rome, but even on the point of departure he was dogged by the consequences of his old spendthrift ways. The procurator of the imperial estate in Jamnia, Gaius Herennius Capito, tracked him down, and sought the recovery of money owed to the imperial treasury in Rome. Agrippa made a hasty escape, reaching Rome in AD 36. En route, he stopped in Alexandria and borrowed a considerable sum from Alexander, the brother of Philo.

When Agrippa reached Puteoli he made contact with Tiberius in Capri, and much to his relief was invited in the most friendly terms to visit the emperor. He almost came to grief when, the day after his arrival on the island, a letter arrived from Capito detailing the extent of Agrippa's debt. Tiberius was determined to shun him, but the situation was saved by the timely intercession of Antonia who provided Agrippa with the money. Josephus says that she was moved by her affection for his mother Berenice and because of his friendship with Claudius, illustrating once again that powerful nexus between Antony's daughter and the ruling dynasties of the East. Agrippa had yet again fallen on his feet, and was restored to Tiberius' favour. So charming and diplomatic was he that Tiberius asked him to take his grandson Gemellus under his wing. It is to be noted that Agrippa quickly assessed that the future lay elsewhere, and began to pay special attention to Caligula. He correctly recognized that where reckless spending was concerned, the two were kindred spirits. Borrowing a million drachmae he repaid Antonia's loan and shrewdly invested the remainder in currying Caligula's favour. Agrippa was now over 46 years old, and the attention of the older man, grandson of the great Herod, would doubtless have aggravated Caligula's sense of self-importance. Willrich has argued that Tiberius sought to train Caligula as a constitutional ruler, free from Hellenistic influences. If so, Agrippa would have undone much of Tiberius' efforts. How much blame can fairly be attributed to Agrippa for Caligula's later conduct is difficult to determine, but it is a reasonable speculation that he did not seek to win the future emperor's favour by promoting ideas of moderation and constitutional government. Harmful or not, there can be no denying that Agrippa's influence was strong and lasting. Of all Caligula's old cronies, he was the only one whose counsel was still followed at the very end.

Agrippa had a knack of bringing trouble onto his own head. He made the mistake of speculating before Caligula on the brilliant prospects offered by Tiberius' eventual demise and his own succession. That Agrippa was involved in direct political intrigue is most unlikely; he was surely involved in no more than laying secure foundations for his personal future. The only weapons he needed were charm and a smooth tongue, and the incident reveals that he understood exactly where Caligula was most susceptible. Unfortunately, there was a witness. When Agrippa's coachman Eutychus was later accused of stealing his master's clothes he declared that he had evidence of treasonable activities. Eutychus was sent to Tiberius, who hesitated at first, then in September 36 summoned Agrippa to Tusculum. He was charged with wishing the emperor's death, found guilty and sentenced to imprisonment. The sentence proved not so harsh as he might have feared. Antonia saw to it that he should enjoy considerable comforts, and procured these through the connivance of Macro.[70]

In his later years Tiberius must have become increasingly concerned about the question of a successor. His options were limited. The Augustan precedent would oblige him to seek someone from within the imperial house, and to go outside it would open up the prospect of chaos and civil strife.[71] Claudius, brother of Germanicus and nephew of Tiberius, had the right family background but was considered mentally incompetent. He had been kept out of public life and sought consolation in his scholarly studies, occasionally enlivened by drinking and gambling. The choice would clearly have to be between Gemellus and Caligula.

Tiberius' failure to make his views clear and explicit has led to much confusion and speculation in the literary sources.[72] Generally there is a sense that Tiberius was far from happy at the prospect of being succeeded by Caligula. Suetonius says that he had fostered the rise of Sejanus to secure the succession for Gemellus, whom he looked upon as his *nepotem...naturalem* ('natural grandson'), against the claim of Germanicus' sons. At best, Caligula's eventual succession was supposedly regarded as an inevitable, but none the less appalling, prospect. Philo reports that Tiberius shrewdly saw through him and recognized that he had an erratic and unreliable temperament that made him unsuited to the task. Similarly, Suetonius says that Tiberius recognized Caligula's destructive powers and felt that he had reared a 'viper for the Roman people and a ruin for all men', which is echoed in Tacitus' claim that Tiberius felt that Caligula would have all of the cruel dictator Sulla's faults but none of his qualities. Others see more personal motives for Tiberius' unease, in particular his concern for the future of Gemellus. He was, of course, Tiberius' natural rather than adopted grandson, and the emperor would have felt a natural anxiety about his fate, one that that went beyond the narrow dynastic issue. Tacitus reports him putting his arm around Gemellus and saying to Caligula, 'You will kill him and another will kill you', an anecdote repeated by Dio. Josephus has Tiberius faced with the inevitability of Caligula's succession and consequently suffering anguish because his own choice was for Gemellus, whose future seemed perilous. Philo claims that there were those who said that had Tiberius lived a little longer, he would have eliminated Caligula, and that only the constant reassurances of Macro held him back.[73] Yet confusingly enough the sources speak also of Tiberius' reservations about Gemellus. Dio reports Tiberius' consolation that Caligula's reign would be so disastrous that his own would look good by comparison, and adds that he suspected that Gemellus was illegitimate. Suetonius also refers to suspected illegitimacy as the grounds for Tiberius' plan to murder Gemellus (along with Caligula).[74] This notion contradicts Suetonius' statements mentioned earlier, and it is possible that we have a reflection of how Tiberius' commitment to Gemellus might have waned because of rumour and gossip fed to him by Macro. Of course the conduct of Gemellus' errant mother, Livilla, would have made Macro's task easier. None of these ancecdotes throws much light on the issue, and perhaps suggest that the confusion arose simply because Tiberius did not make his ultimate intentions clear.

There was, of course, no formal mechanism for the succession. The Augustan approach had been to associate his chosen successor in the powers of his office and thus, as it were, to leave the new princeps in place at his death. But neither young man, in Tiberius' rigid view of constitutional procedure, was yet old enough for this degree of responsibility. All that Tiberius could do, from a strictly legal point of view, was appoint an heir. This he did in 35, but hardly in a manner that clarified the situation, since he bequeathed his estate jointly to Caligula and Gemellus. Did he thereby intend the principate to be held jointly? The lack of a precedent for such an arrangement does not, in itself, invalidate the notion.[75] Dio does speak of his leaving the *autarchia* to Caligula and Gemellus, and Philo describes Gemellus as being bequeathed a 'share' of the rule.[76] But both sources are concerned not so much with constitutional procedure as with the moral impropriety of Caligula's claim to be sole ruler. The main objection to joint rule, however, is that while minor offices and honours were bestowed on Caligula during Tiberius' later years, nothing at all was granted to Gemellus, who was kept completely in the background, even to the extent that he had not yet formally assumed the *toga virilis* by Tiberius' death.[77] It is interesting that the sources place emphasis on Gemellus' great youth. Tacitus can be read to suggest that in the last months of Tiberius' life Gemellus (who was by then 17) had not yet reached puberty. Dio, under the year 33 refers to him as a child (*paidion*). Philo describes him as just entering adolescence in 37. Unfortunately we know virtually nothing about Gemellus' personality or character. The only detail is an anecdote of dubious value recorded by Philo that when he was later handed a sword and instructed to commit suicide he asked where to place the weapon. Now, Gemellus and his twin brother were born late in AD 19 (the year of Germanicus' death). By the time of Tiberius' death he would thus have been 17, hardly a child. It may well be the case that Gemellus was slow for his age and had been sheltered from appearing in public. This could explain Tiberius' concern for his welfare after his own death, and later have provided the senate with a justification for putting aside Tiberius' will. The comments of the sources may thus have their ultimate origins in his mental, rather than his chronological age.[78]

It seems difficult to believe that Tiberius could have thought that there was any serious prospect of his being succeeded by Gemellus. The other contender was the choice of the army and the people, both of Rome and of the empire as a whole. He must have been aware of the tremendous popularity that Caligula commanded as the son of Germanicus, and of the prestige enjoyed by a direct descendant of Augustus. The chance of Gemellus' acceptance as co-ruler on Tiberius' death would have been a remote one at best. For all the scholarly theorizing about a Gemellus party in Rome, his only named supporter was Avillius Flaccus, prefect of Egypt.[79] But since Flaccus had apparently been involved in the prosecution of Agrippina he might have felt that his future under Caligula was not promising, and he can hardly be considered as representative of a large body of feeling. Why then did Tiberius name Gemellus in the will? Balsdon suggests that he wanted to avoid a repetition of the discontent that the senate had felt on his own accession in having its mind made up for it.[80] Also, in making Gemellus Caligula's co-heir, he perhaps had the vain hope that this could somehow protect his grandson.

Although much energy has been expended in the effort to determine Tiberius' intentions, in the end they proved irrelevant. Caligula was accepted as the next princeps by the army, the senate and the people apparently without question, and much of the credit for this rests with Macro, who continued to strengthen his position right to the very end of Tiberius' life. The *maiestas* trials showed no signs of abating. In 37 an Albucilla was arraigned for an act of impiety against Tiberius. Her lovers, Gnaeus Domitius, Vibius Marsus and Lucius Arruntius were associated in the indictment. In the trial of these three, documents were presented to show that Macro had been present at the examination of witnesses and the torture of slaves, leading to the suspicion that because of his hostility to Arruntius he had fabricated much of the evidence. Tiberius was by this stage dying and all three men were urged to use delaying tactics. Arruntius refused. Although he did not come from a distinguished background (his father's consulship in 22 BC was possibly the family's first), Lucius Arruntius was a man much admired not only for his wealth and learning, but also for his integrity. It is said that Augustus speculated that Arruntius had both the capacity and inclination to be his successor. He was a natural target for emnity of both Tiberius and Sejanus, and it was speculated that when he became legate of Hispania (Citerior) Tiberius was afraid to allow him to assume his command and accordingly made him govern the province *in absentia*. In 31 a charge of *maiestas* was brought against him but quashed. By 37 he had come to the conclusion that the death of Tiberius would not herald any improvement in the political situation in Rome. His attitude was an excellent illustration of how secure Caligula's position was by now, although this one senator, unlike many of his fellows, could see through the glamour of the Germanican lineage. While Arruntius realized the certainty of Caligula's succession, he also was conscious that the pretender was barely more than a boy '*ignarum omnium aut pessimis innutritum*' and would be under the control of Macro, who was even more brutal than his predecessor Sejanus. If absolute power had corrupted Tiberius with *his* vast experience, what chance was there for the inexperienced Caligula under the tutelage of Macro? Arruntius' concern over Macro's power is reflected elsewhere in Tacitus, who speaks of his excessive influence (*nimia potentia*) over Caligula, and reports Tiberius' rebuke to the Prefect for 'forsaking the setting sun and turning to the rising sun'.[81] The assessment of Caligula is of great interest for what it tells us about his personality at this time. Arruntius saw the next emperor as a mere boy, corrupted by the evil power behind the throne, Macro. There is no suggestion, however, that Caligula was mentally unstable or inherently cruel or wicked. Indeed, the implication is that under different circumstances Arruntius might have held out hope for an enlightened reign.

About the beginning of March 37, Tiberius fell ill while in Campania. He fought his illness, putting on an appearance of cheerfulness and engaging in physical activities. His condition worsened, however, when he caught a chill and was struck down by a pain in his side. He eventually retired to his fine villa at Misenum, built originally by the great general Marius, with its commanding view of the sea. There he continued with his usual activities and regular rounds of dinner parties and entertainments. Plans to go to Capri were thwarted by stormy weather. He grew weaker and eventually took to his bed. Tacitus reports that when Tiberius' doctor Charicles (who seems to have been acting as Macro's agent) revealed to Macro that the emperor had only two days to live, the prefect made hurried arrangements to set Caligula's succession in motion. He ensured the loyal support of the key figures in the entourage by speaking to them in person, *conloquiis inter praesentes*. The military commanders and provincial governors were given their instuctions by messenger.[82]

Tiberius died on March 16, 37, and his death gave rise to a host of rumours. Suetonius relates several theories, that Caligula poisoned him, or starved him to death, or smothered or strangled him. Dio reflects part of this in his story that, as Caligula pretended to arrange Tiberius' coverlets, he suffocated him, with some help from Macro. Tacitus provides a more detailed account, that Tiberius had apparently died, but while Caligula was already being congratulated showed signs of revival, much to the consternation of everyone present. In Tacitus' report, however, it was Macro, not Caligula, who delivered the *coup de grâce*. The variations in these stories cast doubt on the whole notion of murder. Moreover there was a much less sensational report, attributed to Seneca (supported by Philo), that the death was perfectly natural. Seneca said that Tiberius felt his end approaching and took off his signet ring as if to give it to someone, but seemingly changed his mind. He called for his servants, and when they did not come, stood up. At this moment his strength failed him, and he fell dead near the couch. It might be noted that despite his apparently genuine reluctance to accept the principate in the first place, in his final hours Tiberius could not bring himself to give it up.[83]

· 3 ·

PRIVATE PURSUITS

BEFORE 37 CALIGULA HAD lived out of the public view and little would have been known about him. To give some flesh and blood to the political picture that will emerge in the following chapters, it will be useful at this point to consider him as a private man, with emphasis on his personal idiosyncracies and private interests (with the caution that much of the information is in fact based on incidents from fairly late in his reign and on anecdotal material of dubious reliability).

Fortunately, we have very full accounts of Caligula's physical appearance, which both Seneca and Suetonius describe in vivid detail. While personal descriptions in antiquity are often influenced by the theories of the physiognomists, who claimed that certain types of personality would create a certain appearance, Seneca's account, at least, must be close to the truth, since he was writing for people who, in some cases, would have known at first-hand what the emperor had looked like. He tells us that Caligula had a pale complexion, was prematurely balding, had thin legs and very large feet (the thin legs were probably a family trait, inherited from his father, who is said to have built up his own by constant horse-riding). All these features receive confirmation from Suetonius, who adds that he was very tall and uncoordinated, and had a broad forehead and hollow eyes (these last are confirmed by Pliny, who describes his eyes as *rigentes oculi*). He was supposedly so sensitive to his baldness that he would not allow himself to be viewed from above, objected to hearing the word 'goat', and made any man with a fine head of hair shave it off. Both Seneca and Suetonius describe him as repellently ugly, Suetonius adding that he used to practise before a mirror to make himself look more fearsome, and Seneca asserting that his expression was so fiendish that it could kill a man.[1] These last two observations are essentially value judgements, and can be confidently dismissed. The rapturous reception that Caligula received from the populace on his first journey to Rome, and the near adulation of the senate, would have been unthinkable had his appearance excited either ridicule or repulsion.

The most reliable source of evidence for Caligula's appearance is his coinage. The only certain pre-accession portraits are on the colonial issues of Carthago Nova in Spain, unfortunately with little apparent attempt at realism.[2] The official coinage of Rome sought to portray genuine likenesses, the most useful coins for our purpose being the large bronzes, especially the sestertii, whose field offered the engraver scope for detail and individualization. While some degree of idealization should be allowed, especially in the provision of a rich head of hair, it must be conceded that Caligula's profile on coins is fairly unremarkable, lacking the refined delicacy of Augustus' image, but also the squat ugliness of Nero's. The most noticeable and consistent features are the elongated forehead (confirming Suetonius), a somewhat bulbous nose, a slightly pointed chin, and a mouth with a retracted lower lip.

In the first six months of his reign Caligula behaved with remarkable restraint and modesty. When his true personality was given free rein, it soon became apparent that he was a young man with a taste for the exotic and the outrageous, who was not afraid to cause offence among what Dio calls the *euphrones*, the sober minded who took umbrage at his excesses. As Suetonius comments, he would claim that there was nothing in his own character that he admired more than his *adiatrepsia*, a Greek word, difficult to translate but conveying the notion of 'shamelessness'.[3] This shamelessness would manifest itself in a wide variety of ways. At a basic level it explains his apparent taste in exotic clothing. As a child, probably at the urging of his mother, he began to dress up for public show to entertain the soldiers, and in later life never lost his love of impersonation, imitating Alexander the Great, or a *triumphator*, or a variety of gods and goddesses. But when he dressed as himself, as it were, he would, according to Suetonius, appear in public in embroidered cloaks, covered in precious stones, or long-sleeved tunics and bracelets, with a variety of different kinds of exotic footwear.[4]

For his entertainments Caligula constantly sought out the different or novel. He supposedly invented new sorts of baths, where he could soak in perfumed oils. He devised bizarre and unnatural foods, and could compete with Trimalchio in the way he presented them to his guests. He was said to have laid out loaves and meats of gold, and to have drunk pearls melted in vinegar. The setting for his entertainments were equally novel. He had luxury villas throughout Campania and ships so extravagantly constructed that they contained baths and fruit trees. The surviving vessels at Nemi provide concrete evidence of their opulence (p. 201). Those not inclined towards maritime diversions could join one of his picnics, such as that described by Pliny at Velletri, which took place in a kind of tree house in the branches of an enormous plane tree, large enough to accommodate fifteen guests.[5]

In his personal pastimes his interests were essentially those of the common man. He had a passion for gambling, playing even when he was on his northern trip in Gaul. According to Seneca, when he went off to his Alban villa after the death of Drusilla it was to seek solace in gambling. He was also apparently willing to stoop to a little cheating to ensure a win.[6] He enjoyed good eating and drinking, and one scholar, T.E. Jerome, explains his erratic behaviour as the consequence of alcoholic intoxication, attributing his fainting fits to alcohol rather than to epilepsy. There is no real indication, however, that he drank to excess.[7] He was also, according to the sources, a man with an enormous sexual passion. The targets of his desires were varied. At dinner parties he would select the wives of guests during the course of the meal, have his pleasure, then regale the company with an account of the performance. Some of his supposed mistresses are known: the concubine Pyrallis, Ennia the wife of Macro, Nymphidia, the daughter of Callistus, the wife of Asiaticus. To these we must add his male partners: various hostages, the actor Mnester, his brother-in-law Marcus Lepidus, and Valerius Catullus, with whom he is supposed to have had a particularly vigorous session.[8] Finally, we must not forget his sisters, all of whom supposedly shared his bed. Balancing these tales of sexual dynamism, however, there is the story that his last wife supposedly had to supply him with aphrodisiacs. Moreover he was so narrow-minded that even before he became emperor attacks on his masculinity by such people as Marcus Cotta Messalinus and Sextus Vistellius led to charges of *maiestas*. On his accession he banished the *sphintriae*, sexual perverts, and had to be restrained from drowning them. He was also supposed to have burned the author of an Atellan farce for a *double entendre*. We have a relatively detailed account of only one of his marriages, to his last wife Caesonia, and the sources all acknowledge genuine affection for her, and a conduct both uxorious and monogamous.[9]

Caligula was also addicted to those peculiarly Roman forms of entertainment, the *spectacula*. There were technically three kinds. The least expensive were the *ludi scaenici*, stage plays in the broadest sense of the word. On a more ambitious scale were the *ludi circenses*, whose main event was horse-racing (which could be interspersed with other forms of entertainment). This was the most popular of the *spectacula* during the republic until replaced by the *munera gladiatoria*, the gladiatorial contests, which in the imperial period would be presented on the same days as animal fights. One of the most famous ancient episodes from the arena is the story of Androcles and the lion, which supposedly took place while Caligula was presiding.[10]

Caligula gave many gladiatorial shows, in the amphitheatre and in the Saepta. They were on a grand scale. There had in the past been limitations on the number of gladiators allowed in any one show, but he lifted the restrictions. Gladiators as a profession were much favoured by him. He often gave them money, and even took some with him when he went to the north on campaign. He was a partisan of the *parmularii*, who supported the Thracian gladiators, with their small round shields, and was an opponent of the rival *murmillones*, armed with the larger oblong shields. According to Pliny he had a Thracian in his own school by the name of Studiosus ('Keen'), who had the advantage of a right arm that was longer than the left. He also supposedly owned gladiators who had trained themselves not to blink. He apparently took part in gladiatorial contests himself, without taking any risk, of course. To be his partner might prove a dubious honour. It is said that when practising with a gladiator from the training school with wooden swords, Caligula ran his partner through with a real one. Prominent citizens took part in the contests, reputedly forced to do so but probably voluntarily. Caligula also found that gladiatorial contests could be a lucrative source of income. The responsibility for organizing the shows rested with two praetors chosen by lot, a system that had prevailed under Augustus. He would sell the survivors of the gladiatorial games, preferably to the praetors, forcing up the bids himself, while others pushed up the prices by joining in, in the hope of ingratiating themselves with him. Gladiatorial shows appealed to a particularly brutal side of human nature, but Caligula seems to have been no worse than his contemporaries, and on one occasion even berated spectators who enjoyed the spectacle of a particularly gory episode when five combatants, presumably disabled, were slaughtered by *retiarii*, armed with nets and tridents.[11]

Caligula's real passions, however, were reserved for horse racing. During the republic magistrates were obliged to call upon the established stables, which acquired their own following and were known by the colours worn by their drivers. Originally there were only Reds and Whites. Early in the first century the Greens and Blues appeared, eventually to dominate the others. Julius Caesar often attended the races but took little real interest in the events, preferring to spend his time there working on documents. He was much criticised for his diffidence and later emperors found it politic to show a more personal involvement. Caligula's obsession with racing, however, sprang from a personal passion and not merely from a desire to swim with the tide. He spent enormous sums on horses, and had his own track, the *Gaianum*, on his Vatican estate. One of his fellow drivers there was the future emperor Vitellius, who suffered a spill when driving with the emperor, and had a permanent limp afterwards. Although the factions did not yet command the degree of fanaticism that would lead eventually to riots and bloodbaths, there was certainly a lively partisanship. Caligula was personally devoted to the Greens, and reputedly poisoned the horses and charioteers of the rival factions (Vitellius, for his part, was said to have executed opponents of the Blues). He would dine at the Green stable and would shower their drivers with gifts. One of them, Eutychus, received two million sesterces and was allowed the use of praetorians to build stables for him. Caligula had a favourite horse, the famous Incitatus, which was reputedly provided with a fine stable decorated with marble and ivory and with a fine jewelled collar. Before races soldiers were posted to keep the area quiet. Many stories were spread about Incitatus, originating most likely from Caligula's own humorous quips. The horse was supposedly invited to banquets. Dio claims that Caligula promised to make Incitatus a consul, and Suetonius reports rumours of such a plan. Possibly out of perverted sense of humour Caligula would pour libations to Incitatus' Salus, and claimed that he intended to co-opt him as his priest.[12]

The general public expected their emperor to be a devotee of the races, and would not have been uphappy about the contrast between the behaviour of Caligula and of Tiberius. The number of races in Caligula's day increased. Under Julius Caesar the normal number had been ten to twelve. Caligula increased this so that by 37, at the games commemorating the dedication of the Temple of Augustus, there were twenty races on the first day and forty on the second. By the end of his reign the regular number was twenty four. Suetonius claims that his races in the Circus, interspersed with various entertainments, lasted from morning until evening. The number of festivals when these races would be exhibited also increased. Circus games were instituted in honour of his mother in 37 and Drusilla's birthday was celebrated in 39 with two days of horse racing, athletic contests and the slaying of animals. In the following year, Tiberius' birthday also was celebrated by two days of horse races.[13] Interestingly, it is among Caligula's worthy acts that Suetonius records games in the circus where sand was mixed with red and green and senators drove the chariots. Senators, in fact, were forbidden from appearing in regular circus games by a senatorial decree of 19, but this occasion is presented as a piece of harmless horse-play (in the figurative sense).[14]

Caligula also had a passion for the stage and presented constant *ludi scaenici*, some of them at night, when he would light up the whole city. He loved the company of actors. On the grounds that they were a threat to public order Tiberius had banished a number of them from the city, and one of Caligula's first acts was to recall them. He lavished money on them and was constantly in their company, taking them also on his northern trip. His very last act before his death was to engage in congenial conversation with a troupe of visiting performers. Two favourites stand out. Apelles, the most famous actor of the day, was with him constantly. Also, the pantomime Mnester was said to have been his lover and they were reputed even to kiss in the theatre. Caligula looked upon the theatre as a serious activity. He took a dim view of people leaving or arriving in the middle of a performance, and, to avoid excuses about not being able to attend, postponed lawsuits and suspended public mourning. If anyone in the audience made the slightest noise while his favourite

Mnester was performing, according to Suetonius, Caligula would drag him from his seat and whip him with his own hand. When a knight created a disturbance he was reputedly told to go to King Ptolemy of Mauretania on a fool's errand. As with the races and gladiatorial shows, Caligula was no passive observer. It was claimed that on Capri, amidst various debaucheries, he would disguise himself in a wig and long robe, and devote himself to dancing and singing. When he became emperor he would join in the songs and the dances. One of the most bizarre stories told about him is that on one occasion he summoned leading men from the senate at the dead of night, pretending he had some business to discuss, merely to treat them to an impromptu dance. These anecdotes are, however, difficult to reconcile with Suetonius' statement that on the day of his death he was preparing for his very first appearance on the stage.[15]

Some of Caligula's interests do redeem him somewhat. He was clearly a man of considerable intellectual powers, although allowance must be made for the usual rhetorical embroidering by the ancient sources. His talents may have been exaggerated to emphasize the contrast between his good and evil side. In his early childhood he would have had before him the example of his father Germanicus, a noted orator and man of letters.[16] Germanicus was the author of a number of literary works, including the still extant version of Aratus' *Phaenomena*, and Greek comedies, one of which may well have been performed annually in the reign of Claudius. He could, however, have provided Caligula little in the way of formal education — his son was only seven when Germanicus died. We know that as a child Caligula made some sort of speech to the people of Assos, and delivered the funeral oration for Livia in 29. Beyond this we have no details of his formal education until he moved to Capri at the age of nineteen. Tiberius, under whose guidance he was placed, was deeply committed to liberal studies in both Latin and Greek. He wrote poems in both languages, and spoke Greek fluently. His linguistic interest (or pedantry) ran so deep that on one occasion he is said to have published an edict that contained a word of dubious Latinity, which he took so seriously that he spent a sleepless night worrying about it, and finally called in experts to guide him. He was in addition something of an expert on both sacred and secular law, once expressing a desire that by the end of his life he would have aquired mastery of the subject. Indeed, Tiberius seems to have felt truly comfortable only in the company of scholars. His early 'exile' in Rhodes was prompted in part by the desire to attend the schools of the philosophers, while many of the people in his company on his early eastern mission and on Capri were men of letters. He was very fond of relaxed intellectual gatherings, where he would test his companions on mythology and literary quotations. On one occasion he was much offended when he discovered that the grammaticus Seleucus cheated by finding out from one of Tiberius' slaves what he was reading.[17]

Caligula would personally have found such company stimulating. Josephus testifies that he had a natural aptitude for learning, and, because of the excellent example provided by Tiberius, accomplished great things in this sphere, seeking the company of those who shared his interest in the higher things of the mind. As a consequence of this training he became greatly skilled in the use of both Greek and Latin. He developed a name as one of the best orators of his day, especially good at impromptu speech, and was even supposed to have written a book on oratory. Tacitus concedes that although his mind was disturbed (*turbata*) this did not affect his *vis dicendi* ('power of speech'). He enjoyed the challenge of writing rebuttals of successful speeches, and of composing the defences and accusations of important individuals, such as Domitius Afer, in the senate, arranging special invitations for the equestrians to come and hear him. When he was in Gaul in the winter of 39/40 he held contests in Latin and Greek oratory. Dio has preserved the outline of, and some quotations from, one of Caligula's important speeches, the declaration in 39 before the senate of his intention to restore the charge of *maiestas*. It seems to be well organized and logical, with the standard rhetorical devices, such as calling upon the dead Tiberius to address him, just as Cicero calls upon Appius Claudius in the *pro Caelio*.[18]

Suetonius claims that other than his passion for oratory Caligula showed little interest in scholarly learning (*eruditio*). This is not easily reconciled with Josephus' observations, and is belied to some degree by his apparent interest in literary debates. He is supposed to have considered destroying the works of Homer, claiming the same right as Plato, who excluded him from his ideal state. He threatened to remove the busts of Vergil and Livy from the public libraries, on the grounds that the former had no talent, and the latter was a wordy and shoddy historian. In fact Vergil was criticised, especially for plagiarism, in his own day, and obliged to answer the criticisms personally. Moreover Livy was charged with verbosity also by Pompeius Trogus, the Augustan historian (although the same trait was admired by Quintilian as *lactea ubertas*).[19] This might suggest that Caligula was *au fait* with current trends in criticism, but the idea should not be pressed too hard. The comments look very much like the *obiter dicta* of the young iconoclast. Certainly he had no hesitation in quoting from both Homer and Vergil when the occasion demanded it. It must also be recognized that it was something of a convention to ascribe perverse literary views to emperors. It was said of Hadrian, for instance, that he preferred Cato to Cicero, Ennius to Vergil, Caelius to Sallust, and with the same arrogance passed judgement on Homer and Plato. The allusion to Plato in the disparagement of Homer looks like the possible remnant of a witticism, and hardly meant to be taken at face value, given Caligula's habit of quoting Homer.[20]

In his use of language, Caligula expressed scorn for a relaxed and excessively decorative style (*lenius comptiusque*), and singled out for censure Seneca, who was currently popular, saying that his compositions were mere *commissiones*, and sand without lime. *Commissio* is a difficult word, taken from the language of the theatre and in the narrow sense means the opening act in a theatrical perfomance (then by extension the perfomance itself). Caligula presumably meant that Seneca's writings were just show pieces, aiming at light entertainment without any real substance.[21] It is in any case difficult to see how Caligula's strictures could be validly applied to Seneca's style, especially to a work like the *Consolatio ad Helviam*, which belongs to the Caligulan period. Caligula's views on Seneca might have seemed bold at the time. A century or so later they had become almost mainstream. Aulus Gellius wrote that in his day some considered Seneca to be of little worth, and his style commonplace and trite, lacking real power and relying on contrived cleverness.[22]

In his private pursuits Caligula is probably at his most conventional. All of the Julio–Claudians exhibit to some degree the same combination of a passion for vulgar pursuits and a lively interest in matters of the intellect. In this regard Caligula seems to have been no better, but no worse, than his peers.

· 4 ·

THE NEW EMPEROR

WORD OF TIBERIUS' death would have travelled the 120 or so miles to Rome very quickly. It met with a varied response in the city. Herod Agrippa's freedman, Marsyas, might announce the news to his master with a melodramatic flourish: 'the lion is dead', but Agrippa's jailer simply refused to believe the story, and his reaction was not, in fact, untypical. Romans generally were unwilling to trust what they heard, fearing a trick to test their loyalty, and conflicting rumours were spread that Tiberius was alive and would be coming soon in person. As the truth gradually took hold anxiety yielded to jubilation. The people gave vent to their old resentments, praying that Tiberius' spirit would be damned for eternity. His physical remains were also the subject of lively discussion. Some thought they should be thrown down the Gemonian stairs (the fate of common criminals), or hurled into the river — 'Tiberius in Tiberim!' was the popular slogan — or even taken to the amphitheatre at Atella (near Misenum) and given a semi-cremation.[1]

Such issues did not preoccupy Macro. Once he had sent out instructions to provincial governors and army commanders, he lost no time in setting out for Rome, which he reached by March 18 at the latest. He brought two letters from Caligula. One of them, according to Josephus, instructed Piso, the city prefect, to release Agrippa from his cell into a more comfortable house arrest. Precisely what form such an instruction took is difficult to say. Caligula would hardly have been in a position to *order* Piso to take action, but he may have communicated his wishes indirectly. It is significant that Agrippa was not ordered released outright. Josephus attributes the delay to Antonia, who feared the impression of a slight towards Tiberius. But we might more reasonably suspect the hand of Macro, who would be anxious to avoid any suggestion that Caligula had simply usurped Tiberius' powers without reference to the senate. In due time Agrippa was released, and he was thus more fortunate than a number of convicted criminals whose execution had been scheduled for the very day the news of the death arrived. Their appeals would have to be addressed to the new emperor, and since he was not on hand, their jailers were afraid to break the law and went ahead with the executions.[2]

The other letter was more significant. It constituted the official report to the senate of Tiberius' death. In it Caligula apparently asked the senate to bestow the same honours granted to Augustus on Tiberius, a display of his impiety towards his mother and others, according to Dio, who asserts that he made a special point of describing Tiberius as his 'grandfather'. The request seems to have included divine honours, which was more than the senate was willing to countenance. They were not, however, prepared to risk offending him, and their solution was simply to avoid bringing the issue to a vote, until he turned up in person.[3] The letter also covered what Josephus calls 'his own succession', clearly an exaggeration, since Caligula would hardly have risked provocation by any explicit statement of his ambitions at this early stage. But the formal announcement of Tiberius' death was, in effect, the prelude to a well organized series of moves in this direction carefully planned by Macro. The first problem to be dealt with was the will. Tiberius had made Caligula and Gemellus joint heirs to his estate, and Dio and Philo, as has been observed earlier, suggest that at the same time he bequeathed to them a share in ruling the empire.[4] It is virtually certain that the punctilious Tiberius would not have included any suggestion that he could pass on the principate. Nevertheless, the will was an important political document. Unlike Tiberius in AD 14, neither of the two young men had held any office that would automatically mark him as the next princeps. All that legally distinguished the two of them from any other claimants, apart from their kinship to the Julio-Claudian line, was their designation as Tiberius' heirs, even if heirs only to his estate. In this context, of course, Gemellus' potential claim to the principate would be just as valid as Caligula's.

Macro's solution was to have the document declared null and void, and Dio claims that this was done by the consuls and others (senators) with whom things had been arranged beforehand. Clearly the Prefect had foreseen the potential complexity of the annulment and had been shrewd enough to arrange preliminary discussions with legal experts and with influential senators who would ease its passing in the house. One of the consuls with whom things were arranged, Gnaeus Acerronius Proculus, might in fact have been in a position to combine both roles, since there are good grounds for identifying him with the distinguished jurist Proculus, who gave his name to the 'Proculian'school of law.[5]

The formal basis for the senate's treatment of Tiberius' will is not made clear in the sources. There would seem to be be no legal premise for cutting Gemellus out simply on the grounds of youth. Moreover it seems that the whole will was declared null and void, since there was no legal necessity for Tiberius' other legacies to be paid out.[6] But if the document was simply annulled, the property should have passed to those descendants who came under Tiberius' parental authority, the two young men and

Caligula's three sisters. Clearly this did not happen. The key to the problem may lie in Dio's argument that the annulment was justified essentially on political grounds, namely that Tiberius had demonstrated mental instability in giving authority to a mere boy to rule. Whatever Tiberius' intentions, the notion that the heir of the princeps was somehow automatically designated as the princeps may well have been held as a quasi-legal concept by the senate. The procedure in fact raises an interesting constitutional issue. Since Caligula alone inherited Tiberius' estate after the annulment, it implies that the estate belonged to him *by virtue of his position as princeps*, and that on succession the new princeps would not only acquire imperial powers but also the imperial property of his predecessor, by virtue of his office. This process would be helped by the increasing interdependence of the emperor's personal wealth and the imperial finances under his control. Similar thinking seems to underlie a senatorial decree passed later under Caligula that whoever had bequeathed money to Tiberius and then survived him would be obliged to leave it to his successor.[7] After Claudius, whose will was also suppressed, the emperors seem to have given up the practise of making wills.[8] During the chaos of 68/9 we find that the property of the Julio-Claudians passed into the hands of the men who replaced them. Otho acquired Nero's slaves and held a dinner in the palace in the Palatine. Vitellius enjoyed the imperial properties, and Vespasian was able to sell off imperial palaces in Alexandria.[9] It is clear, then, that for Rome's imperial rulers the ordinary laws of inheritance did not seem to apply, and there is reason to believe that this principle was first 'legally' established on Caligula's accession.[10]

Once the will had been annulled neither Caligula nor Gemellus would have had any kind of formal position in the succession. Caligula's claim now seems to rest on the very Augustan notion of *consensus*, that he was the choice of the Roman people and the senate (and the army, of course). Given that Macro had already brought over the Praetorians and the army commanders, the senate may well have felt that they had no choice but to acquiesce in this *consensus*. But it appears that far from being reluctant partners, they collaborated enthusiastically with Macro. It has been argued that they supported Caligula as the son of Germanicus, and that he represented to them the hopes that the old nobility had placed in his father. Yet it is difficult to believe that the senators could have been so naive. More probably they anticipated that because Caligula was young and inexperienced he would be easily manipulated. This misapprehension could well lie at the root of many of the disasters that were to befall the senate in the next four years. If any did feel lingering reservations about the annulment Caligula knew how to dispel them. He would promptly honour Tiberius' legacies, even adding bonuses to them to ensure that there would be no complaints. Of course, if the will had been declared null and void there would be have been no need for the legacies to be paid at all, making Caligula's act seem all the more generous.

The problem of the will would, of course, have cast something of a shadow over Caligula's claim to power. Tiberius had secured the succession with the active help of the incumbent; Caligula was set to do so against the contrary instructions (however oblique) of his predecessor. It was essential, then, for Macro to proceed with utmost speed to the second stage of the plan, made possible once the will had been revoked — the formal recognition by the senate of Caligula's succession.[11] The Arval records provide a vivid record of the senate's compliance. They show that on 18 March of the following year, 38, anniversary sacrifices were carried out because on that day Caligula 'had been acclaimed Imperator by the senate': *quod hoc die...a senatu imperat[or appellatus est* (or *esset*).[12]

In the Republican period, after a victory in the field a successful general, though already an *imperator* by virtue of the excercise of his *imperium*, might, as a special mark of honour, be acclaimed as *imperator* by his soldiers. He then assumed the title of Imperator after his name, which he maintained during the tenure of his office, or, if one should be awarded, until his triumph. There was a tendency in the later republic for figures like Caesar to retain the title even after their term of office had expired. The senate, as well as the army, had the traditional right to acclaim a victorious commander as *imperator*, and its exercise of this right in the case of Caligula is of great interest.[13] Caligula did not hold *imperium*, nor could he by any stretch of the imagination be said to have won a significant military victory. By using the old republican formula the senate was in a sense acknowledging that its actions were dictated not by profound political considerations but by action that had been taken by the Roman troops, who, even before the first senate meeting, had begun to swear loyalty to Caligula as their *imperator*. The term by now seems to indicate little more than 'princeps', a process that must have started to gain momentum under Tiberius and one that he tried to oppose, to judge from his comment that he would be *imperator* only to his troops.[14] By the time of the senatorial acclamation Caligula had already taken *de facto* power through the coalition, for the first time, between a claimant and the Praetorian guard, a phenomenon that would be repeated through Rome's history. After Tiberius' death Caligula would almost certainly have been acclaimed as *imperator* by the detachment of Praetorian guard at Misenum and by the troops stationed at the marine base there.[15] Macro had also ensured the support of the military commanders and provincial governors. We know that Vitellius, governor of Syria, was in Jerusalem when news of Tiberius' death a month earlier reached him. Macro's despatch must have been clear and explicit, since the governor proceeded at once to administer an oath of loyalty to Caligula.[16] Similar scenes would have been enacted throughout the empire.

From the time of Tiberius' succession the oath of loyalty to the new princeps became an institution. Immediately after Augustus' death it was taken first by the consuls, then by the Prefects of the Praetorian guard and of the Annona, followed by senators, soldiers (presumably Praetorians) and people. Tiberius then ensured the loyalty of the troops of Italy by using the oath of allegiance established by Augustus. Germanicus took the oath personally and administered it to his officials and the Belgic *civitates*, his action probably being typical of provincial governors.[17] We are fortunate in that of the six surviving oaths made to Julio-Claudian emperors at least two belong to the accession of Caligula. One is a fairly routine example from Assos in Mysia, preserved on a bronze tablet together with a congratulatory decree passed by the town.[18] The other, from Aritium in Lusitania is more significant. It was administered on 11 May, fifty-two days after Tiberius' death, by Gaius Ummidius Durmius Quadratus, described as the legate of Gaius Caesar Germanicus Imperator.[19] The swearers bind themselves to be an enemy to anyone who is the enemy of the emperor: 'I shall not cease to pursue in armed warfare by land and sea anyone who brings or might bring danger upon him and his welfare until that person has been punished, and I shall not consider myself or my children more precious than his welfare, and those who have been of hostile intent towards him I shall consider to be my enemies.' It is particularly interesting that in the oath Caligula has been given the title of Imperator, which points to an acclamation by the troops. He is not, however, called Augustus, a title which only the senate could bestow, suggesting that this particular oath administered by Quadratus was taken in response to the instructions sent out by Macro immediately after Tiberius' death, before the senate had bestowed the title of Augustus upon him, and probably, in fact, before they had any say in the matter.[20]

On 18 March the senate was presented with a *fait accompli*. Whatever reservations there might have been about the legality of Caligula's position (none is recorded), there could be no doubt that in practical terms he was in control. The fact that the original communications had been conveyed by the Prefect of the Praetorians would have brought home to them where the real power lay. This had in a sense been recognized at the very outset in Rome, when the convicted criminals were put to death because, even though the consuls were in the city, it was apparently thought that in Caligula's absence the person with the 'correct authority' to grant a pardon was not on hand. Nor would the lesson be lost on future contenders. Both of Caligula's immediate successors, Claudius and Nero, were acclaimed by the soldiers before being recognized by the senate. When the senators were called upon to acknowledge Caligula's claim, they had no real choice but to accede. The acclamation in itself, of course, while an important token of the senate's acquiescence, can have only had symbolic force. They had not bestowed *imperium* on Caligula and his constitutional position was not yet defined. Its definition would await his arrival.[21]

Macro had done his work well. In contrast to AD 14, when Augustus' death led to confusion in the senate and disorder on the frontiers, Caligula's accession was a brilliantly stage-managed affair, apparently brought off without a hitch. The way was now paved for his triumphal progress to the city. After Augustus' death in Nola in Campania his body had been brought to Rome in a stately procession lasting fifteen days. Caligula's procession from Misenum, accompanied by soldiers, went at about the same pace. From Sinuessa the two routes converged, to progress towards Rome by the Appian way.[22] But the reaction of the populace was markedly different on this occasion. As he made his way towards the city, the joy felt over Caligula's accession was made evident. People came out in throngs to meet their *princeps exoptatissimus* (most earnestly desired princeps'), calling him by pet names 'star', 'chick', 'baby', '*alumnus*'. There had not been scenes like this in Italy since the days when Germanicus was mobbed by crowds of admirers when he went out in public. Though dressed in mourning garb, Caligula was greeted rapturously by blazing torches, and sacrifices were made along the course of his route. The offerings over the next three months were said to total 160,000.[23] There is little doubt that to ordinary people along the route it was a foregone conclusion that Caligula would be the new princeps.

This ecstatic reaction was not confined to Italy. The magic of Germanicus' name and Macro's efforts had aroused enthusiasm far and wide. Philo describes vividly the jubilant response that greeted the return of the 'golden age' from every class of society, with banquets, holidays, all night revels, 'every sort of pleasure, appealing to every sense', an unprecedented display of affection for an emperor, and shown in every corner of the empire. Some specific examples outside Italy are known. In Jerusalem and Alexandria Jews offered splendid sacrifices. When the city of Assos took its oath of loyalty, it appointed an embassy to convey it to Rome, and added its congratulations: 'Since the rule of Caesar Germanicus Augustus has been declared, hoped for in the prayers of all men, and the world has found joy beyond limit, and every city and every nation has been eager to look upon the face of the god, since the sweetest era for mankind has now been established...' The League of the Achaeans, Boeotians, Locrians, Phocians and Euboeans offered sacrifices and prayers for Caligula's well-being, and voted that statues be erected in his honour.[24]

Caligula reached Rome on 28 March.[25] On arrival he was very careful, doubtless under Macro's guidance, to show the maximum deference to the senate. Dio observes, in a much-discussed passage, that Caligula seemed most *democraticos* at first, not writing to the senate or to the people, nor assuming any of the imperial titles (*onomata archika*), but that he afterwards turned excessively monarchical, assuming in one day 'all the things' (Dio's Greek is ambiguous) that Augustus had assumed reluctantly and gradually, and some of which Tiberius had not accepted at all.[26] It is usually assumed that *onomata* ('titles') must be taken to mean powers and prerogatives also, but this is probably not the case. At issue here is merely the period of ten days or so that followed Caligula's acclamation as imperator, when he was anxious to maintain an outward show of constitutional deference. As a broad principle, names and titles appropriate to a princeps and family were voted by the senate and not merely usurped. Thus Galba in 68 would be scrupulous enough to use none of the titles voted to him until in the course of his march to Rome he had met at Narbo the embassy sent by the senate. Even as late as the third century Dio was shocked by the way Macrinus and Elagabalus headed their letters with titles that had not been formally awarded them. Thus for Caligula to have observed this nicety would have made a highly favourable impression.[27]

Immediately after his splendid arrival in the city on 28 March, probably on the very same day, Caligula went, for the first time, before the Roman senate.[28] It was a meeting of great significance (so important that Dio gives his precise age), attended not only by senators but also by equestrians and ordinary people.[29] Goodwill seems to have prevailed, and the presence of the visitors was tolerated, and had perhaps even been prearranged to ensure that the formal conferring of powers took place in the presence and with the *consensus* of all three orders, in the tradition laid down by Augustus in the *Res Gestae: per consensum universarum potitus rerum omnium rempublicam ex mea potestate in senatus populique Romani arbitrium transtuli* ('having acquired power in all things through *consenus* I transferred the state from my authority to the jurisdiction of the senate and Roman people'). That some similar phrase might have been used on this occasion is hinted at in the language of Suetonius, who reports that Caligula's powers were conferred *consensu senatus et... turbae* ('with the *consensus* of the senate and the crowd').[30]

At this meeting the senate, in the words of Suetonius, granted to Caligula an awesome authority, *ius arbitriumque omnium rerum* ('power and authority over all things'), which would have included the *tribunicia potestas* and the extended proconsular *imperium*, as well as the special titles that he earlier refrained from using.[31] The gradually accumulated powers of Augustus, as Dio observed, were thus granted to Caligula in a single block. Although the text of the senatorial resolution on this occasion has not survived, it may well have provided the precedent for subsequent enactments of the law that formally defined the imperial power, the *lex imperii*. Part of a senatorial decree granting imperial powers in AD 69 to Vespasian, has in fact survived, recorded on a bronze tablet.[32] The so-called Lex de Imperio Vespasiani, seems to have originated in a *senatus consultum* passed in Rome in December of that year, about six months after Vespasian had been acclaimed imperator by the soldiers. Some of its provisions, almost certainly, go back to Caligula's accession in 37. Part of the original document, unfortunately, is missing, but among those measures surviving is Clause VI which gives the princeps the right and power (*ius* and *potestas*) to do what he thinks to be to the advantage of the state, thus technically giving him the discretion to violate even existing laws. If Brunt is correct in his belief that this clause goes back to a *lex* of 37, the move for Caligula from private citizen to princeps was a sudden and abrupt one, and the careful balance of authority that Augustus had evolved and which Tiberius had struggled to maintain, came to an end at this meeting of the senate. In their enthusiasm the senators gave a legal sanction to power that Augustus had excercised only by virtue of his *auctoritas*. Caligula would be restrained only by his own sense of discretion. Dio in a confused and textually corrupt passage implies that he regularly sought senatorial dispensation from the established laws, but this presumably belongs to his early period, when he went out of his way to treat the senate with deference. Suetonius claims that Caligula strove to transform the principate into a monarchy. But by handing over to him his new power the Senate had in fact done it for him, and when he would later boast that he had 'every power over every person' (*omnia in omnes licere*), this was was not the raving of a madman — he had good constitutional grounds for his notion that he was a *princeps legibus solutus* (a princeps not bound by the laws). It is therefore not surprising that to a Jewish provincial like Philo Caligula was a young man whose authority was unchecked, and his subjects were, in effect, his slaves.[33]

In addition to formal powers, the senate conferred on Caligula the titles appropriate to his new station in life. At the time of his accession his name would technically have been Caius Iulius Caesar Germanicus. Like his father he did not make use of the nomen 'Iulius', but this is not, in itself, particularly significant. In the imperial period it was not uncommon for nobles to drop their *nomina*, which had lost much of their distinction by being transmitted to freedmen and clients.[34] Octavian himself dropped Iulius from his name, and it is rarely used by the male members of the imperial family. 'Caesar' was technically a *cognomen*, acquired by Octavian when he was adopted by Julius Caesar and transmitted to Caligula through Tiberius and Germanicus. Its close association with the imperial family had given it, by the time of Caligula, a special attachment to the imperial function. This must have been the reason why Claudius assumed Caesar in his name from 41 on, although he had not himself been adopted by his predecessor.[35] Of the titles granted by the senate, the most important was Augustus, which embodied the moral and political authority of the princeps, and distinguished the imperial ruler from the statesmen of the republican period. It is claimed by Suetonius and Dio that Tiberius had declined this honour, which had been bequeathed to him, except when he dealt with foreign kings.[36] This may have been Tiberius' intention, but he clearly found that in the minds of most people the title was inextricably bound up with the idea of the principate, and he was obliged to use it almost from the outset, as his coins show. It is similarly used from the very beginning by Caligula. The praenomen 'Imperator', adopted by Octavian, was avoided by Tiberius and Caligula in Rome, although it is attested briefly in the provinces.[37]

Of the other titles bestowed at the discretion of the senate, Caligula may well have postponed accepting that of the Pontifex Maximus, chief interpreter of the sacred law and the high priest of all the gods. The office commanded great respect, and remained inherently bound up with the principate until the fourth century. The delay of the early emperors in assuming it may have been intended as a mark of its prestige. Augustus did not assume the chief pontificate on the death in 13 BC of the incumbent, Lepidus, but waited until the following year. Similarly Tiberius waited almost a year after Augustus' death, until the following March 15.[38] Caligula's delay was not a long one — the abbreviation PM appears on his earliest coins. But he may well have waited until he had recovered the remains of his mother and brother. These he is said to have collected with his own hands, an act which would have been strictly prohibited to a Pontifex Maximus.[39] We do know for certain that he postponed acceptance of one other title, Pater Patriae ('father of the country'). Dio says that this was for only a short time, and, as will be seen, his testimony has been confirmed by a recently discovered fragment of the Arval Record.[40] There is no certain information that the senate granted any other titles, although Suetonius claims that Caligula gave himself several, including Pius, Castrorum Filius, Pater Exercituum, Optimus Maximus Caesar. There is no primary evidence that he did, in fact, adopt any of these. It is possible that he used the expression *castrorum filius* ('son of the armies') to win the affections of the troops when on campaign in Germany, and it, in turn, could have led to confusion about his place of birth. *Pater exercituum* ('father of the armies') might have been similarly used. But the assumption of such nomenclature could have been informal at best, and none of it appears on coins or authentic inscriptions.[41]

There must have been a number in the senate who resented being manoeuvred into handing over both the trappings and the reality of power to an untrained twenty-five year old, and Arruntius would not have been alone in his misgivings about Caligula's dependence on Macro. In the event, their concerns seem to have been to a large degree allayed. Caligula made excellent use of his first senate meeting and displayed a masterly diplomatic skill. The deaths of Germanicus and Agrippina had aroused strong emotions among many Romans, and deep sympathy for their surviving children. Caligula played on these emotions, placing himself under the senators' guardianship, and calling himself their 'son and ward'. In the true Augustan fashion, he offered to share power with them and to work towards commonly desired goals.[42] In the euphoria of the moment many may even have been naive enough to believe that it would happen.

Caligula had to be especially cautious in his attitude towards his predecessor, and needed to maintain a very careful balance. On the one hand, there was a widespread relief that the remote and austere Tiberius had at last left the scene. His successor would need, therefore, to show that he did not intend to model his reign on what had gone immediately before. But *pietas* required that he show respect to his grandfather, and this was probably, in any case, his own personal inclination. Dio attempts to show that Caligula sought constantly to denigrate Tiberius, and has convinced many modern scholars that he felt a deep and abiding hatred for his predecessor. The idea is not, however, borne out by any inscriptional or numismatic evidence, or, indeed, by the other literary sources.[43] Dio, in fact, seems to make much of Caligula's cricitism of Tiberius for the express purpose of emphasizing the new emperor's perversity, and claims that he was ready to criticise him in order to provoke others, who might hope to please him by being critical themselves.[44] Caligula's criticisms would probably not have been any more severe than his usual cynical darts of humour, and Dio's overall verdict seems to be contradicted by events.

Tiberius' body had been left outside Rome, possibly for reasons of security. It was brought into the city under a military guard on the following day, probably before dawn, and laid out for its funeral.[45] Caligula did not pursue the issue of divine honours, and limited himself to providing a public funeral. Josephus and Suetonius record that it was a splendid occasion in the old Roman tradition, and that Caligula personally delivered a tear-filled eulogy, which Dio dismisses as an attempt to remind the people of Augustus, Germanicus and himself rather than to praise Tiberius. After cremation, Tiberius' remains were put to rest, probably in the mausoleum of Augustus.[46] Although the issue of Tiberius' apotheosis seems not to have been reopened, he was granted the distinction of having his speeches read on New Year's day, along with those of Augustus, even though the ritual took up all the senate's business until the evening.[47] In light of this we ought not read too much into the decision that the regular oath taken on New Year's day to uphold Tiberius' *acta* would no longer be taken.[48] Tiberius had personally refused at first to allow the oath in the case of his own *acta*, insisting only that he and others swear to uphold those of Augustus (in 25 Apidius Merula was ejected from the senate for refusing to do so). In AD 32 after the fall of Sejanus, he relented, and his own *acta* were included in the oath. From 37 the old practice that had been in force before 32 was resumed. Clearly, however, it should not be seen as a vicious personal attack on Tiberius, since the symbolic honour of having his speeches read continued.

One manifestation of Caligula's desire to honour Tiberius' memory that would have been particularly popular was his generosity in paying the late emperor's legacies. The most politically important was, of course, the payment to the Praetorians, and he lost no time in dispensing it. They had been left a thousand sesterces each, and this sum was doubled by Caligula from his personal funds. He thus became the first, in a sense, to acknowledge, by such a gift, his debt to the Praetorians for his accession, and he established a precedent for his successors (Claudius paid the enormous sum of 15,000 each). The gift was awarded at a special ceremony attended by senators and perhaps commemorated by a sestertius depicting Caligula addressing a group of five soldiers, with the legend ADLOCUT(io) COH (ortium) (fig.. 17).[50] Caligula may have been taking a leaf from Tiberius' book, since his predecessor, it was claimed, had sought to overawe the senators by arranging for them to be present at an inspection of the Praetorians. Bequests were also paid to the people, possibly in the form of two largesses, as well as to the legions, Vigiles and urban cohorts. In addition, the legacies from Livia's will, left unpaid by Tiberius, were honoured (p. 225) All of this, combined with a lavish new building programme, would place heavy demands on Caligula's resources. In the general thrill of his popularity, he, perhaps understandably, gave little thought to the financial consequences of his extravagant generosity. He would be forced to do so before too long.

During his stay on Capri Caligula had apparently shown no inclination to intercede on behalf of his mother and brothers, and had betrayed a chilling indifference to their fate. Now that he was princeps he could safely assume the role of dutiful son and brother, and he displayed his *pietas* by a brilliant *coup de théâtre*. He went out to Potnia and Pandateria where Agrippina and Nero had died, and brought back the urns containing their ashes. The task would hardly have been an easy one, since Nero's remains had been scattered and buried in such a way as to make recovery difficult. Moreover, he had a stormy passage, which he turned to his advantage, since it made his devotion seem all the greater. The ashes were brought to Ostia, and from there up the Tiber to Rome, where they were carried on biers by equestrians, to join the ashes of Germanicus in the mausoleum of Augustus. Romans would be reminded, of course, of the scene just over seventeen years earlier, when Agrippina with like solemnity brought her husband's ashes to Italy. To ensure maximum effect the display was arranged for the middle of the day, when the streets were crowded. The inscriptions from the funerary urns have survived, and it is noteworthy that Nero on his is called the son of Germanicus, great-grandson of Augustus, with no mention of Tiberius. Whether this reflects Caligula's personal wishes, or whether, given Tiberius' role in Nero's death, he wished to avoid public disapproval, is difficult to say. Cetainly, by the omission of Tiberius' name the inscription as it stands serves to emphasize the brother's Augustan genealogy. In the case of Drusus, there was no trace of any remains, and cenotaphs were erected in his honour.[51] Statues for the two dead brothers were ordered, and responsibility for contracting them was given to Claudius (who bungled the commission). The recovery of the remains was also most likely the occasion of the issue of a dupondius depicting Nero and Drusus (fig. 20).[52] Minted initially in Caligula's first year it shows the two young men riding horses, with their cloaks flying back, possibly as *Principes Iuventutis* ('Leaders of the Youth').

Honours were heaped on Caligula's dead parents. The Arvals sacrificed on their birthdays, even though Agrippina's had been declared a *dies nefastus* by Tiberius, and precious metal coins were issued in honour of each in the first year of the reign, identifying them as his father and mother (figs. 11, 12).[53] The month of September was renamed 'Germanicus'. In a similar fashion Quinctilis had previously been renamed July, as the birth month of Julius Caesar, and Sextilis renamed Augustus, because it was the month of his first consulate. September may thus have been chosen for Germanicus for the simple reason that it came in sequence after two eponymous months, but there was the added advantage that it offered a nice dynastic arrangement — Caesar — Augustus — Germanicus. In Egyptian cities the substitution of names of Germanicus' family for the months became common, such as 'Gaieos' for Phamenoth or 'Drusilleios' for Payni.[54] Games in the circus were established in Agrippina's honour, together with a *carpentum* (carriage) that would carry her image in the circus procession. This is commemorated in an undated sestertius with the bust of Agrippina on the obverse, identified as Caligula's mother, and a *carpentum* on the reverse drawn by mules (Fig. 19). In addition, the villa at Herculaneum where she had for a time been imprisoned was destroyed.[55]

In all these highly popular gestures we should not discount the influence of Macro. Philo has left an account of his role that dwells on the trivial and seems in large part imaginary, but may at the same time reflect the kind of gossip that he himself picked up in Rome. Macro, he claims, would wake Caligula up if he fell asleep during dinner parties. If he got carried away too much at dances or laughed too loudly at ribald jokes or got so excited by the music that he wanted to join in the songs, Macro would restrain him. He would remind him to behave at all hours in keeping with his station. This picture of Macro carefully directing Caligula's public image is probably close to the truth. The Prefect controlled his meetings, and Suetonius says that Caligula refused even Antonia a private interview, insisting that Macro be present also.[56]

Antonia, of course, had played an important role in the downfall of Sejanus, and Macro no doubt knew that she could be dangerous. Despite his caution, however, he would have been fully aware of the great respect felt for her, and would not have discouraged Caligula from paying her all due honours for public consumption, provided they gave her no opportunity to excercise real power. She was granted the rights once enjoyed by Livia. These included the privileges of the Vestal Virgins, who were entitled to occupy special seats in the theatre and at public games.[57] She was also appointed priestess of Augustus, and received Livia's old title of Augusta. She appears to have declined to use this during her lifetime, and it first appears after her death on an Arval fragment of 38, honouring her birthday.[58] The sources speak of Caligula behaving with deference towards Antonia at first, but gradually feeling irritated by her interference. Josephus has her offering advice (on Agrippa) right at the outset, and Suetonius claims that when she tried to offer counsel on one occasion Caligula rebuffed her firmly with the reminder that his power was absolute.[59]

Antonia died on 1 May, 37, at the age of seventy-three. Suetonius and Dio both claim that Caligula drove her to her death by his criticisms and indignities. But since he had not reached Rome until 28 March, and was absent from the city for much of April, collecting the remains of his mother and brother, there would hardly have been much time to drive Antonia to her death by insulting behaviour. It is also difficult to imagine that he would have paid her no honours on her death, as Suetonius implies.[60] She died at a time when the euphoria of the beginning of his reign was still rampant, and quite apart from any question of personal affection, a public slight at this time to the most respected woman in Rome, whose death was marked in local Fasti, would have been politically unimaginable.

The greatest honours of all, however, were reserved for Caligula's sisters. As well as receiving the privileges of the Vestals they were allowed to watch the public games from the imperial seats. They were also included in the standard formula that the consuls used for making proposals to the senate, wishing success to the emperor, as well as in the annual vows taken for his safety. These last have their origin in republican tradition, the *vota pro salute reipublicae* ('vows for the safety of the state'), carried out by the consuls on 1 January. Under Tiberius, Livia's name was included in the formula, and, after her death, so was that of Sejanus; but the privilege was still considered something special, and Tiberius objected strenuously to the unauthorised inclusion of Nero and Drusus.[61] What is perhaps even more remarkable is that the sisters were included also in the annual vows of allegiance to the emperor. There seems to be no Roman model for their inclusion in this type of oath, although the decree passed by the people of Assos at the beginning of his reign does swear allegiance to Caligula *and his house*, showing that there was at least a precedent among the communities of the Greek East.[62] In the first year of his reign (but not in later years) Caligula issued a dramatic sestertius with a reverse depicting the three sisters (fig. 15).[63] They stand side by side, their bodies facing front, and are identified by name. On the left is Agrippina, representing the type of Securitas, with her head turned right, holding a cornucopia in the right hand, with the right arm on a column and her left hand on Drusilla's shoulder. In the centre, Drusilla, as Concordia, has her head turned left, holding a patera in her right hand and a cornucopia in the left. On the right stands (Julia) Livilla, as Fortuna, with her head turned left, holding a rudder in her right hand and a cornucopia in the left. The prominence given to the sisters has no real precedent in the history of Roman coinage, and suggests an extraordinary honour. To the extent that these measures have a political purpose (as opposed to springing from purely personal and sentimental feelings), it is to enhance the prestige of the imperial family and thus of Caligula himself. There is no justification for reading into the honours any notion that he planned to give his sisters a share in the exercising of power.

Caligula's friends also benefited from his accession, in particular Agrippa. The tetrarch Philip had died in 33/4 and Tiberius apparently placed his domain under the authority of the governor of Syria, with its revenues kept aside in a separate fund. Caligula now bestowed the old tetrarchy on his friend, with some added benefits. Agrippa was given the title of king, as well as the revenues that had accumulated since Philip's death. It is possible that at the same time Caligula granted him Abilene, the former tetrarchy of Lysinias, which had similarly remained without a ruler on the latter's death. Also Caligula bestowed on Agrippa the *ornamenta praetoria*, the right to wear the praetor's insignia. While this conferred no actual power, it was a signal honour, and he seems to have broken new ground in bestowing it on a client-king. Antiochus, son of the former King of Commagene, was also rewarded. He must have been on close terms with Caligula, although nothing is known about their earlier relationship. Early in 37 he received back his father's old kingdom (p. 222).

Romans would not have frowned upon Caligula's early involvement in matters outside Italy, especially since he had a stroke of exceptionally good fortune at this point that would enable him to represent a major diplomatic victory as his own. By the time of Tiberius' death, relations with Parthia had reached a critical stage. In early 37 the aggressive Parthian King Artabanus was reputedly planning an invasion of Syria. The province's governor, Vitellius, acted with great courage and energy.

He moved his army up to the Euphrates, and overawed the Parthian king, who decided to yield in the face of superior force and decisive action. The Romans and Parthians met at the Euphrates, according to Josephus, in a luxury pavilion in the middle of the river. They reached an amicable accord, the precise details of which are not clear. Artabanus certainly seems to have made a display of compliance. He gave his son Darius as hostage (thus giving him the opportunity later to accompany Caligula over his bridge at Baiae) and, according to Suetonius, crossed the river and paid homage to the Roman eagles and standards, and even to the statues of Augustus and Caligula. If this last detail is true it suggests that Artabanus' position must have been especially weak. This was hardly Caligula's achievement, but Tiberius had died in the meantime, and the situation might have been helped by the special affection that Artabanus still, apparently, felt for the memory of Germanicus — he was one of the eastern monarchs reputedly much affected by his death, and by the illness, later in the year, of his son Caligula.[64] It is at least to Caligula's credit that he seems to have been willing to be guided by Vitellius in confirming the *modus vivendi* with Artabanus. It is possible that part of the price of the agreement may have been the removal of the Roman candidate Mithridates from the throne of Armenia. He was at any rate recalled to Rome by Caligula and imprisoned, for reasons unstated.[65]

To all appearances, Caligula's policy on the Parthian frontier of refusing to commit Roman arms in pursuit of an obsessive Roman ambition, the control of Armenia, seems to have succeeded. But his success, admired by some modern scholars, was surely illusory. Caligula for the moment probably had no interest in feats of arms against Parthia — his ambition was focused on Germany and Britain. Artabanus for his part may have shown a willingness to compromise largely because the emperor was the son of the great Germanicus, whose diplomatic skills and personal qualities had made such a profound impression on the Parthians. Had Caligula survived for much longer, Artabanus, like the senate, would surely have come to appreciate the difference between the father and the son. We unfortunately do not know what was was decided for Armenia in 37, but there is no sign that the agreement was based on solid and lasting foundations, and, in the event, history shows how ephemeral it proved to be. Caligula's arrangements with Parthia did not survive him, and Mithridates was eventually restored to his kingdom by Claudius.[66]

In fact of all the measures undertaken by Caligula at the beginning of his reign, it would have been a domestic one that proved most popular — the decision to abolish the charge of *maiestas*, the primary cause of fear and resentment under Tiberius. The precise nature of this crime is far from clear. In about 100 BC, in response to the mishandling of the campaign against the Cimbri and Teutones, a *Lex Appuleia de Maiestate* was introduced, apparently intended to punish general incompetence, rather than criminal intent. Sulla's later *Lex Cornelia de Maiestate* seems to have been aimed at restraining ambitious army commanders from taking their troops outside their provinces. Sulla's law was replaced by Caesar's *Lex Julia de Maiestate* (the specific offences dealt with are not clear); its penalty was exile (*interdictio aquae et ignis*), with or without confiscation of property. Caesar's law was modified, or, some would argue, replaced by an Augustan *Lex Julia*. Augustus seems to have extended the concept of *maiestas laesa* to cover verbal abuse or slander, and the *Lex Julia* thus had a double function.[67] It was a law to protect the state against sedition, rebellious magistrates and the like. But there was a second element that protected the princeps against real or imagined injuries, the crime we know as *lèse majesté*; attacks against the princeps were thus dealt with by the same laws as those concerning the security of the state. By a process not fully understood the penalties grew progressively more severe under the principate. Harsh penalties were rare under Augustus, but they became common under Tiberius, especially after 23, often involving banishment and confiscation of property, the death penalty and even *damnatio memoriae*. Many of the *maiestas* trials under Tiberius seemed to have their origin in political or private rivalries, rather than genuine activities either against the state or the princeps. Whether it was true or not, in the public mind Caligula's mother and brothers had fallen victim to this kind of abuse, and there would have been general approval when the sentences passed against them were annulled, and their old supporters recalled from exile.

Caligula went even further. To show that there need be no fear of reprisal, he proclaimed that he had no feelings of malice towards those involved in the earlier attacks against his family, and made a public show of burning in the forum all the papers and letters relating to their cases, swearing with all solemnity that he had never read or touched any of them. Sceptics might have wondered if the originals were really going up in flames, and Dio in fact claims that Caligula destroyed only copies. The papers involved must, presumably, have been private documents in the possession of Tiberius, rather than of the senate, since the trials had taken place *in camera* before the emperor.[68] There actually was a precedent of kinds for Caligula's gesture. After Actium Augustus found incriminating letters in Antony's strongbox and announced that he had destroyed them, although, like Caligula, he had no scruples about making use of them later. But Caligula did not stop here. He did away with all *maiestas* cases, putting aside all those that were still pending and allowing those already condemned to return from exile. This seems a remarkably bold move, and vivid evidence of his self-confidence. Claudius made a similar gesture at the beginning of his reign but took the precaution of going through the records carefully beforehand to ensure that only those charged unjustly should go free. There is no indication that Caligula made any preliminary examination in 37. Clearly under Macro's guidance he was seeking to reassure those who felt reservations about him, and was perhaps trying to disarm any who felt that their loyalties lay with Gemellus. The act of allowing Agrippina's supporters to return, it is argued, would have caused this group some alarm, and the destruction of the trial records would have allayed their concerns to some degree.[69] Whether there was in fact anything that could be called a pro-Gemellus party is far from clear. As noted earlier, his only named supporter was Flaccus, prefect of Egypt, who was not even in Rome in 37. But there are certainly hints of machinations against Caligula from the very outset. Suetonius records that soon after his accession he made a show of refusing to accept a document with evidence of some sort of plot against him, claiming that he had done nothing to make anyone hate him and had no time for informers. We can not rule out totally the possibility that the episode was stage-managed, but it could be an early hint of the opposition that he would later have to face.

Only one person is named specifically among those released as a result of Caligula's amnesty, Publius Pomponius Secundus. Pomponius was a highly regarded man of letters, a very popular playwright, and ranked as one of the great orators of the day in the *Dialogus* attributed to Tacitus. He was the subject of a biography by the Elder Pliny.[70] Charged with sheltering Aelius Gallus (probably the nephew of Sejanus) in his garden after the latter's fall, he was imprisoned for seven years, during which he was badly treated.[71] After his release Pomponius showed his gratitude in a fashion that Caligula would doubtless have greatly appreciated — he invited the young emperor to a banquet with costly and historic wines. Among those who would have benefited from the decision not to pursue the *maiestas* cases would have been Annius Pollio, Vinicianus and Mamercus Scaurus, whose treason cases were postponed in 32, pending the emperor's return to Rome, as well as Cnaeus Domitius and Vibius Marsus, associated with Albucilla on a charge of impiety against Tiberius in 37, but still untried when the emperor died. The abolition of *maiestas* charges became a formality at the beginning of each reign, but the gesture was probably more symbolic than practical. Neither Caligula nor any other emperor would have left himself totally exposed to the dangers of sedition — there were other criminal charges that would still offer some degree of protection.[72]

Caligula's liberality was to go even further. Certain writings had long been suppressed by senatorial decree, and three authors in particular had gained notoriety by having their books banned — Titus Labienus, Cremutius Cordus and Cassius Severus. Caligula apparently ordered that their works be hunted out and circulated, claiming that it was in his interest to have all events recorded for posterity.[73] Titus Labienus was an orator whose vicious attacks on all classes of society had earned him the name of Rabienus ('rabid'). His writings were destroyed by fire on the orders of the senate, and refusing to survive his works Labienus had himself walled up in his ancestral tomb. Cassius Severus, according to Seneca, declared that if they wanted to destroy the works of Labienus they would have to burn him alive as he knew them by heart. Severus was a powerful orator, but enjoyed little success as either defender or prosecutor. Because of his slanderous attacks on distinguished men and women, he was first charged by Augustus under the heading of *maiestas*, and eventually banished to the barren island of Seriphus, apparently with confiscation of property. He died there in 32.[74] The most notorious case of defamatory libel during the reign of Tiberius was that of Cremutius Cordus. He was prosecuted early in AD 25 on the trumped-up charge of publishing a history in which he eulogized Brutus and called Cassius the last of the Romans, although the real cause of his troubles was the emnity of Sejanus. Cremutius gave a noble speech, defending his actions on the basis of precedent (apparently even Augustus had heard a recitation of the offending passages and took no exception to them), then anticipated the verdict by committing suicide. Tacitus reports that his books were ordered burnt by the aediles, but that a few copies survived.Cremutius' daughter Marcia was largely responsible for keeping his works safe until they could be published under Caligula, and when that happened, the melodramatic end of their author inevitably made the interest in them greater. An expurgated copy was available to Quintilian some fifty years later, still marked by its outspokenness.[75] It might be said that the lifting of the ban on these writers was the one truly progressive deed of Caligula's reign. On the other hand, he had not suffered personally from the writers in question, and it is not clear how far he was motivated by genuine liberalism and how far by a cynical desire to draw a contrast with the repressive atmosphere of the previous regime. His later conduct seems to be in stark contrast, since he is even accused of burning alive the writer of an Atellan farce because of a *double-entendre*.

The most intractable problem of this early period of his reign was Tiberius Gemellus. He had been excluded from his inheritance, and there was an obvious danger that he might nurture a constant resentment. To allay any such feeling Caligula treated him with a great outward show of generosity. He was formally granted the *toga virilis*, and on the same day adopted by the emperor as his son, co-opted into the Arval Brotherhood, and given the title of *Princeps Iuventutis*. This old military title, once applied to the commanders of knights under 45 on military service, had acquired special meaning when conferred on Gaius and Lucius Caesar by Augustus on their adoption, and together with his own adoption by Caligula might reasonably be taken as an official recognition that Gemellus was accepted as his heir.[76] Philo saw the adoption as a ploy from the outset, intended to put Gemellus under Caligula's authority (*patria potestas*), and perhaps intended to persuade the senate to go along with the scheme to deprive him of the share that was morally his.[77] It is difficult not to share this cynicism. Caligula had deprived Gemellus of his birthright for his own personal ends, and it was at the very least hypocritical to pretend deep concern for his welfare. By designating Gemellus as his heir Caligula did not concede a great deal. The emperor was still young and could look forward to a lengthy reign, during which he would be able to resolve the question of succession at leisure.

A recently discovered fragment of the Arval record, covering the activities of 38, allows us to add another significant event with some confidence to the first half of 37, since it shows that anniversary sacrifices were held at the altar of Providentia Augusta in the Campus Agrippae on June 26 of 38, almost certainly a repetition of rites that would have been held the year before also. Providentia is essentially the power to plan ahead, and for the early emperors it personified the transmission of hereditary powers, belonging as a quality to the one who chooses the successor in the first place and then by transference to the one who succeeds him. In this sense it was first exercised by Augustus, and the *providentia* of Augustus would become an important propaganda element in the transmission of power to Nero, Galba and the Flavians. The first commemoration of Providentia Augusta took place under Tiberius, as is shown by his coins. A series of asses carries on the obverse the radiate head of Augustus and on the reverse an Altar with a panelled door, and the legend Providentia. Caligula's rites were presumably carried out to mark the anniversary of either the original founding or the actual dedication of the altar, which is clearly associated with Augustus' adoption of Tiberius, on June 26, AD 4. He is seen to be at pains to celebrate the initial founding of the dynasty, and its transmission from Augustus to Tiberius, thus again belying Dio's notion that he pursued a policy of denigrating Tiberius.[78]

Even Caligula's uncle Claudius received his share of honours, when, on 1 July, at the age of 46, he was taken into the consulship with Caligula. Claudius up to that time had been treated with much scorn and contempt, and been kept in the background, remaining an equestrian and heading the deputation of equestrians that went to meet Caligula on his grand progress to Rome. Now for the first time he became a consul and a senator, and was given the additional distinction of presiding at the games in the absence of Caligula. Caligula had in March been voted an immediate consulship, to be repeated annually, but he declined the offer until the incumbents had completed their six month term. The assumption of this office represented for Caligula a highly significant event, and seems to have been marked by the dedication of special statues.[79] The speech that Caligula gave to the senate on his assumption of office reflected the enlightenment of the early part of reign. In it he noted the abuses of the previous regime and gave solemn undertakings that they would not be repeated by himself. The senate was so taken by his words that they ordered that the speech be read every year, hoping, Dio notes, to prevent him from changing his mind.[80] It was probably in this speech that Caligula declared his intentions to publish the financial accounts of the state, a practice established by Augustus but discontinued by Tiberius. We do have good primary evidence for the moderate image he sought to project when an embassy from a number of Greek states came to Rome early in Caligula's reign offering him various honours. In the letter that he sent in reply Caligula accepted some of the honours, but asked them to avoid the expense of setting up an excessive number of statues to him, and to limit themselves to those erected at the sites of the great Panhellenic games, at Olympia, Nemea, Delphi and the Isthmus.[81]

One of the marked characteristics of this early phase was Caligula's enormous effort to identify himself with Augustus, and thus seek to confer a legitimacy of sorts on his reign. This Augustan link was an important element of Caligula's (or Macro's) early propaganda. The awkward presence of Gemellus made it difficult for the emperor to present himself as the natural successor of Tiberius. Instead, he chose to emphasize his direct descent from his great-grandfather, the founder of the principate. Thus a year later, on July 4, 38, and no doubt in 37 also, where the record is missing, rites were carried out by the Arvals to mark the anniversary of the founding (*constitutio*) by Augustus on his return from Gaul in 13 BC of the Ara Pacis, the great monument to peace, and of course to the Julio-Claudian family.[82] As consul, however, Caligula's most important symbolic act was without any doubt the dedication of the Temple of Divus Augustus, which took place over two days, on 30 and 31 August, the latter being Caligula's birthday and the last day of his consulship. It is no accident that the occasion fell on his birthday, just as in 40 he postponed his *ovatio* so that he could hold it on the same date. The coincidence of the anniversary of his birth with the temple's dedication would have emphasised the direct blood line from Augustus to Caligula.

The Temple of Augustus had in fact been decreed immediately after his death in AD 14 and most, if not all, of the construction must have been completed under Tiberius. But the fact that it remained undedicated provided Caligula with a splendid opportunity for extravagant display. Dressed in triumphal garb he carried out the ceremony, accompanied by a choir of noble youths and maids. The event was marked by splendid shows, including a two day horse race and the slaughter of some 400 bears. To commemorate it a splendid sestertius was issued, depicting Caligula carrying out a sacrifice in front of the temple (fig. 18).[83] The obverse of these coins carries the figure of a seated Pietas, draped and veiled, holding a patera in her right hand, and the legend PIETAS below.

Pietas was a highly emotive concept for the Romans, emphasizing the principle of family duty and thus the idea of Caligula's loyalty to his illustrious forbear. Caligula was thus able to depart his first consulship in a blaze of glory, stepping down with Claudius on 1 September to allow the previously designated candidates to succeed him.[84]

The most effective exploitation of Augustan symbolism occurred a few weeks after Caligula had given up his consulship. We are told by Dio that in March he had accepted all the Augustan titles *en bloc*, with the exception of Pater Patriae, which he postponed for a short time. Dio's observation has been confirmed by the new Arval fragment, which shows rites being carried out on September 21, 38 (the record for 37, again, is missing) before Augustus' birthday, to mark the fact that Caligula *consensu senatus delatum sibi patris patriae nomen recepisset* ('had received the title of Pater Patriae offered to him with the consent of the senate').[85] The earliest extant use of the term *pater/parens patriae* is in connection with the famous general Marius, who, Cicero claimed, ought to have received the title. But Cicero was in fact the first recipient, on the suppression of the Catilinarian conspiracy, in addition to which Lucius Gellius Poplicola proposed to the senate that Cicero should also be granted the *corona civica*, the oak-wreath granted to a soldier for saving the life of a comrade in action.[86] Appian lists the title among the honours granted to Caesar in 45 BC, and *parens patriae* is attached to his name on coins of 44 BC. When Augustus received the title he considered it an event of great significance, and in the *Res Gestae* emphasized that the honour was bestowed by the senate and equestrian order and the whole people: *senatus et equester ordo populusque Romanus universus appellavit me patrem patriae.* Suetonius observes that in a speech in the senate when the title was conferred a decree was made that: *senatus te consentiens cum populo Romano consalutat patriae patrem* ('the senate in agreement with the Roman people acclaims you pater patriae') and in reply Augustus told the senate that he hoped he would retain to the end *hunc consensum vestrum.* The language of Augustus, with its emphasis on *consensus*, is clearly reflected in the phraseology of the Arval entry that marks Caligula's acceptance of the title.[87]

It was probably on the occasion of the grant of the title that we should assign the golden shield that Suetonius says was voted for Caligula. He informs us that every year, on the appointed day (presumably 21 September) it was to be carried to the Capitol by the college of priests, escorted by the senate, while girls and boys of noble families sang his praises.[88] The shield would again remind Romans of the famous shield that was awarded to Augustus in 27 BC. He was probably at the same time granted the *corona civica*. In one of the finest sculptural representations attributed to Caligula, in Copenhagen, he is depicted as wearing an oak crown, and he also is described as wearing one at the time of the famous crossing of the bridge on the bay of Naples.[89] The honour of the crown was bestowed by the Senate on Augustus in 27, and in coins and inscriptions (including those of Caligula) the crown, shield and title of Pater Patriae are closely associated.[90] None of the sources specifically states that Caligula received the oak crown in September but Suetonius does observe that the shield was granted *inter reliquos* honores. There are indications that a *corona civica* was a standard fixture on the pediment of the Palatine residence by the beginning of Claudius' reign, although Tiberius had specifically not allowed one.[91] It could very well have been placed there by Caligula in September 37.

The first six months of Caligula's reign constituted a period of near-euphoria. But they exacted their toll on the young emperor. The strain of being at the centre of power and attention, and the adulation of the people, would have made enormous demands on his nerves and stamina, coming as it did after a life spent almost totally out of the public view. Hardly was the summer over, when he fell seriously ill.

Appendix
The legal date of Caligula's accession

The presence of the people at the senate meeting of March 37 can have been no more than symbolic. If the *senatus consultum* conferring Caligula's powers had the full force of a *lex*, it would properly need popular assent. But this could not be given simply by acclamation. Technically it would need to be passed by the popular *comitia*, and before this could happen, strictly speaking, a formal period of time, the *trinum nundinum*, would have to elapse. Its precise duration is uncertain, but the range seems to have been between 17 and 24 days, and the restriction is occasionally ignored (see M. Hammond, 'The Tribunician Day during the Early Empire', MAAR 15 (1938), 36-52, M. Griffin, Nero (London, 1984), 244 n.91, Brunt). Now in the cases of Nero, Otho, Vitellius and Domitian, the Arval record specifically mentions the assumption of tribunician power at dates later than the sacrifices *ob imperium*, which must represent the acclamation by the senate. The later date clearly represents the formal passage of the *lex* by the popular *comitia*; Nero: acclamation, October 13; comitia, December 4 (AFA lxiv.14-15 [Smallwood 19.14-15] see, T.B. Mitford, 'Some Published Inscriptions from Roman Cyprus', ABSA 42 [1947], 220-1); Otho: acclamation, January 15; *comitia*, February 28 (AFA xcii.58-60); Vitellius: acclamation, April 19; *comitia* April 30 (AFA xciv.82); Domitian: acclamation, September 14; *comitia* September 30 (AFA cx.33-4). The Arval record notes only the *comitia tribuniciae potestatis*, but there is no need to assume a separate comitial vote of proconsular power. The terminology must represent the preeminence of one power over the other (see Parsi, 129). Whether or not Caligula's legal adoption of powers is to be dated to the senate meeting of 28 March, or to a later meeting of the *comitia* can not be proved. It certainly comes before 28 April, since a dedication made at Syene in Egypt on 28 April, 39 (*ILS* 8899), shows that by that date Caligula was now in his third tribunician year.

A clue may be provided by a senatorial decree that the day on which his principate began, *dies quo cepisset imperium*, was to be called the Parilia, to mark that the city had been founded a second time (Suet. *Cal.* 16.4). The Parilia was an old shepherd's festival traditionally, though some argue incorrectly, associated with the rustic deity Pales. Originally it seems to have been a festival of purification of the herds and herdsmen, and at some point the rite became an anniversary of Rome's foundation, celebrated on April 21 (Cic. *Div.* 2.98, Varro *Rust.* 2.1.9; Ovid *Fast.* 4. 721–862; Dion Hal. 188. 3; Wissowa, 199–200; Latte, 87–8; Weinstock, 184–91). There was nothing remarkable in the idea of celebrating a great achievement as the rebirth of Rome. Cicero claimed the Nones of December 63, when the senate decided to take action against the Catilinarian conspirators, to be the new birthday of Rome (Cic. *Flacc.* 102, *de Cons.*, *FPL* fr 17M) After the murder of Julius Caesar, Dolabella suggested that Rome's birthday should be moved to the Ides of March (Appian *BC* 2. 122; 3. 35). Similarly, the Assos decree refers to the accession of Caligula as the beginning of a new age, and the same concept of the return of the golden age would be used of the accession of Nero (*IGR* 4.251 [Smallwood 33]; Sen. *Apocol.* 4.9; Cal. Sic. *Ecl.* 1. 42). What is interesting is not that the beginning of Caligula's reign was seen as Rome's rebirth but that it was given the name of a pre-existing festival. It seems unlikely that a well-established festival could have been redated. In fact it speaks very strongly for 21 April as the date of the formal passage of Caligula's *lex imperii*. An analagous situation arose in 45 BC. News of the victory of Julius Caesar at Munda reached Rome on the eve of the Parilia, and it was voted that circus games be held in Caesar's honour as if he were the founder of the city. The date provides an appropriate intermission for the *trinum nundinum* after the senatus consultum of 28/9 March, and such a technical delay before the formal assumption of power would be completely in keeping with Caligula's constitutional behaviour at this early stage.

· 5 ·

SIGNS OF STRAIN

CALIGULA'S ILLNESS WAS clearly serious.[1] Philo reports that news of it caused widespread consternation throughout the empire, even leading to mental distress and severe depression. Suetonius and Dio echo the same excessive reaction. Crowds slept in the open outside the imperial residence waiting for bulletins. The equestrian Atanius Secundus announced that he would fight as a gladiator, and Publius Afranius Potitus vowed publicly to give his life, if the emperor should be spared, extravagant offers but with precedents in similar vows for Augustus' recovery.[2] Some scholars have tended to agree with Philo, that the illness was some kind of nervous breakdown, caused by the stress of the first six months of the reign.[3] Others have sought to diagnose a more specifically physical ailment. Among recent attempts, A.T. Sandison has suggested that Caligula may have suffered from epidemic encephalitis, which leads to symptoms of mental derangement. R.S. Katz, on the other hand, argues that he suffered from hyperthyroidism, which can be triggered by serious stress. He suggests that the strain of rule caused Caligula's thyroid gland to become overactive, thus contributing to his breakdown. One serious problem with his thesis, however, is that hyperthyroidism is usually accompanied by exophthalmia (bulging of the eyes), which conflicts with Suetonius' and Pliny's description of Caligula's eyes as hollow. V. Massaro and I. Montgomery suggest that the illness may have been a viral one that affected the central nervous system, with residual mental symptoms.[4] All these, and other, speculations about the nature of the illness are in the end unprovable, and like the speculations about Caligula's mental state rely on descriptions of symptoms that have been much distorted by the process of source transmission. Nor can we be sure that the illness had any long-term effect. The sources seem to suggest it was a turning point in Caligula's reign, and Philo implies a causative link between it and his subsequent behaviour. But it can have played at best only a contributory role, since there is no evidence of any dramatic change in his behaviour — his serious excesses and clashes with the senate do not begin until 39.[5]

The precise date of the illness is also uncertain. Philo says that it fell in the eighth month of his reign (mid October to mid November) and

73

that news of it was brought by sailors as they returned to their home ports at the end of the sailing season, which Vegetius places at November 11.[6] If the illness occurred so late it would be difficult to fit his recovery, and other events recorded for late 37, into the short remainder of the year. Also, Dio implies that Caligula fell ill not long after his first consulship, which he held up to the end of August. It could very well be that he was struck down shortly after being acclaimed *pater patriae*, on September 21, and that news of his progress through gradual improvement to final recovery continued to be brought by sailors right up to the end of the shipping season. There is a clue also in the calendar of Egypt. One of the honorific months introduced there by Caligula (it did not survive him) was *Soter* ('Saviour'). This is known to have been the equivalent of the Egyptian Phaophi, which began on September 28.[7] Soter might well have been named because during this month he began his initial recovery from illness, which should, accordingly, be placed at some point in October.

News of the recovery brought joy and relief to the empire, and Philo reports that the Jews of Alexandria celebrated it with sacrifices.[8] Not everyone would have cause to rejoice. The first who might have begun to feel regret were those unfortunates who, perhaps in the hope of favours, had offered themselves for the emperor's recovery. It is not immediately apparent what their punishment was. Dio says ambiguously that they were obliged to keep their promises. Suetonius indicates that the would-be gladiator (he does not provide names) was forced to fight in the arena several times before being released, while the other was decked in sacred garlands and conveyed through the streets by slaves before being hurled from an embankment. Again, the ambiguity of the language suggests that probably both lives were spared and that Caligula intended this episode as public humiliation (not totally undeserved) to punish gross flattery.[9]

Any change in his conduct at this time, however, is more likely to be the indirect consequence of the illness, rather than of its residual effect on his mental state. The events of Caligula's reign took a dramatic turn in the period immediately after his recovery. The spirit of universal good will came to an abrupt end, with the enforced suicides of two prominent figures, Gemellus and Caligula's father-in-law, Silanus, in what seems to have been fairly rapid succession, to be followed some time later by the similar fate of Macro. A proper understanding of the circumstances surrounding these deaths would be invaluable for the assessment of Caligula's career as a whole, in that they seem to represent the first serious break in the general euphoria that marked the initiation of his reign. Unfortunately, the sources are frustratingly reticent about the details. We are not even certain about the dates. Suetonius treats Silanus and Gemellus together in a way that suggests that their deaths occurred within the same general period, while Philo groups all three together. Dio actually places the deaths of Gemellus and Silanus among the last events of 37, immediately after the illness, while Macro's is separated from them and placed at the beginning of 38. Replacements for Gemellus and Silanus in the Arval brotherhood were not made until 24 May, 38.[10] It is certainly a reasonable speculation that the deaths of all three were in some way related, but in the final analysis even that simple premise remains unprovable.

The first victim mentioned by Philo and Dio is Gemellus. Dio says that the charge made against him, late in 37, was that he had anticipated Caligula's death, and had waited for a chance to benefit from his illness. Philo explicitly says that the pretended reason was a conspiracy. Suetonius is more anecdotal and less convincing, claiming that Gemellus had a chronic and deteriorating cough for which he took medicine. When the smell was detected it led to the charge that he had been taking an antidote against poison. Soldiers were despatched to order him to take his own life, and when, pathetically, the lad was handed the sword he did not know what to do with it, and had to be helped. It is specifically stated that in Gemellus' case no reference was made by Caligula to the senate.[11] Gemellus was probably buried in the mausoleum of Augustus, to judge from the fact that his gravestone was found in its vicinity. As an apparent mark of the contempt that Caligula felt for him at the time of his death he is not recorded as the emperor's son on the stone: *Ti. Caesar Drusi Caesaris f./ hic situs est* ('here lies Tiberius Caesar, son of Drusus Caesar').[12]

The assertion that he had been taking an antidote (*antidotum adversus Caesarem*) might suggest involvement in a plot, and this is supported by Dio's observation that Gemellus was charged with having 'prayed for and anticipated Caligula's death'. We have only the barest outline of events for the period, and it is easy to forget that during the illness the day-to-day operation of the state would have had to continue. The chief executives would, of course, have been the consuls, who could have represented the concerns of the princeps in dealing with the senate. But there were many tasks whose terms of reference would not have been so clearly established by precedent. These would have ranged from formal ceremonies, like receiving deputations, to such routines as giving the password to the imperial guard. The presence of the princeps was expected at games, at the theatre, at festivals. We know that Claudius deputized for Caligula at games, but it would have been almost inevitable that Gemellus, as the emperor's son, should have represented him at other innocuous and non-political events. Caligula had been treated as one on whose shoulders the fate of the Roman world rested. On recovering from his illness he would have discovered the disconcerting truth that no-one is indispensable and that things had gone ahead no less smoothly than before. The resentment that this would have engendered, along with the natural suspicion of plots and conspiracies endemic to the age, might have made it difficult for him to accept that Gemellus' conduct during his illness had been dictated by circumstances and not by ambition. It also might have been difficult for him to interpret any support that Gemellus received during this period other than as disloyalty. This might explain Dio's cryptic comment, under 38, that several people owed their destruction to Caligula's illness.[13]

The situation would have been aggravated by Gemellus' delicate position. To the extent that Augustus and Tiberius had laid down any sort of pattern for the succession, the only possible candidate during the serious illness would have been Gemellus. Admittedly, he was far from being the ideal successor — his age and lack of experience would have told strongly against him. The senate had apparently shown no reluctance in removing him from the succession, and if there were any pro-Gemellus party in that body it must have been small and not very vocal. Despite this, however, he would still, as the emperor's son, have been seen as the inevitable candidate. This, of course, is no more than speculation. It could well be that Caligula's suspicions were well-grounded, and that Gemellus was at the centre of an embryonic conspiracy. Even Philo suggests that in a sense it was a good thing that Gemellus died — the empire was *akoinoneticon* ('impossible to share') and people were beginning to take sides.[14] When we are told that early in the reign Caligula refused to give an ear to evidence of a plot, we may have been given the public face that he put on the approach to him. In reality, he may have taken the information seriously. While Gemellus' death does seem to foreshadow the rift between Caligula and the senate that would follow later, it is to be noted that Philo admits that the public did not criticise Caligula for this and the other executions that immediately followed his illness.

The possible link between Gemellus and Caligula's father-in-law Silanus is not readily apparent. Before Tiberius' death Silanus was held in great honour, to the degree that the emperor refused to try any case on appeal from his decision and referred such cases back to Silanus. Because of his age and rank he was accorded by the consuls the honour of casting his vote first in the senate.[15] Philo and Dio say nothing of any specific incident that might have led to Silanus' downfall. They seem to believe that Caligula simply grew to resent his father-in-law's attempts to interfere.[16] Suetonius, however, relates the anecdote that when Caligula put to sea (presumably to go to Potnia and Pandateria to seek the remains of his mother and brother), Silanus declined to accompany him because he tended to get seasick, and that Caligula suspected that he had stayed behind in order to take over if he himself should be lost at sea.[17] Tacitus observes that Julius Graecinus, the father in law of Agricola, was forced to commit suicide for refusing to prosecute a Marcus Silanus. If this is the same Silanus, it implies that he faced a *formal* charge and trial before the senate.[18] The anecdote about Silanus' plotting while Caligula was at sea may be a garbled version of one of the charges, which could have involved participation in a supposed conspiracy to replace Caligula with Gemellus. Since Silanus would have been an accessory rather than the figurehead of such a conspiracy Caligula would not have felt the need to act so swiftly, and the case could have gone before the senate. Whatever the political or legal background to Silanus' fall from grace, the outcome is clear enough. He committed suicide with his own razor.[19]

Suspicion of some kind of plot may have prompted Caligula to think more seriously about the issue of his succession. At all events, at some point before the end of 37 he remarried. His new wife's name is uncertain. Suetonius gives it as Livia Orestilla, Dio as Cornelia Orestina. At the time of her marriage she was already engaged to Gaius Calpurnius Piso, who belonged to a family that was still powerful and distinguished and did not seem to have suffered from the notoriety of Germanicus' murder; his cooption into the Arval brotherhood in place of Silanus on 24 May, 38, may have been a reward for his compliance in the marriage. Suetonius reports Caligula's quip that he acquired his wife in the manner of Augustus and Romulus. He was referring, of course, to the fact that they had both snatched their brides from their original husbands (like Livia, Hersilia was already married [to Hersilius] before she married Romulus).[20] He seems to have tired of his new wife quickly and soon divorced her. This happened after a few days, according to Suetonius, who adds that Caligula eventually banished her on the grounds that she took up with Piso again within two years of the marriage. Dio places the banishment after two months, adding that Piso was banished also. Dio must be wrong about Piso's banishment, however, since he was still in Rome until at least June 40 (when the Arval record breaks off). Also it is difficult to see what his crime could have been, since he and his former wife could not have committed adultery unless they had remarried. The whole incident is something of a mystery, since it makes no apparent sense for Caligula to have divorced his wife after a few days. It may be that the two month figure of Dio is actually the period before the divorce, rather than the banishment, and that she was put aside because she showed no signs of pregnancy.[21] But if this reconstruction is correct Caligula was, at the very least, excessively impatient. The incident may simply represent his increasing fecklessness, and a tendency to behave on personal whims.

The year 38 opened with a dramatic occurrence. A slave called Machaon entered the temple of Jupiter on the Capitoline. Climbing onto the god's couch he made a number of frightening predictions, then slew a puppy he had brought into the temple, before killing himself.[22] Machaon was no doubt deranged, and hoped that his self-sacrifice would secure him a brief moment at the centre of attention. But many people in the months to come would doubtless look upon his mad act as an omen of what

Rome herself was to suffer. At some point in the first part of the year, a third figure fell victim to Caligula — his apparently loyal henchman, Macro.[23] The precise date of Macro's death is uncertain. Before it occurred, he received a new office, the Prefecture of Egypt, which he did not live to take up. Dio places his death among the early events of 38, and Philo suggests that news of it arrived early enough in Alexandria for the current Prefect of Egypt, Flaccus, to react and to change his policy before the arrival of Agrippa in the city in the summer of 38.[24]

The death of Macro is particularly problematic, since he had been Caligula's staunchest supporter and would surely have appreciated that his own future interests were closely interwoven with those of the emperor. Philo sees the problem in very simplistic terms, as one that arose from Macro's insistence on trying to control Caligula's conduct. Once again, the account of their relationship owes a very great deal to Philo's own imagination, but it is probably based in part on what Philo himself heard. Philo attributes noble ideals to Macro, whom he presents in the role of Caligula's guide and mentor, giving frank and blunt advice, restraining his excesses in public and even checking him in matters of protocol. Despite Macro's best efforts, Caligula's inclinations were in complete opposition, and his mind would bend in the opposite direction to where it was guided. *Tolmai tis didaskein*? ('who dares teach me?') was his reaction. He was offended by constantly being reminded that the Prefect had saved him time and time again, and that after Tiberius' death he had brought the army over to his side. As Philo puts it, Macro paid the penalty for his act of duty; he had performed zealously on Caligula's behalf and in return he was punished. In this picture Caligula was a William II tiring of his Bismarck, the young ruler no longer wanting to be beholden to anyone older and more experienced. It may be true, and it certainly seems in character, but it can hardly be the whole explanation. Philo in his detailed account gives no hint of any conspiratorial activities by Macro, but we must remember that he was writing a moral tract and wished to display the ingratitude of the emperor. It would not have suited his theme to give any hint that Macro deserved his fate.

It is tempting to speculate that Macro came down as a result of conspiratorial dealings with Gemellus, and possibly with Silanus and others. Dio does imply that several people were put to death in connection with his fall.[25] Again, the event may have been the inevitable by-product of Caligula's illness. If at a critical phase it was anticipated that Gemellus would soon succeed to the principate, Macro would not have scrupled to manoeuvre himself into a position as potential regent, even though this might be construed as a (temporary) shift of allegiance. The full truth of his duplicity might not have been immediately apparent to Caligula on recovery, but even if it had been, his removal would have required the same delicate handling that Macro himself exhibited in the downfall of Sejanus. In fact, Macro would have been forewarned by his predecessor's fate. The appointment as Prefect of Egypt may have been part of this process of deception, a ploy, like the promise of tribunician power to Sejanus, to divert Macro's attention while Caligula prepared his ground.

The issue of Macro's death is further complicated by the earlier affair between Caligula and Ennia. Suetonius simply mentions the Prefect and his wife among the friends and relatives who were rewarded for their services by a cruel death. Dio says that Caligula compelled Ennia and Macro to commit suicide and involved Macro in a scandal, by charging him among other things with pandering his own wife. Bauman has suggested that because the *maiestas* law had been suspended he may have brought an *accusatio adulterii* against Macro, under the specific category of *lenocinium* (pandering).[26] Both Philo and Dio have Caligula laying charges against Macro and Ennia but neither specifies one that would adequately explain their fates. It seems clear that actions against them were begun *in camera* and that details were not made public. The clouding of the political issue by covering up the charges of disloyalty with accusations of sexual misconduct might have been a deliberate ploy to avoid making public just how precarious Caligula's position had been. Macro and Ennia presumably committed suicide to protect their family and estate. It is interesting to note that despite Caligula's later reputation for engineering the deaths of prominent individuals to get his hands on their estates, Macro was able to leave enough money to provide an amphitheatre for his home town of Alba Fucens.[27]

One of the most intriguing aspects of Macro's case is the apparent involvement of the Alexandrian Greek leader Isidorus, a sinister and unscrupulous figure who played an important role in the dispute between Jews and Greeks in Alexandria, Egypt's principal city. The evidence comes from one of the highly coloured tracts produced by Alexandrian Greek nationalists to which the general name of the *Acts of the Pagan* or *Alexandrian Martyrs* is sometimes assigned. These have survived only on very fragmentary papyri comprising the texts of trials before Roman emperors of important Alexandrians who suffered martyrdom to defend the privileges of the city. They dwell on supposed oppression by their Roman masters, in contrast to what is portrayed as the courage and spirit of the Alexandrians, and they are predictably anti-Jewish in tone. While they are based on historical events, the events are much distorted to emphasize the dignity of the accused in contrast to the cruelty of the emperor. In one group of four papyri, the *Acta Isidori*, we have an account of the trial of Agrippa (probably II), prosecuted by Isidorus and Lampo before Claudius, probably in 53. The trial takes place in the imperial gardens in Rome, before a number of spectators, including women. The charge against Agrippa is not clear. It seems to have involved the status of Alexandrian Jews, but in any case it failed, and Isidorus and

Lampo end up being condemned, the sentence apparently intended as vengeance for the death of Claudius' friends at their hands. The proceedings break down into insults, Claudius calling Isidorus the 'son of a whore' and Isidorus insisting that Claudius' mother was Jewish.[28] One of Isidorus' pleas is that in previous prosecutions he acted as agent for Caligula, and in this document he is held responsible for the death of an earlier prefect whom Claudius apparently considered a friend and whose name appears to have been Naevius (Macro).[29]

It is difficult to know just what to make of this information. Macro is said by Philo to have been a friend of Flaccus, the Prefect of Egypt. Now Flaccus was supposedly an adherent of Gemellus (the only individual so identified by Philo), and had played a role in the condemnation of Agrippina. Philo might have added the detail about his supporting Gemellus simply for rhetorical effect, since Flaccus had been in Egypt for the past seven or so years and could hardly have had any close involvement with political events in Rome. It could be that when Gemellus' star was briefly in the ascendant during Caligula's illness Macro communicated with the Prefect of Egypt on ways to ensure that in the event of the emperor's death matters could be arranged to their mutual interest. If Flaccus had been an accuser of Agrippina it seems unlikely that he would have been on intimate terms with Macro, and Philo's supposition about the friendship may be based only on written communications. If Flaccus did compromise himself in his dealings with Macro, this could account for his utter despondency at the news of the latter's death. Moreover, if Isidorus had somehow become privy to the communications, we have an explanation for the strange and sinister hold that the leaders of the Alexandrian Greeks supposedly began to excercise over Flaccus early in 38, and also how they were able to destroy Macro. It is interesting to note that when Agrippa went to his kingdom in 38, on Caligula's advice he did not take the northern route through Greece, but waited for the Etesian winds and sailed via Alexandria. Could he have been sent to investigate Flaccus? It is difficult otherwise to find a reasonable explanation for his presence in Alexandria.[30]

After Macro's death Caligula would probably have felt that it was dangerous to concentrate control of the Praetorians in the hands of a single man, and Balsdon is probably correct in suggesting that it was at this time that he reverted to the principle of divided command of the prefecture. None of the sources specifically mentions a formal change but they do refer to Praetorian Prefects later under Caligula.[31]

The death of Macro and the departure of Agrippa would have removed the major influences on Caligula during the crucial period in his reign, when he first began to show the traits that a year or so later would have developed into overt autocracy. Suspicion of plots would, of course, have brought the euphoric 'honeymoon' period of the early part of the reign to an end. Yet there is no indication that the early executions caused popular resentment or were thought to have been unjustified. With careful guidance Caligula might have retained his good rapport with the senate. It is difficult, however, to see where he might have found this guidance. It had been the regular practice of Augustus and Tiberius to make use of *amici*, as advisors on matters of state, the so-called *consilium principis*.[32] There are slight hints that such a consilium might have existed under Caligula. He called together 'the top men' to hear the announcement of Gemellus' adoption, he would speak to 'close advisors' about the dismissal of the consuls in 39, and on one occasion called' the leading men of the senate' to the palace (only to dance before them).[33] But there is no indication that they were in a position to offer him frank advice and guidance on a systematic basis and thus fill the role previously played by Macro and Agrippa. The only senior statesman known to have been on close personal terms with Caligula was Valerius Asiaticus, and there is no reference to any association between them until just before the emperor's death. We do know that Caligula enjoyed the friendship of Vitellius, the future emperor, while they lived on Capri. They both shared a passion for chariot racing, and Vitellius had a crippled thigh as the result of an accident he suffered when riding with Caligula. But it is unlikely that at this stage the young Vitellius could have assumed the role of political advisor. The suffect consuls for 38, Sextus Nonius Quintilianus and Servius Asinius Celer would presumably have been designated by Caligula personally, and the latter might at any rate have been on close terms with the emperor, since he was the son of Gaius Asinius Gallus and Vipsania, the former wife of Tiberius. Gallus was reputed in his later years to have been the lover of Agrippina, and they perhaps hoped to marry, which might have created a special bond between their sons. The one recorded achievement of Asinius during Caligula's reign, apart from the consulship, suggests that he did have one thing in common with the emperor — wild extravagance — since he paid 8,000 sesterces for a single mullet.[34]

Probably Caligula's closest friend still in Rome, however, was Marcus Aemilius Lepidus, who enjoyed a special status, as Caligula's lover, according to Dio, and as husband of the emperor's favourite sister, Drusilla. She had first been married in 33 to Lucius Cassius Longinus, the consul of 30 (possibly the prosecutor of their brother Drusus). At some point they were divorced and she subsequently married Marcus Lepidus. Caligula had no children of his own at this point, and after Gemellus' death there was no other obvious successor from within the imperial family. According to Dio, Lepidus was publicly marked by Caligula to succeed him, and was allowed to stand for office five years earlier than legally permitted.[35] During the emperor's illness, according to Suetonius, it was Drusilla who was designated as heir to the emperor's estate and the empire, *bonorum* and *imperii*. Perhaps Caligula might have felt threatened by the position, real and imagined, of Gemellus and his supporters, and thought that by making Drusilla his successor he could to some degree weaken Gemellus' prospects.[36] But the tradition may have become confused by the special position of Lepidus, and it was possibly he, as Drusilla's husband, who was designated in the will as successor, as Dio's description of Lepidus' status might imply. Lepidus is the only one of the sisters' husbands to attract any attention in the sources; there is no mention of Caligula even acknowledging the existence of Domitius Ahenobarbus and Marcus Vinicius, husbands of Agrippina and Livilla respectively. Neither is mentioned once in Suetonius' *Life of Caligula*.[37]

Lepidus' family antecedents are not known in precise detail. He was descended from Lucius Paullus Lepidus, a distinguished friend of Augustus, whose eldest son Lucius Aemilius Paullus married Augustus' granddaughter Julia Minor (and went down with her in the scandal of AD 8). Their daughter Aemilia Lepida (ii) was at one time betrothed to Claudius but after the Julia scandal this was broken off, and she married Marcus Junius Silanus (cos. AD 19). Lucius Paullus Lepidus' younger son, Marcus Aemilius Lepidus, was consul in 6 AD, and it was said that Augustus considered him (as well as Lucius Arruntius and Asinius Gallus) as a potential successor, remarking that Lepidus had the capacity for rule but not the desire.[38] Marcus' daughter Aemilia Lepida (i) married Drusus, brother of Caligula, and there is general agreement that Marcus' son was Aemilius Lepidus, husband of Drusilla.[39] Lepidus might thus have entertained ambitions on the basis of his family connections, in particular his distinguished father; he could also have traced a link with the imperial family, in that his paternal grandmother, Cornelia, was the daughter of Scribonia, who later married Octavian. We know nothing of Lepidus' life or priestly offices before his marriage with Drusilla, nor even how old he was at the time. But he certainly did well from the marriage, enjoying an accelerated career and a special relationship with the emperor.[40] A very striking piece of evidence for his privileged relationship to Caligula comes from the city of Aphrodisias. In a statue group of the imperial family from the *sebasteion* associated with the imperial cult, there is a base for the figure of a Marcus Lepidus.[41] In the same group are bases for Germanicus and Agrippina, the latter securely dated to Caligula's reign, and all three, on the grounds of letter style, of the same period. Lepidus' position was clearly so secure that his intimate ties with the imperial family were recognized even in the provinces. It is unfortunate that the only Roman who might have been in a position to influence Caligula had ambitions of his own and was probably not willing to incur the emperor's displeasure by trying to restrain any tendencies towards autocratic behaviour.

Stemma 5
The family connections of M. Aemilius Lepidus, husband of Drusilla

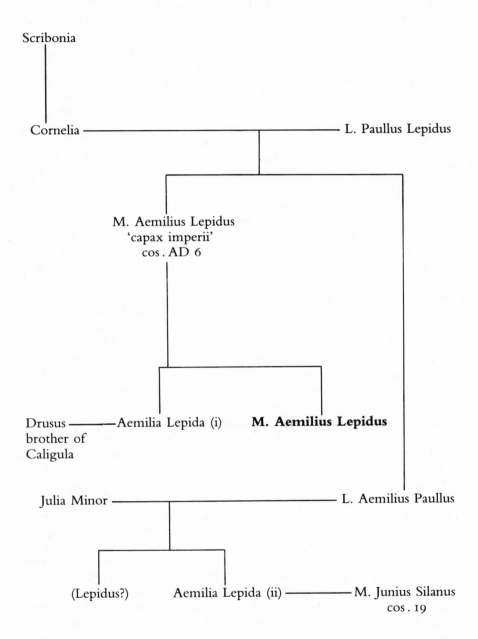

There was no shortage of advisors at the lower end of the social scale. The sources claim that Caligula sought out the company of gladiators and actors. The only one specifically named as having an influence over him is Apelles, the famous actor from Ascalon who supposedly urged an anti-Jewish policy upon him.[42] The most readily identifiable intimates of Caligula, however, were the imperial freedmen, and it was during his reign that this social group first began to enjoy a position of power and influence.[43] Slaves and freedmen tended to pass down within the same home.[44] They, more than any others, represented continuity from emperor to emperor, and thus were able to make themselves indispensable. The most important of these was Callistus, a freedman who inspired great fear and amassed enormous wealth from his position, and may even have pandered his own daughter, Nymphidia, as a means of gaining influence over Caligula. Many years later, there was a rumour that Nymphidius, the unsuccessful claimant for the principate in 68, was the son of Caligula and Callistus' daughter, a rumour that Nymphidius did nothing to dispel. Callistus is seen offering advice on crucial issues, such as the trial of Domitius Afer and the handling of the suspected conspiracy towards the end of Caligula's reign.[45] Another freedman, Tiberius Claudius (the name is uncertain), came as a young slave from Smyrna to Tiberius' court and gained his freedom under that ruler. He was inherited by Caligula and accompanied the emperor on his northern expedition. He received further promotion from Claudius (perhaps a procuratorship) and was made financial secretary (a rationibus) by Nero (probably succeeding Pallas in that office in 55). Granted equestrian status by Vespasian, he finally died under Domitian at the age of ninety. We know of no specific advice that Tiberius Claudius may have given Caligula, but he was apparently able to excercise a moderating influence on him, and is likened by Statius to an animal trainer who controls a savage beast.[46]

Helicon first appears in Philo's account of the initial reception of the Jewish embassy that he headed from Alexandria. By this time he was well-established in the household. He was the leader of a large group of Alexandrian Greeks in Caligula's service (Philo loosely calls them 'Egyptians'). His first master, according to Philo, had given him a smattering of education and handed him over to Tiberius; he then passed to Caligula. He had not made great progress under Tiberius because of that emperor's distaste for childish jokes. But he saw his opportunity for advancement under Caligula because of his great skill at clever witticisms, especially quips with a malicious sting, that combined accusations with ridicule. He was soon inseparable from the emperor. He played ball with him, exercised with him, bathed with him, had his meals with him, and was with him when he retired for the night. He became chamberlain (katakoimistes) and supervised the palace guard. Philo says that he saw the Jews as an appropriate butt of his kind of humour, and prejudiced

Caligula against the Jewish delegation in return for bribes from the Alexandrians and the promise of honours as soon as Caligula visited Alexandria. Philo blames him, along with Apelles, for later encouraging Caligula in his scheme to set up his statue in the Temple at Jerusalem. Helicon was eventually executed by Claudius for various unspecified crimes. Two other freedmen are known during this period. Homilos is said to have been in charge of embassies, when the Jewish deputation tried to see the emperor. Perhaps most sinister of all was Protogenes, who appears towards the end of the reign as Caligula's chief agent in his bloody campaign against the senate. Gelzer attributes many of the woes of Caligula's reign to the excessive influence of these freedmen. It is in fact very difficult to quantify their impact on events, but it is probably safe to say that as a group they would not have seen their role as one of trying to curb the emperor's excesses or urging him towards a harmonious relationship with the senate.[47]

With his brothers and parents dead, and without a compatible wife, it might be expected that Caligula would have looked for affection from his three sisters. The enormous favours that he heaped on them at the beginning of his reign had a political purpose, but they also suggest considerable affection within the family. It was doubtless this affection that led to the stories of incest with all three sisters.[48] Such reports are to be treated with scepticism. Suetonius claims that Caligula was actually caught with Drusilla when they were staying at Antonia's house, but admits that the story was hearsay. Neither Seneca nor Philo, contemporaries of Caligula who both adopt a highly moral tone, make any mention of incest. Also when Tacitus deals with Agrippina's incestuous designs on her son, the emperor Nero, he makes no hint of any improper relationship with her brother — although the context was certainly appropriate — and attributes her moral corruption to her association with Lepidus.[49] The charge of incest has been traditionally levelled against despots, from antiquity to Napoleon. The mother is the usual partner, but, as Willrich observes, since the mother was not available to be blamed in the case of Caligula, the sisters were called upon to fill the role.[50] The noted wit Passienus Crispus, who attended Caligula on one of his journeys, was supposedly asked by him if, like the emperor, he had been intimate with his sister. Passienus diplomatically replied 'Not yet.' Apart from illustrating Passienus' mental agility, the story also suggests that the rumours of Caligula's incest may have arisen from his own jocular remarks. It is interesting that presumably through a textual corruption the story as it appears in the manuscripts is told not about Caligula but about *Nero*, indicating that in the mind of the copyist, any emperor was considered a suitable target for this kind of gossip. It is also worth noting that the conversation, although described in such detail, supposedly took place in private, *nullo audiente*.[51]

Suetonius states that Caligula was especially attached to Drusilla, but did not show the same affection to his other sisters.[52] Allowance must of course be made for the simple fact that the other sisters survived, to be involved in a conspiracy, and the resulting antipathy might well have coloured the tradition about their earlier relationship. But of the devotion to Drusilla there can be no doubt. Throughout his life Caligula had suffered a series of family tragedies, and in 38 he was dealt his most grievous blow yet, when, on 10 June, Drusilla died.[53] The emperor was devastated, and his reaction to her death was, in the view of some, so bizarre that it must have been inspired by oriental precedents. But while his grief may by some standards seem excessive, his behaviour nevertheless was, as Herz has shown, within the bounds of Roman tradition.[54] Drusilla was granted a public funeral, which was not attended by Caligula. He was too overwhelmed with grief to be present, and the eulogy had to be read by Lepidus. The emperor went first to his villa at Alba in the Alban Hills near Rome, then moved on to Campania and Sicily, showing his grief by not cutting his hair or beard. It was presumably while in Syracuse on this occasion that he held 'Athenian games', perhaps in connection with the rebuilding of the city walls and temples. There is no need to doubt that the grief was genuine; only Seneca is sceptical, cynically commenting that Caligula found his chief solace in gambling and other such self-indulgences at his Alban villa.[55]

A *iustitium* (a period of public mourning) was proclaimed, when business was suspended and public and private amusements were banned, as had happened at the deaths of other members of the imperial family. In Drusilla's case at least it was observed also in other parts of the empire, since we know that Jews closed their shops in Alexandria.[56] Individuals who did not show the proper respect during this period stood at some risk — a man who sold hot water (for wine) was convicted. Dio claims that the charge was *maiestas*, but that particular charge was in abeyance at the time, and a lesser prosecution is more likely. In fact, the newly discovered Arval fragment shows life continuing. Celebrations were held that summer to mark the anniversary of Caligula's first consulship (1 July), his birthday (31 August) and the anniversary of the assumption of the title Pater Patriae (21 September). The actual implementation of the *iustitium* was clearly less severe than Dio would have us believe.[57]

The honours granted Drusilla were formally voted in the senate in accordance with precedent.[58] In fact they were not in themselves extraordinary in Roman terms. What is striking is that they were granted to a person of such little political significance. But this does not in itself indicate that Caligula was deranged, or under the influence of eastern practices, any more than, say, Queen Victoria in erecting grandiose monuments for the late Prince Albert.

The distinctions previously voted for Livia were bestowed on Drusilla.

In Livia's case the senate had ordered mourning for the women, without suspension of business, and had voted the unparalleled (for a woman) distinction of an arch, and Drusilla was presumably granted the same honours.[59] In addition, however, Drusilla received a privilege that Tiberius had specifically vetoed in the case of Livia. Once the period of mourning had ended it was decreed that she was to be deified. She thus became the first woman to be consecrated and worshipped as a goddess in Rome itself. Yet even this measure can not have been totally alien to the Roman mind. The senate must clearly have been inclined to grant divine status to Livia, otherwise Tiberius would hardly have felt the need to prohibit it. Also, if deification of a female member of his own family *was* Caligula's innovation, it was certainly followed by his successors, resulting in the apotheosis of Livia in 42, of Claudia, daughter of Nero, in 63, (she was deified by order of the senate with a temple and a priest), and of Poppaea in 65.[60] Again, what is perhaps most significant in Caligula's case is not the consecration of a woman, but of a woman of such little importance or achievement. Livia had, after all, occupied a prominent position in Roman affairs for over half a century. Drusilla's only achievement was to be Caligula's sister. By deciding to elevate her to the status of goddess, Caligula demonstrated his increasing egocentricity, his conviction that the state as an institution was designed to serve his own personal needs, rather than what the communal interests might dictate.

If the generally accepted restoration of the text of the Arval records is correct, Drusilla's consecration probably took place on 23 September, which would link her with Augustus, whose birthday fell on that date.[61] Technically, of course, the consecration had to be preceded by proof of divinity. In the case of Augustus a certain Numerius Atticus had claimed to have seen the soul ascend to heaven, to which he had to swear an oath and for which he was rewarded by a payment of a million sesterces. In Drusilla's case a similar service was performed by Livius Geminus, who was paid the same sum.[62] Next, a golden effigy was ordered set up in the senate house, and it was planned that in the Temple of Venus in the forum she would have a statue the same size as that of Venus, and would be honoured by the same rites. The temple in question would almost certainly be that of Venus Genetrix in the forum Julium, appropriate because of that goddess' role as the founder of the Julian line, and a common cult name of Drusilla was 'New Aphrodite'.[63]

In her divine capacity Drusilla was included in oaths, similar to the ones already made to Divus Caesar and Divus Augustus. Caligula, according to Suetonius, required women to swear to her by name, and did so himself even before assemblies and soldiers. The extension of this honour to a woman may have been an innovation but, again, Claudius would apparently honour Livia in the same way.[64] Drusilla was also to have her own personal shrine with twenty priests of both sexes. In establishing this personal priesthood, Caligula again seems to have adapted an Augustan model, the Sodales Augustales, who were charged with the worship of Augustus.[65] Even the use of both male and female priests was not without precedent, since Livia had been made a priestess of Augustus under Tiberius, as had Antonia under Caligula.[66] We know nothing further about Drusilla's priesthood, since after Caligula's death the college was presumably disbanded.

Caligula declared that Drusilla was to receive divine honours throughout all the cities, and to receive the name of Panthea (all-embracing deity). The use of this cult name is unexplained — it is in fact quite commonly found attached to a number of gods, both male and female. Its connection with the Imperial house is suggested by an undated inscription from Gillium in Tunisia 'Pantheo Augusto sacrum'.[67] There is widespread evidence of divine honours throughout Italy and the empire, and since they greatly outnumber those of her sister Livilla (Agrippina received many such honours by virtue of being the wife of Claudius and mother of Nero), we must assume that most, if not all, followed her death and consecration.[68] In Egypt the month of Payni (26 May–24 June) was renamed Drusilleios, in accordance with the common practice there of renaming months after the imperial family. It was dropped soon after Caligula's death.[69]

The birthday was a very important occasion for the Imperial family, because of its close association with the genius of the princeps, the object of worship (p. 142). Drusilla's birthday was accordingly given special status. It was to be celebrated in the manner of the Megalesia, a two day festival held on April 4 and 5 to mark the arrival of the goddess Cybele in Rome, when the senators and knights traditionally sent out mutual invitations to dinner banquets.[70] The choice of Cybele's festival is not easy to explain, but it must be remembered that this goddess was given important status by Augustus, and when her Palatine temple was destroyed by fire in AD 3 it was rebuilt by him.[71] The fact that the Megalesia was a two day festival would also provide an appeal, since Augustus' birthday celebrations similarly extended over two days.[72] As an illustration of Drusilla's birthday festival we have the account of the celebrations held in the following year. The month is uncertain but it probably marked the first anniversary of the birthday since her death.[73] The events lasted two days. On the first there were horse races, and 500 bears were slain, while 500 elephants met their end on the next day (both the games and the slaughtering of animals echo Augustus' birthday celebrations). There were athletic contests, feasting for the public and gifts for senators and their wives in the tradition of the Megalesia.

The climax of the festivities occurred when the image of Drusilla was brought into the circus on a car drawn by elephants. There were Roman precedents for this also. In 45 BC Caesar was granted the honour of an ivory statue carried in a chariot at the games, and similar honours were granted, after their deaths, to other members of the imperial family, such as Germanicus and Britannicus.[74] The original inspiration for the elephant cart probably came from Hellenistic models, such as the famous procession arranged in Egypt by Ptolemy II, in which the figure of Alexander appeared in an elephant-drawn car.[75] But it had been used in processions in Rome from the time of Pompey, and among the divine honours voted for Augustus was a chariot drawn by elephants.[76] A year later, moderation prevailed. Early in January 40 it was decreed that the birthdays of Tiberius and Drusilla should be celebrated in the same manner as that of Augustus. Tiberius had in fact during his lifetime checked the celebration of his own birthday. It seems to have been marked by Arval sacrifices, but when it was proposed that it be celebrated with ten horse races and a senatorial banquet, he firmly turned the offer down, although reluctantly allowing the addition of a single two-horse chariot to the pre-existing games that happened to coincide with his birthday.[77] The restrained level of Drusilla's subsequent birthday celebrations after the extravagance of the original anniversary shows that once Caligula's initial bout of grief had abated the treatment of his dead sister was kept within reasonable bounds. It is also striking that he honoured Tiberius' birthday with greater distinction than his predecessor had himself been prepared to countenance.

Caligula married for a third time in the course of 38.[78] The date of the marriage is very uncertain. After describing the death of Drusilla Dio states that 'after a few days' the emperor married Lollia Paulina, which presumably should be taken to mean a few days after the consecration and end of the *iustitium*, thus probably after 23 September. The third wife belonged to a wealthy family, possibly from Pompeii. She was a fine-looking woman whose beauty went back at least three generations, according to Suetonius, and Caligula was reportedly first encouraged by reports of her looks, but he may also have been motivated by an increasingly difficult financial situation, since she was a woman of great inherited wealth. The elder Pliny saw her at a modest dinner party, covered with emeralds and interlaced pearls over her head, neck and fingers, the total amounting to 40 million sesterces. For those who doubted that such wealth could belong to one woman, she reputedly carried the proof of ownership on her person. She was also married already. Her husband, Publius Memmius Regulus, had been suffect consul of 31, and had been involved in the overthrow of Sejanus. At the time of Caligula's wedding he was governor of Moesia, Macedonia and Achaea, to which he had been appointed in 35 and where he would stay until 44.[79]

Suetonius says that Memmius was called from his province to participate inthe ceremony, to which Dio adds a very curious comment. He says that Caligula forced Memmius personally to give his wife in marriage to Caligula, in case she would not be 'properly married, contrary to the laws'. This may well simply be a garbled version of some joking comment by Caligula about how appropriate it was for Memmius, the former husband, to be present to give away his own wife.[80] Memmius was in the city by 23 September, 38, when he participated in the Arval rites, and his presence was probably a result of his being summoned from his province for the wedding, as Suetonius suggests, an eager compliance that would doubtless cause him embarrassment later.[81]

Memmius came from a simple provincial background (he may have originated from Narbonensis), and, according to Tacitus, his modest demeanour, and lack of wealth or family distinction protected him from envy.[82] He was suffect consul from 1 October, 31, an important appointment since it was during his term of office that Sejanus fell, a sign of the high trust in which Memmius was held by Tiberius, although he was criticised by his colleague for his lack of enthusiasm on that occasion. The wedding seems not to have done his career any harm. He retained his governorship until his provinces were eventually handed over to the senate in 44. In 40 he was ordered to bring the famous statue of Zeus from Olympia to Rome. He supposedly delayed carrying out the order, conduct which would have cost him his life had it not been for the timely death of the emperor.[83] This story of the opportune rescue of Memmius, and, at the same time, of his reputation, should perhaps be viewed with some suspicion.

Late in 38 the governor of Egypt, Aulus Avillius Flaccus, was arrested at the time of the Jewish feast of the Tabernacles in late October, by a centurion Bassus sent by Caligula with a detachment of troops (p. 187). We are given no information in the sources whether he was charged after his return with poor administration and failure to quell the riots, or whether the case was purely political.[84] It is noteworthy that after his arrest the charges were taken up by his new enemies Isidorus and Lampon, who not much earlier had supposedly been treating him as a close friend and benefactor. Their presence adds weight to the notion that Isidorus might earlier have been privy to communications between Macro and Flaccus, which he had used first to bring down Macro and which were now being turned against Flaccus.[85]

Flaccus was condemned and his property confiscated, but through the intercession of Lepidus was exiled to the relative comfort of Andros rather than Gyarus, possibly the bleakest of the islands of exile. The fact that he did not receive the death penalty suggests that the evidence at this stage did not extend beyond a general association with Gemellus and Macro, and did not indicate active involvement in a supposed conspiracy. The intervention of Lepidus is striking and our total ignorance of his links with Flaccus is a great handicap, since the arrest was in some ways a prelude to the repression that was to come in the following year, and which would ultimately bring down both Flaccus and Lepidus.

· 6 ·

CONSPIRACY

AT THE BEGINNING of AD 39 Caligula entered into his second consulship, an event of some political significance. Once Augustus had stepped down from his annual consulship in 23 BC he held the office on two occasions only after that, in 5 BC and 2 BC, in order to introduce his grandsons Gaius and Lucius to public life. Similarly, after assuming the principate, Tiberius held the consulship only in 18 (with Germanicus), 21 (with Drusus) and 31 (with Sejanus). Caligula had at the beginning of his reign declined the perpetual consulship, and did not resume the office in 38, possibly to demonstrate an attitude of constitutional moderation. Beginning in 39, however, he held the consulship for each of the last three years of his life. In terms of practical power it meant little, since on each occasion he soon stepped down to allow a suffect to replace him. But as a symbolic gesture it tells much more than the literary accounts of extravagant behaviour and blood thirsty cruelty. It demonstrates that from now on he was quite overt in his determination to assert a predominant role in the government of the Roman state. The illusion of the princeps as merely an equal partner with the senate had by now been dispelled.

His choice of colleague for 39 was an interesting one. Lucius Apronius Caesianus was the son of the Lucius Apronius who had been a legate of Germanicus on the expedition to avenge Varus, and had received the *ornamenta consularia*. From AD 28, at the latest, the father held the command of Lower Germany; Gaetulicus, commander of upper Germany and an old adherent of Sejanus was thus the new consul's brother-in-law, and Caligula's colleague is himself identified by Dio as a former intimate of Sejanus. But the younger Apronius had qualities that would have made up for this particular skeleton in his political closet. He was lively company, and had an outrageous sense of humour. He had made fun of Tiberius during the festival of the Floralia by inviting only bald-headed men to participate, and even Tiberius, apparently, took the joke in good part.[1] After thirty days Caligula steppped down from office, although he allowed Apronius to complete his full term of six months, indicating that some degree of deference to the senators was still being displayed at the beginning of 39. He was succeeded by Sanquinius Maximus, Praefectus Urbi, who had already held a consulship some time before 32. He was the first man in over fifty years (apart from the emperors) to have held the consulship twice. It is not clear why he was singled out for the honour, and he may well have owed his nomination in part to the presence of Memmius Regulus in Rome during the previous year for the marriage of his former wife to Caligula, since the two appear to have been friends.[2]

The previous year had seen Caligula dealing with what he apparently perceived to be a conspiracy formed during his illness, and had ended with growing mistrust and suspicion, when Flaccus was recalled from Egypt and condemned to exile. In 39, according to Dio, the selective ruthlessness was transformed into a campaign of savage brutality. The despatch of Gemellus and his supporters, and the consecration of Drusilla, would have brought home to the senate the reality that Caligula was not the compliant and malleable youth they had hoped for. Inevitably there would have begun to arise in the minds of many the hope that he might some how be replaced. Most senators would have kept this desire muted through fear, but a number may now have started to form the beginnings of a small but active senatorial opposition. The most serious development came when, at some point in the year, Caligula entered the chamber and delivered a savage denunciation of its members.[3] The confrontation is suprising for its ferocity, but unfortunately there is nothing to show what specific event provoked the new outburst. No doubt, as some have noted, when building up his evidence against Macro and the others Caligula would have gone back through the records of earlier trials that he pretended to have destroyed, records that would have revealed the complicity of some of the senators.[4] The difficulty is that such a search would probably have taken place about a year earlier, and can hardly be seen as the immediate cause of the events this year. The latter part of 39 would be marked by the conviction of a number of conspirators and it is tempting to think that this speech may have been provoked by the discovery, for the first time, of evidence against the plotters. This new evidence might have prompted Caligula to take a fresh look at the papers from the trials. Much of the hostile information against individual senators must have been conveyed to Caligula in secrecy, and it is therefore not remarkable that it should remain concealed from us. All of this, however, is mere speculation. We can simply record that in 39 the tension between emperor and senate came to a critical point, resulting in a major confrontation. Adding to the uncertainty, Dio is especially vague about the chronology of that particular year, and it is far from clear when during its course the dramatic speech was given.[5]

During the speech, in what Balsdon describes as the most momentous scene in the senate since the denunciation of Sejanus, Caligula attacked the senate for their hypocrisy in finding fault with Tiberius simply because their emperor had done so; his action did not give them such a right, and, indeed, such behaviour on their part might well be construed as *maiestas*. He then took up the case of each individual who had lost his life. The general theme of his presentation was that the prosecution in each particular instance had rested not with the emperor but in fact with the senate. His evidence for this claim, it was revealed, came from the very documents that he was supposed to have destroyed. Most chilling of all was his denunciation of the senators' earlier fickleness in honouring Tiberius, and even Sejanus, since any honour that they might pay to Caligula would be similarly specious and could hide the possibility that they hated him. Dio's account is given some support by Suetonius who says, in a general context, that Caligula called all senators alike *Seiani clientes* ('clients of Sejanus') and *matris ac fratrum suorum delatores* ('informers against his mother and brothers'), on the basis of documents supposedly destroyed, and justified Tiberius' actions on the grounds that his predecessor could hardly have refused to believe the cumulative testimony of so many accusers.[6] Dio goes on to say that Caligula dramatically introduced an imaginary Tiberius speaking to him to show that he would have approved of his present response. He concluded that he saw no protection for himself in trying to please the senators — the only wise course was to make them fear him. It is likely that he ended this speech with the famous line of the tragic poet Accius, *oderint dum metuant* ('let them hate provided they fear').[7] The return of the *maiestas* trials was the most striking indication of how serious a turn events had taken. Caligula had, of course, been able to protect his position without the need for such legislation, as early as 37. But his actions in that year seem to have been taken against a very limited circle of very prominent individuals. The threat of *maiestas* accusations would now hang over all senators, and the news must have caused alarm. But they remained true to type. The restoration of the *maiestas* charges, like their earlier abolition, would have required their approval.[8] This they granted, without apparent hesitation, and made clear the depth of their humiliation when they reassembled the next day.

At this next meeting the senators heaped praise on Caligula as a sincere and pious ruler, each individual member doubtless feeling grateful that he had thus far escaped punishment. They voted to offer annual sacrifices to the emperor's Clemency in commemoration of his speech, when his golden image was to be carried up to the Capitol and hymns sung in his honour by boys of noble birth.[9] In addition, rites to Clemency were to be performed on the anniversary day of his address. The concept of Clementia was an important one for the Julio-Claudians. As a virtue it had gained a special Roman connotation in the context of how to treat a vanquished enemy. It became an important catch-phrase towards the end of the Republic and was particularly associated with Caesar. The concept persisted under Tiberius, appearing on coins of 22/3 with a type of laurel wreath and shield, and the senate set up an altar to Clementia in 28.[10] The emphasis on this concept in 39 adds weight to the notion that Caligula had suppressed some sort of conspiracy, and then made a show of not being vindictive towards those who had made their loyalty patent.[11]

Given the general obscurity that surrounds these events it would be dangerous to try to evaluate the precise intentions of the senate in 39. Some two years ealier they apparently believed that they had a young ruler who could be manipulated and manoeuvred so as to collaborate with them. It seems remarkable that two years later they could still have been under this illusion. Perhaps more significantly, Caligula seems to have appreciated the effect of fear on their collective mentality. The individual senator who became the target of the emperor's displeasure would know that in the end there was little that could protect him. His instinct would be to join the herd, which, having no immediate resources for attack, would be reduced to cringing flattery. It is clear that throughout 39 the emperor felt the need to assert himself with the senate. Dio places the episode of the Bridge over the Bay of Naples just after the speech, and the spectacle might be seen as a demonstration by Caligula of how completely he controlled affairs. This may have been his second trip to Campania in 39, since in a different context Dio states that in anger with the conduct of the mob at the games, Caligula had withdrawn in a fit of pique to Campania, returning to celebrate the birthday of Drusilla (date unknown). So confused is our knowledge of the year that there is no way of telling if this and the episode of the Bridge at Baiae are one and the same.

While these events were taking place a change occurred in Caligula's private life also. At some point he divorced his wife Lollia and remarried. The sources are much confused over when this happened. Both Suetonius and Dio claim that the divorce from Lollia followed very soon after the marriage, which was probably solemnized in September 38.[12] Now in a separate passage Dio places the divorce just before Caligula's next and final marriage, to Caesonia, but this he seems to date towards the close of 39, after the emperor had departed for an extended stay in the north. There have been suggestions that this last marriage might have taken place in Gaul, a notion that receives some slight support in a recently published inscription from Lyons that indicates a female of some prominence (name missing) in Caligula's company at the dedication of a building in that city.[13] His new wife did make public preparations in Rome for the triumph that would greet his return, but she could well have returned to the city when he went on to the German frontier in

39. But there are serious objections to the idea of a marriage in Gaul. Caligula was present in Rome when their daughter was born, a short time after the marriage, and took part in a formal dedication on the Capitol.[14] Immediately after his account of Caligula's marriage to his last wife Dio notes that the weather was so hot that awnings had to be placed over the forum, which better suits the middle of the summer than the weeks following October 39, and the likelihood is that the marriage in fact took place in the summer.[15] We must assume that Dio tacked on the reference to the marriage and the hot summer as an afterthought, rounding off his account of 39 with a few details about affairs in Rome, like the oddments that Tacitus will often insert at the end of a year.[16]

What then, of the divorce from Lollia? Dio states that Caligula got rid of her on the pretext that she was barren, but that in reality he was tired of her. It is worth noting in this context that according to Tacitus a later argument in favour of Lollia as a prospective wife for Claudius was that she was apparently barren, and would not present a threat to the succession.[17] If this is the case, the divorce probably occurred in the spring of 39, perhaps not long after Caligula's mistress had become pregnant. Suetonius states that Caligula forbade Lollia from having intercourse with another man in perpetuity, and Meise suggests that the prohibition might have been to avoid the danger that she might have children and thus have the charges of infertility turned back on Caligula.[18] On the other hand Caligula's first wife had been pregnant at the time of her death, and his fourth bore his child just before their marriage. He thus had no need to fear gossip about his potency. Moreover it will be recalled that there were reports of similar restrictions imposed on his second wife, and it is possible that we have a garbled account of some restrictive period he placed on one of them before remarriage would be allowed.

In his next wife, Milonia Caesonia, Caligula seems to have found a true soul-mate. She was the daughter of Vistilia, a woman married six times and whose remarkable gestation periods earned her a place in Pliny's *Natural History*. Presumably one of Vistilia's relatives was the Vistilia who registered herself as a public prostitute, probably to avoid a prosecution for adultery.[19] Caesonia was herself born of the sixth marriage.[20] Suetonius says she was not beautiful, nor young, and had a reputation for high living and low morals. Moreover, she had already produced three daughters. She was probably born about AD 5 and thus was some seven years older than Caligula, which was unusual for Romans.[21] Her portrait has recently been identified on a coin of Herod Agrippa (fig. 31). Depictions of Caligula on Agrippa's coins appear to be fairly realistic; if this is true also of Caesonia we see a rather severe and authoritative face of a woman who does, indeed, look somewhat more mature than Caligula.[22] Suetonius claims that she was promiscuous, but has to admit to Caligula's devotion (he apparently remained faithful) and his pride in her, which was so intense that he supposedly showed her off nude to his friends and paraded her in cloak, helmet and shield to the soldiers. Contemporaries could not understand her appeal, hence the stories that she had ensnared him with a love potion.[23] Of course the fact that she had borne three daughters already might well have been a positive recommendation, since it would show that she was fertile. She was far pregnant when he married her, and according to Suetonius the marriage took place on the day of her daughter's birth (a month before, according to Dio). Caligula was devoted to the child, whom he named Julia Drusilla in remembrance of his late sister. She is depicted standing with a small figure of Victory on the reverse of the coin issued by Herod Agrippa, mentioned above, identified by the legend, 'to Drusilla, daughter of Augustus'. On her birth Caligula carried her to the Capitoline temple, where he placed her on Jupiter's knee (to establish her paternity, according to Dio and Josephus), then on Minerva's, commending the child's education to the goddess. Some modern authorities see in this an imitation of Egyptian practice, but it appears to be within the Roman tradition. Quintus Catulus, for instance, dreamt that he saw a child (Augustus) in the lap of Jupiter Capitolinus and was told by the god not to remove him, as he was being reared to be the saviour of his country.[24] Caligula may well have spoiled her, as she seems to have developed a savage temper, even on one occasion viciously scratching the eyes of her playmates, which her father humorously cited as absolute proof of his paternity.[25]

The problems between Caligula and the senate came to a head in September. Just after the third day of that month Caligula removed the two consuls from office. They, of course, would be the suffects, who would probably have taken office on July 1. He gave two reasons. One was that they had failed to order a thanksgiving for his birthday. The usual races and annual shows had been held, as in previous years, but they were deemed insufficient. The other reason was that they had celebrated the traditional festival for the victory at Actium. Caligula declared that he would no longer allow the victory games for Actium and Sicily, held on 2 and 3 September, to be celebrated, as they were events that had been disastrous for the Roman people.[26] His stated explanation was almost certainly hypocritical (see p. 218) but he went ahead and dismissed them in any case, breaking their *fasces*, or symbols of office. One of them took the whole affair so much to heart that he killed himself, and his excessive reaction suggests that Caligula might well have suspected them, possibly on good grounds in at least one case, of some serious misdemeanour. The latter part of 39 was marked by plots and treachery, and the involvement of one or both of the consuls in some sort of conspiracy can not be ruled out.[27] In Dio's account of the incident the two suffect consuls for 39 are not named. In a different context, however, he states that Gnaeus Domitius Corbulo was consul in this year and the only place available for him would be as one of the dismissed suffects.[28]

The name Corbulo is familiar as one of the great generals of the Neronian age, and the standard view is that Corbulo the consul of 39 is the father of the famous general.[29] What qualifications would he have had? We know that he was the fifth husband of Vistilia, mother of Caligula's wife Caesonia, and this family link may have helped. Tacitus tells us, under AD 21, that Corbulo, as senator of praetorian rank, quarrelled in the senate about his precedence, and also (not necessarily in the same year) complained about the roads and was appointed road commissioner, and Dio adds that Caligula used him to prosecute corrupt road commissioners and that this work earned him a consulship.[30] This sequence, however, would make the gap between Corbulo's praetorship (before AD 21) and consulship (39) a long one, and he could hardly in any case still have been youthful even in 21. Moreover, in his list of the children of Vistilia Pliny emphasizes that Corbulo (the general) had consular rank, as if to distinguish him from his father.[31] It is thus possible that the surviving consul of 39 was the famous Corbulo, and not his father, and that Dio has confused the father and the son. But there can be no certainty on the issue.

Suetonius observes that the state was without consuls for only three days, and Dio provides the information that the new suffect was Gnaeus Domitius Afer, who was appointed *eythys* (immediately)[32]. His colleague is attested in recently discovered *tabulae cereatae* from Pompeii as Aulus Didius Gallus, who is shown to have been in office by at least 15 September.[33] Afer's rise to the consulship was an extraordinary episode, and, as reported (our main source is Dio), is an object-lesson in the art of survival. He was noted as one of Rome's greatest speakers, and his urbane witticisms became so famous that they were collected together and published in a work mentioned by Quintilian.[34] Under Sejanus he had been willing to act against Caligula's family and had conducted the charges against Agrippina's friend Claudia Pulchra (charged with treason and adultery) and her son Quictilius Varus, for which Caligula is supposed to have borne him a grudge. At some point in 39 he himself was charged on the grounds that he had set up a statue of Caligula and placed on it an inscription that the emperor had reached his consulship already for the second time in his twenty-seventh year. It would have been meant as a compliment, but Caligula apparently thought otherwise and saw it as a sarcastic comment on his extreme youth. Proud of his own oratorical skills Caligula personally conducted the case. Afer's tactic was supposedly not to attempt a response but to express astonishment at the quality of his opponent's speech. He made no defence, but merely repeated the accusation point by point, praising it.[35] He finally threw himself to the ground in supplication, expressing fear of Caligula as orator rather than emperor. The latter then dropped the prosecution, pressed to do so by the freedman Callistus, whose favour Afer enjoyed. When asked why he had launched the prosecution in the first place Caligula is supposed to have answered that it would not have been right to keep such a fine speech to himself.[36]

The story clearly can not be taken at simple face value. Afer was raised to the consulship at one of the most precarious moments in Caligula's reign, when the emperor was planning to leave Rome and needed someone in whom he had complete trust, to preside over the senate and keep a general control over events in his absence. If Caligula was willing to reverse his position and promote Afer it was because he thought that he might be of use. Moreover Afer's contribution must have been extremely valuable. It is perhaps no accident that his period of office saw the exposure of conspiracies against Caligula both in the provinces and within the imperial house. Afer, along with the powerful Callistus, may have played a key role in bringing to light plots against Caligula. Certainly a store of political secrets that could bring its possessor power and influence would have carried more weight with Callistus, who championed his cause, than a display of oratorical skills.

Afer's colleague, Aulus Didius, had already been marked for favour in the second half of 38, the previous year, when he apparently replaced Marcus Porcius Cato as Curator Aquarum, head of the three man board originally appointed by Augustus to supervise the water-supply. He remained in office until 49.[37] This position ought to have been reserved for consulars, but since Didius did not receive his consulship until 39 he must still, in 38, have been of praetorian rank. The appointment of a non-consular to the position suggests that Didius might have had special talents, the kind of ambitious and able administrator that appealed to Caligula.[38] Didius was a solid career man, a loyal and industrious servant of the kind typified by Memmius Regulus. If Afer's consulship was a reward for some kind of political collaboration, Didius' came as a reward for hard work and competence, and it may have been his steadfast reliabilty that Caligula sought in late 39.[39] Domitius Afer adopted a rather patronizing view of his industrious and ambitious colleague. Quintilian reports that on one occasion Didius actively campaigned for a province (possibly Britain), and when he acquired it grumbled as though it had been forced on him. 'Do it for the good of the nation!', was Afer's ironic reaction.[40]

It is evident that in 39 Caligula felt himself threatened from several quarters. Dio reports that the building of the Bridge at Baiae had proved so costly that he was forced to bring a number of bogus charges against various individuals as a way of raising funds. Many died in prison, he claims, and some were hurled from the Tarpeian rock, or committed suicide. The financial motive is not convincing, since in a different passage, clearly referring to the same incidents, Dio speaks of the general fear of the populace, many of whom,including aediles and praetors, were being forced to resign their offices and stand trial because of friendship with the emperor's enemies.[41] It is in fact clear that there was serious opposition to Caligula at this time, and equally clear that his response was ruthless, suggesting that any financial benefits that the deaths might have brought must be no more than bonuses. Unfortunately very few victims are identified by name. Dio mentions Titius Rufus, otherwise unknown, who was charged with denigrating the senate by claiming that it thought one way and voted another, and committed suicide. In view of the charge, it may be that his case was instigated by some of the more obsequious senators, rather than by Caligula himself. The praetor Junius Priscus was also accused, on unspecified charges, the real target supposedly being his wealth. On learning after Junius' suicide that he was in fact of modest means Caligula apparently quipped that he had suffered a pointless death.[42] It is also to this year that Dio assigns the banishment of Carrinas Secundus, in the context of the emperor's envy and suspicion towards everyone. The fate of Carrinas illustrates the dramatic change of attitude towards censorship and freedom of publication, since his apparent sin was to deliver a speech against tyrants as a rhetorical exercise. It seems that he chose Athens as his place of exile and committed suicide there later. His fate could mark the beginning of the difficulties between the emperor and philosophers, of which there is more evidence in the following year.[43]

A number of changes in military commands are known to have occurred in this year, and it is often assumed that they reflect insecurity on Caligula's part. Philo does claim that he was very afraid of those provincial governors who had large armies at their disposal, and it is probably to this year that we should assign the reorganization of the province of Africa, when control of its one legion was removed from the hands of the senatorial governor (p. 122).[44] Some of the changes, however, may well have been routine in nature, without political overtones. Lucius Volusius Saturninus is identified in inscriptions as governor of Dalmatia under Tiberius from at least 29. He was replaced about 40 but clearly not in disgrace. He was already seventy-three in AD 39, and on his return to Rome he was appointed Praefectus Urbi. He is described by Tacitus as an *amicus* of all the *principes* under whom he served, and is in fact a good example of a Tiberian career man who continued to do well under Caligula. His replacement is also interesting. Lucius Arruntius Camillus Scribonianus (consul 32) was the adopted son of the same Lucius Arruntius who was accused of *maiestas* under Tiberius and chose to commit suicide rather than live under Caligula. Scribonianus seems to have served Caligula loyally, but raised a rebellion under Claudius and died in Dalmatia in 42.[45]

Ummidius Quadratus was governor of Lusitania at the time of Caligula's accession and we see him administering the oath of allegiance to the new emperor early in 37. This governorship regularly offered a speedy progression to the consulship, which Quadratus seems to have held as suffect in 40.[46] Thus while Quadratus may well have been recalled in 39/40 his tenure of the consulship soon after indicates that there was no question of disgrace or mistrust. The governor of Hispania Citerior (his identity is unknown) was apparently replaced in 39/40. Gaius Appius Junius Silanus, consul of 28, seems to have been sent out to replace him at this time. At any rate Appius is present at the Arval rites for the beginning of 39, when he is Magister, but there is no mention of him after that.[47] Interestingly enough, Appius Silanus is another one of those who were accused of *maiestas* in 32, presumably as a Sejanian, but he did not seem to suffer under Caligula.

It was almost certainly in 39 that Lucius Vitellius was replaced by Publius Petronius as governor of Syria.[48] Syria was a highly important command, its four legions matched only by those in each of the two Germanies. According to Dio's account Vitellius had performed well but his achievements made Caligula suspicious. Vitellius supposedly escaped with his life only as a result of his low cunning, by performing *proskynesis* before the emperor and worshipping him as a god, deftly excusing his inability to see the moon in Caligula's presence by the comment that only a god could see another god. So charmed was Caligula by this that Vitellius not only survived but prospered. This is clearly another example of the concocted narrow escape, to enable Vitellius to explain afterwards why he seemed to be so favoured by Caligula. Certainly he later had a reputation for sycophancy, and was considered a model of *adulatorium dedecus* ('flattering disgrace'). His son, Aulus, the future emperor, was a close friend of Caligula, and it is more than likely that Vitellius' recall was simply a routine one. His successor Publius Petronius was a man of unquestioned ability, well suited to the position, and in fact with close ties to Vitellius, since he was married to the daughter of a Vitellia, and his own daughter was married to Vitellius' son, Aulus.[49]

At least two of the command changes, however, are far from routine, and do suggest an attempt by Caligula to disarm his opponents. The first of these involved Calvisius Sabinus, appointed governor of Pannonia some time after late 36.[50] When Sabinus returned to Rome in the summer of 39 he was indicted, along with his wife Cornelia. Sabinus was no stranger to trouble. He was one of the group of five, including Vinicianus, accused of *maiestas* in 32 after the fall of Sejanus. He and Appius Silanus had been freed, through the intercession of Celsus, a tribune of the urban cohort. Sabinus emerged apparently unscathed from this affair; he was not to be so fortunate in 39.[51] The charge laid by Caligula against him is not made explicit, but Dio does provide some details on Cornelia's misdeeds. It was claimed that she had 'gone the rounds' of the sentries and 'watched the soldiers in manoeuvres'. The former charge is expanded by Tacitus, who says that she went to visit the camp dressed as a soldier, and had sex with the guards, but was caught with Titus Vinius 'in the headquarters ' (in principiis).[52] Tacitus reports that Vinius was charged with adultery and thrown into chains, but was later released (probably after the death of Caligula) and went on to command a legion, and to be a close friend of the future emperor Galba, along with whom he was murderered. It is possible that Cornelia was charged with the same crime as her husband, and that the claim of sexual misconduct is the traditional cover for political wrong doings. The allusion to the 'headquarters' is especially suggestive and it is possible that her presence at the manoeuvres of the soldiers, not indictable in itself and with a precedent in the behaviour of Agrippina and Plancina, may suggest that she participated in an attempt to suborn the Pannonian legions. But absolute certainty is impossible.[53] In any case, the charges were serious enough for Sabinus and his wife to commit suicide. He seems to have been succeeded in Pannonia by Aulus Plautius, who was later to win acclaim as Claudius' commander in the initial phase of the invasion of Britain.[54]

Sabinus was linked with another figure who looms large in the events of 39, in that in 26 he had been a colleague in the consulship with Cornelius Lentulus Gaetulicus. This is a tenuous enough link, but it is possible also that Sabinus' wife Cornelia may have been the sister of Gaetulicus, Cornelia Gaetulica.[55] Gaetulicus, legate of Upper Germany, was the son of Cossus Cornelius, the consul of 1 BC, who added the element Gaetulicus to the family name by a victory over the Gaetulians in Africa in AD 6, and passed it on to his son, whom Velleius describes as an example of an adulescens in omnium virtutum exempla genitus ('a youth born for every type of excellence').[56] In common with other members of the Roman nobility he combined a political and military career with literary activities, becoming a poet of some note, mentioned as such by Pliny and cited by Martial as one of the precedents used to justify a free use of language.[57]

Gaetulicus held the praetorship in 23, and was consul with Sabinus in 26.[58] In 29 he became legate of Upper Germany.[59] His position there would have been a powerful one. In the first place, there are good grounds for believing that he succeeded his brother Cossus Cornelius Lentulus in the command. The four legions of Upper Germany would thus have owed their loyalty to two successive commanders from the same family. Moreover, his father-in-law Lucius Apronius had been legate of Lower Germany from 24, and Tacitus suggests strongly that Gaetulicus' influence extended also to the four legions under Apronius.[60]

Clearly Gaetulicus' direct or indirect control of eight legions would have weighed heavily with Tiberius in his sensitive dealings with the commander after the fall of Sejanus. Accused in AD 34 because he had betrothed his daughter to Sejanus' son, he had managed to escape conviction. Tacitus reports a claim that Gaetulicus wrote a letter to Tiberius from Germany pointing out to the emperor that his connections with Sejanus had been made at Tiberius' instigation, and that his own error of judgement was no different from Tiberius'. His loyalty to the emperor, he asserted, remained unshaken, and just as Tiberius had retained the principate, so he should retain his province. Tacitus admits that this story seems unbelievable, but is inclined to give it credit because Gaetulicus was the only person so closely associated with Sejanus who survived.[61]

Gaetulicus had thus earlier shown, after the fall of Sejanus, an appreciation that he owed the continuation of his military command in no small part to political considerations. He would presumably have spared no effort to ingratiate himself with Caligula. The device he seems to have used in his case was flattery. He was a poet of some distinction, and somewhere in his writings he sought to curry favour with Caligula by inventing the notion that the emperor was born in Tibur, implying that the city, sacred to Heracles, would reflect some of its glory on to him. Now the comparison between Heracles, a mythical hero who journeyed afar and smote down powerful enemies, and Caligula best suits the context of 39, when Caligula was in fact planning to campaign against the Germans and Britains. Given that Gaetulicus, as commander of Upper Germany, might reasonably have hoped to be involved in these events, it would have been appropriate for him to glorify the projected expedition in a poem.[62] A fragment of this work may have survived in the commentary by the late first century grammarian, Probus, on the Georgics of Vergil. On *Georgic* I. 229 *haud obscura cadens mittet tibi signa Bootes* ('by his setting Bootes will send you clear signs'), Probus cites Gaetulicus, *cum ait de Britannis* ('when he says of the Britons'):

> Non aries illum verno ferit aere cornu,
> Cnosia nec geminos praecidunt cornua, tantum
> Sicca Lycaonius resupinat plaustra Bootes.
> ('In the Spring air the ram does not strike him with his horn,
> Nor do Cretan horns cut off the twins;
> Lycaonian Bootes is content to tip up carts that are dry').[63]

These lines convey very well the scope of Caligula's ambitions in 39. The images describe the phenomenon of circumpolarity, whereby the further a traveller in the northern hemisphere moves north, the greater will be the number of stars that rotate around the pole above the horizon without setting at any point during the year (the converse is true of the southern hemisphere). The topos of the remoteness of Britain is an old one in Latin literature, and the motif of circumpolarity is a highly poetic way of expressing it, effective in a poem dedicated to a ruler planning to set off to conquer this remote region.

It could not be said that the affairs of Upper or Lower Germany had been well managed by either commander, and Rome had suffered a number of military setbacks in both districts, largely because of a general lack of discipline (see p. 130). Gaetulicus had been more interested in currying favour with his troops than in keeping them in fighting trim.[64] Given his record of incompetence, it would not have been remarkable for him to have been relieved of his command. But the circumstances of his removal constitute another of the great mysteries of Caligula's reign. We know that in 39 the emperor departed for the north to participate in the military campaigns against Britain and Germany. By October 27 news of Gaetulicus' execution had reached Rome (see below). It is not known precisely when Caligula actually set out, but it must have been after the new consuls had taken office, early in September. Both Dio and Suetonius suggest that he took his leave suddenly and that the actual departure was not in fact from Rome itself. Dio claims that it was from a 'suburb' (*proasteion*), while according to Suetonius he went first to Mevania on the bank of the river Clitumnus, a beauty spot about 100 miles north of Rome. The site was famous for its oracles, which supposedly advised Caligula to add to his German bodyguard, thus prompting him to depart for Germany. Suetonius adds that from there he journeyed north hastily (*festinanter et rapide*), and that it may have been to improve his speed that the inhabitants of towns on his route were required to sweep the steets for him and to sprinkle them to settle the dust. He did not, however, skimp on his personal comfort, and rested on the route on a litter carried by eight bearers.[65] Why he should have chosen to depart in this fashion remains a mystery. The speed and place of departure might indicate that he wanted to keep his plans secret and to conceal his intentions from Gaetulicus until the last possible moment. But it is difficult, in practical terms, to see what difference this would make. Once Gaetulicus had learned of Caligula's arrival, whether sooner or later, he would hardly have been likely to expose himself to unnecessary danger. In any case the organization of the imperial train for an absence that would last over six months would have required extensive preparations, even if Dio's account of the lavish arrangements is exaggerated.

On his journey north, Caligula was supposedly accompanied by actors, gladiators and women. He also took with him at least part of the Praetorian guard, who, because of the need for haste, transported their standards on pack animals. Their presence need not, however, imply extraordinary security, as Claudius also had Praetorians with him in

Britain, and two Praetorian cohorts even fought alongside Germanicus during his campaigns in Germany.[66] The only specific individual who can be identified as having travelled the whole journey with him is the freedman Claudius Etruscus (p. 84). The assumed presence of Passienus Crispus on the northern journey is based on no more than the information that he attended Caligula on foot when the latter was making a journey, *iter facientem*.[67] On the possibility that Caligula was accompanied by his sisters and Lepidus more will be said later.

The events of late 39 are obscure, but we do know that by 27 October a supposed conspiracy of Gaetulicus had been exposed and suppressed, and noted in the Arval record of that day *A.d VI K. Novembr./... ob detecta nefaria con[silia/ in C. Germani]cum Cn. Lentuli Gaet[ulici* ('on 27 October... because of the wicked plots of Cn. Lentulus Gaetulicus against Gaius Germanicus').[68] This Arval entry is clear enough, yet we have no explicit information on how and why Gaetulicus fell foul of Caligula. In his narrative of the events of 39/40 Dio briefly dismisses the emperor's military achievements in the north, and notes that while he did little damage to the enemy, he inflicted great harm on citizens and allies, putting some to death on the grounds that they were 'rebelling', and others because they were 'plotting' (*neoterizontas... epibouleuontas*), but the real reason being that they were rich. Unfortunately Dio says that he will spare the reader by not listing specific victims, except those of historical significance. The first he mentions is Gaetulicus, and the reason given for his death is his popularity with the soldiers. Suetonius, in the seven consecutive chapters that he devotes to the northern campaign, makes no reference to Gaetulicus, and in the whole *Life of Caligula* mentions him only as the author of flattering verses. In the section of the *Life of Galba* dealing with that future emperor's career in Germany, Suetonius limits himself to noting that Gaetulicus was Galba's easy-going predecessor in the command.[69]

Any discussion of the reasons behind Gaetulicus' death will be, by necessity, speculative. It is agreed that he had been executed before 27 October, when the exposure of the conspiracy was reported in Rome. It is also generally assumed that the execution took place in Mainz, Gaetulicus' headquarters, although a meeting between Gaetulicus and Caligula, if indeed there was a meeting at all, could equally well have taken place, in, say, Lyons.[70] What is especially problematic is that it can hardly be expected that Gaetulicus would have exposed himself to risk if he had any suspicion of what Caligula was about, and conversely it is inconceivable that Caligula would have risked the danger of placing himself in the enemy camp. In fact, the only indication we have that Caligula might have been in Germany when the execution took place is that he is not recorded as present at the Arval ceremonies at the end of October. But, in fact, this indicates only that he was not in Rome. We do know that he spent some time in Mevania, and it seems more than likely that agents (including Galba?) were despatched to Germany to eliminate Gaetulicus before the emperor's arrival. Caligula, then, may well have remained in the relative security of Mevania, protected by the Praetorians, until the deed was carried out. Once word arrived that it had been done, he could send a report to Rome, for it to be recorded by the Arvals, then depart at once for Germany. This is, of course, speculative, but it is to be emphasized that there is no evidence that Caligula was present in Germany (or Gaul) when Gaetulicus died, and that the traditional view is in itself also speculative.

Even more puzzling than the 'mechanism' of Gaetulicus' elimination is the reason behind it. Now it should be observed that Gaetulicus was a commander who would have made any ruler feel uneasy. He had direct control over four legions on the Rhine, indirect influence over another four and would presumably have had some authority over the two new legions, XV and XXII Primigeniae, that were currently being raised in connection with the planned invasion of Britain (p. 126). He had shown himself to be a general who constantly sought the popularity of his own troops and who, on past form, would probably resist any attempt to dismiss him. Dio says that he was killed because of his popularity, and this may in a sense have been true, if misleading. In view of the coming campaigns against the Germans and Britain he could not be left in his command. If it was felt that he was likely to resist dismissal, as he had done before, the safest course would have been to eliminate him, and to pretend to the world afterwards that he had been involved in some sort of dark plot. The claim of rebellion, as Dio suggests, may just have been a pretext.[71]

Many scholars have seen in Gaetulicus' downfall more than the mere dismissal of an incompetent commander. It has been argued that because of his earlier associations with Sejanus he would have felt himself endangered, and was part of a much larger threatened group of old adherents of Tiberius and others unhappy with Caligula's conduct. Meise even sees him as an adherent of the old pro-Gemellus party.[72] But there is no indication that former adherents of Sejanus were in fact suffering during this period. After all, Lucius Apronius had been made consul for the first half of 39. Nor is there anything to suggest that Gaetulicus had contact with any larger political grouping. Indeed there is no evidence for any of his activities or contacts outside of Germany in the previous ten years. Nor is there anything to substantiate the notion that old Tiberians were suffering. Figures like Memmius and Sanquinius certainly seemed to be enjoying unimpeded careers.

Some have sought to find an immediate connection with the execution of Sabinus, Gaetulicus' partner in the consulship in 26. The possible combination of Sabinus' two Pannonian legions and those under Gaetulicus' direct or indirect charge could have put potential conspirators in control of about half of the available legionary troops. But there is no hard evidence of any intimate link between the two men — their close family relationship is purely speculative, based on little more than wife and sister sharing the common *nomen* of Cornelia. This would not, of course, rule out the possibility that the fate of Sabinus might have caused Gaetulicus to feel some alarm over what might be in store for other legionary commanders, and could have driven him to some desperate plot. Certainly it would have put him on his guard, definitely making it even less likely that Caligula would have wanted to risk going to Germany while he was still alive.[73]

The most interesting possible association between Gaetulicus and some kind of organized conspiracy goes right to the centre of the imperial family, and to Caligula's close friend Lepidus. In his list of those victims whose historical significance justifies their being identified by name, Dio places Gaetulicus first. Then, without indicating any connection between the two, he names none other than Lepidus, Caligula's old friend and husband of the late Drusilla. Dio provides no explicit reason for his downfall, but hints that an illicit affair with Caligula's two sisters may have played a part. Finally, he notes that to celebrate Lepidus' death Caligula sent three daggers to the Temple of Mars Ultor in Rome. Suetonius' account may go back ultimately to the same source. In the context of Caligula's supposed relations with his sisters, but not in the chapters dealing with the northern campaign, Suetonius mentions a *causa* of Lepidus. During this *causa* the emperor made public certain letters of his sisters, which he had obtained fraudulently, showing that they had committed adultery with Lepidus and become involved in plots against their brother. Suetonius also refers to the dedication of the three daggers. Lepidus was executed, and Seneca provides the detail that his throat was cut, by a tribune named Dexter. In a bizarre travesty of the return of Germanicus' remains to Rome, Caligula's sister Agrippina was given Lepidus' bones in an urn and forced to carry them back to the city. On their arrival in Rome the bones were not placed in the traditional columbarium, but the senate decreed that they be cast out unburied, on the motion of Vespasian, the future emperor. This can hardly refer to Gaetulicus whose remains would presumably have been disposed of in the north. Both sisters were then deported to the Pontian islands. Suetonius claims that in the winter of 39/40 Caligula sold their furniture, and constantly terrified them with threatening messages, such as the grimly humorous quip that as well as islands he also had swords, giving rise to a later tradition that he had planned to execute them, and they were saved by his death.[74]

Again, the simple circumstances surrounding the death of Lepidus elude us. All modern treatments make the assumption that he and the sisters travelled to Gaul/Germany with Caligula. None of the sources explicitly states this, and the inference is drawn from a number of passages. Dio states that Caligula accused Lepidus and his sisters in a communication to the senate; this implies that there was no formal trial in the house, merely a statment from the emperor of the grounds on which he had acted. This is almost certainly the *causa Lepidi* to which Suetonius refers, and the publication of the letters between the sisters and their lover presumably took place at the same time. This admittedly does not prove, but does suggest very strongly, that the condemnation of Lepidus and the sisters took place when Caligula was outside Rome. Suetonius tells us that he afterwards auctioned off the belongings of the sisters, including slaves and freedmen. Since the sale took place in Gaul it is presumed that these were the belongings that the sisters had taken along with them. The humiliation imposed on Agrippina of carrying Lepidus' remains back to to Rome shows that he died somewhere outside the city. Finally, as will be seen, Claudius and others were sent out from Rome to congratulate Caligula on the suppression of the conspiracy, indicating that this must have postdated the emperor's departure from the city.[75]

While it is clear that the disgrace and death of Lepidus took place outside the city, none of the sources gives any indication of its occurring in Gaul or Germany. The auction of the sisters' goods in Gaul proves nothing. Caligula found the provincials in Gaul so keen to acquire items that had an imperial connection that he commandeered carriages and animals and transported all the goods from the old imperial residence on the Palatine. This supposedly caused such a strain on the transportation system that it resulted in a shortage of carts for transporting bread! Thus he in fact imported items to Gaul from Rome *after* his arrival, and these could have included the jewels, furniture and slaves of his disgraced sisters. Also, it must be remembered that Caligula did not depart for the north immediately from Rome but from Mevania, some 100 miles north of the city. Mevania does in fact seem much better suited for the execution of Lepidus than Gaul/Germany. It is a much more suitable starting point for the dramatic procession of Agrippina carrying the bones of Lepidus– the great distance from Lyons or Mainz would surely present problems for such a piece of theatre. It is also hard to see why Caligula should have thought fit to take a party of suspects on a journey of over 600 miles, with all the attendant problems of security. That Lepidus was put to death by a tribune in no way proves that he was in a legionary camp, since the executioner Dexter could well have been a tribune not of a legion of the Rhine army but of the Praetorian guard, a detachment of which accompanied Caligula to Germany, and which would presumably have been in Mevania beforehand.[76]

Once more, the actual mechanism of Lepidus' execution is less intriguing than the motives behind it. The despatch of the three daggers to the Temple suggests that Caligula believed that he had survived a very serious attempt on his life. The charges of adultery laid against the two sisters may well have been the traditional device of covering up political intrigue with the claim of sexual indiscretion. Dio's observation that people in Rome were brought to trial simply on the basis of their friendship towards the sisters implies that they were suspected of some sort of conspiracy. Certainly the gesture of the daggers was repeated by Nero when he put down the conspiracy of 65 and dedicated the dagger of Scaevinus in the Temple of Jupiter on the Capitol.[77]

It has been argued that Lepidus became involved in some sort of intrigue because of considerations beyond his own immediate ambitions, and that he was the leader of an evolving opposition to Caligula, made up, according to Bergener, of the old adherents of Tiberius, and probably including at least one of the consuls removed in 39.[78] But there is, in fact, no hint in any of the sources of such a broader role for him, beyond Josephus' observation that he was friendly with Lucius Annius Vinicianus, the 'noblest of the Romans'. This man plays a conspicuous role in the final conspiracy and its immediate aftermath.[79] He was probably the son of Gaius Annius Pollio (cos.21 or 22) and possibly Vinicia, the daughter of Lucius Vinicius (cos. of 2 AD), which would make Vinicianus the nephew of Livilla's husband Marcus Vinicius.[80] Together with his father Annius Pollio, as well as Appius Silanus, Mamercus Scaurus and Sabinus Calvisius, he was among those accused of *maiestas* in 32, probably because of suspected ties with Sejanus. Moreover, according to Josephus, he believed that his old friendship with Lepidus was a source of danger to himself. But Caligula did not apparently see him as a threat. In 24 May, 38 Vinicianus was coopted into the Arval brotherhood and seems to have held a consulship sometime before Caligula's death.[81] He was the first member of the Arval brotherhood recorded as having been coopted by the instruction of the emperor as opposed to the vote of the college, and of the men named to the brotherhood from 37 by Caligula, only he does not belong to a patrician family and is not from one of the traditional 'Arval' families. This, if anything, suggests special favour.[82] His involvement in the later plot against Caligula was supposedly motivated by his desire to avenge Lepidus. But if Josephus' testimony is to be taken at face value Vinicianus had not been involved in the opposition prior to Lepidus' death, and it was only as a consequence of what happened to the latter that Vinicianus was moved to act. Indeed, the whole story of the friendship with Lepidus and the desire to avenge him may have been a later fabrication to enhance Vinicianus' role during this period. In any case, the presence of the cult statue of Lepidus in the imperial sanctuary at Aphrodisias is an indication that he may not have been as free of personal ambitions as would be expected in the leader of an opposition movement.

Nothing indicates that either of the husbands of Caligula's sisters was involved, and they seem curiously to be left entirely in the background. Domitius at any rate was still in Rome in late October, since his presence is attested at the meeting of the Arval brothers a day or two before the key 27 October ceremony.[83] There is no mention in any of the sources of the whereabouts of Livilla's husband, Vinicius.[84] The explanation for Lepidus' actions probably does not lie in his connections with any larger movement, but in his own personal ambitions.

If Lepidus and the sisters plotted to overthrow Caligula it could only have been because they thought it would serve their own best interests. Caligula's marriage to Caesonia might have provided them with such a motive.[85] The death of Drusilla would have marked a set-back to Lepidus' own dynastic ambitions, but he seems at the outset to have remained on close terms with Caligula, to judge from the fact that he gave the funeral speech for Drusilla. Moreover, on the return of Flaccus from Egypt in the autumn of 38 it was through the intervention of Lepidus, according to Philo, that Flaccus was exiled and not executed, and through him again that Flaccus was able to exchange the bleak Gyaros for the more hospitable Andros, showing that Lepidus' influence was still strong in late 38. Lepidus could have continued to entertain some hope for the future. Caligula's earlier illness might have led his associates to believe that his health was not strong, and up to about the middle of 39 he had not produced a surviving child. There would hardly have been any serious contenders for the succession from within the imperial family at that time. Claudius, who had probably the best claim in terms of family connections, was never considered a serious candidate, and apart from him there were only marginal possibilities.[86] But though Lepidus might have felt that his own prospects were not unpromising, the absence of a direct link with the imperial family would have been a serious obstacle. This he may have sought to overcome through a connection with one (or both) of the surviving sisters, and the poet Namatianus (1.303) says of him that: 'while he desired to insinuate himself into the kingdom of the Caesars, he paid the penalty for foul adultery' (*Caesareo dum vult irrepere regno/ incesti poenam solvit adulterii*). It is likely that the excessively ambitious Agrippina played the more dominant role; certainly Tacitus later speaks of her committing adultery with Lepidus *spe dominationis* ('in the hope of power').[87] Agrippina's son Nero, the future emperor, was born in 37 and she no doubt felt that after Drusilla's death his prospects would be strengthened. Her husband Gnaeus Domitius Ahenobarbus, who had been more of a political liability than an asset, was probably ill by 39, since he died of dropsy in 40. A marriage with Lepidus after her husband's death would strengthen her position, and her son's, at the same time. Like her mother, Agrippina Minor was highly ambitious, and it would not have been out of character if she had begun to scheme for Nero's accession from the very outset. At any rate, soon after his birth in December 37 she asked her brother to give the child a name, probably hoping that he would give his own, as a sign that Nero was marked as a possible successor. Caligula suggested 'Claudius', either as a family name, and thus as a mark of distinction, or from some perverse sense of humour (he is said to have looked at his uncle when he said it). Whether Agrippina was in fact offended we shall never know, but in any case she did not take up the suggestion.[88]

Agrippina's ambitions in this direction would have had to be all-consuming. She and her sister enjoyed enormous privileges from Caligula and presumably only the prospect of becoming the new Livia would have been sufficiently enticing to persuade her to act against him. Livilla's motivation is baffling. Lepidus could have married only one of the sisters, and unless he was engaged in a complex love triangle that kept each sister in the dark about the other's involvement (hardly likely), it would have meant that one of the sisters, probably Livilla, would have had to act in the full knowledge that she was to be left on the sidelines. There must surely be something wrong with the account as it has come down to us. Nor does it seem likely that Livilla's involvement could have been through her husband, Vinicius, who is not mentioned by the sources and, more significantly, emerges unscathed from the whole conspiracy.[89]

Caligula's marriage to Caesonia, whose mother Vistilia had been a marvel of fecundity, and who herself, with the birth of Drusilla, had borne four children, would have dealt a serious blow to the plans both of Lepidus and Agrippina. If this marriage is placed in early/middle 39 it provides a reasonable chronological setting for the break between Lepidus and Caligula. There may also have been some estrangement between the two friends at this time because of Avillius Flaccus. The former prefect of Egypt had been given a comfortable place of exile in Andros, largely through the intercession of Lepidus. According to Philo Caligula regretted this decision and eventually decided to eliminate Flaccus. This may have been because of new evidence, but it is also possible that in the general paranoia of 39 Caligula was removing those whose past behaviour rendered them suspect. Lepidus realized that further intervention would only bring risk on himself, without helping Flaccus, and finally gave up the effort. Agents were despatched to Andros. Flaccus observed their arrival and tried to hide in the wilder interior of the island. They pursued him there and eventually tracked him down, stabbing and clubbing him to death, and depositing his remains in a crude pit.[90] If Philo is right in placing Flaccus' death before that of Lepidus, it is quite clear that the order to execute Flaccus would mark an important change in Lepidus' fortunes and in his relationship with Caligula, and may have have been what finally drove Lepidus to plot against his former old friend. Of course it is also possible that Lepidus died first and that after his fall action was taken against his old associates, including Flaccus (although nothing, apparently, happened to Vinicianus). The death of Flaccus in fact followed a pattern. As the threat of conspiracy grew, Caligula became increasingly less tolerant towards those who had previously been involved in apparent acts of disloyalty. Philo claims that Flaccus headed a list of men who had, in the emperor's estimation, escaped death for a life of comfortable exile. The list may also have included Anteius, father of a senator by the same name who died during the final plot against Caligula. According to Josephus the elder Anteius had originally been exiled, then, like Flaccus, killed by a gang of soldiers sent out to deal with him (the charges are not stated). He is otherwise unknown.[91]

By far the most intriguing aspect of the 'Lepidus conspiracy' is a single reference in Suetonius' *Life of Claudius*, where we are told that Claudius was sent to Germany as part of the embassy despatched to congratulate the emperor, on the exposure of what Suetonius calls the *Lepidi et Gaetulici coniuratio* ('the conspiracy of Lepidus and Gaetulicus').[92] This is the only reference in any of the sources that suggests any kind of collaboration between these two men, and there has been much speculation about what form their co-operation might have taken. No plot could possibly hope to succeed without military backing, and Lepidus, it might be argued, would have sought out a leader who could provide it. The German Legions offered the most promising power base.[93] For his part, Gaetulicus might have felt himself threatened on two grounds. He had a reputation as a lax disciplinarian. Moreover, his old links with Sejanus might have seemed especially dangerous in the light of Caligula's fiery speech in the senate. The fate of Flaccus would also have shown that there was little prospect of clemency towards old opponents. If Gaetulicus was to look for protection it might have seemed to him that Agrippina and Lepidus formed the nucleus of the group that was best able to provide it. But there are also good reasons to doubt that Lepidus and Gaetulicus acted together in a concerted and organized fashion. Dio makes no suggestion that there was any formal link between them, although he does see both men as victims of the same general purge. More significantly, Suetonius says nothing of any joint action in the *Life of Caligula*, and refers specifically to the case of Lepidus alone. Perhaps most significant of all is the omission of Lepidus' name from the celebrations indicated in the Arval record. The entry is, admittedly, fragmentary, but there are simply not enough letter-spaces to accommodate Lepidus' name. This can hardly be explained by the desire to down play publicity about Lepidus' role, given that Caligula wrote to the senate denouncing him. It may well be that in alluding to the conspiracy of Lepidus and Gaetulicus in the *Life of Claudius* Suetonius telescoped two generally contemporaneous episodes under a broad heading; his concern in this part of the *Life*, after all, was to explain basically why Claudius travelled north when he did, rather than to give a detailed account of events in Caligula's career.

Other prominent figures also suffered at this time. Among the last events of 39 recorded by Dio is the fate of Tigellinus Ophonius, familiar as the evil Praetorian prefect of the reign of Nero. Suspected of having an affair with Agrippina, he was banished. We are told by a scholiast on Juvenal that Tigellinus came from a poor family in Agrigentum but became an acquaintance of Marcus Vinicius and Gnaeus Domitius Ahenobarbus, husbands of Julia and Agrippina. How much reliance we can place on this testimony is uncertain, nor is it clear what light it would throw on any possible role for him in any conspiracy.[94]

Another man who attracted Caligula's wrath, in very obscure circumstances, was the hypocritical orator and philosopher Seneca. Dio claims that Seneca's only sin was to plead a case well while the emperor was present. He was condemned to death but spared, according to Dio, when Caligula learned through some female associate that he was in an advanced state of consumption and would die before too long anyway. It is possible that Seneca was involved on the fringe of the opposition to Caligula, in which case the speech in the senate may have been in defence of a fellow-conspirator. His later conduct certainly suggests that he was very close to the people who fell from grace. In 41 he was banished by Claudius for an affair with Livilla, who was herself exiled, for a second time, to Pandateria. Also, he was later suspected of having an affair with Agrippina. It has even been suggested that she was the mysterious 'female associate', although there seems to be no good reason why her name would have been concealed.[95] But the story of Seneca's escape seems basically implausible, and very much in the tradition of the eleventh-hour reprieve so common in the careers of those who served Caligula. It could very well have been concocted by him to explain how he managed to survive a tyrant he professed to abominate. Certainly, Seneca showed a great talent for accommodating his principles to the outlook of successive rulers, later abusing those he had earlier sought to flatter. In what is probably his earliest extant work, the *Consolatio ad Marciam*, written under Caligula, we find no hint of criticism of the contemporary emperor, but a violent denunciation of Sejanus, as compared with Seneca's vitriolic abuse of Caligula in his later works and a corresponding absence of strong feeling about Sejanus.[96] All in all, it would have been quite out of character for Seneca to have exposed himself voluntarily to danger. If he received the slightest hint of the emperor's displeasure this probably would have sufficed to bring him quickly into line and to abandon his dangerous friends.

A much more cogent case can be made for the involvement of Seneca's friend Lucilius Junior. This man, somewhat younger than Seneca, was born in humble circumstances in Campania, possibly in Naples or Pompeii. Through his own efforts and hard work he rose to equestrian rank and became a successful man of letters, noted for his elegant style. He was also a philosopher, the recipient of a number of Seneca's works, notably the *Epistulae Morales*. In the *Quaestiones Naturales*, which Seneca dedicated to Lucilius some time after 62, he praises the courage that Lucilius showed in adversity, and suggests that he was tortured, or threatened with torture, by Caligula, but that the emperor 'did not tear away his loyalty in the matter of his friendship with Gaetulicus' (*non... in amicitia Gaetulici Caius fidem eripuit*). This is an intriguing piece of evidence that must in the circumstances be based on the truth. It provides further proof that Caligula suspected that Gaetulicus was involved in a plot and that it involved collaborators outside of Germany. What role might Lucilius have played in such a conspiracy? In an ambiguous passage of the *Epistulae Morales* Seneca speaks of Lucilius' holding at one time a procuratorship in the Alpes Penninae and Graiae, the great mountainous buffer area between Gaul and Italy.[97] This would have given him a very strategic role in guarding the passes of the Little and Great Bernard had Gaetulicus been considering any kind of action against Rome.[98] If, as Seneca suggests, Lucilius was a personal friend of Gaetulicus he would become a natural object of suspicion, even if, in fact, innocent.

By his prompt action Caligula seems to have suppressed an embryonic conspiracy, whose precise character and scope eludes us. His activities were conducted against a background of problems outside of Italy, especially in North Africa and Northern Europe. It is to these that we must now turn.

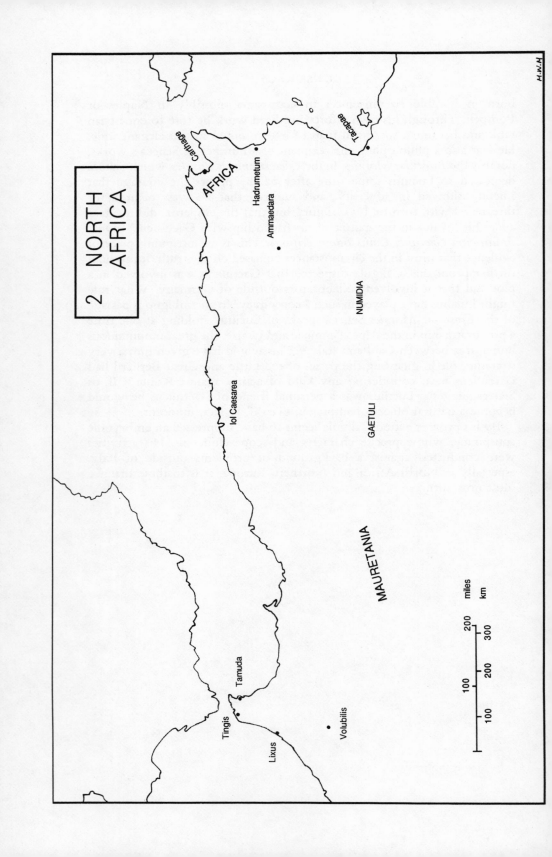

2 NORTH AFRICA

AFRICA

Carthage

Hadrumetum

Ammaedara

Tacapae

NUMIDIA

Iol Caesarea

GAETULI

MAURETANIA

Tingis

Tamuda

Lixus

Volubilis

miles
km

200
300

100
200

100

100

· 7 ·

NORTH AFRICA

DURING THE REPUBLICAN period two senatorial provinces were located to the west of Egypt-Cyrene (with Crete) and Africa. The original province of Africa (Vetus) lay in modern Tunisia. Since its conquest in the second century BC it had attracted a steady stream of immigrants from Italy, with the founding of colonies and the establishment of a prosperous merchant class. It was bordered by Numidia, the last of whose kings, Juba I, a man of excessive ambitions, had designs on the province. They came to nothing, and Juba was forced to commit suicide in 46 BC, after Julius Caesar's victory at the battle of Thapsus. Caesar created a new province, Africa Nova, from Juba's kingdom, and some time before 27 the two Africas were combined by Augustus into a single province.[1] Under Augustus, with some changes of boundary, the united province of Africa Proconsularis became a prosperous, but anomalous part of the empire. Its agricultural wealth gave it great economic importance, but it was at the same time a region under constant threat. Economic development entailed a persistent tendency to push further and further south and to displace the nomadic tribes from their traditional grazing lands, creating a constant potential for conflict. Much of the investment in the province had been made by rich members of the senatorial class — in fact by Nero's day half of Africa was reputedly owned by six landowners.[2] Augustus thus had to balance senatorial interests with military necessity, and in his settlement Africa was granted a special status. As a 'senatorial' province it was governed by a proconsul designated by the senate, but it was also protected by a Legion (II), under the command of the proconsul, rather than of an imperial legate. Although applied on a limited scale elsewhere (Macedonia, for instance), only in Africa did this peculiar arrangement survive Augustus.

West of Africa lay Mauretania, covering the western half of the Atlantic range, some 800 miles in length, between the Ampsaga and the Atlantic coast, with an ill-defined southern boundary. On the death of its last King, Bocchus, in 33 BC, his kingdom fell under the control of Rome, though its precise status is far from clear. Roman influence was spread by the establishment under Augustus of no fewer than twelve colonies, and in 25 BC the territory was transformed into a client kingdom, ruled by Juba's son, although the colonies remained outside his jurisdiction. To compensate Juba II for the loss of his ancestral territory in Numidia Augustus seems to have granted him additional territory of the Gaetulians, the nomadic tribes to the south of Numidia, described by Sallust as savage nomads, living on milk and raw flesh.[3] Juba had been taken to Rome by Caesar as a child and brought up in Augustus' household. A highly educated and sophisticated ruler, he saw himself as a monarch from the Hellenistic mould. He married Cleopatra Selene, daughter of Marc Antony and Cleopatra, and together they established a Hellenized court with fine architecture and a library at their capital of Iol-Caesarea (Cherchel).

For all his sophistication Juba showed little skill at exercising control over his own people, especially the Gaetulians to the south, and continuous military unrest forced him to seek constant help from Rome. There was intermittent fighting, until 17, when the most serious revolt of the period broke out, under the leadership of Tacfarinas, a Numidian who had served in a Roman auxiliary unit.[4] He became the champion of the disaffected Musulamians and fought a vigorous, and, for a time, successful, guerilla campaign against the Roman armies. The commanders sent by the senate were no match for him, until finally, in 20, the appointment of the brilliant commander Quintus Junius Blaesus turned the tables in Rome's favour, and the resistance was largely broken.

Juba's son, Ptolemy, seems for a time to have been associated as joint ruler with his father, and to have succeeded in his own right in 23. Under Ptolemy, fighting flared up again, when his subjects rebelled against the despotic behaviour of the court favourites and threw in their lot with Tacfarinas. The rebellion was finally suppressed in 24 by Publius Cornelius Dolabella. Little credit for this could be claimed by Ptolemy, who does not seem to have applied himself with much energy to his kingdom's problems. Yet he was clearly a figure of some distinction in the outside world. His statue stood in Athens in the gymnasium of his ancestor Ptolemy Philadelphus, and the koinon of Lycia also voted him one at Xanthus.[5] But, as a ruler, he seems to have been feckless and incompetent, and although he participated in the campaigns against Tacfarinas he possibly did more harm than good. The Romans, however, knew the importance of diplomacy. As a demonstration of good will a member of the senate was dispatched in 24 AD to present Ptolemy with the traditional gifts of an ivory sceptre and a *toga picta*, the triumphal toga with gold stars on a purple ground, which his father may also have won earlier. On his coins we see the ivory sceptre, together with the curule chair that must have been part of the gift as well as the *toga picta* and gold crown.[6]

Ptolemy's involvement in the campaign against the rebellion of

Tacfarinas is the last recorded event of his reign. Just before a major gap in his text Dio briefly informs us, under 40, that Ptolemy was murdered by Caligula. The date receives support from the numismatic and epigraphic evidence.[7] The literary sources provide two further details. Suetonius says that Caligula invited Ptolemy to his presence and received him with honour, but suddenly had him executed for the simple reason that, when he was presenting a show, he noticed that Ptolemy, on entering the theatre, attracted general attention by the splendour of his purple cloak. Also, Seneca claims to have seen him in prison before his execution. This seems to suggest that Ptolemy was summoned to Italy, imprisoned, and executed after Caligula's return from the north, sometime after the spring of 40.[8]

This straightforward scenario is cast into some doubt by Dio, who places Ptolemy's death between Caligula's stay in Lyons and his 'campaign' on the English channel, before the return to Rome.[9] But Dio will often treat material in a thematic rather than strictly chronological scheme, as when he includes the brief notice of the British 'campaign' under 39 though it belongs, in fact, to 40.[10] If the summons brought Ptolemy from Mauretania in early 40 Dio may well have lumped the description of a later execution with it. Certainly the index for the missing chapters seems to show that he dealt generally with the *whole* topic of the incorporation of Mauretania, presumably including the rebellion that broke out afterwards, before the description of Caligula's exploits on the channel. Since the uprising in Mauretania was apparently suppressed before Caligula's death, all of which would have required a considerable passage of time, Ptolemy's execution perhaps is best placed in the early part of the year. Under this reconstruction, then, he was summoned in early 40 to Italy to meet the emperor on the latter's return from the north. This meeting took place outside the city limits, after which Ptolemy was denounced and imprisoned in the city, where he was seen by Seneca. Some time later, he was executed.

The incorporation of Mauretania into the empire can be defended on strategic grounds, and reflects a concern about military security that is matched also by change in the command structure in Africa. But the usual fate of loyal kings who lose their provinces is honourable exile, often in considerable comfort. Ptolemy is the only client-king to have been executed. Why should he be the exception? We can not put it down to arbitrary cruelty. Seneca points out that Mithridates (of Armenia) was imprisoned at the same time, and suffered only exile. Dio suggests that Caligula wanted Ptolemy's wealth, his standard explanation for almost all of Caligula's activities at this time, and surely belied by the emperor's generosity to Herod Agrippa and Antiochus IV of Commagene.[11] Hofmann sees the clue in the story of the purple cloak. He argues that Ptolemy had been invited to Rome to consecrate the sanctuary of Isis in the Campus Martius and wore a long flowing robe for the occasion, which aroused Caligula's rivalry.[12] But such a complex and ingenious scenario is not necessary to explain the cloak. Ptolemy would probably have been lured to Rome in the hope of receiving some kind of honour, as hinted in Suetonius' account. He was a ruler who lived in some splendour in a court run on the lines of Hellenistic monarchs, and would have worn robes that he felt appropriate to the occasion. Under Augustus client-princes had worn the white toga. This regulation had been relaxed under Tiberius, and they were then allowed to wear purple. The son of Cleopatra Selene (Antony's daughter) and thus a relative of the emperor might have been expected to avail himself of this privilege.[13] The splendid robes would have added a particular irony to Caligula's denunciation of him.

Given the context of Ptolemy's execution, and the severity of his punishment, it is difficult to avoid the suspicion that he might somehow have been involved in the plots against the emperor. The father of Gaetulicus, the supposed conspirator, had campaigned alongside Juba II, and this family association might have helped Gaetulicus involve Ptolemy in his intrigues. Ptolemy might have been induced to join by the promise of an independent kingdom.[14] Alternatively he might have been drawn in by Caligula's sisters, his relatives. Certainty in the whole matter, as so often in the affairs of Caligula, is unattainable, and the death of Ptolemy remains yet another of the mysteries of 39.

The decision to incorporate Mauretania into the empire is not too difficult to understand, in the light of its previous history. The rebellion of Tacfarinas had shown how exposed Africa Proconsularis was to its west, and the lacklustre performances of Ptolemy and his father before him had demonstrated how incapable the Mauretanians were at providing any protection to the province, or to the Roman colonies within Mauretania itself. In this light Caligula's action can be seen as a prudent and reasonable act. But, not surprisingly, it met with resistance among Ptolemy's old supporters at his court in Mauretania. Pliny informs us that on Ptolemy's death a revolt broke out under Aedemon, one of his freedmen.[15] This seems to have involved a fairly widespread rebellion against Roman authority, and is attested in the archaeological record.[16] Part of the city of Volubilis was destroyed by fire. There is evidence of destruction in the SW area of the forum at Lixus, and Tamuda was burnt to the ground, pillaged and abandoned by the population. In the last two there is a long gap in the numismatic sequence after the last coins of Ptolemy, suggesting that the destruction immediately followed the end of his reign.[17] In parts of the kingdom there was clearly popular support for the Romans. From Volubilis in the west an inscription has survived honouring Marcus Valerius Severus, son of Bostar (the father's name is a Latinised form of the Punic Bodastart or Bod'star). He was a local worthy, a *sufes* (a Punic term for an official) and duovir, and first priest in the imperial cult. He is recorded as having commanded the auxiliary forces in the war against Aedemon (this is the only mention of Aedemon's name apart from the reference in Pliny). This show of loyalty stood Marcus and Volubilis (which suffered in the fighting) in good stead with Rome. He afterwards was sent on an embassy to Claudius and secured Roman citizenship and other rights for the inhabitants.[18]

Mauretania was organized into two separate provinces, Mauretania Tingitana and Mauretania Caesari ensis in the territory around Tingis and Caesarea respectively, separated by the river Malua. The sources are in disagreement about when this division took place. Pliny claims that it was the work of Caligula. Dio, however, explains that in 42 fighting broke out once again, to be subdued by the vigorous campaigns first of Suetonius Paulinus then of Hosidius Geta, and only after this, according to Dio, was the territory divided into two administrative districts, by Claudius.[19] Clearly, the appointment of the regular equestrian governors can hardly have occurred earlier than 43; the first of whom we know was Marcus Fadius Celer Flavianus, in office in 44.[20] Pliny may simply have got the chronology confused; at best it might mean that Caligula made the decision to divide the province, but that the implementation had to be postponed because of the uprising.

The constant rebellions in the region revealed not only the weakness of the rulers of Mauretania but also the unsatisfactory arrangement by which the defence of Africa Proconsularis remained a senatorial responsibility. It was only a matter of time before the anomaly would have to be removed, since apart from any strictly strategic considerations there was also the political danger of concentrating into the hands of a single governor the control both of troops and of an economically powerful province. Caligula took the necessary step, taking the command of the legion from the proconsular governor and placing it under an imperial legate.

The precise circumstances of the change are unclear. Tacitus, in describing the difficulties at the beginning of the reign of Vespasian in 69, and the murder of the proconsul of Africa by the commander of the legion, explains that when Marcus Silanus was proconsul (at an unspecified date) Caligula was afraid of him, so took the legion away and gave it to a legate. This, he says, resulted in increasing power for ambitious legates, while the proconsuls showed less and less initiative. Dio, on the other hand, says (under 39) that when Lucius [Calpurnius] Piso, son of Gnaeus and Plancina (who were charged with Germanicus' murder), was chosen to be governor of Africa, Caligula feared that he would lead a revolt, and so divided the province into two parts, assigning the military force and the Numidians in the area to a legate, an arrangement that continued down to Dio's own day.[21]

The contradictions between Tacitus and Dio have attracted much scholarly attention (see below), but the broad outlines of the change are clear enough. There is no reason to question that Caligula's action was a sound one, dictated by a sober evaluation of the circumstances, rather than by fear or hatred, as Dio and Tacitus suggest. Moreover, he seems to have sought to introduce a minimum of disruption to the established system. He could, after all, simply have taken Africa from the senate. The province, in a different way, continued to be an anomaly. While Tacitus' claim that the shared command created widespread confusion may be exaggerated somewhat, to explain the disasters of 69, the later history of Africa shows that there was an awkward overlap of functions, mainly because of the need for the legionary legate to retain strategic flexibility. He would have to intervene wherever the military situation demanded, as shown from Vespasian's time on by the presence of the legate's name alone on the milestones throughout the province, where he was involved in settling internal territorial disputes.[22] The legate provisioned his troops in the granaries of Hadrumetum or Utica (in the civil zone), and had the responsibility for the division of the tribes into cantons.[23] Also, curiously, the proconsul might occasionally have special powers. Galba, for instance, seems to have been given command in Africa of an army to deal with internal strife.[24] A cohort could be detached from the legion and placed under the command of a proconsul, as appears in a speech of Hadrian.[25] There was also an urban cohort in Carthage.[26] As Dio explains the arrangement there was a division not only of powers but also of territory. The proconsul would administer the district around Carthage, with the legate basically taking the less settled region of Numidia. But the division could not have been hard and fast. For instance, in Cirta, which must have been in the legate's zone, we find Quintus Marcius Barea, proconsul 41-3, making a dedication to the divine Livia.[27] The measure taken by Caligula was, in fact, only one step in a much longer process, which reached its natural conclusion at the end of the second century under Severus, with the creation of a separate province of Numidia.

Appendix 1
The Roman commander during Aedemon's rebellion

The most likely candidate as commander of the Roman forces is Marcus Licinius Crassus Frugi. According to Suetonius he received the *ornamenta triumphalia* a second time in 43 AD for his exploits in Britain (Suet. *Claud.* 17.3). That the first occasion might have been in Mauretania is suggested by an inscription which, as restored, records Crassus in M[auretani]a as legatus of Claudius (ILS 954: on the restoration, see Gascou, 300-301). Against this identification it is argued that there is no mention of Crassus in Dio's account, in contrast to the detailed information he provides about the commands of Suetonius Paulinus and Gnaeus Hosidius Geta, whose successive campaigns finally crushed the rebellion by 42. The title of legatus would be without parallel in Mauretania since the kingdom was organized into two Mauretanias governed by equestrian prefects. Also, there would not have been enough time for Crassus to have been given office by Claudius, since Suetonius Paulinus seems to have been appointed in 41. Those supporting the notion of Crassus as commander include: R. Cagnat, *L'armée romaine d'Afrique* (1913²), 30; *PIR¹* L.130; Carcopino *op. cit.*, 182, 191; Romanelli, 260, H.G. Pflaum, *Procurateurs équestres sous le Haut-Empire Romain* (Paris, 1950), 37 n.2 M. Rachet, *Rome et les Berbères: un problème militaire d'Auguste à Diocletian (Brussels, 1970), 133*. Those against include: Groag, 'Licinius Crassus', *RE* 13 (1926), 342; 133; St. Weinstock, 'Mauretania', *RE* 14 (1930), 2373; B. Thomasson, *Die Statthalter der römischen Provinzen Nordafrikas von Augustus* bis Diocletianus (Lund, 1960), 241, Fishwick *op. cit.* VII n.9, 479.

A clue may be provided by Dio 60.8.6 (see Gascou, 303). He tells us that Claudius was persuaded to adopt the *ornamenta triumphalia* for his exploits in Mauretania even though he had not achieved anything there and the war had been brought to an end before he came to power. If Crassus had been appointed by Caligula after the outbreak of the rising of Aedemon and had crushed it by the end of January 41, it is quite conceivable that his command would have been extended by Claudius, thus making him that emperor's legatus. If Claudius claimed the credit for the earlier victory, Dio's comment would make sense (although the *ornamenta triumphalia* normally went to the commander in the field). Crassus clearly enjoyed Claudius' favour, as evidenced by his later role in Britain and the fact that in 41 Claudius gave his daughter Antonia in marriage to Crassus' son Gnaeus Pompeius Magnus (Suet. *Claud.* 27.2, 29.2, Dio 60.5.7). The use of the title 'legatus' need not be a problem. J. Gascou, 'M. Licinius Crassus Frugi, légat de Claude en Maurétanie', (*Mélange P. Boyancé*, Paris, 1974), 308 argues that between the death of Ptolemy and the organization of the two provinces Mauretania was governed by a single legatus instead of two equestrian prefects, as it would be in a time of emergency under Vespasian in 75 (ILS 8969). Moreover, the absence of any reference to Crassus in Dio's account could be explained by the fact that there is a gap in Dio's manuscripts after his coverage of the death of Ptolemy, and the *Index* shows that the missing section dealt with the incorporation of Mauretania into the empire.

Appendix 2
Procurators of Africa under Caligula

Lucius Calpurnius Piso might for a time have suffered the stigma of parents widely believed to be the murderers of Germanicus. All the same his career was not seriously hampered, since he achieved the consulship in 27 and was *praefectus urbi* in 37 when Caligula came to power. Dio indicates that he was proconsul in Africa in 39, but we have no further evidence for this appointment and do not know if his term was 38/39 or 39/40 (newly appointed governors of senatorial provinces normally left Rome with their staff by mid-April to allow them to begin their term of office by mid-summer; see Dio 60.17.3). Among others, A. Pallu de Lessert, Fastes des Provinces Africaines (Paris 1896-1901), 120; S. de Laet, De Samenstelling van den Romeinschen Senat (Antwerp, 1941), nr. 555; P. Romanelli, 248 support 38/9; E. Groag *PIR²* C 293; Thomasson. 2.30 support 39/40. He may afterwards have been governor of Dalmatia under Claudius, and seems to have survived until the reign of Vespasian (*ILS* 5952, on which, see Groag, *loc.cit.*; J.J. Wilkes *Dalmatia* [London, 1969], 443).

Marcus Junius (M.f.) Silanus was consul in 19 and was married to Aemilia Lepida, daughter of Aemilius Paullus (cos 1 AD) and Julia. Apart from providing the consular date of 19 AD he is not mentioned in Tacitus' *Annals*. He is identified by inscriptions as governor of Africa, but they do not provide his dates (*PIR²* I 839, Benabou, *op. cit.* VII n.1, 131). One of his officers in Africa was the *praefectus fabrum* C. Maenius Bassus. In an inscription from Tibur this man is said to have served Silanus *sexto*, which seems to imply the sixth year of the latter's governorship (*ILS* 6236). Dio 58.23.5 speaks of a six year proconsular term for P. Petronius in Asia (29/30- 34/35). Now Vibius Marsus was governor of Africa to 30, and Silanus seems to have been in Rome in 32 (Tac. *Ann.* 6.2.2). The period 32-38 or 33-39 would thus seem to accommodate best a six-year term (see, E. Hohl, 'M. Junius Silanus', *RE* 10.1098). Unfortunately, the inscription from the Triumphal Arch of Tiberius at Leptis indicates that the proconsul in Africa in 35/36 was not Silanus, but Gaius Rubellius Blandus, husband of Julia, the widow of Caligula's brother, Nero Caesar (*IRT* 330ab, 331; Syme, *Papers*, 1357, 4.188-9). We know that Blandus was in Rome towards the end of 36, and if Silanus succeeded him it could have been at the most for three years, from 36 to 39. If, however, we assume that Bassus served his own sixth year as *praefectus fabrum* under Silanus, but had served earlier under other proconsuls, then a three year term for Silanus could be made to harmonize with the inscriptional evidence; see, B.E. Thomasson, 28, *id.* 'Verschiedenes zu den Proconsules Africae', Eranos 67 (1969) 179–84. Romanelli, 248, suggests that on Caligula's accession Silanus was already proconsul in Africa, having been appointed in the summer of 36, and that his term was prorogued for a year (until July 38). Under this construction Silanus' successor Piso took office in July 38.

On the question of the change of legionary command the two sources seem to be mutually contradictory. One way of reconciling them is to assume that the two men succeeded one another, that Silanus was proconsul when the decision was made and that Piso was the first to be subjected to it (Romanelli, 248 Thomasson, vol. 1. 11, vol. 2. 30, Benabou, VII.n.1, 132). Syme, however, suggests that in fact the term of Silanus had nothing to do with Caligula, and and that he served from 30 to 35 (to be succeeded not by Piso but by Rubellius Blandus). Proconsular years run from summer to summer, and Silanus would thus have served for only five proconsular years, while Bassus' *sexto* might refer to a calendar year. The confusion over the change in command, Syme believes, stems from a simple mistake of Tacitus. The historian may have conflated Silanus, governor of Africa, who probably did not survive Tiberius, with Caligula's father-in-law of the same name, Marcus Junius Silanus, who, as has been shown, did indeed incur the resentment of the emperor (Syme *Papers*, 1362, followed by Vogel-Weidemann, 103-105).

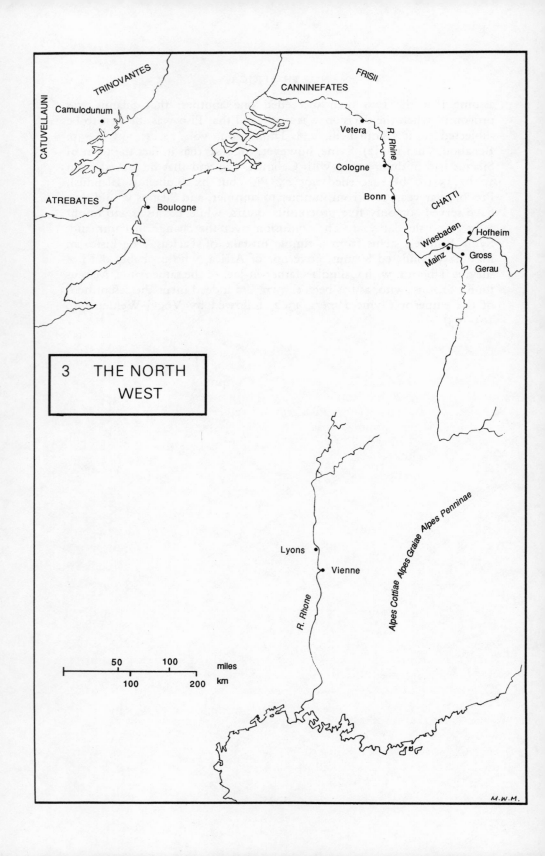

3 THE NORTH WEST

· 8 ·

BRITAIN
AND GERMANY

CALIGULA CAME FROM a line of celebrated military commanders. Both
his father Germanicus and his grandfather Drusus had enjoyed enormous
reputations as soldiers, probably in excess of their talents. His evident
penchant for riding in a chariot dressed as a triumphator or Alexander
the Great suggests that he himself was not immune to the attractions of
military glory, and it was inevitable that he would feel the need to
emulate his forbears.[1] It was on Rome's northern frontier that they had
won their laurels; Caligula set his sights on the same part of the world,
but aimed to achieve a feat of arms that would eclipse even theirs. He
would take Rome's *imperium* beyond the Ocean into Britain. In the
process he would be the first emperor to lead his troops into battle since
Augustus' campaigns in Spain in 26–25 BC.

The sources depict Caligula's northern expedition as little more than
a frivolous whim, undertaken on the spur of the moment, either to
exploit Gaul for its wealth, or to raise recruits for the imperial bodyguard.
On the contrary, the seriousness of his intentions is proved by the
extensive preparations that he made. Suetonius reports that he 'held levies
every where with utter strictness, and brought together supplies of every
kind on a scale never before matched' and speaks of the forces 'drawn
together from all provinces'. Dio says that he had gathered together,
depending on the source, 200,000 or 250,000 troops. Even the lower
figure is actually more than twice the normal garrison strength on the
Rhine. Tacitus' denigrating comments on Caligula's military ventures
tend if anything to confirm the extent of his preparations, since he speaks
of *ingentes adversus Germaniam conatus* ('enormous efforts against
Germany') and the *ingentes Gaii Caesaris minae* ('enormous threats of
Gaius Caesar').[2]

It may be possible to identify some of his specific preparations. In the
later Claudian invasion of Britain in 43, three of the Rhine legions were
used (in addition to Legio IX from Pannonia): II Augusta, IX Hispana and

XX Valeria. Clearly it would not be safe to remove a force of this size and leave a defensive vacuum. There is sound evidence that their replacements were provided mainly by the raising of two new legions XV and XXII Primigeniae. The first literary reference to these units is in connection with the events of early 69, when XV was stationed on the Lower, and XXII on the Upper Rhine. Epigraphic evidence points to their earlier presence there, mainly at Vetera and Mainz respectively, during the later Julio-Claudian period.[3] They are not among the twenty-five legions in existence in AD 23, and the absence of any reference to their formation in Tacitus' *Annals* suggests that they were raised in the period 37-47 (missing from the Annals). They seem, then, to have been raised to fill the gaps that would be left when the German legions departed for Britain. Who raised them? The notion that it might have been Caligula, and that Claudius in 43 essentially implemented a policy already initiated by his predecessor, was first put forward by Ritterling in the 1920s.[4] His most important evidence was epigraphic. The tombstone of a centurion Tiberius Julius Italicus records that he served (in this order) in Legio VII Macedonica, XV Primigenia and XII Germania.[5] Now Legio VII Macedonica received the title of Claudia Pia Fidelis for its role in suppressing the mutiny of Scribonianus in Dalmatia in 42. The absence of the honorific from the legion's name on the inscription suggests that Italicus had already left that legion before 42 and that XV Primigenia, in which he next served, was already formed before then. Now while it is just possible under this reconstruction to squeeze the raising of the latter into Claudius' reign, the references in Suetonius and Dio to the raising of Legions makes the case for a Caligulan date very strong. On the west bank of the Rhine, about a mile south of Mainz at Weisenau there is tentative evidence for a short lived legionary base of the Caligulan period. Since tombstones of Primigenia XV have been found in the area, there is a strong suggestion that the legionary base at Mainz was extended at Weisenau to accommodate the newly raised legions.[6] Moreover the new commander, Galba, after his appointment to Germany by Caligula, was involved in the training of raw recruits.[7] At any rate it is clear that the massive preparations preclude the notion, found not only in the ancient sources, but also among modern scholars, that the northern expedition was anything other than a campaign that had been seriously planned.

Britain had been invaded by Julius Caesar in 55 and 54 BC. He achieved some military success, but clearly decided that continued Roman presence in the island would place an unduly excessive strain on his resources. He made treaties and imposed tribute, and was able to present his limited victories as a conquest of sorts. Given the dynamics of imperialism it was inevitable that Romans would one day return to the island. Augustus for a time envisaged its reconquest, a hope that would have been shattered by Varus' defeat in the Teutoburg forest in AD 9. Tiberius adopted a generally cautious policy on the Roman frontiers and would have considered an expedition against Britain a reckless venture. Caligula doubtless shared with many Romans an impatience with Tiberius' restraint, and clearly had the temperament to take up the expansionist banner once again. But quite apart from his personal desire for glory, circumstances in Britain were such that an invasion might well be politically and strategically justified.

Information on this period of British history is based largely on coin evidence, and great caution must be exercised in drawing political conclusions from the discovery of particular coins in particular locations.[8] The chief opponents of Julius Caesar had been the Catuvellauni, located in the Hertfordshire area. After his departure they seem to have lived up to their agreements with the Romans and to have paid regular tribute. Between about 20 and 15 BC, however, Tasciovanus came to power, the first British king to mint coins inscribed with his name. He initiated an aggressive policy and by the time of his death between AD 5 and 10 the Catuvellaunian territory stretched from Northamptonshire to the Thames. One rare coin issue shows the mint of Camulodunum (Colchester), perhaps indicating expansion east into the kingdom of the pro-Roman Trinovantes of Essex. The presence of Augustus in Gaul in 16 BC may have prompted Tasciovanus to withdraw.

To the south of the Catuvellauni, beyond the Thames, lay the Belgic kingdom of the Atrebates, with its capital at Calleva Atrebatum (Silchester). It appears to have been founded by Commius, the Gallic Atrebatian, who had fallen out with Julius Caesar and fled from him. Ironically it was to become pro-Roman under Commius' son, Tincommius, and to act as a curb to Catuvellaunian expansion. From the mid 30's to the 20's, talk of an invasion of Britain was very much in the air in Rome, to judge from the pronouncements of poets like Horace. At some point, however, Augustus decided to postpone the plans for invasion in favour of a diplomatic policy, probably to leave himself free to embark on conquest beyond the Rhine. Strabo says that the Romans could, in fact, have taken Britain but that it was considered not worth it. He also notes that leading British figures paid honours to Augustus and made offerings on the Capitol, thus making the whole island in a sense Roman property.[9] It is possible that the change in Augustus' policy can be dated to his visit to Gaul in 16 BC, which could have resulted in some sort of agreement with Tincommius. Roman pottery does begin to turn up in large amounts in Atrebatic territory at Calleva from about that time. Tincommius was obliged to flee to Rome before AD 7 (his arrival is recorded in the *Res Gestae*) probably because of internal problems. He was succeeded by his brother Eppillus (for a short time), then by another brother Verica, who reigned through until the accession of Claudius.

North of the Atrebates, Tasciovanus of the Catuvellauni was succeeded

Stemma 6
The family of Cunobelinus

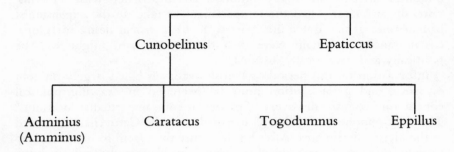

by his son Cunobelinus (Cymbeline), the most famous of the British kings of the period. Under him the ancient conflict with the pro-Roman Trinovantes seems to have been brought to a final conclusion, since we eventually find Cunobelinus minting coins from the old Trinovantian capital of Camulodunum. It is probably no coincidence that this development seems to date roughly to the time of Varus' defeat in AD 9. After the disaster, Augustus may well have decided to seek an accommodation with the powerful king. This is suggested by the considerable trade with Rome, evidenced at Camulodunum by large quantities of imported amphorae (mainly Italian but some from Spain), used to bring in oil and wine, as well as plates and drinking vessels.

Tiberius would certainly have been inclined to continue Augustus' policy of accommodation and indeed his diplomatic approach seems to have paid dividends, when, in AD 16 Roman soldiers cast ashore in Britain were returned to the continent by British princes. On the negative side, however, he would have been little inclined to check Cunobelinus' expansion into the pro-Roman territory of the Atrebates, south of the Thames. Cunobelinus' brother Epaticcus seems to have established himself at Calleva by AD 25. The regular silver coins of Epaticcus have on one side a head of Hercules and on the other an eagle with a snake in its talons. Silver coins of an identical type are found, but with the reading CARA instead of abbreviations of Epaticcus' name. These coins almost certainly belong to Cunobelinus' famous son, Caratacus.[10] The Atrebatic kings may well have appealed for aid to Rome to resist this hostile expansion, but they would not have found in Tiberius a very receptive audience.

We know that at least by the time of the Claudian invasion in 43 Cunobelinus was dead, and had been succeeded by his two violently anti-Romansons, Togodumnus and Caratacus, and that the Atrebatic kingdom was on the verge of defeat. Before the invasion the last king Verica had sought refuge with Claudius, and their enemies had penetrated the kingdom thoroughly — pedestal urn material of the Catuvellaunian type has been discovered even at Selsey, the southern tip of Atrebatic territory.[11] There was an obvious danger by 39 that the whole of southern England could fall into hostile hands, and could threaten constantly to foment trouble in Gaul. If ever direct Roman intervention could be justified strategically, it was now.

In the propaganda leading up to Caligula's departure Germany figures at least as prominently as does Britain. Suetonius claims that there were rumours that the massive scale of the bridge at Baiae was intended to overawe both the Germans and the Britons. Dio suggests that while Caligula intended to plunder Gaul and Spain he professed a campaign against *Germany*. Philo, moreover, reports that the Jews demonstrated their loyalty to Caligula by sacrificing three times, first on his accession, next after his recovery from illness and third 'for the hope of a victory in Germany'.[12] Yet it seems inconceivable that Caligula could have entertained any notion of a major expedition into Germany, whose only strategic purpose could be to extend Roman power beyond the Rhine. The disaster of Varus would have been a constant reminder of the risks involved, and Caligula was probably shrewd enough to appreciate that his father's campaigns had come within a hair's breadth of disaster. Britain, where Julius Caesar had shown that the military opposition was not nearly so powerful, must have seemed to Caligula, as it would later to Claudius, a potentially more rewarding theatre of operations. It would, of course, have been disastrous to attempt an invasion of Britain and a major launch into Germany at the same time. But the two regions are strategically intertwined. To place an army in Britain without securing the eastern flank against German incursions would be to court disaster, since a successful breach of the Rhine frontier by the enemy would cut off the Roman supply line and leave the Romans isolated. For a successful British campaign the frontier would have to be secured. Caligula's German policy, while tactically aggressive, would thus ultimately have a defensive purpose.[13] Now while the overriding necessity of securing the German frontier before invading Britain might, arguably, have been beyond Caligula's grasp of military strategy, it would certainly have been evident to the man he appointed to be his commander of the German operations. Servius Sulpicius Galba was a professional soldier, who had previously fought a successful campaign in Aquitania and who, after his German victories (culminating in the *ornamenta triumphalia*), was so valued by Claudius that a rumour of his illness in 43 was said to have persuaded the emperor to postpone the British campaign. Later in the 40s he was sent to handle a serious uprising in Africa.[14] Galba was an excellent choice for the post, and it is likely that at the same time as his appointment Lucius Apronius was replaced in Lower Germany by Publius Gabinius Secundus, another competent and professional soldier.

Galba would have recognized that to strengthen Rome's position in the frontier area would be no light task. There are clear signs that there had been a general laxity on the frontier in recent years. In 28 the Frisii took advantage of the neglect and revolted, crucifying some of the Roman troops sent to collect taxes. Apronius was unable to maintain control and summoned reinforcements from Upper Germany. He travelled down the Rhine to Frisian territory, where he suffered a great disaster. The Romans were forced to retreat without burying their dead, and it was discovered only later that 900 men had held out until the next day and then were taken as exhausted prisoners and slaughtered in the grove of Baduhenna. Some 400 committed suicide. No proper measures were taken to deal with the disaster, and its true dimension was kept hidden from the public. Problems were also rife in Upper Germany under the casual control of Gaetulicus. He seems to have been unable to contain the pressure of German tribes to the east; they broke over the Rhine and caused major devastation in Gaul, apparently in the latter part of Tiberius' reign.[15] One problem was Gaetulicus' inability, or unwillingness, to impose discipline, and it may be that he was seeking to strengthen his political base by courting the popularity of his troops. Dio, though meaning to compliment him, hints at this, observing that Gaetulicus was a man of honour, who had remained governor of Upper Germany because he was acceptable to thesoldiers. Tacitus is more blunt, stating that *mirum amorem adsecutus est* ('he had sought excessive popularity') and that he was a man *effusae clementiae modicus severitate* ('of much clemency, restrained in handing out punishment').[16] The archaeological record seems to confirm that the army of Upper Germany was unable to control the movements of German tribes. There are signs that German settlers moved into certain regions that should have been under the control of the Roman army, on the Neckar near Ladenburg and in the Gross Gerau area; R. Nierhaus has argued that they represent local militia, granted land in return for their services in protecting the frontier.[17]

Galba's prime task on taking up his command would have been to impose strict discipline. He blocked requests for leave and raised the soldiers into a good fighting condition by hard work. He gave his troops minutely detailed instructions on their behaviour — even to the degree that they were not allowed to applaud at festivals. Commanders who were dilatory in mustering their men promptly were dismissed. Centurions who had grown too old for the task or whose health was not up to their duties were relieved of their office. A number of unsatisfactory soldiers were discharged, receiving only 6000 sesterces, half the normal discharge pension. The soldiers themselves offer the best testimony for the impact of the new regime: they soon began to recite the tag, *disce miles militare, Galba est non Gaetulicus* ('learn to be a soldier, soldier, don't make a fuss, Galba's here, not Gaetulicus!').[18]

Galba is unlikely to have taken over his new command much earlier than 27 October, when Gaetulicus was executed. Thus apart from the general strategic considerations against a major invasion of Germany, it would in any case have been too late in the season for such a venture in 39/40, especially since Galba would have to invest considerable time in restoring discipline. Balsdon is quite right in arguing that the Romans had not contemplated a major penetration of Germany, but this does not mean, as he implies, that the campaign was not 'serious'. The propaganda that surrounded the undertaking, as well as Tacitus' references to the *ingentes conatus* and *ingentes minae*, and the literary evidence for the resistance of the Canninefates (see below), can not be reconciled with Balsdon's suggestion that essentially routine training manoeuvres were involved, and that the only contact with the enemy was in skirmishes. No doubt Galba would have been involved to some degree in training, especially if new legions were being raised. But this can not be the whole picture. Training, for instance, can not account for the reports of the slaying of prisoners. The Romans were almost certainly involved in important, though limited, military activity, designed to inflict serious losses on the Germans and to deter them from any thought of further incursions over the frontier. The first task would be to deal with those elements that had already made inroads into Gaul.[19] This would no doubt have been followed by engagements with tribes bordering the river, accounting for the references in the literary sources to activity on the east bank of the Rhine. Dio claims that the Romans went a little beyond the Rhine, then turned back, while Eutropius reports that Caligula undertook a war against the Germans, and having entered Suebia carried out no vigorous action. Galba's operations seem to have been successful, and Suetonius comments that he achieved brilliant successes before Caligula's arrival.[20] Because Caligula's reign is so short it is difficult to assign military remains confidently to his period. The legionary base at Mainz-Weisenau has already been mentioned. Ritterling has made a strong argument for a Caligulan base at Hofheim at the junction of the Main and Wetter, in a good forward defensive position to prevent movement towards the east bank of the Rhine.[21] Wiesbaden, located on the east side of the Rhine from Mainz may also have been a Caligulan fort, and it has also been suggested that there could have been a Caligulan base at Gross Gerau.[22] All of this might well suggest that Galba's main concern was control of the fierce Chatti, who seem to have displaced the pro-Roman Mattiaci in the regions north of the Main-Wetter. The fact that Galba was still campaigning against the Chatti in 41, when he won a major victory over them, strengthens this supposition. In Lower Germany a Caligulan base for Legio I has been tentatively identified at Bonn, but the main opponents seem to have been the Canninefates down on the North Sea coast east of the Rhine, opposite Batavia. Their ruler is identified by Tacitus as holding out against the Romans during this campaign, and thus bringing his family an acclaim that they still enjoyed during the military uprising in 69.[23]

The chronology of Caligula's personal role in the northern expedition is highly confused in the sources. We can say that he left Italy in the autumn of 39. Precisely when is uncertain, because we do not whether he had already crossed the Alps when Gaetulicus' death was reported on 27 October. Certainly his departure could hardly have been before early September when he dismissed the consuls for paying insufficient attention to his birthday (31 August) and too much attention to the celebrations of Actium (2 September). He moved with great haste, *festinanter et rapide*, but also in considerable comfort, one feature of which was that he required the inhabitants of the town to sweep the streets for him and sprinkle them to keep down the dust.[24] His first destination would probably have been the city of Lyons, a journey of over 600 miles, and he did not apparently move from there for several months, until Galba could ensure that the Rhine frontier was safe enough to visit.

The accounts of Caligula's stay in the north present a picture of military absurdity combined with personal extravagance and decadence. He made his headquarters at Lyons. Among his activities there, he organized oratorical competitions where the losers had to erase their entries with their tongues, or be beaten with rods and thrown into the Rhône. Suetonius includes these activities among the pursuits of the 'princeps', and they may convey harmless horseplay, rather than serious punishment.[25] But Caligula is also charged with more sinister activities. Dio states that he spent much of his time gambling and putting to death wealthy Gauls to get his hands on their money. A certain Julius Sacerdos is also said to have died even though he was not particularly wealthy, but simply because of his name. It has been suggested that Sacerdos might have been one of the Gauls suborned by Gaetulicus. His name would thus have created trouble for him later, since 'Julius' might suggest that he was a freedmen or descendant of a freedman of the imperial family, which would make his treachery seem even greater.[26] In reality, Caligula seems to have had no difficulty in extracting money from the provincials, who were eager to ingratiate themselves with the emperor, even paying enormous sums just for an invitation to dinner. They were also easy victims at auctions set up by him, willing to bid extravagantly on any items that had an imperial connection, such as the victory prize at Actium.[27]

While he was in the north Caligula seems to have continued regular business, keeping up a continuous stream of correspondence with Rome. Individuals came to deal with him from all quarters of the empire. Agrippa and Antiochus seem to have paid court, a situation that disturbed many people, who felt that Caligula was coming under the influence of 'tyrant-teachers'.[28] He also received representatives sent by the senate to offer him congratulations on his escape from the plot on his life, and to report that he had been granted an ovation. The ovation would be an appropriate way to celebrate the victory over Gaetulicus. Augustus, for example, had celebrated three full triumphs for victories over foreign enemies in Dalmatia, Actium and Alexandria, but an ovation only for his defeat of fellow-citizens at Philippi and Sicily.[29] The embassy was not a success. Caligula was by now apparently paranoid about the risk of conspiracy and he refused to meet some of the envoys, suspecting them as spies. Those who were accepted were treated with ill-grace, in particular his uncle Claudius. The deputation had been chosen by lot, with the exception of Claudius, who was appointed directly. The choice seems to have upset Caligula, and he claimed to be insulted at the implication that he needed his uncle as guardian. His experiences with his sisters had perhaps soured him towards his immediate family, and he declared henceforth that none of his relatives was to be honoured. According to Suetonius there were 'some who claimed' (*non defuerint qui traderent*) that he threw Claudius into a river fully dressed, perhaps a confusion with the penalties for the losers in the oratorical contests. There is in fact epigraphic evidence that Caligula's treatment of Claudius may not have been so cavalier. An inscription, probably of 39, discovered at Lyons seems to suggest the presence of Caligula and Claudius together at the dedication of some important building. Even more intriguing is the allusion to a female figure, clearly a person of some importance. She can hardly be one of the sisters, and it opens up the possibility that Caligula's wife Caesonia (or their recently born daughter Drusilla), was in Gaul for some time with him, perhaps returning to Rome once he departed for Germany.[30]

At the beginning of 40 Caligula entered his third consulship. He did so without a colleague, but both Dio and Suetonius are at pains to point out that this was not intentional as some critics claimed, but because the consul- designate had died just before assuming office and no one could be appointed in his place at such short notice. This created a hiatus in the conduct of affairs, since the praetors, who should have stood in for the consuls, seem to have been afraid to act. Finally, by the twelfth day of the year Caligula resigned his office, and the suffect-consuls designate were able to succeed to their position.[31]

At some stage, probably in the new year, Caligula departed for the German frontier. His first destination was probably the legionary base at Mainz, where Galba's men seem to have made a fine impression on him, and Suetonius comments that of the forces assembled from every province none other received greater commendations or greater rewards.[32] Again, there is evidence that even in the military zone Caligula continued to conduct official business. A recent inscription from Julia Gordos in Asia records the embassy of a certain Theophilus, who travelled with both an administrative and domestic staff 'to Rome, in Germany and with the emperor'.[33] A memento of his stay in the Rhine area has been identified in locally produced glass medallions of the period, thought to bear the emperor's image.[34] The high point of his time there would no doubt have been the opportunity to lead his troops in battle, but it is safe to assume that the affair would have been stage managed to present a minimum of danger, as it would be for his uncle Claudius when he personally led the Roman troops into battle in Britain in 43. But this does not make it frivolous. It would serve to strengthen the bond between soldiers and an emperor willing to share with them the hardships of campaign.[35] We have very garbled accounts in Suetonius. He reports that Caligula went across the Rhine with a small detachment of his bodyguard, and that the enemy approached while he was there, but he personally saw no action. As a consequence of this exploit he devised new crowns for those soldiers who had distinguished themselves, *coronae exploratoriae* ('scouting crowns'). In a section of the *Life* dealing with Caligula's timidity Suetonius seems to describe the same event, telling how the emperor found himself in a narrow pass on the east bank of the Rhine and fled in panic on the rumour of the enemy's approach, escaping over a crowded bridge by being passed over the heads of his troops. According to Dio, Caligula was acclaimed imperator seven times, without winning a battle or killing a foe. These acclamations are not, however, reflected on his coinage, and seem to be contradicted by Dio's later assertion that Caligula's successor, Claudius, was hailed imperator several times contrary to precedent.[36] It is hardly surprising that Caligula should have presented these achievements in Rome as great victories, and within their limited context they probably were. 'A laurel has been sent by Caesar for the outstanding defeat of the German youth', wrote the poet Persius, in reference to the *tabellae laureatae*, letters covered in laurel leaves, in which reports of great victories were traditionally sent to the senate. It was constitutionally appropriate for emperors to claim the credit for the achievements of their legates, although Caligula seems to have gilded the lily somewhat in describing himself as 'on campaign and exposed to great dangers,' while the Romans enjoyed 'the pleasures of the circus and the theatre, and their fine villas'. The senate certainly did nothing to discourage such excessive claims; Vespasian proposed in the house that there be special games to honour Caligula's victory over the Germans (he added a personal thanks to the emperor for an invitation to dinner). The victories also seem to have been celebrated throughout the empire, to judge from a relief found at Koula in Lydia. Crudely cut, it depicts a Roman cavalryman with couched spear facing a woman, Germania, whose hands are tied behind her back; it is dedicated to Gaius Germanicus

Caesar.[37]

From Germany Caligula proceeeded to one of the most celebrated ventures of his whole reign, his supposed invasion of Britain. It is difficult to sort out fact from fantasy in the descriptions of this undertaking. It is fairly safe to assume that his personal 'campaigns' against the German frontier tribes would have belonged to the same phase of activities as his march to the English Channel, thus necessitating one rather than two separate treks across Northern Europe. The sources, moreover, associate the two episode. Dio implies that what he calls the ineffective operations against the Germans were immediately followed by the British episodes. Suetonius, while chronologically vague, also associates the British and German campaigns.[38] Unfortunately there is a gap in Dio's narrative at the critical point. At the beginning of his account of 40 we are told of events in Rome itself, then of the death of king Ptolemy of Mauretania. The narrative then breaks off, and when it resumes we find Caligula on the shores of the Channel, possibly in the Boulogne area. What takes place next is described in colourful terms in Dio's epitome, to which a few details are added by Suetonius.[39] We are told that after Caligula had drawn up his soldiers in battle line on the shore, along with ballistae and other siege weapons, he went out to sea in a trireme, and then sailed back again. He next took a seat on a high platform and gave the battle signal, suddenly ordering his soldiers to gather up the sea-shells in their helmets and folds of their tunics as spoils of the Ocean. These he sent to Rome to be exhibited on the Capitol and Palatine as booty. This episode has provided much grist for the scholarly mill. Most scholars assume that a real invasion was planned, but cancelled at the last minute. Gelzer suggests that the Britons united in the face of attack, while Balsdon claims that, as happened in 43, the soldiers were simply afraid to undertake the crossing of the channel, and that the emperor ordered them to pick up the shells as a form of humiliation, which, to say the least, would have been a courageous gesture on Caligula's part.[40]

It seems, in fact, highly unlikely that an invasion could be involved. In the first place, despite Galba's successes the German frontier clearly was not yet secure enough to warrant an invasion of Britain. The resistance of the Canninefates has already been noted. Even Caligula's own words to the troops in Germany suggest serious problems, since he would quote the line of the Roman hero Aeneas, who rallied his men at a time when their fortunes were at their lowest ebb: 'Bear up, and preserve yourselves for better times!'[41] Campaigns against the Germans were still going on in 41, when Galba overcame the Chatti and Publius Gabinius conquered the Cauchi.[42] It is also curious that in the fairly detailed descriptions of the episode no mention is made of the enormous numbers of transports that would have been needed to move the legions to Britain. Caesar, for instance, had over 800 vessels for his invasion.[43] A much more important factor, however, is the time of the year when this episode was played out. As will be shown later, Caligula had returned to the vicinity of Rome by the end of May, 40. To get there from the channel (over 1000 miles by the shortest route) at the rate of twenty miles a day would require a journey of some two months, even if there was no interruption. Suetonius, in fact, indicates that the return to Rome did not occur immediately after the British episode, and implies that the return journey was quite leisurely, since the emperor was met en route by envoys from the senate who begged him to hasten his return. Thus the very latest that the emperor could have departed from the channel was the end of March, and the likelihood is that he did so some time earlier. This means that he was there at a time when it would have been for practical purposes impossible for him to contemplate an expedition against Britain. Vegetius shows that up to March 10 the seas were closed to shipping (*maria clauduntur*), and were considered unsafe until 27 May.[44] This restriction would be especially applicable to a notoriously dangerous passage like the channel (and Caligula, we must not forget, was no lover of the sea, and could not swim!)[45] Also, Suetonius reports that as a monument to his victory Caligula constructed a lighthouse, likened to the Pharos of Alexandria. Thus he places the construction of this monument, located at Boulogne (Gesoriacum) and intended to aid the return of ships ferrying men and supplies to Britain, *after* the incident at the channel. The logical conclusion to draw from this, if Suetonius' sequence of events is correct, is that the actual invasion was planned for a later date.[46]

What then did happen at the Channel? Recently P. Bicknell has suggested that although there were actual operations involved they were not intended as part of a British expedition, but against the Canninefates. But, if this is so, the sources are at the very least misleading; a Roman would naturally understand a victory over Oceanus to have some connection with Britain, not a tribe at the mouth of the Rhine. In any case, the account as it stands is still basically absurd, wherever the location. R.W. Davies has argued that no serious operation was involved, but rather training manoeuvres along the channel coast. There are problems in this thesis also. It is not clear why the troops should have gone to this particular location, and it hardly seems likely that they would have used shells as missiles.[47] But while these recent suggestions might not be wholly convincing, they have the merit of recognizing that an actual planned invasion of the island at this time is to be ruled out. The solution might be to carry the argument further, and to recognize that the episode may not have been military at all, but rather political and diplomatic.

In a different context Suetonius mentions that Caligula's only accomplishment in the north was to receive the surrender of 'Adminius', son of Cunobelinus. Suetonius says that this ruler was driven out by his father, but it is more likely that the anti-Roman faction had gained the upper hand in the aging Cunobelinus' kingdom (if indeed he was still alive). Adminius was first tentatively identified by Allen with a ruler minting coins in Kent with the legends A, AM or AMMINUS, before the Claudian invasion of 43, and this identification has been recently confirmed by D. Nash. The affinity of some of the coins of Adminius (or Amminus, as he should strictly be called) with issues of Cunobelinus suggests that he may have obtained his kingdom through the aid and protection of his father, and would have continued to pay allegiance to him. Also, the discovery of a small number of silver minims found in Sussex inscribed with an A, and stylistically similar to Adminius' Kent issues, suggests that he may not have fled directly to Caligula, but have sought refuge for a time in Verica's kingdom in Sussex.[48] Suetonius does not connect Adminius with the specific episode at the channel (he is not mentioned in the surviving epitomes of Dio's missing text), but it is not too difficult to understand that a hostile tradition might have downplayed the connection, at which Suetonius does indeed hint, in calling the defection an actual achievement of Caligula, as if the emperor was somehow directly involved in it. A tradition linking the two seems to survive in the fifth century writer Orosius, who says that Caligula set out with a large force, scouring Germany and Gaul, and stopped at the edge of Ocean in view of Britain, and that when he had received the surrender of the son of Cunobelinus he returned to Rome because of a deficiency of war material.[49] Caligula on his departure from Rome would have raised expectations about victories in Britain as well as Germany. To an extent Galba's achievements on the frontier satisfied the latter need. But they clearly had not eradicated the problems sufficiently to justify the risk of an invasion of Britain. This is reflected in a passing remark of Tacitus, who said that the invasion plan fell through because of Caligula's fickle temperament and because his great campaigns against Germany had not worked.[50] Caligula thus faced the prospect of an enormous loss of face if he should be obliged to return with expectations unfulfilled.

The 'defection' of Adminius offered a heaven-sent opportunity. It was a development that could be presented as the surrender of a British king, one that rendered armed intervention unnecessary. The 'surrender' would have been staged with due military pomp- a surrender, after all, can properly be made only to superior military forces. Afterwards Caligula granted gifts to the soldiers, specified by Suetonius as 100 denarii each, and characterized as mean. As a reward for a military campaign this may have been a very modest amount, but was quite ample for participation in an essentially cermonial occasion, and also, incidentally, completely inappropriate if the troops had mutinied.[51] It might have been arranged that the submission would take place at sea, with Caligula sailing out to receive Adminius in the trireme mentioned in Dio, and it is noteworthy that Caligula arranged that the trireme should be taken back to Rome to be part of his triumph.[52] A victory over Britain in such circumstances would represent in the Roman mind a victory over Oceanus. Thus a symbolic collection of shells, the 'booty' of Oceanus, to be part of the offering of spoils for the Capitoline, would not be out of order. Some support for this reconstruction is in fact given by Suetonius, who says that after Caligula had received the submission of Adminius he sent a loftily worded letter by swift courier to Rome, which was to be presented to the consuls at a full meeting of the senate in the Temple of Mars Ultor. The general content of the letter is indicated by the phrase *quasi universa tradita insula*, ('as if the whole island had been handed over'), in other words that he was representing the incident as the surrender of Britain. The Temple of Mars had been intended by Augustus to be the location where the senate would consider claims for triumphs, and where victors on their return would bring their triumphal insignia.[53] At their meeting the senators no doubt received his report with appropriate reverence, even if in private there might have been a tendency to scoff.

Suetonius tells us that Caligula had planned a triumph on a scale never before known and even selected some well-built Gauls who were to dye their hair red and let it grow long, and to learn German, to pass for the conquered enemy in the emperor's triumph. Persius describes Caesonia making lavish preparations for the event. In the end Caligula settled for the much more modest ovation, to celebrate the victory over the conspirators. The decision to postpone the full triumph must have been his own, despite Suetonius' assertion that the Senate cheated him of it. Caligula's decision has generally been passed over in silence by scholars, but it was surely significant. It can mean only that the projected invasion of Britain had been rescheduled, not cancelled, and that no triumph was to be celebrated until Caligula's total military programme in the north had been completed.[54] Moreover, he almost certainly did not assume the title of Britannicus as some scholars maintain.[55] Dio does say that Caligula was called Germanicus and Britannicus, but he also stresses that these titles were given as a jocular tribute (probably by the soldiers) to his great erotic conquests, as if he had 'possessed' the whole of Britain and Germany.[56]

According to Suetonius Caligula intended to complete his stay in the north with a wild scheme, not reflected in any other source. He claims that the emperor planned to eliminate those legions that had taken part in the mutinies of 14 and had behaved aggressively towards himself and his father. Although dissuaded from this mad enterprise, he supposedly would not give up his plan for a decimation of the legions. On the point of carrying out the exercise, however, he noted signs that the troops might resist. He therefore fled the area and turned his ferocity on the senate instead.[57] The story sounds like fantasy, and has all the hallmarks of Suetonian exaggeration: the first scheme would have been impossible (there could have been few troops still serving from AD 14 in any case), and the second, typically, Caligula did not actually undertake but was only, we are told, *planning* to undertake. These stories may well have had their origin in some grimly humorous comments he might himself have made to the soldiers, when it became clear that the legions had not made enough progress against the Germans to make the British campaign feasible in the spring of 40.

We do not know if Caligula returned to Lyons after his 'campaigns' or if he proceeded directly to Rome. At any rate the senate sent a second deputation, much larger than the one previously headed by Claudius to offer congratulations. They brought with them the report of special honours and distinctions (possibly the offer of a triumph) and were received civilly. They also delivered obsequious requests from the senate that he hurry home.[58] Caligula's response could not have been comforting. He supposedly slapped his sword in its belt and declared loudly, 'I'm on my way, and so is this'. On his way back he issued a proclamation that he was returning only to those who wanted him, the equestrians and the people, but not to the senators, whom he could never again regard as fellow-ctiziens. It may well be at this time that he made sardonic comments about eliminating the whole body.[59]

As he left the north Caligula must have felt considerable disappointment. His dreams of great conquest and of emulating or even surpassing his ancestors had gone unfulfilled. In his frustration he would have sought scapegoats, and have looked for some target for his anger. The senators were the obvious choice. He had already shown his hostility towards them before his departure and his bitterness had clearly increased, not abated, during his months of absence. His return to Rome would test the senate's loyalty even further, by demands that he be recognized in Rome not only as princeps, but as a princeps who had special divine attributes, and who might even be an actual god.

· 9 ·

DIVINE HONOURS

OF ALL THE manifestations of wild and extravagant behaviour during Caligula's brief but colourful reign, nothing has better served to confirm the popular notion of his insanity than his apparent demand to be recognized as a god. Cruelty and incompetence may be unattractive traits of a despot, but they do not in themselves prove mental instability. A claim to divinity, however, seems inseparable from madness. The evidence for the supposed cult of Caligula in Rome is characteristically confused and incomplete, and must be evaluated with perhaps even more than the usual scepticism. Most importantly, however, we must be careful not to impose on the ancient world our own preconceptions of what constitutes a sound and healthy relationship between the human and the divine.

Among the Romans the distinction between man and god was not a sharp one. While this blurring is usually associated with the phenomenon of emperor worship in the Imperial age, its origins go back to the republic. Thus Cicero could record his gratitude to Publius Lentulus by calling him *parens ac deus* ('parent and god'), and Mucius Scaevola could say to Crassus *te in dicendo semper putavi deum* ('I have always thought you a god when you speak'). It was thus well within the bounds of Roman tradition for Vergil to include Octavian among the *praesentes deos* ('gods among us'), or for Scribonius Largus to refer to Claudius as *deus noster Caesar* ('our god Caesar').[1] In the Roman mind such expressions probably convey a recognition not so much of a divine being but of divine qualities that we normally associate with a god, but may in exeptional cases recognize in fellow humans. In the eastern provinces this fine line was easily crossed. Many of the eastern peoples, notably, but not exclusively, the Greeks, had long been accustomed to honouring their rulers with the tokens of divinity and to identifying them during their lifetimes quite explicitly as gods made manifest on earth. When Roman officials replaced these rulers, they in turn became the object of worship. Thus after Titus Flamininus defeated Philip of Macedon and proclaimed the liberation of Greece he began to receive homage from cities throughout the region, as did many Roman generals after him.[2] Even Cicero had temples decreed for him in Asia, which he refused.[3]

The Roman emperor became the natural focus for such adoration, and Augustus was obliged to accommodate somehow those communities of the Greek East who expressed a desire to worship him during his lifetime. At the formal provincial level his official policy seems to have been to allow worship of himself only in conjunction with Rome, a practice that was transported to the west; for instance the famous altar at Lyons was dedicated to Rome and Augustus.[4] At the local level, however, he was not nearly so scrupulous, and cults of the emperor himself are found throughout the eastern communities, while members of the imperial family travelling in the east regularly received divine honours.

This policy of restraint at the official level was maintained, as would be expected, by Tiberius. Thus he refused a temple to himself and Livia in Baetica in 25. He also declined the offer of divine honours from Gytheum, suggesting that more modest tokens of respect would not be out of place.[5] He did, however, allow a temple at Smyrna to himself, Livia and the Senate. Again, he seems to have turned a blind eye to local manifestations of worship. When the inhabitants of Alexandria, for instance, sought to heap divine honours on Germanicus he refused them, but said that they would be appropriate if made to Tiberius and Livia.[6]

In Italy it is clear that Augustus was worshipped during his lifetime at the municipal level. There are inscriptional references throughout Italy of temples, priesthoods, festivals, and games in his honour. There is evidence of a temple at Puteoli, a temple and sacred games at Naples, a sacerdos at Pompeii, and a flamen at Pisa, Verona and Praeneste.[7] Even in Rome there seems to have been a popular notion, reflected in the Roman poets, that the emperor should be equated with, if not exactly identified with, the gods.[8] Nevertheless Rome stood apart from the rest of the empire in this matter. In the city itself there was an aversion to the overt and official worship of a man as a god. Whether this sprang from profound theological considerations is difficult to say — it may have more to do do with the traditional Roman virtues of moderation and sobriety (*gravitas*). During an emperor's lifetime there might be private or unauthorized worship in Rome, which seems not to have been checked, but there could be no official or state worship. Thus when Agrippa completed the Pantheon in 25 BC and wished to consecrate it as a temple to Augustus, the princeps refused his request, and even Nero much later refused to allow a temple proposed to his divinity. Dio claims that generally speaking no emperor had been worshipped in Rome and Italy up to his own time, although he seems to have ignored the municipal cults.[9]

At the official level in Rome there were several ways of dealing with the popular impulse to look upon the princeps as a god. One possibility was to postpone apotheosis until after death. Whether or not Julius Caesar personally sought deification during his lifetime is much debated by scholars, but the recognition at a formal state level that he had become a god afterwards clearly served two important purposes. His successor, while outwardly foreswearing any desire for divinity, could at least present himself in his public pronouncements, on his coins and on his inscriptions, as son of a god. Moreover Caesar established a precedent that offered some consolation to the incumbent of the principate that he would, in the fullness of time, be recognized as a god in Rome itself. At a purely theological level the attitude seems inconsistent, but it would satisfy the need to stay within certain bounds of moderation.

There was another way of dealing with the issue, which allowed the emperor in a sense to be worshipped, albeit indirectly, while still alive. Every individual Roman had a *genius*, a spirit with its own divine qualities, to which prayers and offerings could properly be made. In 30 BC, among the honours voted after the battle of Actium the senate passed a decree that a libation should be poured to Octavian's *genius* at every public and private banquet, and we see from Augustan poetry that these libations became associated with the ones poured to the household Lares, the gods of the hearth.[10] At some point between 12 and 7 BC the worship of the emperor's *genius* was elevated to a more formal level, as part of the rearrangement of the municipal system of Rome. Romans had long worshipped the Lares, the gods of the household, not only in private homes but also at the crossroads (compita), in the form of the Lares Compitales. During the republic their shrines had fallen into disuse; in the reorganization, statues of Augustus' *genius* were set up between those of the Lares, which were known from then as the *Lares Augusti*. Several altars of the reorganized cult have survived, showing the sacrifice of victims, pigs for the Lares and bulls for the emperor.[11] The worship of his *genius* comes very close indeed to the direct worship of the emperor himself. Intimately associated with the worship of the emperor's *genius* is the veneration of his *numen*. Basically, *numen* signifies the power in any thing or person, but tends to be associated with the power of a god, and by natural linguistic development had become by the Augustan age essentially synonymous with 'god'. To worship the *numen* of Augustus was in a sense to worship the divine property in him without crossing the line completely and acknowledging him as divine, although it is far from certain that the unsophisticated were aware of the distinction. In literature the *numen* and the *genius* of the emperor seem to be used interchangeably, although strictly speaking they are different.[12] Probably in AD 6 Tiberius dedicated the altar of the Numen Augusti at some location in Rome in association with the abstract personification of Felicitas.[13] Information on the actual form of worship of the *numen*, however, is provided from outside Rome. In AD 11 a municipal altar was dedicated to the Numen Augusti in the forum of Narbo. A board of three knights and three freedmen was established to offer incense and wine and the sacrifice of victims to the emperor's *numen* on his birthday and other significant anniversaries.[14]

It is against this background that Caligula's claim to divinity must be evaluated. In the East he was, of course, identified as a god from the outset. Thus when the league of the Greek states sent an embassy to Rome to offer him congratulations it could refer to him as the *neos theos sebastos* ('the new god Augustus'), while a decree of Cyzicus refers to him as *ho Helios neos* ('the new sun').[15] These manifestations are completely within the tradition of the Greek east and could only have been spontaneous, since there would hardly have been time for him to send instructions on the form of worship required.[16]

There are two striking illustrations of Caligula's policy towards his cult in the east, the planned temple at Miletus and his threat to convert the Temple in Jerusalem to his own worship. According to Philo the decision to dedicate the Temple in Jerusalem to Caligula in the guise of Zeus Epiphanes was taken in the middle of 40.[17] While the move seemed to Philo, as a Jew, the acme of lunacy, from a Roman point of view it can be regarded at worst as a major political and diplomatic blunder; in quasi-theological terms it merely represents the extension of a practice that had long operated in the east, where there were already numerous dedications to Augustus as Zeus. At most the departure from the norm lies in Caligula's demanding as opposed to acquiescing in worship in his own right, unassociated with 'Rome' or 'the Senate' or the like. This demand, however, seems to have been in response to aggressive activities by the Jews at Jamnia, and it may have had a political as much as a religious purpose[18] The details of this famous incident are set out in Chapter 12, but it is worth pointing out here that in the end Caligula was persuaded to abandon his plan.

The cult centre of Caligula at Miletus in Asia is of great interest in itself in that it provides us with a detailed picture of how Caligula's worship was organized in one eastern province. In the list of his admirable achievements Suetonius notes the plans to finish the temple of Didymaean Apollo at Miletus. In Dio's account Caligula's project is shown to be far less altruistic. He says that the emperor ordered a precinct to be set aside for his worship at Miletus, and planned to appropriate for his own use the splendid temple that the Milesians were building to Apollo. The basic story that Caligula allowed the province of Asia to establish a temple at Miletus for his worship is not disputed. The further information that he planned to take over the temple of Apollo for himself is to be treated with some caution, but in light of what was envisaged in Jerusalem it is by no means implausible. It had a precedent of sorts in the scheme of certain eastern client kings who contributed funds to complete the Temple of Zeus in Athens and to dedicate it to Augustus' *genius*.[19] It breaks with tradition in one respect. Of the other major temples in Asia, that at

Pergamum was to Augustus and Roma, that at Smyrna to Tiberius, Livia and the Senate. The Imperial cult at Miletus was reserved for Caligula alone.

The famous Temple of Apollo was not actually located at Miletus but at Didyma (Branchidae), not a separate city, but within the territory of the Milesians and about ten miles south of Miletus itself. The original temple was destroyed by the Persians, under Darius in 494 BC, according to Herodotus, by Xerxes in 479, according to Strabo, and a new temple was begun after the visit of Alexander the Great.[20] The reconstruction apparently went on under Caligula but was still not yet completed when Pausanias wrote his description of the site, and the excavated ruins suggest that it remained incomplete. The temple was called by Strabo the largest in the world, and it is not be difficult to understand why it might have appealed to Caligula. It was in the Ionic order with a frontal colonnade of ten columns. The cult statue was a seated figure of Apollo, situated in a small, roofed Ionic temple at the rear of the cella.[21] Did Caligula incorporate this temple? A coin of Miletus depicting Caligula on the obverse and a temple on the reverse is generally taken to represent Caligula's temple (fig. 29).[22] The temple on the coin is hexastyle (six frontal columns) rather than decastyle (ten), which has been taken to show that Caligula did not make use of the Temple of Apollo, although the difference could be explained as a compromise of the engraver working in a limited field. In fact it seem unlikely that the coin depicts Caligula's temple at all. The same reverse type recurs frequently under later emperors for many years after Caligula's death, and presumably represents either Apollo's temple, or the shrine that held the god's cult statue. It thus has no bearing on the question of whether or not Caligula used the Temple of Apollo.

One of the most significant features of the site at Didyma at this period is an inscription found near the south-west corner of the temple, describing the dedication by officials of a cult statue of Caligula. The inscription provides excellent information on how Caligula's cult was organized, and does establish that Caligula's sanctuary, like Apollo's, was located at Didyma, not Miletus proper.[23] The first official mentioned is the *archiereus*, a chief priest, as in every major branch of the imperial cult. He is Vergilius Capito. At the time of the inscription he is noted as the high priest for the third time of a sanctuary of the provincial cult in Asia, but for the first time at Miletus.[24] The second official mentioned is the *neokoros*, Tiberius Julius Menogenes. The *neokoros* is the temple warden, responsible for keeping the building clean and pure. The third individual named is Protomachus from the city of Julia. He has three titles. The meanings of the first two, *sebasteneos* and *sebastologos*, are unclear; the third, *archinepoios*, involved supervision of the officials who tended to the fabric and expenses of the temple. The officials' names are appended, with the information that they covered the expense of the dedication from their own resources.

So much for the eastern empire. In Rome and Italy Caligula's formal religious policy was in some respects fairly conservative. He held the office of Pontifex Maximus from almost the outset of his reign. When at the beginning of 39 the oath was taken in the senate he pedantically prevented the Flamen Dialis from participating in it, as it had always been considered *nefastum* for that particular priest to swear any oath. At Nemi he revived a tradition that had fallen into disuse. The priest of Diana in the ancient grove, by tradition a runaway slave, remained in office until a challenger came along and slew him. The practice had long been neglected. In Caligula's reign the incumbent was elderly, and the emperor is said by Suetonius to have found a contender for the position. The neglect of Suetonius to mention any physical attack suggests that the violent takeover was essentially ritual.[25] As Pontifex Maximus he seems also to have undertaken the reorganization of the Salii, the priests of Mars. This is shown by a fragment of the list of the members of the college found on the Aventine at the beginning of this century.[26] Five names appear there, in two sections. In the second the appointment of Gnaeus Pompeius Magnus, in 40, is recorded. The four names in the preceding section, Cornelius Dolabella, Marcus Asinius Marcellus, Decimus Torquatus Silanus and Lucius Iunius Silanus (this last restoration is especially dubious) were clearly all appointed together in a single year, missing from the inscription but earlier than 40. Mommsen argues plausibly that Tiberius had neglected to fill vacancies to the college while on Capri and that at least four had accumulated to be filled by the beginning of Caligula's reign.

At the outset of his reign Caligula behaved in religious matters, as in all else, with great decorum. He is said by Dio to have forbidden anyone to set up images (*eikones*) of himself and also to have requested that a decree ordering sacrifices to his *genius* be annulled, asking that this last measure be inscribed on a tablet.[27] All of this was to change. We are told later of a dramatic reversal of the practices of Augustus and Tiberius in Rome itself, where, it is claimed, temples were erected to Caligula and sacrifices offered to him as a god.[28] This would represent, of course, a significant development, going far beyond the spontaneous and popular tendency for the emperor to be perceived in divine terms. Dio seems to date the establishment of a fomal cult to mid 40, the first manifestation being Caligula's anger on returning from the north at the senate's failure to vote him *ta hyper anthropon* (literally, 'things above a human').[29] His supposed earlier rivalry with Neptune at the time of the bridge at Baiae should probably be seen as bragadoccio rather than as evidence of a cult.

This claim that there was an official cult of Caligula in Rome must be examined carefully. As evidence of Caligula's madness Philo gives a lengthy description of his practice of impersonating different gods. He supposedly started with the demi-gods, Dionysus, Hercules, Castor and Pollux, changing costume to fit the character. As he grew more mad he went on to the major gods, beginning with Hermes, then Apollo, complete with radiate crown, while choirs sang hymns of praise to him. Then he would take up weapons as Mars. Dio also speaks of these impersonations, and includes such female deities as Juno, Venus or Diana. There may be a basis of truth to these accounts, but while they tell us much about Caligula's penchant for transvestism, they say almost nothing about any claim to divinity. Caligula certainly did have a predilection for dressing up, as Alexander, as a triumphator, even as a woman.³⁰ To dress up as a god was a natural progression. Suetonius mentions his dressing up as gods or goddesses in the general context, not of his religious ideas, but of his exotic costumes, and Dio notes that dressing up as Jupiter was a front adopted to seduce numerous women. Such behaviour was not unique to Caligula. Suetonius reports an unfortunate dinner party held by Augustus when all the guests appeared in the guise of gods and goddesses, Augustus being made up to represent Apollo.³¹ Antony made much use of this in his propaganda, presumably representing it as a breach of taste and propriety, rather than a serious claim to divinity. That is how such behaviour should be regarded also in Caligula's case. In any event, stories are told that, if based on fact, suggest that Caligula did not expect these performances to be taken too seriously. He is said by Suetonius to have stood beside a statue of Jupiter and to have asked the actor Apelles which of the two was greater. When Apelles hesitated Caligula did indeed have him flayed (possibly a confused account of a joke on Apelles' name, see p. 217). Significantly, however, Suetonius lists this behaviour not among his religious eccentricities but as one of his pranks, *inter varios iocos.* Dio reports that on another occasion Caligula stood on a high platform uttering oracles. A Gallic shoemaker who saw him was moved to laughter, and when asked by Caligula 'What do you think I am?', replied, 'an idiot!'. But because he was humble he came to no harm.³² Caligula seems clearly to have taken the impersonations more lightly than did Philo or Dio.

The evidence for an official cult of Caligula in Rome is provided essentially by Suetonius and Dio. We are told by Suetonius that the emperor established a Temple to his *numen*, which, Dio indicates, was voted by the Senate and was thus associated with an official cult. This was to be served by a priesthood, for which the richest competed and paid considerable amounts. Dio notes that Caesonia and Claudius, among other prominent persons, became members, and in return for the honour Caligula received from each of them an enormous sum, put by Dio at ten million sesterces. In order to pay his obligation Claudius was required to pledge his estates for security, and when he could not meet his debt, he was forced into bankruptcy.[33] This priesthood seems to have been inspired by the Augustales, who served the worship of Augustus. But in one sense it was different from this, and from all other priestly colleges. Talbert notes that generally while senators who were priests could be called upon to contribute to the games given by the colleges on special occasions, there is no evidence of *summae honorariae* payable on entry to the colleges in Rome. There is one known example of a summa honoraria for a municipal priesthood in Italy, an apparent payment of a modest 5,000 sesterces for a flaminate at Lanuvium.[34]

The evidence for the actual site of the temple in Rome is much confused. Dio even seems to suggest that there might have been two of them. The first, he suggests, was established on the Capitoline by the vote of the senate. He then states that Caligula built a *katalusis* ('lodge') on the Capitoline to dwell with Jupiter, but decided to build a second temple, at his own expense, on the Palatine. Suetonius speaks of only one temple, to the emperor's *numen*, but he does not specify the actual location. He does, however, allude to foundations of a new home begun on the Capitoline, where Caligula had decided to live with Jupiter, and to the emperor's plan to build a bridge from the Palatine over to the Capitol.[35] It seems safest to assume that there was only one temple, and most modern scholars believe that it was on the Palatine, where a shrine to Augustus had been built after his death.[36] It was said that Caligula planned initially to have Pheidias' famous statue of Zeus at Olympia transferred as a cult image, but when practical difficulties arose had a new one of himself made. Suetonius adds that the statue was lifesize and made of gold, dressed up each day in different clothing.[37]

What form did this cult take? Dio says that Caligula styled himself Jupiter Latiaris, an ancient cult figure first worshipped on the Alban Mount. Suetonius reports that Caligula would stand between the statues of Castor and Pollux in their temple in the forum to be worshipped, and that some passers-by would greet him as Jupiter Latiaris.[38] It is difficult to know what this signifies; there is a possibility that he used the temple as a vestibule to his residence and may have enjoyed striking a pose as guests entered. There is a possibility, however, that Caligula had his statue placed in their cella. The tradition of a ruler having his statue among those of the gods, not as a cult statue, strictly speaking, but as an offering to the gods, was common throughout the empire, as was pointed out to the Jews who were reluctant to accept the worship of Caligula. But it was also well established in Rome. Cicero speaks of Julius Caesar's being placed in the Temple of Quirinus in Rome. Tiberius made a point of insisting that if his own statues were to be placed in the temples they should be among the *ornamenta aedium* ('the adornments of the temple'), rather than among the gods, suggesting that the latter arrangement was not generally considered inappropriate. Caligula did not share Tiberius' restraint, but he may not have been the only one to yield to temptation. In 54, for instance, the senate voted Nero a number of honours, including a statue, or statues, in the temple of Mars Ultor, to be the same size as the cult statue of the god, suggesting that Nero's would stand next to it in the cella. Moreover, the representation of emperors in the guise of Jupiter has been shown by Niemeyer to have been part of the imperial propaganda from Augustus on.[39] Suetonius does not seem in this context to speak of official worship — the *quidam* ('some') of his text suggests either a popular or casual reaction, or even the response of obsequious courtiers. Also the charge that someone had represented himself as Jupiter would have been a handy form of political abuse. Clodius, for instance, asserted that Cicero called himself Jupiter and claimed that Minerva was his sister.[40]

One piece of evidence that has been adduced in this context is that one of the titles acquired by Caligula, according to Suetonius, was *optimus maximus Caesar*. It has been claimed that this shows that he was worshipped in the guise of Jupiter Optimus Maximus.[41] But while the formula may associate the emperor with the attributes of the god it certainly does not identity him as such. The formula *optimus maximus princeps* may well appear in fragmentary inscriptions as early as the Augustan period, and it can certainly be confirmed for Nero, who refused divine worship in Rome.[42] That Seneca did not find its application to a human offensive is shown by his observation to Nero, that the princeps should be considered the greatest, *maximus*, by virtue of being the best, *optimus*.[43]

The overall testimony of Dio and Suetonius is difficult to assess. The information is vivid and detailed, and it is not easy to dismiss the basic picture, even if allowance is made for distortions of some of the details. Yet their accounts present some serious difficulties. In the first place there is not the slightest hint in a single inscription of the cult of Caligula in Rome or in any western province. An undated dedication, for instance, from a freedman at Bourges in Aquitania to a local god Etnosus (presumably Etussus) and the emperor, where we might have expected divine attributes, alludes to him simply as C. Caesar Germanicus. At least one inscription, on a milestone from Santiago de Compostela in Spain, can be dated to Caligula's fourth tribunician year, thus no earlier than March/ April 40, and, again, it contains no divine attributes. An inscription recorded at Coimbra, dated after his third consulship (January 40 at the earliest) seems to describe him only as Caesar, without further attributes.[44] An interesting pair of inscriptions has survived from Narbonese Gaul. Each record a dedication to Tiberius and Caligula by Sextus Aelianus Pisinus. The dedicator is identified as a sevir Augustalis, a member of the priestly college charged with organizing the worship of Augustus, and thus, presumably attuned to the issue of the Imperial cult. The inscription to Caligula is securely dated to 40 and yet, again, gives no indication of any cult or worship.[45] The Arval record, which is extant for 39 and almost certainly for part of 40, gives no hint of any claim of divine status, even though later Claudius, while still alive, is described by the Arvals as a *divinus princeps.*[46] Also, while his father Germanicus is identified on inscriptions in the east as Zeus/Jupiter, there is no known inscription identifying Caligula with this particular god.[47]

The emperor could not, of course, play a direct personal role in the recording of inscriptions at a local level, where official policy might not be reflected accurately. Also, it is probably the case that a western inscription bearing divine attributes would have been a likely candidate for destruction after the emperor's death. But it is still remarkable that not a single one has survived. Moreover, these reservations do not apply to Caligula's official coinage. Neither in their types nor in their legends do the coins even hint at a formal cult. Especially significant here is the absence of any example of the radiate crown in the official coinage.[48] This device is borrowed from the worship of the sun god by the Kings of Egypt, and Syria and is used on the gold coins of Ptolemy III and Euergetes I of Egypt and Antiochus IV of Syria.[49] In Rome it is the distinctive attribute of the deified emperor, and found on the coins bearing the head of Divus Augustus minted by Tiberius, Caligula and Claudius.[50] Even though he specifically refused a temple in Rome, Nero allowed himself to be depicted radiate on the reverse of precious metal coins and the obverse of lower denominations.[51] Caligula was, in fact, highly progressive in the types of his official coinage. It is surprising that no new type marked the presumed establishment of his cult, and remarkable that he did not at the very least, like Nero, depict his own head with the radiate crown.

It is also striking that there is no explicit allusion to a formal cult of Caligula at Rome in either Seneca or Philo, both of whom were hostile to the emperor and were actually in Rome during the latter part of his reign. Philo, who takes it as a sign of Caligula's madness that he demanded worship as a god, makes no reference to an official cult in the city. Although this is an argument from silence it is a compelling one. Since much of his *Legatio* is dominated by Caligula's plan to be worshipped as Zeus in Jerusalem, it seems astonishing that Philo should have omitted to draw a parallel with the situation in Rome, where he stayed at the time the cult was said to be established. Interestingly enough, he does not even include Jupiter among the gods supposedly impersonated by Caligula. In the works of Seneca, who had a highly personal antipathy towards Caligula not shared by Philo, there is only one passage that some scholars have felt contains an allusion to a cult. In describing the execution of the philosopher Julius Canus, Seneca reports how, on the way to his death, he came close to the tumulus on which a daily sacrifice was offered to *Caesari deo nostro* ('our God Caesar'). There is no way of telling if the 'Caesar' here refers to Julius Caesar, Augustus or Caligula, and, if the last, it seems difficult to imagine that Seneca could have intended such an expression to be taken seriously. Several centuries ago Julius Lipsius stated that this passage was meant as a piece of bitter irony, and that the 'sacrificial victims' were in fact opponents who had been put to death by him.[52]

One aspect of Caligula's reign that has confused the issue of his association with the establishment of his cult is the introduction into Rome of the ritual of obeisance known as *proskynesis*. This had been practised before the kings of Assyria, and in Assyrian documents there are references to subjects prostrating themselves and kissing the king's feet. It was followed also in the Persian court of the Acheminds. Its function seems initially to have been little more than a social formality, the greeting appropriate to one higher in rank, but when adopted in Greece it was chiefly a form of worship.[53] Only in extreme cases would a Roman prostrate himself. Lucullus is recorded as falling to his knees before Julius Caesar, and Quintus Haterius threw himself down before Tiberius, accidentally causing the emperor to fall flat on his face in the process.[54] At the outset of his reign Caligula showed such personal modesty that he forbade Romans from giving him even a formal greeting when he went out in public. It was later in his reign that proskynesis became common, and it was apparently introduced by the notoriously obsequious Lucius Vitellius. After his successful peace with Parthia Vitellius was summoned home, supposedly falling under the general suspicion that Caligula felt for those who had been successful (p. 236). He apparently knew how to save himself. He fell at the emperor's feet with tears and lamentations, calling him divine names and vowing that if he were allowed to live he would offer sacrifices to him.[55] Vitellius' gesture is the only one cited from Caligula's reign that seems to have any connection with worship. Dio mentions that Caligula was in the habit of extending his foot (or his hand) in order to avoid kissing those who greeted him. He met with the required response not only from humble people, but also from those who considered themselves to be in high repute.[56] When Dio goes on to say that these things happened 'as though to a god' he seems to suggest not so much worship as god-like treatment. Several specific instances (apart from Vitellius) are known from Caligula's reign. Domitius Afer supposedly prostrated himself as a suppliant, when overwhelmed by Caligula's superior talent as an orator. The prefects of the guard, and the freedman Callistus, on being accused by Caligula of plotting against him, prostrated themselves and denied any such evil intention. Seneca says that Caligula offered his foot to the suppliant senator Pompeius Pennus to kiss, thus seeking to introduce Persian tyranny.[57] Vitellius apart, all these instances imply not worship but rather servile flattery. This is surely confirmed by the fact that even when the Jews of Philo's embassy came into Caligula's presence they bowed to the floor in reverence. The senatorial embassy sent to Claudius after the assassination fell to their knees in his presence, clearly not in recognition of his divinity. Claudius banned the practice after his accession.[58]

Perhaps the most interesting example of *proskynesis* occurred when Caligula was absent in the north. We are told that the senators went in a body to the Capitol to perform sacrifices and to do homage to Caligula's throne set up in the temple. In Rome the gods had thrones, carried in processions and used at banquets, and taken to the theatre with their symbols, such as thunderbolts placed on them. Under the year 30 Dio records that men brought gilded chairs into the theatres in honour of Sejanus and Tiberius, at a time when Tiberius, at least, was absent in Capri.[59] But these are not strict precedents. The incident occurs in the context of the procedural problems caused by the absence of Caligula from Rome and the death of the consul-designate immediately before the new year. The senators paid homage to the chair not so much as an act of worship but to maintain some sort of fiction that Caligula was still in Rome. This is indicated by Dio's report that they left money behind as though they were giving it to the emperor. The closest parallel to homage *in absentia* is reported by Servius, the fourth century commentator on Vergil. He observes that when Romulus was acting in an official capacity he would set up an empty curule chair next to himself, with the sceptre and crown of Remus, to indicate their common rule. In 40 Roman officials were afraid to act independently, and they similarly behaved as though Caligula was somehow present.[60]

Was there, then, an official cult of Caligula at Rome? The possibility can certainly not be ruled out, but even so it would reflect a breach of tradition and protocol rather than a manifestation of madness. It may, in any case, be possible to reconcile in some degree the testimony of Dio and Suetonius with the silence of the epigraphic and numismatic record. R. Fears has suggested that Caligula sought only to associate himself with Jupiter, to suggest that he was that god's 'divinely appointed viceregent', and that the idea was distorted by the hostile sources.[61] But there is another possible explanation. It is to be noted that Suetonius reports that Caligula established his temple to his *numen*. Now this could simply mean *numen* in the sense of 'godhead'.[62] But it is also possible that Suetonius reflects a tradition in which the temple to Caligula was dedicated not to himself personally but to his *genius* (the terms *genius* and *numen* would be almost interchangeable in this type of context by Suetonius' day). There is a hint of this in Persius, who says that among the festivities prepared in Rome for the return of Caligula from Germany games were to be celebrated *dis...genioque ducis* ('to the gods and to the *genius* of the emperor').[63] Also, Dio's narrative, if examined carefully, may shed some light on this issue. On his return from Gaul in early 40 Caligula was angry with the senate for its delay in granting him *ta hyper anthropon* ('things above a human'). Dio uses the very same expression later, in the context of events leading up to the final assassination (at the end of 40?). We are told that he had *earlier* demanded to be considered *hyper anthropon* but at this time flattering courtiers paid him even greater honours, and began to call him a god, or a demi-god.[64] Now in doing so, they, for their part, behaved no differently from the Augustan poets, who could describe the emperor as a *praesens deus*. What is significant is that Dio at the very least implies that Caligula's earlier claim fell short of outright recognition as a god.

There is evidence that there might have been a cult of Caligula's Salus in Rome. The cult of the Salus ('welfare') of Augustus had been established in that emperor's day. Oaths were sworn to it, and it had a priest at Alabanda. The formula Salus Augusta appears also on coins and inscriptions of Tiberius. Games seem to have been introduced in Rome for Caligula's Salus; on his accession Claudius banned similar honours for himself.[65] Weinstock suggests also that the claim that Caligula swore by the Salus and Genius of his horse Incitatus also implies strongly the existence of such a cult.[66] It could well be that when the senate voted Caligula festivals after his deliverance from the conspiracy of Scribonius Proculus, one would also have been to his Salus.[67]

The cult of Caligula's Salus would have been something of an innovation — there is no evidence that Tiberius allowed the cult of his own Salus. But it would hardly have caused deep offence. The worship of the emperor's *genius* in Rome would have been even less remarkable. Where Caligula may have crossed the line was in introducing into Rome a practice unknown in the city and only sparsely attested in the Italian municipalities.[68] In Rome the *genius* of the emperor had been worshipped privately. It had no temple of its own, nor did it have its own priesthood. It could be that in Caligula's case worship of his *genius* was elevated to the level of an official state cult, with a temple and body of priests to serve it.

It had probably been difficult in the best of circumstances for many people to draw, at a non-intellectual level, the distinction between worship of the divine element within the emperor and the emperor himself. If this cult was now elevated to the level of a state institution, with the trappings associated with the regular gods, the confusion would be even further compounded, a confusion that a hostile tradition would not have tried to clarify. On the other hand, there is no compelling reason why the innovation should necessarily be reflected on coins or inscriptions. Whatever the precise form of the worship of Caligula, whether of his *genius* or of himself, it is clear that he did not *impose* it on the Romans. There is only one hint of opposition in the sources. Caligula is said afterwards to have punished people who would not swear by his *genius*. Swearing by the *genius* of the emperor had by this time become routine, and the reference supports the notion that Caligula's *genius* had a special status and that there might have been problems with some who refused to countenance the new form of worship.[69] Generally, however, there seems to have been no reluctance to accommodate Caligula's wishes. Dio does specifically identify those connected with the stage as setting up images to Caligula and Drusilla, but he also notes that the honours paid to him as a god came not only from the mob, used to flattery, but from people of reputation.[70] The sources show that Vitellius and other obsequious courtiers fell over themselves in addressing him in terms appropriate to a divine figure, and it was by a decree in the senate that a temple was formally devoted to his cult or that of his *genius*. That Caligula did nothing to discourage this behaviour, unlike Augustus or even Nero in similar circumstances, is no credit to him, but it is hardly a sign of madness.

· 10 ·

ASSASSINATION

CALIGULA WAS ONCE again in the vicinity of Rome by the end of May 40, although he seems to have stayed outside the city limits and delayed his official entry into Rome proper until the end of August, when he celebrated his ovation.[1] It was probably not very long after his return from the north that the Jewish embassy from Alexandria, led by Philo, first met him, in his mother's gardens by the Vatican Hill (also outside the city limits).[2] Whatever setbacks the emperor may have encountered in the previous months, he seems to have been in an affable mood on this occasion. He smiled at the delegation, giving them an encouraging wave of the hand and the promise that he would deal with them when he had the time. We should not take this as a hollow excuse. Considerable public business would have accumulated while he was in the north, and apart from the Alexandrians there were several foreign rulers and deputations awaiting him.[3] At some point after this he seems to have moved south to Campania, travelling from one villa to another. If he hoped to escape from the tedium of meeting foreign deputations, he was to be disappointed. It was almost certainly in this summer that Herod Antipas, tetrarch of part of his late father's (Herod the Great's) dominion, and his wife Herodias (sister of Herod Agrippa) made their journey to see the emperor in Campania, lured by the prospect of Antipas being granted the title of king. In the meantime, however, Caligula had received damaging evidence from Agrippa, who still nursed a grudge against his brother in law, and Antipas found himself accused of treachery, originally with Sejanus, and more recently with the Parthian King Artabanus. He was sentenced to exile, probably in Gaul (p. 183).[4] Philo's deputation from Alexandria also tried to meet Caligula while in Campania, and it was there that they heard the devastating news that he had ordered his own statue to be placed within the Temple at Jerusalem (p. 188).

Finally, Caligula entered Rome to celebrate an ovation on 31 August. In timing the event for his birthday he followed precedent. Pompey similarly delayed his triumph in 61 until his birthday, as, apparently, did Messalla in 27 BC.[5] While the symbolic association between the two events would have weighed heavily with him, Caligula's absence may

154

also have been at least in part dictated by a fear of assassination. The activities of Gaetulicus and Lepidus must have made him deeply suspicious of the senate, and no doubt aggravated his autocratic behaviour. It was probably about this time that he began to insist on the official cult of himself, or of his *genius*, in Rome. He may have decided to foster his popularity with ordinary Romans as a protection against a perceived growing threat from the nobility, although ironically the elections previously restored to them reverted about now to the senate (p. 231).[6] Caligula perhaps appreciated that the Roman people were not too concerned about abstract political gains that had little political importance in any case. He understood the appeal of a more concrete demonstration of his favour, and carried out another *congiarium*, showering gold and silver on them from the roof of the palace for several days in succession. Many people in the crowd were injured in the crush, and Dio adds the malicious rumour that they were killed by the pieces of iron that the emperor tossed down with the coins. The Chronographer of 354 records that in the rush 32 men, 247 women and one eunuch died.[7]

Caligula did in fact meet his death as the result of a conspiracy, and it could be said that his persistent fears were, in the end, vindicated. He had first felt threatened after his illness in 37 by a group centred around Macro and Gemellus. The second major threat came in the form of Lepidus, perhaps in concert with Gaetulicus, in 39. Both of these 'conspiracies' are shrouded in obscurity, and, given the nature of a conspiracy, this is not surprising. The plots against Caligula in the final six months are better documented, but their precise nature and the true motives of the participants still elude us. Generally two separate phases of conspiratorial activity are identified, one dated loosely to late 40, the other culminating in January 41.[8] It might, however, be more appropriate to view them both as phases of a single process. A political conspiracy, unlike a straighforward military coup, is often a complex event, and may involve individuals with disparate aims and ambitions, united only by the common determination to be rid of a particular ruler. The more widespread the dissatisfaction, the greater the number of individuals likely to be involved. It is claimed, for instance, that there had been sixty conspirators working for the assassination of Julius Caesar. In such a large operation, there are likely to be sub-groups. Branches of the conspiracy could act almost independently, and part of it might be exposed without betraying the central core, which could continue with its plotting.[9] This approach might help to explain an apparent contradiction in our sources. Both Dio and Josephus emphasize that the final conspiracy was widely known. Yet this seems to conflict with Tacitus, who speaks of a secret plot (*occultae insidiae*) implying that it succeeded because of the very fact that it was secret. These two notions can be reconciled if we think in terms of a conspiracy that attracted a wide range of diverse interests whose inner group retained their secrecy, even though Caligula managed to catch a number of people on the fringe. Josephus does indeed comment that many of the conspirators were operating *allelon agnoia* ('in ignorance of one-another').[10]

The obsessive fear of a major conspiracy might to some degree account for the apparently ruthless behaviour of Caligula in the final six months of his life. Seneca, in particular, provides horrific descriptions of his brutality, especially towards senators, of how he scourged them to death, tortured them by fire and the rack, gagged their mouths with sponges to prevent them from crying out, beheaded them, and even executed them in the evening because he was too impatient to wait until the next day. But when the texts are examined carefully, relatively few specific details or names emerge. Three of the cases as transmitted in the sources involve what seem to be variants on one of the conventional behaviour traits of the tyrant, who traditionally adds refinement to his cruelty by executing a son in the presence of his father, or even executes them together. Similar stories were told even about Augustus.[11]

One of these father-son stories involves a certain Pastor, who is otherwise unknown. Seneca is the only source. He claims that Caligula decided to execute Pastor's son because of the youth's foppish manners and elaborate hair-style. When Pastor begged for his son's life, the emperor had the lad executed at once and that same evening invited the old man to a banquet, giving him perfume and garlands, proposing his health and keeping watch to make sure that he drank the wine. Pastor did so, we are told, because he had another son, and feared what might happen to that boy too, if his father offended the emperor.[12]

The second case, that of Sextus Papinius, is much confused in Dio's account. Under 40 he tells us that Papinius and his 'father' Anicius Cerialis were both discovered in a conspiracy and tortured by Caligula, and that Cerealis maintained his silence, while his son Papinius was induced to speak by the promise of a pardon. On the testimony of the son, according to Dio, Cerialis and others were executed in his presence.[13] Seneca gives us a quite different report. He claims that it was Papinius, son of an unnamed consular, who was tortured to death by Caligula, for amusement.[14] He says nothing of his being being betrayed by another accuser, but this may well be because he wishes to create an impression of the nobility of the victims. Dio is almost certainly in error here. Anicius Cerialis may well have been involved in the incident, but his role would have been quite different from that of the executed father. Tacitus reports that when Anicius was forced in 66 to commit suicide on suspicion of disloyalty to Nero, the evidence on which the charge was based may well have been forged, but the case aroused little sympathy because he had earlier betrayed a conspiracy to Caligula. He certainly had a record of sycophantic collaboration. It was Anicius who, as suffect consul, proposed in 65 the erection of a temple to Divus Nero.[15] It seems probable that on this occasion he betrayed some of the conspirators, including Papinius, and that Dio confused the story, with the added touch of the murder of the father before his son.[16]

The last group involves Betilienus Bassus, a quaestor, and his father, the procurator Betilienus Capito. Both Seneca and Dio (who provides most of the details) imply that their deaths belong to the same occasion as that of Papinius. It is tempting to conclude that these men too might have been betrayed by Anicius Cerialis.[17] Dio adds the detail that Capito was forced to be present at his son Bassus' execution, although not personally guilty of any crime. When Capito asked to be allowed to close his eyes Caligula ordered him slain also; in an attempt to save his own life Capito now offered to disclose the names of others. Dio implies very strongly that the people identified by him were in fact involved in a conspiracy, namely the Prefects of the guard and the powerful freedman Callistus, and that these might have come to a sticky end had not Capito gone too far and added Caesonia to the list of the accused!.

Among the others implicated in the 'early' phase of the final conspiracy was Julius Canus, a Stoic philosopher.[18] The Stoics adhered to a creed that stressed the paramountcy of nature and a rational life lived in accordance with nature. They did concede the necessity of order and structure in society, and had accommodated themselves to the notion of monarchy, provided the ruler was enlightened. Under the Julio-Claudians, (especially Nero), the Stoics became the focal point of courageous opposition to rulers they considered far from benevolent. Seneca hints at Stoic opposition in the pre-Neronian period, but Canus is the first identifiable example of what was to become a familiar type on the imperial scene.[19] According to Seneca he had a long quarrel with Caligula and presumably got the better of him. As he was leaving, the emperor told him not to be too pleased with himself, as he had ordered him executed, to which Canus is said to have replied, 'Thank-you, excellent prince,' a bon mot which impressed Seneca but whose precise significance eluded him. Seneca clearly implies that the death penalty came about as a whim of Caligula's, but it is noteworthy that an interval of ten days elapsed between verdict and execution, which happened to be the statutory period between sentence and execution in senatorial trials. It is thus likely that Canus was actually convicted by the senate.[20] Seneca adds that as Canus went to his death he was accompanied by 'his philospher' (suus philosophus), whom Syncellus identifies as Antiochus of Seleucia, otherwise unknown.[21] Canus is said to have foretold to him that within three days of his death another philosopher Rectus would die, and that this did in fact come to pass, although nothing further is known of Rectus (but see p. 00).[22]

Another senatorial to die was Julius Graecinus, father of the Agricola who would later win fame in Britain. He was a philosopher, and perhaps also part of the embryonic Stoic opposition. Seneca claims that Graecinus, a *vir egregius*, was executed because he was a better man than it suited a tyrant he should be. Tacitus however relates the execution to his refusal to prosecute Silanus.[23] Since Graecinus died in AD 40/1, surviving the trial of Silanus by two years, Tacitus' account can not be taken at face value, although it is possible that if he had refused to be party to Silanus' condemnation, this might have earned him Caligula's displeasure, and could have sealed his doom when his name was later linked to a conspiracy.

The senators as a group seem to have shown a distinct lack of zeal in protecting those willing to take a stand against Caligula. Canus the philospher does appear to have behaved with a certain courageous dignity, but the most impressive story of heroism is told of someone much lower on the social scale, a story that provides a useful link between the apparently early and later phases of the final conspiracy. Pomponius, a man of Epicurean leanings, who had held a number of political offices and was of consular rank, was betrayed by a disloyal friend Timidius. The main witness was Quintilia, a beautiful actress and Pomponius' mistress.[24] She was tortured, but held firm, suffering horrific punishment that left her disfigured. So moved was Caligula by her courage and wrecked body that he gave her a gift of money as compensation, put by Suetonius at 800,000 sesterces. Pomponius (if he is correctly identified as Seneca's Pompeius) did not match Quintilia's bravery, and was so overwhelmed with gratitude when his life was spared that he kissed Caligula's foot. What is particularly interesting is that during her torture Quintilia is said to have given a secret signal to reassure Cassius Chaerea, the Praetorian tribune, a gesture that suggests that her lover was, in fact, involved with the conspirators. Now Cassius Chaerea was the protagonist in the final phase of the attempt on Caligula's life, and the tradition that he and Quintilia were involved together strongly suggests that the supposed 'earlier' and 'later' conspiracy were both part of the same operation.

Caligula's investigation does seem to have smoked out one figure, about whom very little is known, the senator Scribonius Proculus. The emperor's tactic seems to have been to isolate him. He called a meeting of the senate and made a show of granting amnesty, saying that there were only a few members against whom he retained any anger. This statement caused even greater general anxiety since each individual senator now feared for himself. This was Caligula's intention, and its least harmful result was an outbreak of abject sycophancy. At a more serious level, he succeeded in turning the senators against one-another. One of Caligula's freedmen, Protogenes, took to carrying around two books, called *Gladius* and *Pugio* ('sword' and 'dagger'), supposedly containing lists of those marked for execution. He was used, it seems, in a careful plan to take Proculus unawares. The freedman apparently entered the senate one day on some pretext, and as the senators were greeting him, rebuked Proculus for addressing him, even though he hated the emperor. This rebuke appears to have been a pre-arranged signal, since a number of senators now set upon the unfortunate man and brutally murdered him. The report that he was hacked to pieces is an indication that a good number of senators must have been willing to lend themselves to the savage plot.[25]

The death of Proculus marked a setback to that small element in the senate prepared to stand up against Caligula. The senators now seem to have scrambled to ingratiate themselves with him. They voted festivals in his honour, presumably thanksgivings for his deliverance, and at a more practical level provided a platform in the senate house for his security, and allowed him to have a bodyguard when attending senate meetings.[26] Senators were theoretically not allowed to carry arms in the house, but they clearly did not always adhere to the rule. Augustus, for instance, was afraid of assassination and would wear a breastplate under his clothes at senate meetings (although he doubted its real effectiveness), and had senators searched before they came into his presence. In 32 Tiberius had been granted an armed guard of twenty men when he was in the house but he had declined the offer, partly because it was without precedent and partly, according to Dio, because he was hardly so foolish as to hand out swords to men who hated him. In 33 the senate acceded to his request that when he entered the house he should be allowed an escort of Praetorians, although he could hardly have benefitted from the privilege, as he was never again in the city. Caligula's bodyguard thus had precedents in the reigns of Augustus and Tiberius; the additional provision, however, of a special unit to guard even Caligula's statues seems to suggest that matters had taken a particularly serious turn.[27] It may be that at this time Caligula increased the number of the Praetorian guard from nine cohorts to twelve. An inscription predating the Claudian invasion of Britain shows that the increase had certainly taken place by 43.[28] For his security Caligula seems to have relied mainly on a special corps of Germans, noted for their physical strength and brutality. It was Augustus who had first made use of German bodyguards, Batavians specifically. He had called them into service against Antony and was much impressed by their skill, especially in cavalry. They formed a distinct unit, quite separate from the Praetorians, but had been removed from Rome in AD 9 after Varus' defeat because of concerns about their loyalty. Suetonius claimed that Caligula's expedition to Germany was in part intended to recruit a Batavian bodyguard, an unlikely story but perhaps suggesting that he brought a unit back with him.[29]

Opposition to Caligula from certain quarters of the nobility was not especially surprising, and he could deal with it to some degree by playing on either the insecurities or the ambitions of individual senators, and by pitting one member against another. The most remarkable development in the conspiracy is that Caligula also lost the support of his own household staff. As noted earlier, Capito, in order to save his own life, revealed the names of a number of conspirators, including the freedman Callistus, the two Prefects of the guard, and the emperor's wife Caesonia.[30] While the inclusion of Caesonia's name is surely absurd, the rest of Capito's charges appear to have had some basis in fact. Josephus implicates Callistus specifically, and in a later context Tacitus tantalisingly implies that he had a major role in Caligula's death, dealt with in one of his earlier (lost) books. Suetonius suggest that Callistus found allies among the other important freedmen, (*non sine conscientia potentissimorum libertorum*). Callistus was the most influential and wealthy of the freedmen whose very success, according to Josephus, had made him feel exposed to danger. Josephus adds that he had started to pay court to Claudius, anticipating that in the event of Caligula's removal the empire would pass to the emperor's uncle, and even claimed later that he had been instructed to poison Claudius but found excuses for constantly postponing the deed — a claim that provokes Josephus' scepticism. In any case, after Caligula's death Callistus did remain a powerful figure at court, and became secretary *a libellis* to the emperor Claudius.[31]

Suetonius claims also that the Prefects of the guard were involved.[32] Josephus provides the name of one of them, Marcus Arrecinus Clemens, father-in-law of the future emperor Titus. Clemens' son (suffect consul in 73) was appointed commander of the guard in 70, partly on the grounds, as Tacitus ambiguously and perhaps ironically informs us, that his father had performed the same duty 'splendidly' (*egregie*) under Caligula.[33] The name of the second Prefect is unknown to us, and if he was involved, he may have played a more passive role. Rather implausibly, Josephus claims that when Clemens was approached he gave his enthusiastic support to the endeavour but asked to be excused from active participation on the grounds of age![34] It is more likely that he was shrewd enough to distance himself from the actual mechanics of the assassination and to let his subordinates run the real risks.

Both Suetonius and Dio suggest that the individuals named by Capito were in fact innocent of the charges against them (Dio even has Caligula meolodramatically inviting them to kill him on the spot). So obsessed was the emperor by his suspicions, however, that he supposedly tried to arouse divisions between them, ingratiating himself with one then the other in turn, and created such indignation on their part that they eventually betrayed him. Again, this seems implausible, and the insistence that the emperor's staff was not originally involved in the plot may spring from a desire to enhance the role of the senatorial conspirators, and to put Capito in a good light, as not giving away real participants.

Caligula's final weeks are more fully documented than any other period of his life, because of the detailed account provided by Josephus in the *Antiquities*. Unfortunately, Josephus is frequently confused, and his report is vitiated by the corrupt state of the manuscripts. In Josephus, and the other sources, the actual execution of the deed is engineered by military figures, the most prominent role being given to Cassius Chaerea, a tribune of the Praetorian guard. He is already familiar to us from his action during the disturbances on the Rhine following the death of Augustus, when he courageously cut a path through a mob of mutineers. No other details of his life are known, except that by 41 at the latest he held a tribunate in the Praetorian guard.[35] In Josephus' portrait Chaerea is depicted as a noble idealist, motivated by a profound commitment to Republican liberties. Moreover Josephus makes him not merely the actual agent of the deed but the inspiration and organizational power, serving a useful moral purpose as a virtuous man helping to carry out God's will. But all the sources, including Josephus, admit that Chaerea did in fact have a personal grudge against Caligula. Although very manly in his personal tastes, he had a weak, high-pitched, voice, that sounded effeminate. As a consequence he was made fun of by Caligula who called him a *gynnis* ('lass').[36] According to Dio, when asked for the daily watchword by Chaerea, the emperor chose suggestive expressions, such as 'Venus' or 'Priapus', causing much ribaldry among Chaerea's fellow Praetorians. When Chaerea had occasion to thank him for anything, Caligula would offer his hand to be kissed, then at the last moment move it in obscene gestures. At a more mundane level, there are also grounds for believing that Chaerea had come under scrutiny for poor performance of his work. He was made a tax collector for the imperial treasury, but was lax in carrying out his duties, Josephus providing the unconvincing explanation that he felt pity for the debtors.[37] Chaerea had the support of some of the other members of the guard. He won over the tribune Papinius, otherwise unknown, but perhaps related to the Sextus Papinius earlier executed by Caligula. His right-hand man in the actual execution of the deed was another tribune, Cornelius Sabinus.[38] Doubtless behind the military figures there lurked idealistic or ambitious senators. Josephus in fact distinguishes two senatorial conspiracies. He says that one was led by Aemilius Regulus of Cordoba, otherwise unknown, who was motivated by his commitment to the ideals of liberty and was determined to eliminate Caligula either by his own or a colleague's hand. He evidently chose the second option, since after Josephus' introductory comments Regulus simply disappears from the narrative.[39]

A much more sustained role is given by Josephus to the senator Annius Vinicianus.[40] According to Josephus, Vinicianus was motivated partly by his friendship for the executed Lepidus, and partly, we are led to believe, by the realization that he was himself a potential target of the emperor's anger. Most implausibly Josephus suggests that Chaerea and Sabinus approached Vinicianus, declared the watchword 'Liberty' and presented their plan. He praised the undertaking and pronounced that he was ready, if necessary, to follow Chaerea's lead. Again, there is the hint that Chaerea was perhaps the dupe of much more powerful figures who, for the most part, remained in the background. Several modern scholars see an important role for Vinicianus, and consider him the heart of the plot from the outset, motivated not by a desire to restore the republic but by the determination to stage a take-over, by exploiting ill- feeling against Caligula.[41]

Another senatorial figure with some role in the conspiracy was Valerius Asiaticus. Messalina's agent Sosibius later described him as its *praecipuus auctor*. An Allobrogian from Vienne, much admired by Tacitus, he was the first Narbonese to attain the consulship (suffect in 35), followed by a second in 46. Seneca describes him as a personal friend of Caligula, and since he was a devoted follower of Antonia, it may have been in Antonia's house that the friendship began. Be that as it may, Asiaticus developed a personal grudge against the emperor. Seneca tells of how Caligula's taunts at public banquets over his wife's lack of prowess in bed drove Asiaticus into the arms of the conspirators. Asiaticus' later conduct gives weight to the possibility of his involvement, since after Caligula's death he responded to the furious popular demands for the assassin's identity by the declaration that he wished it were he.[42]

Another possible participant was Gaius Cassius Longinus (suffect in 30) governor of Asia. Dio tells us that Caligula recalled him after supposedly being warned by an oracle to beware of a Cassius (in fact, Cassius Chaerea). He was the brother of Lucius Cassius Longinus who had been married to Drusilla and had an unfortunate habit of boasting that his ancestor had assassinated Julius Caesar. He did escape with his life (perhaps being recalled too late), since he went on to become governor of Syria, and eventually to be exiled by Nero.[43]

Two of the senators involved in the plot lost their lives along with Caligula. Very little in known about them. Publius Nonius Asprenas held the suffect consulship of 38, probably designated for the office by Tiberius.[44] He was the first to be cut down by the guard after the assassination. Lucius Norbanus Balbus was also killed alongside Caligula. Josephus gives him the usual encomium awarded the conspirators, saying that he was among the noblest of the citizens, and could boast many generals among his ancestors. He is otherwise unknown.[45]

In Josephus' account Chaerea was eager for action and had to be restrained by the others, until it was finally agreed that they would make their move during the celebration of the Palatine games, which began on 17 January. The games provided good tactical opportunities for the conspirators. A temporary theatre was erected in front of the imperial residence and thousands of spectators would be crowded into a confined space. Hence, if an attempt should be made upon Caligula as he entered or left, his bodyguard would be hampered when it tried to come to his aid. The theatre would also enable a large number of fellow conspirators to congregate in one location. These seem to be more serious considerations than the rumour that Caligula intended to sail to Alexandria after the games, thus making immediate action essential.[46]

The event was foretold by a fair share of portents, fortunately for the conspirators not recognized by Caligula. They supposedly occurred as early as the Ides of March of at least the previous year, when the Capitol of Capua as well as the room of the doorkeeper of the Palace at Rome were struck by lightning. According to Suetonius a man called Cassius claimed in a dream that he had been bidden to sacrifice a bull to Jupiter, while both Suetonius and Dio report that the oracle at Antium warned Caligula to beware of Cassius, leading to the recall of Gaius Cassius Longinus, the governor of Asia.[47] Astrologers were naturally on hand to foretell the event. Suetonius reports that a certain Sulla informed Caligula that his inevitable death was near, and Dio reports that Apollonius 'of Egypt' foretold the death of the emperor to his fellow countrymen, and was supposedly brought before Caligula on the very day of his death, surviving only because his punishment was postponed.[48]

As the fateful day approached there was no abatement in the ominous signs. The statue of Jupiter at Olympia, which Caligula had ordered Memmius to transport to Rome, was said to have burst out in a peal of laughter and the workmen trying to dismantle it took to their heels. On the eve of his death Caligula himself dreamt that he was in heaven beside the throne of Jupiter and that the god struck him with the toe of his right foot and hurled him to earth. By the time the actual day had arrived the portents were flying thick and fast. The very plays presented at the Palatine games were seen as portentous. The dancer Mnester presented the Cinyras, in which the hero and his daughter are slain, the latter for incest, and much blood was shed during the performance. Suetonius claims that the Cinyras had been performed by Neoptolomus during the games where Philip of Macedon was assassinated, and Josephus gilds the lily by asserting that it is 'generally agreed' that Caligula died on the very same day of the year as the murder of Philip.[49] Another presentation was the farce of Catullus, called the Laureolus, in which the chief actor falls while trying to escape and vomits blood. In a farcical reprise after the performance secondary actors (secundarum partium) competed to show their skills, and the stage in the end reeked of blood.

Caligula entered the temporary theatre on the Palatine in the morning when it was already crowded. He was in high spirits and an affable mood. No special seats had been set aside that day and everything was a jumble of confusion, senators and equites, freedmen and slaves, men and women, all of which seems to have amused him. He started the day's procedures with the sacrifice of a flamingo in honour of Augustus, and when he struck the bird the blood spurted out, spattering, depending on the source, either his own toga or that of Publius Nonius Asprenas.[50] After the sacrifice he took his seat, eating and drinking with his companions, the consul Pomponius Secundus at his feet taking his fill of food. Caligula remained in good spirits. Fruit had been dispersed among the spectators, which attracted exotic birds, and afforded much entertainment as the public scrambled to catch the creatures.[51] Among the spectators, behaving, we assume, with more diginity, was the consular Cluvius Rufus, usually identified with the historian of that name. In a famous exchange, he was asked by another consular (otherwise unknown) if he had heard of the planned coup, which led Cluvius to admonish him with the words of Homer, 'Be silent, sir, lest some other of the Achaeans hear the report'.[52] If the story is true (and it may only have been an attempt by Cluvius afterwards to range himself on the side of the angels), it means that knowledge of the conspiracy was widespread enough for it to be the subject of casual gossip in the theatre.

Caligula was in the habit of leaving the show at midday to bathe and have lunch (*prandium*) before returning. The scheme of the conspirators called for him to be attacked in one of the narrow passages that led from the theatre to the palace, where his guard would find it difficult to come to his aid. On the day planned for the assassination, a problem arose. Either because it was the last day of the performances or because of stomach troubles caused by excesses on the previous night, Caligula showed signs of staying on through the lunch hour. Chaerea impatiently made his way to the exit. Vinicianus, feeling that the opportunity might slip from their fingers got up to urge Chaerea, as Josephus puts it, 'to be bold'. At this Caligula tugged at his toga in a friendly manner and asked where he was going, and Vinicianus was obliged to resume his seat for a while. It was apparently Nonius Asprenas (although the reading of the name in Josephus' MSS is far from certain) who finally persuaded Caligula to leave, at the seventh hour, and just in time, according to Josephus, since Chaerea was on the point of abandoning the original plan and of returning to the theatre to take his chances at assassinating Caligula where he sat. As the imperial party left the theatre his uncle Claudius, brother-in-law Marcus Vinicius and friend Valerius Asiaticus were at the front. The crowd was held back- they were told to show the emperor proper respect, but in reality the conspirators wanted to prevent anyone getting close enough to protect him.[53]

Caligula followed behind with an individual whose name is so confused in Josephus' manuscripts that he is unidentifiable (the usual reconstruction is 'Paulus Arruntius'). For some unknown reason he decided on a shorter route to the baths than that taken by his retinue, which happened to be the only one guarded. Once he had left the theatre he entered a narrow passageway, where there were no guards, and he stopped to inspect a group of young performers from the province of Asia. They were going to take part in the show, although their precise role is unclear, either to perform in mysteries to be celebrated by Caligula, or to sing a hymn in his honour, or even to participate in the Pyrrhic dances. Josephus says that they were rehearsing in the actual passageway, although they seem to have chosen a strange spot. Caligula engaged the lads in conversation, and was impressed enough to ask for an immediate performance, which the leader had to decline because he had a chill. It was at this moment that the emperor met his end.[54]

The precise details of Caligula's death have been handed down in different traditions. According to Josephus he behaved in a characteristically mischievous fashion. Chaerea asked for the watchword and Caligula offered him the usual mocking reply, whereupon he slashed the emperor between the neck and shoulder. Chaerea's blow was not a mortal one and as Caligula, groaning in agony, tried to make his escape, he was confronted by Sabinus, who struck him to the ground, whereupon a crowd of assassins set upon him. Suetonius clearly knew of two accounts of his death (*duplex fama*) that differed in their details. One is basically that Chaerea crept up on him as he was speaking to the youths, and stabbed him in the neck, crying out the ritual formula of the sacrifice '*hoc age*', followed by Sabinus, who stabbed him in the chest. The other account has Caligula giving the password 'Jupiter', god of the thunderbolt and sudden destruction, at which Chaerea responded with '*accipe ratum*' (an obscure phrase, perhaps textually currupt and possibly meaning something like 'accept the fulfilment of your vow') and drove his sword through the emperor's jaw.[55]

Whatever the exact circumstances, the sources agree that the first blow was not a mortal one. Yet Caligula stood little chance. Suetonius asserts that in the ensuing *mêlée* he was stabbed no fewer than thirty times, although Josephus is able confidently to identify an Aquila as the individual who struck the fatal blow. Dio's subsequent claim that the assailants ate Caligula's flesh clearly deserves to be treated with caution, but few would quarrel with his closing observation that on this day Caligula received a practical demonstration that he was *not* a god.[56]

The strategy of isolating Caligula from his aides had worked. The only resistance offered was from his litter-bearers, who courageously tried to fight off the assailants with their litter poles, an interesting demonstration that Caligula could command loyalty from at least the humbler members of his staff. The passages back to the theatre were by now blocked by attendants and the members of the bodyguard, so the assassins took another route into the palace, finding refuge in the 'House of Germanicus' one of the individual houses that made up the palace complex. In the confusion Vinicianus was seized, presumably by Praetorians not involved in the plot, and had the good fortune to be hauled before Clemens, who allowed him to leave unharmed.[57] This account, which stresses the great perils to which Vinicianus was supposedly exposed, may cover the reality that he, in fact, sought Clemens' protection at the first sign of danger. Most of the conspirators seem to have escaped by the time Caligula's German bodyguard were able to force their way through to the scene, led by Sabinus, a former Thracian gladiator (to be distinguished from Sabinus, the Praetorian tribune involved in the assassination).[58] When the Germans saw what had happened they were enraged, and sought indiscriminate revenge. Several of the assassins were cut down, as well as some quite innocent bystanders.[59] The first person they set upon and killed was Asprenas. If his toga had indeed been spattered by blood during the sacrifice its presence may have attracted their attention, although it is not clear why he should have stayed near the body.[60] They then attacked Norbanus, who tried to fight back, but stood no chance against the great mob of assailants. An Anteius was also killed, unknown to us, but whose father of the same name had been driven by Caligula into exile and later executed. Josephus tells us that he was caught because he could not resist the pleasure of looking at the emperor's dead body and left it too late to escape.[61] A number of conspirators who succeeded in evading the German guard owed their lives to the ingenuity of a physician called Alcyon. He was obliged to treat some wounded men, and smuggled some of the conspirators out of the passgeway, on the pretext of looking for supplies.[62]

The Germans clearly realized that they had not caught all of the assassins. They guarded the exits to the theatre and a number of them rushed in, carrying the heads of Anteius and others, which they placed on the altar, leading to scenes of utter confusion. It is interesting that Josephus concedes that there was by no means universal joy at the news of the assassination, and that many people were, in fact, stunned by the event. The situation was further confused by conflicting rumours, that Caligula was alive and being tended by his doctors, that he had escaped to the forum and was addressing the people, even that he had made up the story of his death as a test of loyalty. The Germans were finally brought to order, probably because they were persuaded that the anguish of the ordinary people over Caligula's death was genuine.

In the meantime, others were to fall victim to the plotters. Josephus related that the tribune Lupus was despatched to the palace to eliminate Caesonia and her daughter. When he entered, he found Caesonia stretched by her husband's corpse, stained with his blood, with her daughter Drusilla beside her. Caligula's wife died bravely, run through by Lupus' sword, and Drusilla died after her, her head smashed against a wall.[63] The accounts of Caesonia's murder present two serious difficulties. In the

1 The Grand Camée (Bibliothèque Nationale, Paris). The boy at left centre has been identified as Caligula

above **2** Agrippina Major (Archaeological Museum, Istanbul)

above right **3** Gemellus (Museo Archeologico Nazionale, Luni)

right **4** Drusilla (Staatliche Glyptothek, Munich)

5 Caligula (Schloss Fasanerie, Fulda)

top left **6** Caligula (Metropolitan Museum, New York)

left **7** Caligula (J. Paul Getty Museum, Malibu)

above **8** Caligula (Virginia Museum of Fine Arts)

9 *Obv.*: Caligula   *Rev.*: Augustus   **10** *Obv.*: Caligula   *Rev.*: Augustus

11 *Obv.*: Caligula   *Rev.*: Agrippina   **12** *Obv.*: Caligula   *Rev.*: Germanicus

9–13 Aureii and Denarii

13 *Obv.*: Caligula   *Rev.*: SPQR/PP/OB CS

14 Quinarius

Obv.: Caligula   *Rev.*: Victory

15 Sestertius

Obv.: Caligula   *Rev.*: Caligula's Sisters

All coins on this and following pages are reproduced actual size, by courtesy of the British Museum

16 *Obv.*: Caligula   *Rev.*: SPQR/PP/OB CS

17 *Obv.*: Caligula   *Rev.*: Allocutio Cohortis

18 *Obv.*: Seated Pietas   *Rev.*: Temple of Augustus

19 *Obv.*: Agrippina   *Rev.*: Carpentum

16–19 Sestertii

20 *Obv.*: Nero and Drusus

Rev.: SC

21 *Obv.*: Augustus

Rev.: Enthroned Augustus

20–21 Dupondii

22 *Obv.*: Caligula

Rev.: Vesta

23 *Obv.*: Germanicus

Rev.: SC

24 *Obv.*: Marcus Agrippa

Rev.: Neptune

22–24 Asses

Obv: Pileus   *Rev:* RCC   *Obv:* Germanicus   *Rev:* Germanicus/Zeno

25 Quadrans   **26** Didrachm

   27–28 Drachms

Obv: Caligula   *Rev:* Implements   *Obv:* Germanicus   *Rev:* Augustus

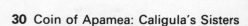

29 Coin of Miletus: unidentified temple

30 Coin of Apamea: Caligula's Sisters

31 Coin of Herod Agrippa: Caesonia

first place, in the narrative of Josephus (the only source to give an indication of its timing), it was not carried out until the evening of the murder, after the senate had called an emergency meeting. Yet it seems almost inconceivable that Caesonia would not have sought to escape, and totally inconceivable that the conspirators would have delayed until the evening and allowed her the opportunity to do so. Another, even more serious, problem is that Lupus was sent by Chaerea to the palace to murder her, yet the palace seems to have been under the control of the Praetorian guard almost immediately after the assassination. The likelihood is that the murder of Caesonia had been decided upon well in advance, to avoid the danger that she might become a focus of resentment and resistance, just as Agrippina and her sons had been in the previous reign, and that it had been planned to follow almost immediately after Caligula's. It will be recalled that the conspirators were said to have escaped 'into the palace'. It had probably been arranged beforehand that Lupus was to kill Caesonia then, and that the account of her body being draped over her dead husband's corpse (not mentioned in Dio or Suetonius) is a poetic elaboration.

Before evening fell Caligula's body was taken to the gardens of the Lamii, the imperial property on the Esquiline hill just outside the city limits. The arrangements were apparently made by his old friend Agrippa, who remained loyal to the end. He went to the Esquiline to take care of the corpse, giving it a hasty cremation and a temporary grave under a light covering of turf. On their return from exile Caligula's sisters are said to have exhumed him to give him a proper cremation and burial. In the literary sources, this became a tradition for autocratic emperors. Nero's remains were supposed to have been similarly deposited by his nurses, Egloge and Alexandria, helped by his mistress Acte; Domitian was cremated by his nurse Phyllis. Caligula's final resting place is unknown. It is unlikely, but not impossible, that his remains were deposited in the Mausoleum of Augustus. Even in death he could not resist mischief. His ghostly apparition was frequently to be seen in the Lamian gardens, until he received a proper burial, and the part of the palace where he died continued to be haunted until it was burnt down, presumably in the devastating Palatine fire in 80.[64]

Appendix 1
The Date of AFA li

The Florentine copy of *AFA* 1i is riddled with errors, and carries no explicit indication of its year. It records a sacrifice for the birthday of Germanicus on May 24, the next ritual mentioned was performed in the Arval cult centre at the shrine of Dia, in the presence of Caligula, as well as Vinicianus and others, some time before 1 June. The grove of Dia lay on the Via Campana some four miles to the west of Rome, outside the city limits, and Caligula's presence there would not contradict Suetonius' claim that he did not enter the city until 30 August. Caligula and Vinicianus were thus present at some ritual between 24 May and 1 June. Vinicianus was not a member in 37, and the Arval record for 38 is extant; the fragment must thus belong to 39 or 40. Now during the ceremonies the magister of the college is absent (his place is taken by the promagister), but his name is recorded, and is seen to end in -ulus. Since the magister for 39 is known to have been Appius Silanus (*AFA* xlviii.3 [Smallwood 7]), the inscription can therefore belong only to the following year, 40. The only member of the college in 40 whose name fits is Memmius Regulus, former husband of Caligula's third wife, who was, of course, absent in his province at this time. On 5 June, or slightly before, there followed a sacrifice for the birthday of someone of prominence related to Caligula, whose name has been erased (OB NATALEM/]C. AUG), but is probably Caesonia (see E. Pasoli, *Acta Fratrum Arvalium* [Bologna 1950] 14, Dabrowski 420-1). For objections to this dating of the fragment: H. Dessau, *Geschichte der römischen Kaiserzeit* (Berlin, 1924-30), 2.1.128 and more recently E.J. Philips, 'The Emperor Gaius' Abortive Invasion of Britain', *Historia* 19 (1970), 371.

Appendix 2
Marcus Cluvius Rufus as a Source for Caligula's Reign

Of the lost contemporary senatorial writers known to have been used by later authors the most likely source of information on Caligula is Marcus Cluvius Rufus. He was supposedly suffect consul under Caligula, and the herald of Nero when that emperor performed as a singer (he accompanied him on his tour of Greece). He was also legate of Hispania Tarraconensis under Galba and afterwards was prominent under Vitellius (Tac. *Hist.* 1.8.1; Suet. *Nero* 21.2; Dio 62.14.3) References by later authors to Cluvius' work all relate to the reign of Nero. He was Tacitus' source for the information that the loyalty of Burrus towards Nero was not in doubt, and that Agrippina was responsible for the attempt at incest with Nero (Tac. *Ann.* 13.20.3, 14.2.4; Pliny *Ep.* 9.19.5.) In his account of the assassination of Caligula, Josephus reports, as the manuscripts read, that a 'Clauiton' of consular rank (the emendation 'Cluvius' is generally accepted) during the Palatine Games reproved a certain 'Bathybius' (Vatinius?), for talking openly about the plot, with a (mis)quotation of Homer. (Jos. *AJ* 19.92). Th. Mommsen, 'Cornelius Tacitus und Cluvius Rufus', *Hermes* 4 (1870), 322 suggested on the basis of this incident that the source of Josephus' account of the assassination was the historian Cluvius, since the anecdote must have come from Cluvius' own writings. M.P. Charlesworth, 'The Tradition about Caligula' *CHJ* 4 (1933), 105-19 (see Syme, *Tacitus,* 287) added weight to the suggestion by noting that the highly rhetorical and metaphorical style of Josephus' account of

Caligula's death is untypical of him, and must be based on a Latin original. Momigliano, *Osservazioni*, 305 has gone even further, and identifies Cluvius as the source of Suetonius and Dio also. G.B. Townend, who believes that Cluvius was embarrassed by his involvement with Nero and tried to show his independence by writing a 'farrago of scandals and lampoons', suggests that he was used only for subsidiary information ('The Sources of the Greek in Suetonius', *Hermes* 88 [1960], 99-100, and 'Traces in Dio Cassius of Cluvius, Aufidius, and Pliny', *Hermes* [1961], 230-32, 248). But we must be cautious. As Syme has pointed out, there is no certainty that the histories of Cluvius included Caligula (Syme, *Tacitus*, 179, 287, 293); Syme suggests Servilius Nonianus as a source for Josephus. For further cautions see W. Steidle, *Sueton und die Antike Biographie* (Munich, 1951) 77-8,; L.H. Feldman, 'The Sources of Josephus' 'Antiquities' Book 19', *Latomus* 21 (1962), 320-33; Balsdon, 227–8. Indeed, we can not even be sure that the Cluvius present at the Ludi Palatini on the day of the assassination is identical with the historian. Groag *PIR*² C 1202 suggests that he may have been his father. Clearly, however, if Cluvius was a source for Caligula's reign he would have been a hostile one. He must have been aware of the plot, or, at the very least, have wanted to pretend to his readers that he was somehow involved in it.

Appendix 3
The Date and Location of Caligula's Death
(See also Chapter 13)

The evidence for the date and place of Caligula's death is very confused. All the main sources (Jos. *AJ* 19. 77; Suet. *Cal.* 56.2; Dio 59.29.5) agree that the event took place during the *Ludi Palatini*. Dio 56. 46. 5 says these games had been established after the death of Augustus by Livia, who held a private festival (*idian...panegyrin*) lasting for three days, a festival celebrated also by subsequent emperors. The fourth-century calendar of Philocalus and the fifth-century calendar of Silvius indicate that the *Ludi Palatini* began on January 17 (*Inscr. Ital.* 13. 2. 239, 264). 17 January was a significant day, since it was the anniversary of Augustus' marriage to Livia. It is therefore reasonable to conclude that it was Livia who established the 17 January date. By the time of Philocalus the games lasted for six days, but we do not know when the length was first extended.

Jos. *AJ* 19. 77 says that the original plan called for an assassination on the first day of the festival, but when the three statutory days of the games had passed [the manuscripts are very corrupt] the deed was carried out on 'the last'. Dio 59.29.5-6 says that the conspirators restrained themselves for five days. But when Caligula decided to participate in the performances and announced a three day extension they could stand it no longer and acted at once. This last detail must be for dramatic effect. Chaerea would be able to strike only on the specific day when his cohort assumed guard duty, or gave it up to his relief. Suet. *Cal.* 54.2 says that on the day of his death Caligula ordered a *pervigilium* (an 'all night' performance) to take the opportunity to appear on the stage. Suet. *Cal.* 58. 1 states that the assassination took place at the seventh hour *VIIII Kal. Febr.* (January 24). Manuscript variants give the date as 25 or 26 January).

Clearly Caligula decided to extend the festival in 41, but the precise nature of the extension is confused in the sources. Dio seems to suggest an extra three days, in which case the assassination would have taken place on the 22 January. The situation is even further confused by Josephus' comment that the choir of boys was still rehearsing but not planning to go on that day because the leader had a chill, suggesting that there was at least one more day. Perhaps the reference is to the *pervigilium*, which might have been intended to go beyond the three extra days already decreed. It is difficult to defend Suetonius' 24 January (or either of the variants) unless the festival was already six days long in 41, and Caligula extended it even further on this particular occasion.

Suetonius' 'seventh hour' is probably fairly accurate. The assassination took place as Caligula was asked for the watchword. The praetorian guard changed every twenty-four hours at about the eighth hour, when a new cohort would take its place as guard, and the tribune received the watchword from the princeps (Mart. 10.48.1–2; Suet. *Nero* 8).

Josephus' description of the arrangements for the games is one of the most confused of his whole narrative and rendered even more incomprehensible by textual corruption. It has so far eluded coherent explanation. A temporary theatre was set up each year for the shows. Josephus seems to suggest, among other things, that it had two entrances, one leading *eis aithrion* (into the open air, or into an open space or courtyard), the other leading into a portico, with entrances and exits, so that those inside would not be disturbed. The stage building itself had its own complex system of exits. What does seem to emerge from this garbled account is the notion that somehow access to the seats was available from a portico, arranged in such a way that the spectators would not be disturbed. A clue might be provided by the actions of Caligula himself. According to Josephus he sacrificed to Augustus, then turned to the show and took his seat in the right 'wing' (*keras*). The most likely place on the Palatine for the sacrifice would have been at the altar before the Temple of Apollo, and if Josephus is correct it took place in the vicinity of the performances. It was presumbly on this altar that the German guard deposited the heads of the suspected assasins. The area south of the Temple was of course occupied by the famous portico of the Danaids, the most suitable candidate for the portico of Josephus' account, and large enough to accommodate the great number of spectators present (p. 205).

When Caligula left the theatre, if he had entered the area occupied by the later Domus Tiberiana he would have done so through the house of Augustus. The symbolism of his death occurring in that part of the Palatine would have been dramatic. Since none of the sources mentions it, however, it is perhaps more likely that he went to the part of the residence later occupied by the Flavian palace, and therefore would have left the theatre through the east range of the portico of the Danaids. The strong possibility that Claudius was found afterwards in that part of the palace adds weight to the notion (p. 173).

· 11 ·
AFTERMATH

WITH THE DEATH of Caligula the senators could enjoy a brief moment of euphoria. Once again, for the first time in living memory they felt about to be called upon to play the great role that had been theirs during the Republic, answerable in a vague sense to the Roman people, but at the whim and mercy of no single individual. They were convened on the Capitol by the consuls. This had happened also after the deaths of Augustus and Tiberius, but on this occasion the consuls' role was seen as more than a mere formality, but almost a declaration of newly regained independence.[1] The consuls also took the precaution of transferring funds from the treasuries (presumably the Aerarium Saturni in the Temple of Saturn in the forum) to the Capitol, and set guards over them.[2] The senators seem to have been full of confidence.[3] A decree charging Caligula with unspecified crimes was passed, and there were even demands that all the Caesars be condemned to *damnatio memoriae* and their temples destroyed. There was, of course, an element of self-interest in the apparent senatorial idealism. They no doubt appreciated that the ending of the imperial system would, in fact, lead to a restoration of their own powers and privileges, a development foreseen also by the Praetorians and the people. Josephus comments that the kind of government they would have instituted was an 'aristocracy, as the government of old had been,' and notes that they met in a spirit of excessive arrogance, as if power already lay within their hands.

While the senators were congratulating themselves, the ordinary people were expressing their anger. As was soon to become apparent, there was considerable distress over the death of Caligula and a distinct lack of enthusiasm for the idea of a return to the republican system and to the privileges of the old nobility.[4] A noisy meeting took place in the forum, with angry demands from the crowd for the identity of the assassins, and the tension was increased by disorderly soldiers roaming about.[5]

The key to the future, however, lay neither with the senate nor the people, but with the Praetorian guard. The precise course of events from this point is far from certain, as we have to rely on Josephus' detailed but often jumbled account, which seems to be an inconsistent pastiche of two different versions. In the first version the Praetorians had a coherent plan of action from the outset. After the murder they gathered together to work out what steps to take to maintain their privileged position. Convinced that the principate would be retained in some form or other, they were determined that it fall to a candidate of their own choosing. Only one name seems to have been considered, Caligula's uncle Claudius, who as son of Drusus and brother of Germanicus would have enjoyed the prestige of a distinguished family name, and they went to the palace to seek him. But in his description of the actual events at the palace, Josephus clearly used a different source, one followed in the main also by Suetonius and Dio, that implied that the Praetorian action was much more spontaneous, even accidental. The earlier plan of the Praetorians is now forgotten.[6] We are told that after the murder, Claudius fled in panic to the palace, where he hid himself in an alcove of a room called by Suetonius the *Hermaeum* ('chamber sacred to Hermes'). This use of the Greek name 'Hermes' for a sanctuary dedicated to the Roman Mercury is very unusual, and the room may have been named after the *Hermata* found in Egypt, at Hermopolis or Alexandria, dedicated to Hermes-Thoth. It could be that Claudius was hiding in the *Aula Isiaca*, the room decorated with mythical Egyptian (but not necessarily Isiac) motifs in the east wing of the original palace complex, and later incorporated into the Flavian palace (p. 221).[7] He was found there by one of the soldiers, named by Josephus as Gratus. Claudius apparently thought at first that he was about to be put to death for killing Caligula. Nothing could have been further from the truth. Gratus, we are led to believe, had the brainwave of persuading his fellow soldiers to acclaim Caligula's uncle as emperor. They then led the much-relieved Claudius out of the palace, to the large area open to the public on the north of the Germalus, the Area Palatini. Bystanders who saw the incident misread it, and thought that Claudius was being taken off to his death. Misleading reports of this incident may well have reached the senators, and could account for their overconfidence during the latter part of this first day.[8] In Josephus' second version it was not until this point that the Praetorians as a body determined to make Claudius emperor, influenced by the still powerful force of Germanicus' name and the patent ambition of some of the powerful senators. Above all, there was the fear that even if the imperial system continued, someone might seize power independently of them. Convinced by their own logic, the Praetorians took Claudius off to their camp at the Porta Viminalis. This second version is reflected also in the accounts of both Suetonius and Dio, who stress the chance discovery of Claudius by Praetorians who simply happened to be in the palace, prowling about or seeking plunder.[9] As Suetonius puts it, Claudius became emperor *mirabili casu*, 'by an astonishing accident'.

Whichever is the true version of events on the Palatine, the aftermath is clear enough. Once Claudius was secure in their camp, they acclaimed him as emperor. Reports of this began to reach the senate, where the consul Saturninus advised a firm line against Claudius, and delivered a lengthy speech, praising Chaerea and extolling the notion of liberty.[10] Again, it was liberty in a limited sense, since he seems to have been mainly concerned with the suffering of the nobility, and spoke of the history of threats to *to gennaion* (the nobility).[11] It is hard to believe that Saturninus, whose family had done so well under the principate, was moved by the republican ideals described so glowingly by Josephus, who adds two anecdotes that might confirm our scepticism. During the course of his speech it was noticed that Saturninus was still wearing a signet ring with the image of Caligula; Trebellius Maximus rose, tore it from his finger and smashed it to the ground. More seriously, Josephus admits that despite his public posture and pretence of unwillingness, Saturninus was really a candidate for the principate himself!

In the meantime Claudius received a new visitor. Herod Agrippa had initially gone to the Esquiline to tend to the body of Caligula. From there he made his way to the nearby praetorian camp at the Porta Viminalis. Agrippa had a keen political eye, and appreciated at once the strength of Claudius' position. Characteristically, he had no hesitation in enlisting himself firmly on what he saw as the winning side.[12] He urged Claudius to stand firm, then went on to the senate, pretending to arrive casually from a banquet (suggesting that the meeting of the senate was probably taking place on the evening of the assassination). Once there he sought to impress upon the members the hopelessness of trying to take a military stand against Claudius and the powerful Praetorians.

A compromise was eventually arranged, that Agrippa would accompany a deputation of 'men of lofty character', to try to reason with Claudius.[13] By now night had fallen. Josephus relates that when Chaerea asked for the watchword and the consuls gave the reply of '*Libertas*' the symbolism was not lost on the spectators, who realized that the watchword had at last passed back to the consuls a century after their liberty had been lost (dating this event to 59 BC, the first consulship of Julius Caesar).[14]

Despite their apparent bravado the senators must have realized their impotence. Next day, when they reconvened, a mere one hundred turned up. They now accepted that the imperial system could not be abolished, and in an air of unreality proceeded to debate who would be the best candidate, wasting further time on fruitless bickering. As noted earlier the consul Saturninus was one man who made a bid. There were at least two other candidates, Marcus Vinicius, the husband of Livilla, who was discouraged by the consuls, and Valerius Asiaticus whose candidacy was blocked by Vinicianus. We have no idea what role, if any, Vinicius might have played in the assassination. As noted earlier, despite the apparent involvement of his wife in the conspiracy of 39, his name is nowhere associated with the events of that year. His marriage connection would make him an appropriate candidate, but he had a reputation for being amiable and unambitious, and his apparent lack of drive might explain why the consuls deemed him unsuitable (one of them, of course, had ambitions of his own). Asiaticus had addressed the people immediately after Caligula's death, and his ambiguous assertion that he wished that he could claim to be the assassin might have been an attempt to play a double game, evading responsibility before the people but seeking to establish his credentials before the senate (and history). The reason for Vinicianus' opposition to Asiaticus is not clear. The general scholarly view is that he had entertained his own personal ambitions at the outset, but felt the need to hold back for appearances' sake. But by this time he may well have felt that events had overtaken him, and having allowed the opportunity to slip from his own hands could not bear to see another candidate succeed.[15] It may be, however, that he had decided to throw his support behind his relative Vinicius, and indeed one reading of Josephus' manuscripts (so corrupt at this point that lengthy speculation is fruitless) would have Vinicianus supporting Vinicius against the consular opposition.[16] It is difficult to assess Suetonius' claim that Galba, the future emperor, was urged to make a bid but expressed a preference for the quiet life. He would, presumably, have been in Germany, and could have received news of the assassination only after Claudius had become firmly established.[17]

The senatorial deliberations were in fact pointless, and the deputation sent to Claudius failed utterly in its original purpose. Immediately on their arrival they would have seen the enormous military advantage that Claudius enjoyed over the senate. Any hope of bluffing him was negated by Agrippa who advised his old friend of the disunity and weakness of his opposition. On coming into Claudius' presence, according to Josephus, they fell on their knees before him. Claudius had taken concrete measures to strengthen his position among the Praetorians. He administered an oath of loyalty to the troops, made more attractive, no doubt, by an enormous donative, 15,000 or 20,000 sesterces, depending on the source, but a massive amount in any case, and a proportionate amount for each officer. Similar sums were apparently promised for the legions.[18] Although Suetonius claims that Claudius established a precedent in fostering the loyalty of the soldiers by bribes, this is true only in a narrow technical sense. In essence Caligula had made the same gesture when on the death of Tiberius he added to the sum bequeathed to the troops an equal sum from his own funds. That Augustus and Tiberius had left money for the soldiers in their wills in not strictly relevant; what was significant was that Caligula had provided money in anticipation of future services, and it might even be argued that his father Germanicus had shown the lead in using the money under his personal control in Germany to bribe the mutineers after the death of Augustus. Claudius may have taken another measure at this time to strengthen his position, by the appointment of Rufrius Pollio, and possibly Catonius Iustus, as Prefects of the guard.[19] All of this would have had an unsettling effect on the senators, not helped by the shouts of the people outside the house calling for the retention of the principate, and even calling for Claudius by name. Despite the urgent pleas of Chaerea, the remaining soldiers abandoned the cause and drifted over to join the Praetorians. The senators then began to quarrel and to blame one another for the calamity. They also began to move over to Claudius. When Quintus Pomponius Secundus, Saturninus' colleague in the consulship went to his side, it marked the end of any serious opposition.[20] Claudius was escorted to the Palatine, and the remaining senators summoned before him (he did not attend a formal senate meeting for thirty days). The speed and thoroughness with which the resistance had collapsed is illustrated by the apparent ease with which he persuaded them to condemn the hapless Chaerea. For all the praise that had been heaped on him, no one seems to have spoken on his behalf when his fate was put to the vote. He was condemned, and forced to commit suicide, which he did bravely. Claudius recognized that he owed his own elevation in no small degree to Chaerea, but also saw the danger in the precedent of regicide. Others died with him, but the only one identified is Lupus.[21] Surprisingly, Chaerea's fellow tribune Sabinus was neither charged nor dismissed from his office, although he committed suicide not long after. Others involved were pardoned, and some reputedly even attained high office.

Claudius succeeded in taking power within twenty four hours of his nephew's death, in an operation that was so remarkably smooth that it provokes quesions about the possible role of Claudius himself, or at least of those around him. Although none of the sources speaks of his direct involvement, Josephus does reflect a tradition that his rise to power did come about through a cohesive plan, at least in the immediate aftermath of the assassination. Could this plan also have preceded the assassination? The supposedly chance discovery of Claudius in the Palace could well have been deliberately arranged, as Josephus' alternative source seems to suggest. If we apply an appropriate scepticism to Josephus' notion that the participants were motivated by the ideals of liberty, we must wonder why several tribunes and at least one Prefect of the Praetorian guard should have become involved in a plot to restore a system that would have reduced their own privileges. Even more baffling is the conduct of Callistus. As an imperial freedman he would hardly have hoped to benefit under a restored republic, and his switching of allegiance to Claudius, whom he saw as Caligula's successor, betrays a foresight that is, literally, incredible. In a later context Tacitus refers tantalisingly to an earlier reference (now lost) that implies that Callistus played an important role in Caligula's murder. He was certainly well rewarded by Caligula's successor. He became a *libellis* to Claudius, and went on to become even richer than before. Pliny comments that the four small onyx columns erected by Cornelius Balbus in his theatre caused a sensation, but that he had personally seen no fewer than thirty columns of the same material, and large ones at that, in Callistus' dining room.[22]

The plot was a complex one involving many individuals acting in some cases out of idealism, in others out of self-interest. But there may have been at its centre a small group who had a clear idea of where events should lead, and who were happy to exploit and manipulate others, like Chaerea, to their own ends. The Praetorian guard and the imperial freedmen would not have served their self-interest by abolishing the principate. They might, however, have seen the merit of removing a specific princeps whose behaviour threatened to discredit the whole institution, and of replacing him by a more suitable incumbent. Claudius may or may not himself have been a party to such a plot from the outset, but he would in any case have been anxious to prevent any general knowledge about it afterwards, and to foster the notion that the principate came to him only by an accidental twist of fate.[23]

A serious decision facing Claudius on his accession was the official attitude to be adopted towards his predecessor. The resentment felt by the nobility towards Caligula would take time to abate, and he clearly needed to be sensitive to the strength of their feelings. The books of the freedman Protogenes, along with the papers that Caligula pretended he had burnt but had kept in the palace, were destroyed, and Protogenes himself was put to death. Poisons that had been stored in the palace were also destroyed. Caligula's *acta* were rescinded, and his name, like that of Tiberius, was taken from the lists of emperors mentioned in oaths and prayers.[24]

Yet Claudius was prepared to go only so far. When the senate attempted to declare Caligula a *hostis* and to subject him to an official *damnatio memoriae*, as they would do later to Nero, Claudius blocked the attempt.[25] His reasons would have been twofold. It would clearly have been dangerous to condone an act of regicide, which might have provided a precedent for malcontents during his own reign. Moreover, Claudius had to keep in mind the feelings of ordinary people. Caligula had enjoyed considerable popular support and the newly established emperor would hardly have wished overtly to risk alienating a large segment of the population. Thus there was no official *damnatio memoriae*. But on the other side of the delicate balance Claudius needed to show that Caligula's assassination came about largely as the result of his own shortcomings, not because the office of princeps deserved to be eliminated. Apart from this, Claudius seems himself to have been subjected to a certain amount of personal humiliation by Caligula towards the end of the reign. This helps to explain why he set out on a subtle campaign of denigrating his predecessor, a campaign that would continue throughout his reign.[26] Thus the inscription recording the repair by Claudius of an arch of the Aqua Virgo makes the point that it had been damaged by Caligula. He seems to have removed Caligula's name as the dedicator of the repaired Theatre of Pompey, and to have taken the credit for Caligula's victories in Mauretania.[27] This 'smear' campaign began soon after Caligula's death, when, on his own initiative (as distinct from a senatorial decree), Claudius ordered that the statues of Caligula, over which the senate had ironically at one stage set a guard, be demolished stealthily at night. A similar fate would be meted out to the statues of Nero's wife Poppaea and his mother Agrippina after their deaths, but significantly in Caligula's case it could not be carried out in the open.[28]

It is interesting to note that the head of the fine togate statue of Caligula now in Virginia seems to have been removed by deliberate chiselling.[29] The sculpted bodies could, of course, be recycled as other Romans, and one of of the statues from the shrine at Velleia seems to be made up of the head of Claudius on the body of Caligula. A small bronze bust in private possession which Jucker has identified as Caligulan shows signs of deliberate disfigurement. Its eyes were hacked out and the face mutilated by a metal object on the nose and lips. It was then thrown into the Tiber.[30] There are some inscriptions where Caligula's name has been erased, but they are not numerous enough to prove anything beyond local spontaenous action. Within Italy they are found in Milan, Bologna, Pompeii, from the rest of the empire in Dalmatia, Africa, Egypt, Asia (Samos).[31]

Perhaps the most intriguing issue is Claudius' treatment of his predecessor's coinage. In the context of the honours paid to Claudius for his victory over Britain in 43, two years after the assassination, Dio states that the senate, in hatred of the memory of Caligula, decreed that all the bronze coinage bearing his image should be melted down. The bronze was supposed to have been converted to no better purpose since Messalina used it to make statues of the actor Mnester to reward him for satisfying her lust.[32] It is curious that if such a measure was enacted it should have been postponed for two years. Of course since Claudius took power quickly such a measure might have been difficult to implement at the very beginning of the reign because it might have led to a currency shortage, and Caligulan bronzes would have had to remain in circulation. D. Nony has even shown that in Gaul local mints may have continued after 41 to issue bronze asses with a portrait of Caligula rather than Claudius, perhaps to 43, when the demonetization might have been ordered.[33]

Wholesale demonetization of Caligula's aes coinage seems implausible, but not impossible.[34] Scholars often cite in this context Statius, who, writing towards the end of the century, describes an article bought very cheaply *plus minus asse Gaiano* ('for about a Caligulan as').[35] This abusive phrase might at first sight suggest that the Caligulan as had been debased, but there is no evidence of any decline in aes standard in Caligula's coinage; there may in fact have been a slight improvement.[36] But the Statius passage need not consequently indicate out and out demonetization. To emphasize the cheapness of certain second hand books bought as a gift, costing only an as, Statius wants simply to show how despicably low an amount the as represents. 'Gaian' may thus be merely a generally pejorative term.

The argument for demonetization has received some support from the scarcity of coins in hoards with Caligula's image, even though contemporary coins of Germanicus, Agrippina and Agrippa are numerous enough. The Pozzarello hoard, near Bolsena, for instance contains 719 copper and orichalcum coins from the Republic to Nerva, but no aes of Caligula in any denomination.[37] The scarcity is not, however, confined to bronze (casting doubt on the Messalina story, if doubt be needed). It applies also to precious metals. Three hoards from various areas of the empire illustrate this. At Bredgar, in Kent, which Carson dates to 43 and associates with the Claudian invasion, the aurei number Tiberius 19, Claudius 4, Caligula 0.[38] The hoard of aurei discovered in 1976 in Patras Greece, dated after 47 revealed Tiberius 22, Caligula 2, Claudius 11.[39] A hoard from Pudukota in India, probably Flavian, shows Tiberius 169, Claudius 152, Caligula 14.[40] The evidence is far from simple however. The coin list from the early conquest fort at Hod Hill in Dorset shows a marked preponderance of Caligulan 'Vesta' dupondii relative to the issues of other reigns. The fort does, of course, have a very brief period of occupation, and the contrast with Bredgar might be explained by the longer time it would take to demonetize aes coinage.[41]

Countermarks common on other reigns occur rarely on Caligulan coins. The mark NCAPR attributed to the mid-years of Nero and found on sestertii from the beginning of Tiberius' reign until Claudius, is never found on bronzes with the head of Caligula. The inference might be that many of the sestertii of Caligula had been withdrawn by the time the countermark was applied. There were exceptions. There is, for instance, a group of Caligula's Vesta asses with the countermark TICA (Tiberius Claudius Augustus) employed in such a way to obliterate the *praenomen* and *nomen* C [ie. Gaius] *Caesar*. It has been suggested that this was done in Gaul for the use of soldiers on the Rhine, where Claudius would have felt the need to assert his authority.[42] There are also coins where whole Claudian types have been overstruck on Caligulan. Thus we find a restriking of Caligula's asses with the Pallas type of Claudius (BMC 140) on Caligulan asses (BMC 45)[43] Whether the mint of Rome was engaged in such overstriking, or whether it involved only the local imitations is uncertain, and the value of these pieces as evidence for demonetization is dubious, since Giard observes that Tiberian coins were also overstruck, sometimes by Caligulan types![44] At a much simpler level there exist several coins that manifest attempts to deface Caligula's image with a chisel. There is also a relatively high proportion of Caligulan coins where individual letters from the name have been removed (such as the C standing for the praenomen Gaius), as a means of obliterating his identity.[45]

There is no clear consensus on whether an actual demonetization was carried out. That such a policy can not be considered totally unfeasible is suggested by the decision of Vitellius not to demonetize the coinage of his immediate predecessors.[46] While an immediate and wholesale recall would hardly be a practical proposition, it may be that after a couple of years, when feelings had grown less intense, Caligulan coins were routinely melted down and restruck as they came into official hands, particularly in the military zones, in a gradual process.

History has been unkind to Caligula largely because he deserves to be thus treated. But there can be little doubt that his successor, probably for personal rather than political reasons, was determined, by both overt and subtle means, to suppress any lingering trace of kind memory that Caligula might have enjoyed. The treatment that Claudius seems to have meted out to the physical reminders of Caligula gives us some idea of the impact that the new emperor might have had on the written record.

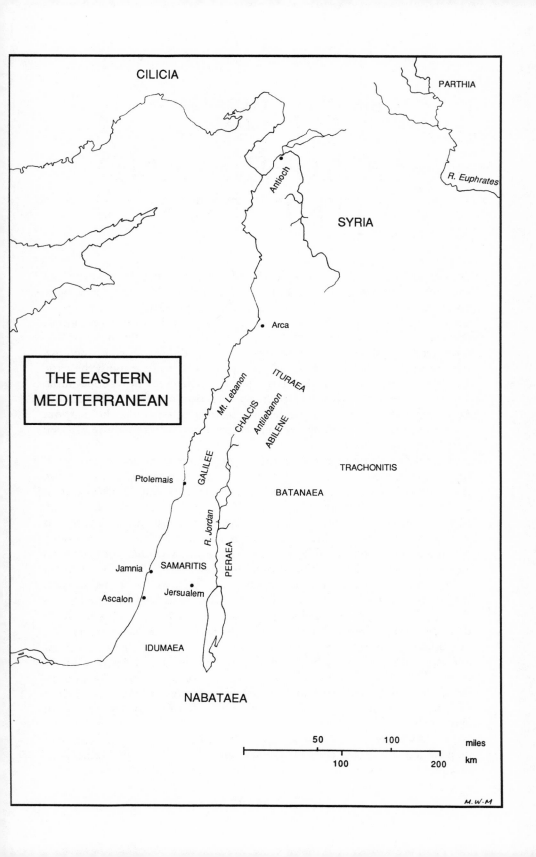

CILICIA

PARTHIA

R. Euphrates

Antioch

SYRIA

Arca

THE EASTERN
MEDITERRANEAN

ITURAEA

Mt. Lebanon

CHALCIS

Antilebanon

ABILENE

TRACHONITIS

GALILEE

Ptolemais

BATANAEA

R. Jordan

PERAEA

Jamnia

SAMARITIS

Ascalon

Jersualem

IDUMAEA

NABATAEA

50   100   miles

100   200   km

M.W.M

· 12 ·

CALIGULA AND
THE JEWS

IT WAS DURING Caligula's reign that the relations between Rome and
the Jews reached their first serious crisis. The difficulties that arose were
complex, involving two different branches of Judaism. There were, on
the one hand, those Jews who continued to live in the original region of
Jewish settlement, loosely referred to as Judaea, with its main city of
Jerusalem. There were also, presenting a wholly different set of problems,
the Jews of the diaspora, the result of a process that began with the exile
and the subsequent creation of large Jewish settlements in Mesopotamia.
There had been periods of emigration since, most notably the influx into
Egypt after the time of Alexander. By the age of Caligula, the diaspora
Jews were scatttered among the various provinces of the empire, as well
as in Rome and Italy.

Although there had been occasional earlier contacts, it was not until
the mid-first century BC, and Pompey's eastern campaigns, that the
Romans began to deal with Jews as a national group. Judaea at first
remained a client-kingdom ruled by King Herod. On Herod's death,
probably in 4 BC, his son Archelaus succeeded him in Judaea proper, as
well as in Samaria and Idumea, as 'ethnarch', a title deemed preferable
by Augustus to Herod's title of 'king.' Herod's two other sons, Antipas
and Philip, succeeded to lesser domains, as tetrarchs. Archelaus proved
an incompetent ruler, and in reponse to the appeals of his subjects
Augustus banished him to Gaul in AD 6, and organized his territory as
the province of Judaea, under an equestrian procurator, answerable to
the governor in Syria. When Philip died in 33 or 34 his territory was
put under the administration of the legate of Syria, with the revenues
kept separate, and was subsequently bestowed on Herod Agrippa in 37.
Agrippa thus acquired a kingdom made up of Auranitis, Trachonitis,
Batanaea and Paneas, and may also have acquired Abilene, a portion
of Ituraea east of Antilebanon, which was still ruled by Lysanias until
about 27.[1]

Herod's other son, Antipas, reputedly called a 'fox' by Christ, was
bequeathed the tetrarchy of Galilee and Peraea by his father, an
arrangement subsequently confirmed by Augustus. With his brothers he

had been brought up in Rome, and became a good friend of Tiberius, later naming the city of Tiberias after him.[2] He was married, probably for diplomatic reasons, to the daughter of Aretas, king of Nabataea, the wild area south of Judaea. Some time before 30 he fell in love with Herodias, sister of Herod-Agrippa, and in order to marry her discarded his wife, who fled to her father.[3] This would have aggravated an already tense situation, and the military clash between Antipas and Aretas that followed some years later over a border dispute was probably inevitable.[4]

Tiberius instructed Vitellius, the governor of Syria, to go to the assistance of his old boyhood friend Antipas. When he received news of Tiberius' death, Vitellius broke off his preparations, possibly on his own initiative. Caligula would clearly not have been enthusiastic about the notion of going to war against a king who was an old friend of his father Germanicus.[5] There was, indeed, a change of policy. Support for Herod Antipas was withdrawn. Also, it is interesting to note that from the end of Tiberius' reign to the beginning of Nero's the municipal coinage of Damascus in Syria ceases, and that during Caligula's reign there was an ethnarch of Aretas in the city. It is he who supposedly set a guard at the gate to arrest St. Paul.[6] This is sometimes taken to indicate that Damascus was in this period under Nabataean control, and might indicate an award of territory by Caligula to Aretas.[7]

Antipas' connection with Herodias was to cause him yet further problems. At his wife's urging he had helped her brother Agrippa with his financial problems. The help was apparently rather grudging, and Antipas made the mistake on one occasion of casting Agrippa's destitution in his teeth when they were in their cups. When Agrippa's fortune improved under Caligula the success of their former dependent must have incited the envy of Herodias and Antipas, who went to Italy, probably in the summer of 40, to request that he be made king instead of merely tetrarch.[8] Agrippa had not forgotten his earlier humiliation, and, to thwart the plan, intimated to Caligula that Antipas had been plotting against him, and had built up an arsenal of supplies for 70,000 soldiers.[9] Caligula believed his old friend and banished Antipas, probably to Lyons, although it is difficult to imagine the two of them spending the winter of 39/40 together in the same town.[10] Herodias was spared (presumably out of regard for Agrippa) but nobly chose to share her husband's exile. Agrippa, as often, came out the winner, and was rewarded with Antipas' personal property and his tetrarchy.

In dealing with individual Jewish rulers Caligula could claim a degree of success. The problems presented by the Jewish people as a whole proved much more intractable. Many of the communities of diaspora Jews, of course, had come within the Roman orbit before the time of Herod and his sons. The main problem that they presented was the ill-will between their various communities and often hostile neighbours.

The rigidity of the Jewish faith tended to create local friction and unpopularity, since contrary to the general trend of Greco-Roman religions, they refused to recognize the validity of any god other than their own. This was not, of course, of primary concern to their Roman rulers. While the Romans considered Judaism a superstition, they did not regard it as a political threat and were prepared to tolerate it, and even to protect Jewish rights.

To the extent that there was anti-semitism among the Romans before Caligula, it generally took the form of fairly good-natured mockery of what were considered their outlandish religious views. There is no evidence of serious anti-semitic outbursts under Augustus or Tiberius. When Germanicus made his distribution of grain in Alexandria the Jews were not allowed to share in it, but that was because they were not citizens, and Josephus is at pains to stress that it was not a provocative exclusion.[11] Philo speaks of Sejanus' hatred of the Jews and his plan to attack them throughout the empire. But there is only one serious move against them recorded in Tiberius' reign. Suetonius, Josephus and Tacitus tell of the expulsion of the Jews from Rome, and the use of 4,000 Jewish men of military age who were conscripted to go to Sardinia to fight brigands.[12] Only Josephus mentions any reason — financial corruption among individual Jews, involving Romans close to Tiberius, and Smallwood suggests that proselytism from the ranks of the Roman upper classes may have caused the problems. The expulsion seems to have been restricted to Rome and is mentioned by all three sources in the context of actions against the worship of Isis, Suetonius adding the banishment of astrologers. It does not seem to have been a narrowly anti-semitic action as such.[13]

Serious antisemitism was in fact a prejudice not of the Romans, but more typically of the Greeks, and its most serious manifestations seem to have been in Alexandria. The association between the Jews and Egyptians was a very ancient one, going back to the second millenium and the period of the captivity, and there had been a sizeable Jewish community in Egypt since at least the early sixth century BC. The arrival of the Ptolemies and the foundation of Alexandria, with its enormous commercial potential, encouraged extensive Jewish immigration from the third century on. The Jews seem to have enjoyed the favour of the Ptolemies, being especially prominent in the army, which may account for the undercurrent of hostility noticeable in Alexandrian literature from as early as the third century BC. The annexation of Egypt after the battle of Actium aggravated this situation. The Greeks felt offended that their proud and independent kingdom, with its illustrious capital of Alexandria, had come to an end, to be replaced by foreign domination.[14] There remained a hostility towards the alien ruler, and while in the main it expressed itself in merely passive contempt, there also grew up a great tradition of Alexandrian martyrdom, hallowing the memory of those who died in active opposition to the Romans. This could not fail to affect the Jews also. As H.I. Bell observed, anti-Jewish feeling grew among the Greeks because it offered a 'safer and less direct way of attacking the authority of Rome'.[15] The Jews for their part must have welcomed the arrival of the Romans, and with it a degree of protection. Indeed, after the annexation, Augustus had erected in Alexandria a bronze stele to announce the safeguarding of Jewish political and religious rights.[16]

The situation was complicated by the legal status of the Jews within the city of Alexandria, the precise details of which are hotly disputed by scholars. Jews living in the city at the time of the Roman conquest do not appear to have held Alexandrian citizenship as a community, although some may have managed to acquire it as individuals. The Jews had their own independent citizen body, or politeuma, with their own ethnarch (until that position was eliminated by Augustus), their own council of elders, their own assembly, and even their own courts for dealing with cases that involved only Jewish law. They were thus able to enjoy the benefits of civic life without being forced to become part of the gentile community, with the inevitable religious tensions. This arrangment was apparently complicated by the attempts of individual jews to acquire Alexandrian citizenship, and with it certain coveted privileges such as exemption from the *laographia*, a capitation tax introduced by Augustus from which Greek citizens of Alexandria were exempt.

Apart from a riot in 29 BC there were no serious disturbances in Alexandria until Caligula's reign, by which time the tensions had become severe. Our main source for the events is Philo, and as valuable as he is, it must always be borne in mind that he was a spokesman for the Jews, and would not have felt the modern historian's obligations to objectivity. It is clear that anti-semitism had by now achieved a focal point in a party of rabid Alexandrian nationalists, led by demagogues like the crafty Isidorus. The governor of Egypt at the time was Aulus Avillius Flaccus. Born and educated in Rome, Flaccus was known to members of the imperial house and considered among Tiberius' closest friends. Appointed to succeed Hiberus in AD 32, Flaccus handled his responsibilities ably and conscientiously during his early years of office. In particular he sought to control the actions of the extreme nationalists, even forcing Isidorus to leave the city. Tiberius' death must have caused him concern, as he had apparently played some role in the banishing of Agrippina, Caligula's mother, although he is also said to have been a friend of Macro.[17] Preoccupation with his future may, according to Philo, have caused him to lose his grip on affairs. When the Jews, for instance, probably at the beginning of the reign (or on his recovery from illness), passed a resolution honouring Caligula, Flaccus omitted to forward it to Rome. But it is clear that Caligula did not bear a serious grudge against him. He was allowed to remain in office until 38, when he was due to be replaced by Macro, and on the death of the latter his prefecture seems to have been extended (see below).

By early 38 Isidorus had returned to Alexandria, and it is claimed by Philo that he began to exercise some sort of curious hold over the governor, despite their previous differences. To Philo it seemed that the Greeks offered Flaccus 'protection' against Caligula should he be willing to sacrifice the Jews. What form the protection could have taken we do not know, but Isidorus may have played a part in Macro's downfall, and if Flaccus had been involved in some compromising association with Macro, the hold over him, probably much exaggerated by Philo in any case, may have been by way of blackmail, rather than protection. Flaccus should have been wary of any dealings with Isidorus, since he had previously caught him out in intrigues, but he may have had little choice. As Philo saw it, the Prefect now began to show a distinct partiality towards the Greeks in lawsuits and the like. The spark that ignited this increasingly tense situation was the arrival of Agrippa in Alexandria in August 38. At the urging of Caligula he had abandoned his plans of returning home by the northern route through Greece, and had waited until the summer for the Etesian winds, heading for his kingdom by way of Alexandria.

The Jews supposedly found out that Agrippa was among them and asked him to forward to the emperor their declaration of loyalty that Flaccus had suppressed. This was done, and as they waited for a reply, Agrippa behaved in what appears to be a deliberatively provocative manner. He paraded through the streets of Alexandria with his bodyguard, perhaps intending to convey to the Greeks the message that whatever the attitude of the governor the Jews enjoyed the protection of a friend of the emperor. The results were quite different. Agrippa's presence did remind the Greeks of their now reduced status and the fact that they, unlike the Jews, no longer had a king. But they felt no deference towards Agrippa — to them he was merely a defaulting debtor. They collected in the Gymnasium to deliver insults against him, staging a parody of his procession, with the local idiot impersonating Agrippa in the character of king Carabas ('cabbage'). Too late, Agrippa realized that his presence would bring the Jews more danger than protection, and decided that it would be prudent to slip away to his kingdom.

The Greeks now went on a campaign of violence, and the Jews would look in vain for help from Flaccus, who seems to have resented Agrippa's interference. The Prefect, according to Philo, did nothing to check the Greeks, who rampaged through Alexandria, burning and demolishing isolated synagogues, and erecting statues of the emperor in others. But Flaccus' response suggests that he did not believe that the Jews had been mere passive victims. He issued a proclamation to regulate their right of residence in the city. Alexandria had long been divided into five quarters, each named after a letter of the Greek alphabet. Technically, permanent Jewish residence seems to have been legal in only one zone. Before Flaccus' proclamation Jews had been concentrated into two quarters, with a scattering in the three remaining. From 38 the law was to be strictly obeyed, and the Jews were obliged to reside only in the single Delta section.[18]

It is possible that Flaccus saw his ruling as a positive measure to maintain order, but the results for the Jews appear to have been disastrous. The overcrowding in the confined single area caused serious problems. People were forced to live on the beaches and even in the cemeteries. They lost many of their possessions, some of which were looted by the Greeks, and the terrible living conditions inevitably led to the spread of disease. Yet as shocking as the creation of history's first forced Jewish ghetto might seem, it is overshadowed by stories of the unchecked savagery of the Greeks, when they caught those Jews who had strayed outside in their search for help. Even allowing for exaggeration in Philo's account there is no doubt that they were subjected to cruel treatment. Jews were set upon by the mobs, who haunted the edge of the ghetto for their victims and, according to Philo, beat them or burned them to death, or, perhaps worst of all, bound them together and dragged them through the market, kicking and trampling them until their bodies were mutilated beyond recognition.[19] There is no hint in Philo that the Jews took any kind of retaliatory action whatsoever, but the subsequent conduct of Flaccus (and the attitude demonstrated later by Claudius) suggests that this is a false picture. Flaccus arrested members of the Jewish council and implemented a search of Jewish houses for weapons. At the end of August, on Caligula's birthday, arrested Jews were marched through the streets to the theatre where they were beaten and forced to eat pork. An uneasy calm finally seems to have settled over the city.

Little more is known of events in Alexandria before October 38, when a detachment of troops arrived to arrest Flaccus.[20] He was replaced as Prefect by Gaius Vitrasius Pollio, who stayed in the city for the remainder of Caligula's reign, possibly dying there in 41. Pollio seems to have been considerably more diplomatic than Flaccus, and the situation eased to a great degree. The Jews were at some point allowed to return to their old quarters and to resume their former livelihoods. Certainly, by September 39, just less than a year later, they were sufficiently wealthy to contribute towards the sacrifice of a hecatomb to Caligula for his success in Germany. It was decided that the status of the Jews should be determined by the emperor, and that delegates be sent to present both the Greek and the Jewish arguments. Philo led the Jewish delegation, the notorious anti-semitic writer Apion and Isidorus and Lampon forming part of the Greek team.[21] The chronology of the embassies' arrival in Rome is greatly confused. Philo indicates that the Jewish group sailed in 'mid–winter', but does not specify the year. It is probably safest to assume that this means the winter of 39/40, although 38/9 can not be ruled out completely.[22] Caligula initially gave the embassies a brief, but polite hearing. As he was leaving the Vatican gardens of his mother Agrippina on the bank of the Tiber, he waved affably at the Jewish delegation and told them that he would see them when he was free. This first step might have heartened them, but their confidence was surely shattered later in the summer when devastating news reached them from Jerusalem, that Caligula had decided to convert the Temple into a centre of the imperial cult. In these disheartening circumstances, the meeting finally took place in the emperor's residence on the Esquiline Hill and ended without any clear resolution. Afterwards, the Jews waited in some trepidation for his final adjudication, but whether or not he gave serious thought to the issue will never be known, since no decision had been reached when his assassination made his attitude irrelevant. The death of Caligula and the accession of Claudius seems to have been welcomed by the Jews of Alexandria, as well as by those of the homeland, to whom attention must now be addressed.

The chronology of Caligula's plans regarding the Temple at Jerusalem is much confused because of contradictions between Philo and Josephus, and the version followed here is basically the one adopted by Smallwood.[23] We can be sure that the incidents described took place in 40, since they are confirmed in Tacitus' brief survey of events in Judea leading up to the siege of Jerusalem.[24] The basic problem is that in Josephus' version the demonstrations in Judaea that provoke Caligula's reaction occur in the latter part of 40, while, if we follow Philo, they would belong to the earlier part. Philo's version is generally followed here, with the recognition that both writers are careless with the details of chronology and both tend to get the facts muddled.

In his summary of events in Judaea, Tacitus makes the famous comment that 'under Tiberius all was quiet'. This is, of course, an overstatement since under Pontius Pilate there was considerable unrest, but the problems then were essentially of a local nature, with no repercussions outside the province. They were settled with the suspension of Pilate by Lucius Vitellius, the governor of Syria. Vitellius then appointed a temporary procurator, Marcellus, and visited Judaea in person to ensure that order was being maintained. While Vitellius was engaged on his diplomatic efforts, the death of Tiberius was reported. Caligula sent out a Marullus as a permanent governor of Judaea.[25] Nothing further is known of him, to a large degree because the affairs of Judaea took such a serious turn that they required the personal intervention of the governor of Syria. At some point, probably during the winter of 39/40, riots broke out in

Jamnia, a coastal town with a mixed population of Jews and Greeks almost due west of Jerusalem. The resident Greeks erected an altar to the imperial cult, which was torn down at once by the Jews. Jamnia was part of an imperial estate inherited by Livia from Salome, and as such came under the jurisdiction of the procurator Gaius Herennius Capito, the same man who had encountered such difficulties in trying to persuade Agrippa to meet his debts. Capito reported the affair to Caligula, who responded with a vengeance, supposedly acting on the advice of Helicon and Apelles. He decreed that the Temple of Jerusalem would be converted into an imperial shrine, with an enormous statue of the emperor in the guise of Jupiter. The governor of Syria was by this time Publius Petronius, who probably took up office in the autumn of 39. Possibly by early 40 Petronius had been instructed to have a statue of the emperor made for the Temple, and to use half the army in Syria (where four legions were regularly stationed) to handle any unrest that might ensue.[26]

The Byzantine historian John Malalas recounts a riot that took place in Antioch, the administrative seat of Syria, in 39-40 (dated by the presence of Petronius in the province). What began as a fracas developed into an attack on the Jews and the burning of their synagogue. Phineas the high priest in Jersualem is supposed to have called in 30,000 men to seek vengeance. There is obviously much distortion and exaggeration in this report which is found in neither Philo or Josephus, but it is just possible that it echoes events connected with the threat to the temple.[27]

It was a fortunate circumstance that Syria was governed by a legate who matched his predecessor not only in his competence but also in his diplomacy and tact, a man who had prepared himself even to the degree of a preliminary study of Jewish philosophy. Petronius made good use of the time required for the manufacture of the statue, which was being prepared in Sidon. He invited the Jewish leaders to a meeting (the precise location unknown) in a forlorn attempt to persuade them to submit to the desecration. While they did not offer violence, their adamant refusal to accept the new measure would hardly have come as a surprise to him. He moved two of his legions south, possibly in May 40, in accordance with his imperial instructions, but on reaching Ptolemais, just before the border of Galilee, he was met by a massive demonstration of Jews, who made their convictions known so forcefully that he realized that Caligula's plan was likely to cause a major riot. He shrewdly suggested to the sculptors in Sidon that they take their time with the statue.[28] According to Josephus (the incident is not mentioned by Philo) he then left his army at Ptolemais and went to the Galilean capital, Tiberias, where he met a deputation of Jewish officials led by Aristobulus, nephew of Antipas, who had perhaps just left for Italy to press his claim with Caligula for the title of King. Further demonstrations pressed home how serious the situation had become, and Petronius was persuaded to write to Caligula to present the Jewish case.[29] Apart from the threat of force, the Jews used powerful economic arguments. They neglected their harvest and threatened even to destroy the corn in the fields, which would induce a famine at the very time when Caligula was making his visit to Alexandria.[30]

Philo and Josephus portray Jewish reaction to Caligula's plans as restrained and responsible, and there is no suggestion that a single life was lost.[31] But of course they are at pains to show the Jews in a good light. Tacitus, in fact, points out that they were quite prepared for a violent armed clash if necessary.[32] It is difficult to sort out precisely what happened next. Caligula's reply to Petronius seems to have been far from conciliatory, and he suspected that the governor had taken a bribe.[33] The emperor ordered him to carry out his instructions, and to set up the statue at once. The events that follow are much confused. According to one version Agrippa played a key role.[34] He seems to have reached Italy in the summer of 40, having no idea of what was taking place. When he learned of the planned desecration of the Temple he was utterly dismayed and fell ill. While recovering from his illness he wrote a carefully worded letter, seeking to persuade Caligula to continue the principles laid down by his predecessors and to continue the protection of the Jews.[35] Agrippa would have had good reason to intervene, beyond any general concern for his people, since his own kingdom was likely to be affected. His influence on his young protégé had not waned. Caligula, out of regard for his friend and fellow king, consented to abandon his plans. Josephus claims that Agrippa saved the temple by entertaining Caligula at a splendid banquet and when offered a favour in return, seized the opportunity. The emperor wrote to Petronius, telling him to abandon the project but insisted that the Jews must repay toleration with toleration, and not oppose further attempts by non-Jews to establish the imperial cult outside Jerusalem.[36] As a result, Petronius was able to withdraw with his army to Antioch. This version of events, in which Caligula behaved rationally, did not suit Jewish tradition or Petronius' later reputation. Another version was circulated, in which Petronius continued to delay matters and made excuses (not known) for further delay, holding his army back at Ptolemais. Caligula in fury ordered him to commit suicide, but the order was held up by bad weather, and by the time it had reached Petronius he had already received news of the assassination.[37]

Although they disagree on details, both Josephus and Philo confirm that Caligula's decision to set up the statue was prompted by his claims to divinity. From a Jewish standpoint this clearly was not an unreasonable conclusion. But Philo adds the further assertion that Caligula hated the Jews and was preparing a vast war against them. This is clearly absurd. Roman policy was basically one of reciprocity, and Roman protection of the Jewish religion was conditional on their limiting their zeal. The behaviour of the Jews at Jamnia might well have been looked upon as a hostile political act rather than merely a bout of religious fervour. How far Caligula could be held personally responsible for the problems that arose in this period is difficult to say. He did recall Flaccus and appoint a capable successor, and this action seems to have eased matters in Alexandria somewhat. The Jews must certainly share part of the blame. They lacked political tact in their dealings with the Greeks, as evidenced by the parade of Agrippa through Alexandria, while the destruction of the Altar at Jamnia seems to suggest the development of a religious zeal that must have been largely independent of Caligula. But whether through his own doing or not, there can be no doubt that Caligula's reign does mark a turning point in Romano-Jewish relations. Events showed how difficult the position of the Jews had become and how they could find themselves at the mercy of what they considered an arbitrary tyrant. All of this strengthened the hands of the Jewish nationalists.

On news of Caligula's death the Jews of Alexandria, who seem to have been stockpiling weapons, decided to even scores, and went on a rampage against the Greeks, possibly calling in Jews from Egypt and Syria, until the Prefect put the rebellion down.[38] In fact Claudius, probably under pressure from Agrippa, had issued an edict for Alexandria, which must have arrived too late. In it he criticized the policy of Caligula for its 'madness and lack of understanding' and stated that none of the rights of the Jews should be lost because of this. He also instructed both parties to make sure that following the posting of the edict there should be no further disturbances.[39]

A similar edict was sent to Antioch, and some time later a further edict was addressed to the Jewish communities throughout the empire, of which we have only the summary of Josephus; there is much in the way of kind words to the Jews, and a confirmation of the privileges throughout the empire similar to those enjoyed by the Jews in Alexandria. At the same time there is a warning of the need for mutual toleration, and an admonition to the Jews that they were not to scorn the religious beliefs of others.[40] Claudius was able to combine tact and firmness in a way that was quite beyond the capacity of his predecessor. His reign saw further edicts and further embassies, as he struggled for some formula that might restore permanent order. Yet despite his good intentions sporadic disturbances continued in both Alexandria and Judaea. Clearly the difficulties had not disappeared with Caligula's death. The stage was already set for a final confrontation that would culminate less than thirty years later in the devastating sack of Jerusalem by the Romans.

· 13 ·

CALIGULA
THE BUILDER

WHILE AUGUSTUS' BOAST that he found Rome a city built of brick and left it one of marble is not, of course, literally true, there can be no denying that his reign was marked by a series of magnificent architectural schemes, many of them initiated under the direction of Marcus Agrippa.[1] By contrast, while Tiberius was conscientious about keeping existing buildings in good repair and in assisting cities in genuine financial need, he did not share his predecessor's zeal for transforming the physical face of Rome, and, in keeping with his decidely austere and frugal view of life, felt an aversion towards unnecessary public works. It is hardly surprising that Caligula did not take his lead from his immediate predecessor, but sought to revive the family tradition begun by Augustus and Agrippa — he seems to have taken a genuine personal interest in the visual arts, and would have seen in architecture a chance to grace the Roman world with a tangible symbol of his greatness.

At all periods Romans seem to have felt an obsessive need to own precious *objets d'art* and Caligula was no exception; he appears to have combed the world in his search for beautiful pieces to adorn his capital city. The sources all consider his zeal to have been directed towards perverted ends. Pheidias' great statue of Zeus, we are told, was to be brought to Rome from the temple of Olympia to be converted into a cult statue of Caligula himself.[2] Where no such quasi-political purpose can be detected, his erotic obsessions are cited — his lust supposedly drove him to ruin two beautiful nude paintings of Atalanta and Helen at Lanuvium when he tried to remove the plaster from the wall. The seizure of the famous Cupid of Thespiae was popularly thought to have placed him under a fatal curse, since his murderer Chaerea was in part motivated by taunts about his sexual inclinations. The Cupid was returned by Claudius, repossessed by Nero, and eventually destroyed by fire in Rome. It is only fair to add that in plundering works of art Caligula behaved no differently from many other emperors.[3]

The most vivid illustration of Caligula's personal obsession with art is provided by the meeting in 40 between the emperor and the Jewish delegation seeking to promote the cause of their fellows in Alexandria.

It took place at Caligula's villa on the Esquiline, and Philo has left us a first-hand account of what took place. As the Jews, confused and terrified, scurried behind him, Caligula rushed from room to room, inspecting the furnishings and fittings, and on occasion ordering replacements for those that did not meet his standards. A discussion on the political rights of the Jews was cut short by a tour of a large room, where he ordered the windows to be replaced; no sooner had the discussion resumed than they were shepherded into another room where he made arrangements for pictures to be hung.[4] Although allowance must be made for exaggeration, Philo's basic portrait of Caligula as would-be connoisseur and aesthete is probably not very wide of the mark.

Caligula's eagerness for public works seems to have left a firm impression on the public imagination, and Suetonius records feats of almost Biblical proportions, of moles built out into the depths of the sea, of passages carved through crags of the hardest flint and even of mountains levelled.[5] Suetonius' hyperbole is perhaps understandable, since Caligula's record is, in fact, remarkable for one who had so short a reign.

Some of the projects serve to remind us that despite his exaggerated and erratic behaviour the routine and prosaic functions of the state continued. Caligula showed, for instance, a keen interest in the upkeep of the roads. In 20 BC Augustus had been placed in charge of the roads in Italy and reorganized (if he did not create) a board of ex-praetors as road-commissioners. As early as AD 21 a senator Gnaeus Domitius Corbulo (on his identity see p. 193) began to prosecute the commissioners because of the damaged condition of the highways, and those found guilty were obliged to make the appropriate repairs at their own expense, even though in some cases it meant that they had to sell their personal property.[6] Caligula apparently welcomed Corbulo as an ally in his policy of attacking the incompetent commissioners. In a confused report Dio seems to suggest that he charged those who had let fraudulent contracts and those who had negligently omitted to make use of the funds budgeted.[7] These measures seem to have caused some resentment. At any rate Claudius later stopped the prosecutions and returned the money taken in fines, either from the public treasury or from Corbulo personally.[8]

Caligula's concern with communications was not restricted to Italy. He revived the project of building a canal across the Isthmus of Corinth and had even reached the point of sending a military surveyor to carry out the preliminary work before he died.[9] Also in the sphere of communications was the lighthouse built at Boulogne, intended to assist the movement of transport ships between Britain and the continent for the supply of the invading Roman army. The structure was still standing until the mid-sixteenth century, and surviving drawings provide a general impression of its original appearance, although it is likely that much of the finished project should be credited not to Caligula but to Claudius and later repairs. It took the form of a polygonal pyramid in twelve stages, with a base of 19.5m, reaching a height of over 35m (some authorities say as high as 60m); each stage had eight openings, consisting of seven windows and one large door (on the north face). The stages were constructed of alternating bands of yellow stones, red bricks and grey stones, bonded with concrete.[10]

Suetonius' suggestion that he planned to found a city high in the Alps, when combined with his separate comment about levelling mountains and tunnelling through flint, may suggest that there was road-building in the Alpine regions, presumably to improve communications with Gaul and Germany. In Strabo's day the Little St. Bernard Pass was paved– the Great St. Bernard leading to the Vallis Pennina was not, but would be by at least the time of Claudius, and the paving should perhaps be attributed to Caligula — dedications to him are known from the Vallis Pennina.[11] Spain provides evidence of his roadbuilding activities there. Nor was his interest limited to construction and maintenance. He seems to have been particularly obsessed with cleanliness. The future emperor Vespasian, when aedile, had reportedly neglected this aspect of his duties and as punishment Caligula ordered mud to be heaped into his toga, surely a humiliating experience for Vespasian at the time, but one that he could later represent as an omen that Rome was destined to be entrusted to his care.[12]

The water supply was also one of his concerns. The seven existing aqueducts supplying Rome were no longer adequate and Caligula began the construction of two more, the Aqua Claudia and the Anio Novus.[13] These were left unfinished at the time of his death, and Claudius completed the work. The Claudia, which was considered by Pliny to be one of the great engineering feats of his day, may have been completed as early as 47, but it was not dedicated until 52, by which time the Anio Novus was finally completed (and dedicated at the same time).[14]

Almost as important as the water supply was the adequate provision of grain for Rome. Responsibility for its supply lay with the *praefectus annonae*, the position being occupied under Caligula by a Gaius Turannius, who had held it since the time of Augustus. Caligula tried to edge him out of office (he was now in his nineties). Turannius clearly felt himself indispensable, and engaged in a spectacular publicity stunt, laying himself out as if he were dead, while the household mourned him. The emperor, perhaps against his better judgement, relented, and Turannius lived to serve under Claudius.[15] Problems connected with the grain supply had plagued Tiberius, leading to riots in 32, and that these problems continued under Caligula can not be doubted. Suetonius says that several times he 'condemned the people to hunger' by shutting up the granaries, and suggests that by commandeering all the transport facilities to move goods to Gaul for auction he caused problems in the bread supply. There seems to have been a particularly serious crisis in the winter of 40/1. Seneca claims that when Caligula died there were supplies of grain sufficient for only seven or eight days because the resources had been channelled into the Bridge at Baiae, and Dio makes a similar accusation.[16] Clearly, this specific charge is absurd, since the bridge was built in 39, too early to have had any effect in the period immediately before Caligula's death. Probably what was a genuine grain crisis was simply blamed on the most outlandish episode on hand. Certainly the problems recurred under Claudius in 42, finally persuading him to begin the reconstruction of the new harbour at Ostia.[17] It was with the problems of the grain supply in mind that Caligula undertook the large-scale improvement of the harbour at Rhegium, which Josephus considered to be his only public work worth mentioning, and which he believed would have been of enormous benefit to ships transporting grain from Egypt (it was not finished). Suetonius' allusion to the moles in the deep sea could well be to this project. One might wonder why the harbour needed to be extended in the first place. It was too far south to have been of use to Rome, and may have been intended for the supply of grain to southern Italy.[18]

Many cities throughout the empire will have benefited from Caligula's generosity, although in some cases we have only scattered allusions. At Syracuse he repaired the dilapidated city walls and temples. At Bologna he seems to have undertaken the repair of a bath house given to the town originally by Augustus. Antioch also seems to have been favoured by him, after a major earthquake in 37, although the evidence is to be treated with caution, since the source is the Byzantine scholar, John Malalas, who is often confused and unreliable.[19] However, Caligula would certainly have been well-disposed towards the city, which had shown its affection for his father Germanicus at the time of his death.

Inevitably it was in Rome that Caligula's policy was to have its greatest effect. Many of his projects were of a type that would have been bound to increase his popularity with the masses. There is one possible exception, the improvement of the Tullianum, Rome's oldest surviving prison. This building, known in the Middle Ages as the Carcer Mammertinus, lies beneath the small church of San Giuseppe dei Falegnani at the foot of the Capitoline Hill, northwest of the Forum Romanum. It may have begun its history as a cistern but eventually housed some of Rome's most distinguished criminals and captives, as they awaited execution. It was here that Jugurtha died of starvation in 104 BC, and Vercingetorix was beheaded in 46 BC. According to Christian tradition St Peter and St Paul were detained for a time in the Tullianum. Two levels are distinguished, an original lower circular room with a domed ceiling, and an upper trapezoidal room added later. The upper chamber underwent improvements and was decorated on the exterior by a facade of travertine slabs, dated by the inscription on its cornice to the consulship of Gaius Vibius

Rufinus and Marcus Cocceius Nerva, probably suffect consuls in 40.[20]

Most of Caligula's work, however, involved buildings that had a more popular appeal. The theatre of Pompey, the first permanent stone theatre of Rome, built in 52 BC, had been destroyed by fire in AD 22. Repairs were begun under Tiberius and seem to have been completed in different phases. Tacitus implies that the theatre was finished by Tiberius; Dio indicates that it was finally restored and dedicated by Claudius, who credited Tiberius with the restoration of the stage building. Suetonius explicitly states that the work on the theatre was completed by Caligula, and it would certainly have been in character for Claudius to have begrudged his immediate predecessor any credit for the work.[21] Probably the favourite forms of entertainment in Rome were the animal and gladiatorial shows, and Caligula sought to make further provision for these, in the area of the Saepta, which had been completed and dedicated by Agrippa in 26 BC as a voting place, close to the Pantheon. He demolished many large buildings in the area, at great expense, erecting temporary wooden stands. No further progress was reported and the plan was abandoned by Claudius, who proudly records his repair near the Saepta of the arches of the Aqua Virgo damaged by Caligula.[22]

Of all Caligula's building projects none has caught the imagination more than the circus, or race-course, that he planned out in the *Ager Vaticanus* (ill. 5). This area, on the right bank of the Tiber, constituted the 14th administrative region set up by Augustus. Agrippina, or her husband Germanicus, laid out gardens here, between the *mons Vaticanus* and the river. The estate passed down to Caligula, and it was in its grounds that Philo's embassy was greeted cordially by the emperor at their first meeting. Seneca provides evidence of architectural structures, referring to a covered passage that separated a portico from the river bank.[23] On the level ground in this area Caligula was able to indulge his passion for chariot-racing. Dio refers to the place which he used for practice as the *Gaianum*, which bore the same name until Dio's own day.[24] Far more important than the Gaianum is the circus that the sources indicate Caligula also laid out in his mother's gardens, known as the Circus of Gaius and Nero.[25] It was here that the Christians were put to death by Nero, and from an early date Christian tradition revered it as the site of Peter's martyrdom. It was probably this tradition that led Constantine in the fourth century to locate the great church of St Peter at the southeast foot of the Mons Vaticanus, where he created an enormous level platform by cutting away part of the hill on the north and using the spoil to build a ramp, burying a number of pagan tombs in the process.

The topography of the Vatican area suggests that the circus had an east–west orientation, and for generations it was believed that the south wall of Constantine's church stood on the north walls of Caligula's circus,

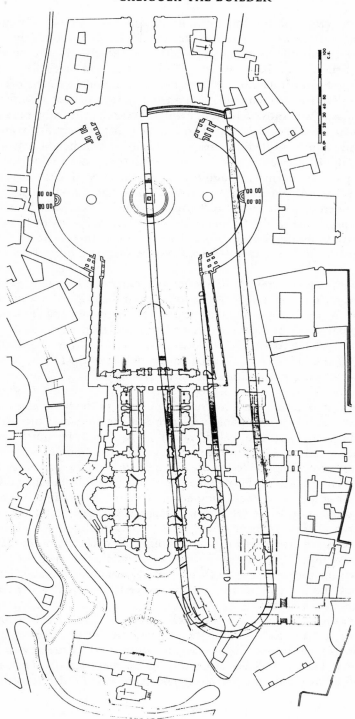

5 AGER VATICANUS

a notion strengthened by the position of the obelisk that Caligula transported from Egypt to stand in the enclosure, one assumes in the traditional location on the spina, the central barrier that ran down the long axis of the circus. The Vatican obelisk, which had originally been located in the Forum Julianum at Alexandria, was made by Nencoreus, son of Seosis, and stands 25m (82 ft) high. Pliny records that it suffered damage when it was moved (it weighs over 300 tons); there is no sign of the damage today, and Magi has speculated that the obelisk was in fact originally 45m (148 ft) high, nearly twice its present height.[26] It was set up in Calgula's circus, where it stood until 1586, to be relocated as the centre piece of Bernini's magnificent portico in St. Peter's Square, where it has become one of modern Rome's most famous landmarks. It was surmounted by a gilt bronze ball with a small obelisk-shaped pointer. The ball is preserved in the Conservatori museum, and in its place now stands a cross, supported by the original acanthus ornaments. At the base of the obelisk were four astragal-shaped bronze supports, now concealed by lions.

The obelisk was transported to Rome in a ship built for the purpose, where the surface of the stone was ground off and the original inscription replaced by a new one, with a dedication to Augustus and Tiberius, unusual in that it brings together a deified and undeified emperor: DIVO CAESARI DIVI IUL II F. AUGUSTO, TI CAESARI DIVI AUGUSTI F. AUGUSTO, SACRUM ('sacred to the Divine Caesar Augustus, son of the Divine Julius, and to Tiberius Caesar Augustus, son of the Divine Julius').[27] It was then set up in the Vatican gardens. Its location, known from drawings predating its removal in 1586, provides the position of the transverse axis, which in turn allows a reasonable conjecture of the course of the walls, strengthening the long-held belief, noted above, that the north wall underlay the wall of Constantine's church. In 1939, however, when preparations were being made for the tomb of Pius XI, the pagan tombs were discovered beneath the original floor of the old church, and a systematic programme of excavating and restoring was initiated. One of the most significant discoveries, for our purposes, was that no trace could be discovered of the circus, or of the road (Via Cornelia) that had been presumed to run to the north of it, providing the necessary access. The foundation walls of Constantine's structure seem in the main to have stood on virgin soil, and the south row of the tombs (generally dated between 125 and the end of the century), were located where the road had been presumed to run.[28]

Although this evidence at the time dealt a serious blow to old theories about the circus' precise location, the excavations did provide striking confirmation for the notion that it was somewhere in the general vicinity of St. Peter's. The mausoleum of Gaius Popilius Heracla, located in the northern street of the necropolis, still retained the marble slab recording his final arrangements for burial, which include the instruction that his tomb was to be located *in Vatic(ano) ad circum*.[29]. The obelisk remains the most crucial piece of evidence for the circus' setting. When Pliny located the monument in *Vaticano in circo* he seems to have meant that it was located specifically in the actual circus rather than just in the geographic region associated with it- at any rate he uses a similar phrase *in circo maximo* in the same context to refer specifically to another obelisk in position inside the Circus Maximus. If located within the circus, however, the Vatican obelisk would almost certainly have had to stand on the spina, and in that case the north walls of the circuit would be expected to underlie St. Peter's.

G. Townend has suggested a simple solution, that Caligula erected the obelisk in his gardens in the area where he drove his chariot, but that there were no actual structures, perhaps wooden ones being added later by Claudius or Nero. As the obelisk was originally set up, the inscriptions faced east-west, and would not have been seen by the spectators (facing north or south) in the completed circus, adding weight to the notion that it was erected when the track was still a private preserve. The area would thus share some affinity with the garden hippodromes of the kind that Pliny the Younger describes.[30] Townend's suggestion obviates many of the archaeological difficulties. There does, however, remain the problem that, in drawing a parallel between Caligula's circus and the Circus Maximus, Pliny at the very least implies a substantial structure in the case of the former, whether or not it was actually completed by Caligula.

Since the Vatican excavations there has been further important archaeological work. In 1959, F. Castagnoli carried out a study of the initial location of the obelisk. He found what he believed was the original surface of the track, consisting of sand, over gravel, clay, charcoal and ashes, with a bedding of cobbled stone; unfortunately, there is no way of proving that this surface belonged to the arena. Most interesting, however, was the failure to find the spina, which, Castagnoli concludes, must not have been continuous.[31] Another important study was published by Magi in 1973, with a report on drilling cores carried out around St Peter's Basilica, along with a reinterpretation of walls discovered earlier. Magi's conclusions are by no means the final word, but they do deserve close consideration. Especially interesting are the two parallel curving walls found in 1949 to the east of the end of the southern colonnade of St Peter's Square. The outer wall is 1.5m thick, 3.23m (10½ ft) high, convex in shape, bulging to the east. To the west of it, about 2.3m distant, runs a parallel wall, 2.2m (2ft 3in) thick. The space between would presumably have been vaulted. The convex curves of the walls are what demand attention, since they would suit the foundations for the row of starting gates (*carceres*) for the competitors. The need to double up as retaining walls for the platform of the circus may explain why these foundations are so massive (the west wall would, of course, need to be heavier for this purpose). The wide platform above the foundations could well have accommodated both the starting booths and a connecting corridor running behind them. Apart from this structure, Magi also reinterpreted a wall (1.2m, 3ft 11in, wide) found in 1937 at the base of the steps of St Peter's. This he relates to the walls reported in the sixteenth century at the time of the building of the new Basilica. Magi thus might claim to have given some new life to the old view that the north wall of the arena would have run south of the tombs beneath St Peter's nave, and only further excavations beneath St Peter's will be able to decide the matter. As reconstructed on the basis of the drillholes Magi's arena would extend as far west as San Stefano, where the hill slopes steeply, on the assumption that the obelisk stood mid-way along the axis. Its length would be some 560m (1850 ft), only about 20m (60 ft) shorter than the Circus Maximus, a similarity that Humphrey suggests may not have been accidental.[32]

The reconstruction is, of course, very tentative, and it is far from certain that even if correct it indicates the extent of the arena as actually completed by Caligula. The monumental structure could have been completed by one of his successors, either Claudius or Nero, and Pliny's reference to the circus *Gaii et Neronis* certainly implies that Nero had some part in its construction. We can not be sure that in Caligula's time it was used for anything more than private chariot racing. But Claudius certainly gave public races *in Vaticano*, with beast-baiting between every five races. Nero seems at first to have used the area for private races, but by at least 64, when the Christians were executed in the Vatican Circus on the charge of setting fire to the city, he put on public games at which he drove a chariot himself. No specific references to games there postdate Nero, and it has been speculated that the grounds, like Nero's Domus Aurea, may have been given to the public by Vespasian, as a move to win popular support. The later history of the circus remains obscure. It was apparently still in use in the second century, to judge from the reference on the tomb of Heracla. The literary sources remain silent except for a single entry of doubtful reliability on Elagabalus (218-22), who, like Caligula and Nero, had a passion for chariot- racing. He is said to have driven chariots drawn by four elephants *in Vaticano*, knocking down tombs that blocked his way. No further reference is known, suggesting that the building did not long survive Elagabalus.[33]

There is one final chapter to the story of Caligula's circus. When the obelisk was moved to its current location, in 1586, the undertaking was considered a major engineering feat. This serves to emphasize the magnitude of the task of bringing it from Egypt to Rome in the first place. A massive transport ship was designed, modelled probably on the great grain carriers used on the Ostia–Alexandria route, and described by Pliny as the most wonderful sight on the sea, so huge that it required 120,000 modii of lentils for ballast[34] After it had fulfilled its initial purpose, the ship proved to be commercially impractical; it was kept for some time by Claudius as a curio, before being sunk at Ostia, as part of the mole to support the lighthouse in the great Claudian reconstruction of the harbour. When Rome's airport was constructed between 1957 and 1960 the Claudian harbour was recovered, revealing the boats that had been filled with concrete before being sunk to form the north mole. In the central section the great mass of concrete used for the foundation of the lighthouse has survived, thus preserving a solid mould of the original ship, providing approximate dimensions of some 100m (330 ft) by 20m (60 ft).[35]

Many of the architectural projects of Caligula, while on a grandiose scale, did serve a utilitarian purpose, or at least provide a public amenity. Others can be categorized as exercises in luxurious self-indulgence. These would include, for instance, the rebuilding of the palace of Polycrates at Samos, which Willrich speculates may have been intended to provide accommodation on his eastern tour.[36] To this category also belong his 'Liburnian galleys', vividly described by Suetonius, 'with jewelled sterns, multicoloured sails, extravagant baths, colonnades, banqueting halls, with even a diversity of vines and fruit trees. He could recline on them from the daylight hours and roam the coast line of Campania amidst songs and choruses'. None of these sea-going vessels has survived, but Suetonius' account receives some degree of confirmation from the two famous ships recovered from Lake Nemi in the Alban Hills. The beauty of Nemi explains its attraction for Romans like Julius Caesar, who had a Villa there (he tore it down because he was not satisfed with it). It has since remained a popular haunt for artists, visited by the likes of Turner and Lear. In ancient times it was the setting for the grove of Aricia, where the goddess Diana was worshipped with savage rites. Her priest was a runaway slave who by tradition attained office by killing his predecessor in single combat, a practice that fell into disuse in the historical period, although Suetonius claims that it was revived by Caligula.[37] The presence of ancient ships in the depths of Lake Nemi has been known for centuries, and attempts to lift them date from the fifteenth century. Beginning in the late 1920's, in a major engineering project, the lake was drained and the vessels recovered, only to be destroyed in 1944, together with the museum that housed them, by retreating German soldiers.

The ships are large for pleasure craft, 73m (241 ft) by 24m (79 ft) and 71.3m (235 ft) by 20m (66 ft), and have aptly been described as floating villas.[38] Their construction under Caligula is virtually confirmed by his name on inscribed water pipes, but it seems likely that they were redecorated under Nero, to judge from the style of the mosaics.[39] They have added greatly to our understanding of Roman naval design and construction techniques. The quality of workmanship is extremely high. Careful use was made of nails, small copper ones for the lighter work, iron ones for the heavier joins. Where iron nails were used, holes were bored and filled with soft wood to avoid the danger of splitting. The planks were fitted by carefully worked mortises, not caulked, but packed with tow and smeared with clay. The whole surface was then covered by woolen cloth dipped in pitch and resin for waterproofing and finally by thin plates of lead. The latter is an unusual feature, since as a precaution against marine borers it would hardly have been necessary in fresh water. The quality of the interior decoration matched that of the construction. The boats were served with running water (as evidenced by the lead pipes) and the quarters were lavishly decorated, although we can not be sure how much is owed to later restoration, since much of the decoration is what we would associate with the Neronian period. The floors were covered with mosaics, the walls revetted in some places with marble, in others with mosaics, although the discovery of wood with traces of painted design and inlaid ivory shows that there was a good deal of variety. In places the walls were crowned by a terra-cotta frieze. The wooden ceilings were inlaid with roof tiles on which copper plates were set and gilded. Throughout, exquisite bronze decorations were used, even for the utilitarian parts. A fine Medusa head, for instance, topped the rudder pole of one of the ships. Some of the architectural splendour associated with the 'Liburnian galleys' is echoed by the discovery of four matching columns of africano marble; a single spiral-fluted column with a Corinthian capital is also known, one of the earliest recorded instances of this style of fluting, unless it belongs to the later Neronian refurbishment.[40] On the later history of these vessels we can only speculate. They were not simply abandoned, as the remaining bronze decorations, which would have been stripped away, were left in place. There are numerous legends, even including one that Caligula sank them during a drunken orgy. The coin finds suggest, however, that they continued in use until the Flavian period, when they may have gone down as the result of a storm or an earthquake.

Caligula clearly appreciated the pleasures of fine living when visiting spots like Nemi or his villas in Campania. He also sought the same level of luxury when he was obliged to stay in Rome. The extent and extravagance of his personal residences in the city are illustrated by an observation of Pliny that in his lifetime he had seen the city ringed by the houses of emperors, namely Caligula and Nero. The latter allusion, as Pliny goes on to explain, is to the Golden House of Nero, a luxurious range planned after the great fire of 64 to link the Esquiline with the Palatine. Caligula's projects must have made a similar visual impact but their extent and nature are more difficult to determine. He inherited estates in at least three areas of the city. His mother's gardens in the

Vatican area, with their portico and covered walkway, have already been mentioned. There may also have been a villa on the slope of the Mons Vaticanus, from which he was able to watch Antonia's funeral pyre in the Campus Martius.[41] In addition, he had properties on the Esquiline, which he inherited from Tiberius. They lay just outside the city limits, and it was here that he met the Alexandrian embassies, described so vividly by Philo. The grounds were made up of two adjoining estates. The Horti Lamiani were possibly laid out by Lucius Aelius Lamia, consul in AD 3, and left by him to Tiberius, to become imperial property, since there is epigraphic evidence that they were managed by a procurator. In these gardens Caligula's body received its first, temporary, burial immediately after his death. Adjoining them were the Horti Maecenatis, laid out on the Esquiline by Maecenas, transforming the area into a beautiful promenade, and possibly containing Maecenas' hot swimming pool, the first such amenity built in Rome. These became imperial property after the death of their founder, and Tiberius lived here on his return to the city in AD 2. The precise location and geographical relationship of these two estates are uncertain, and later rebuilding over the centuries in the Esquiline area makes the chances of their recovery unlikely. Scattered finds have been attributed to the complexes. These include a large collection of very fine gems, originally inlaid, and strips of gilt with wood fibre adhering to them, suggesting gilt panels or furniture. It has recently been argued that these formed part of a splendid throne of Caligula — Dio certainly speaks of a throne placed on the Capitol to symbolize Caligula's presence when he was away on his northern campaigns.[42]

By Caligula's day the 'official' imperial residence, as opposed to merely the private estate of the emperor, was firmly established on one of the most significant historical areas of Rome, the Palatine Hill. Since it was here that Caligula met his death, the topography and architecture of the region merits close study. The Palatine, which rises some 40m to the south of the Forum Romanum, gives the appearance to the modern visitor of a level plateau, an impression created to a large extent by the massive palace complex, the Domus Augustiana, built over a large part of the area by Domitian after 80. In fact there are two distinct summits, still visible in Caligula's own day, the central and higher one being the Palatine, to the north and west of which lay the Germalus. Indeed, there is strictly speaking a second lesser slope, the Veleia, connected with the Esquiline by a saddle through the forum. Although the whole group is loosely referred to as the Palatine (as in this book) it is clear from Varro that strictly speaking that term was used specifically of the main summit.[43]

The Palatine Hill, especially its south-west corner, had close associations with Rome's earliest history, and was the original location of the ancient walled city (ill. 6). During the republic much of the Hill became a prime

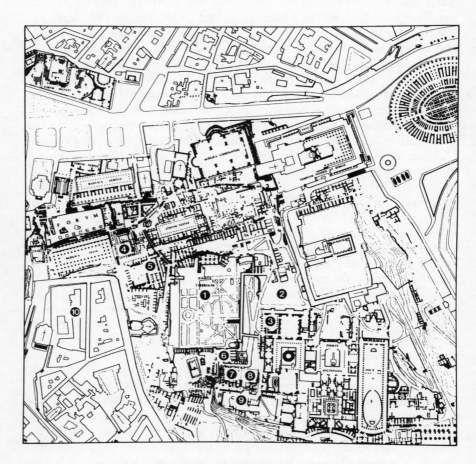

6   THE PALATINE HILL

residential area for distinguished Romans, such as Marcus Livius Drusus, plebeian tribune in 91 BC, the demagogue Clodius, his murderer Milo, and the orator and statesman Cicero. Marc Antony may also have owned a house there.[44] Augustus was born there and made arrangements to move there after his marriage to Livia, and deliberately chose to be near the ancient south-west corner. The remains of his first house were excavated in the nineteenth century, south of the eastern side of the later Domus Tiberiana, east of the Temples of Victory and of the Magna Mater, Cybele. It was a somewhat unconventional residence in the size of some of its rooms, and was clearly intended for someone who needed to entertain on a large scale. After 36, on the grounds that part of the house had been struck by lightning and was desired by the gods, Augustus dedicated the area to a new Temple of Apollo, and to compensate him for this act of generosity the senate constructed a new house at public expense.[45] The new residence was built south of the first house, which seems to have remained as a self-contained unit and part of the imperial complex. Lead pipes found nearby and stamped Iulia Augusta suggest that the first residence remained the private apartments of Livia, where she probably lived after Augustus' death, and where the young Caligula no doubt stayed for a time after his mother's arrest.

Excavations of the new residence from 1961 onwards have revealed a splendid complex made up essentially of a small palace joined by a ramp to the Temple of Apollo to the east.[46] The whole structure was open to the south and would have presented a splendid spectacle to those who approached it from the south. The union of residence and temple is not Roman in conception, and seems to take its inspiration from the great complex built by the Attalid kings of Pergamum.[47] The Palatine residence soon was recognized as a kind of 'official' imperial house, and already in the Augustan period 'Palatium', strictly speaking just a residence on the Palatine, had acquired the the modern connotation of 'palace'.[48]

The Temple of Apollo was dedicated in 28. The podium has survived, 44m (145 ft) by 22m (66 ft), reached on the south side by a flight of steps. Excavation has confirmed the literary testimony that it was built on the site of republican houses.[49] The Temple was enclosed by the magnificent portico of the Danaids, with statues of the fifty murderous daughters of Danaus, none of which has survived. This was a structure of some considerable splendour, to judge from the descriptions in the literary sources. It was here that Augustus met the rival delegates from Judaea after Herod's death in 4 BC, when the court accommodated a crowd put by Josephus at several thousand. Along its western range of the portico were located the Greek and Latin libraries, rebuilt in the later Domitianic phase. Unfortunately, none of it has survived.[50]

Between the area of the Magna Mater–Victoria complex and the north slope above the forum the Germalus was to be covered by the platform of a massive residential complex, some 15,000m², the Domus Tiberiana. This area was built over by the Farnese gardens in the fifteenth century and systematic excavation has thus not been possible. The northen range has been the most intensively examined. From here, in particular, clear evidence has emerged, from tile stamps, that after 80 Domitian rebuilt the original Domus Tiberiana, as part of his own palace, and that Hadrian made further alterations. A fundamental question to be resolved is whether or not the palace that stood originally on the platform was built by Tiberius, as the name implies. This is of some importance for present purposes, because of the literary evidence that Caligula somehow extended Tiberius' palace. Tiberius was born on the Palatine, and lived there after becoming emperor. There are good grounds for believing, however, that the construction of the massive palace that bears his name was probably not undertaken by him. The name itself, Domus Tiberiana, is actually used for the first time in the context of the assassination of Galba in 69, and may have arisen from the need for writers to distinguish this structure when the general term 'palatium' had been taken over by Domitian's great complex. Tiberius' aversion to extravagant architectural projects makes it unlikely that he would have undertaken a luxury project of this magnitude. Moreover, in Josephus' very confused account of the assassination of Caligula it appears that the imperial residence was still, in 41, made up of the accumulation of individual houses acquired by various members of the imperial family.[51] Could this mean that Tiberius merely began work on the palace? Previous studies have indeed inclined to the view that the palace developed piecemeal from Tiberius on. However, a recent archaeological survey of the Domus Tiberiana by the Swiss Institute in Rome has concluded very emphatically against this idea, claiming that the geometric structure of the palace argues very strongly for its being the uniform concept of a single individual. It does seem to have been built by at least 54, when Nero was proclaimed emperor. On this occasion, Tacitus reports that the doors of the palace were dramatically flung open for him to emerge, and Suetonius says that he was proclaimed *pro gradibus palatii*, an allusion to the steps that would have been needed to make the podium accessible from the ground level. The building technique, a mixture of tile and travertine blocks certainly suits a late Claudianic date. The structure of the podium may also be a model for the similar platform of the Temple of Claudius, begun after that emperor's death by Agrippina at the northwest corner of the Caelian hill, opposite the site of the Colosseum. It thus seems probable that Tiberius lived in the house of his father, rather than in a newly built palace. This may seem a modest arrangement, but the old Claudian residence was in fact very extensive, and seems to have covered a whole block (*insula*) in a central location on the Germalus. It was doubtless here that Caligula on 27 May, 38 carried out sacrifices 'in the open air, in the house which had belonged to his grandfather Tiberius Caesar', as noted in the Arval record.[52]

Could, then, the Domus Tiberiana have been built by Caligula? His palatine residence was certainly extensive. It held art treasures, was the setting for banquets and was even, so it is reported, converted into a bordello.[53] But Josephus' account argues against a single, organically planned palace at this time. Also there is no reference to Caligula actually building a palace on the Palatine. His planned new residence is placed by Suetonius on the Capitoline, and on the Palatine he speaks merely of his extending the palace as far as the forum. Since there does not seem to be a single unitary palace at this time, Suetonius' words can not be taken in their literal sense. There are two developments to which he might have been referring. Along the northern edge of the hill, the platform of the Domus Tiberiana overlies republican houses. Recent excavation has shown that these were restored during the imperial period, and the mosaics in the pavements and walls suggest that the repairs were made after Tiberius. The restorations provide one possible context for Caligula's 'expansion' — the extending of the imperial property by buying up republican houses along the north range of the Germalus and refurbishing them. The imperial complex would thus now spread from the Houses of Augustus and Livia in the south, through the Claudian block in the centre to the houses overlooking the forum on the west edge, exactly the kind of arrangement described by Josephus. Caligula also seems to have acquired property, the Domus Gelotiana, on the southern slope of the Palatine over-looking the Circus Maximus, from which he would order races down below in response to the appeals of his neighbours.[54]

There is, however, another candidate. In his description of the extension of the imperial property to the forum Suetonius claims that Caligula turned the Temple of Castor (and Pollux) into a vestibule. Dio goes even further, saying that he cut the temple in two and made the approach to the palace run through it, to have Castor and Pollux as doorkeepers.[55] This has led some scholars to believe that the extension to the 'palace' may have moved off the Palatine proper, into the area that lies beneath the Santa Maria complex, located below the north-west corner of the Palatine between the forum and the north edge of the great granary complex built by Agrippa, the Horrea Agrippiana (ill. 7). Strictly, speaking this is not part of the Palatine, but the emphasis in Suetonius' expression *usque ad forum* ('right to the Forum') does seem to suggest a structure that went beyond the Palatine proper. The later history of this sector is fairly well known. Domitian established a complex here in alignment with the orientation of the forum, converted later into the church of Santa Maria Antiqua. Systematic excavation was carried out after 1900 by Boni and the work was resumed by a joint British–Italian project in 1983. The excavations have revealed remains of republican

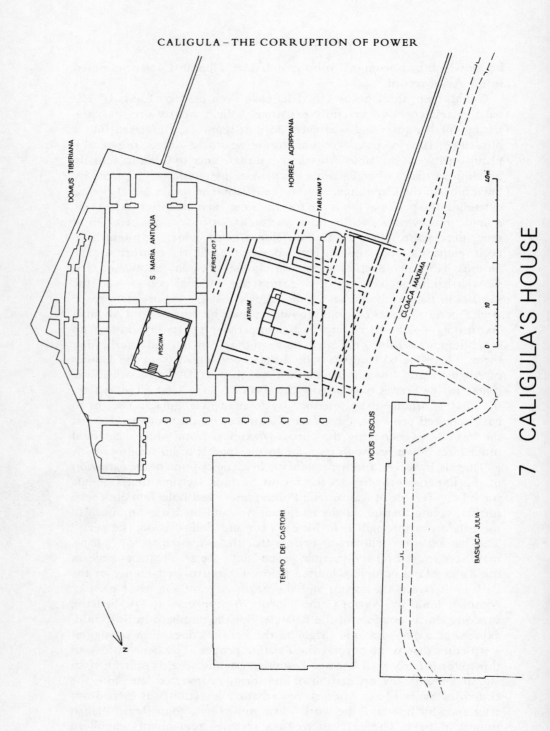

7 CALIGULA'S HOUSE

DOMUS TIBERIANA

S MARIA ANTIQUA

HORREA AGRIPPIANA

PERISTILIO?

TABLINUM?

ATRIUM

PISCINA

CLOACA MAXIMA

VICUS TUSCUS

TEMPIO DEI CASTORI

BASILICA JULIA

40 m

10

0

N

buildings under the Domitianic complex, sealed by herringbone floor, and remains of a tufa threshold. These may be contemporaenous with the Horrea Agrippiana, which has a similar herringbone floor. Overlying the floor is a later structure, aligned with the Domus Tiberiana and Horrea Agrippiana, rather than with the forum. Its most striking feature is a forecourt, or atrium, with an outer wall 26.5m (87 ft) x 22.3m (74 ft), thus the largest atrium known from either literary or archaeological sources in the Roman world. Within this are massive concrete foundations, up to 2.4m (8 ft) wide, for travertine blocks to support the four columns at the corners of the collecting-basin, or impluvium. There are traces of a gallery (*tablinum*) on the south side. To the east of the atrium is another room in which excavation has revealed a large foundation, perhaps for a peristyle, and possibly contemporaneous with the large atrium. This would have been built around a piscina, 25m (82 ft) by 8m (26 ft). The long sides of the pool are broken by alternating circular and rectangular niches, with steps down the short sides.

Since the excavations at the beginning of the century this complex has been interpreted as a kind of extension of the palace above. The discovery in the piscina of a fragment of marble tablet (perhaps from a statue base) with the legend in fine lettering [GER]MANICI F[ILIUS] ('son of Germanicus') confirmed the general assumption that the structure is Caligulan.[56] Current excavations do not seem to contradict this view, although for the moment any tentative conclusions must be regarded as speculative.[57] Sealed finds associated with the construction of the atrium seem to be mainly Augustan in character, which is certainly compatible with a Caligulan construction. H. Hurst, the current excavator, notes that the central axis of the temple of Castor passes through the mid-point of the atrium. The north walls of this residence could have abutted on the Temple of Castor, possibly with an entrance from the rear of the cella (not well enough preserved to allow certainty), and possibly with a more conventional entrance from the Vicus Tuscus.[58] Of course, the pre-Domitianic structure strictly has a northeast-southwest orienntation, while the Temple of Castor has an east–west orientation, producing an oblique juncture between the two, which, according to Tamm, would have been avoided by someone of Caligula's artistic sensitivity.[59] But since the residence was aligned with the Domus Tiberiana and the Vicus Tuscus, an exact orientation with the temple would be impossible. The difference of level, some 6m between the cella and the atrium, is not a serious objection, since it could have been exploited so as to provide a grand entrance into the atrium. P. Wiseman has suggested a quite different way of looking at Caligula's claim that he used Castor and Pollux as his door-keepers. He proposes that Caligula may have revived a plan first adopted by Augustus. This would have involved the use of the triumphal arch erected over the minor street leading to the Temple of Vesta as the entrance to his palace.[60] If Caligula did seek to implement such a scheme, the Dioscuri would thus have stood at the base of this grand entrance, and their description as doorkeepers may have arisen from a typically Caligulan quip. Wiseman's reoconstruction would certainly resolve a number of the difficulties. But Dio's comment, if it is to be taken at all seriously, that Claudius later 'restored their temple to Castor and Pollux', does seem to imply that the temple had somehow previously been incorporated into the structure, rather than that a decision was made to change the general access to the palace.[61]

Suetonius tells us that Caligula also laid foundations for a new house on the Capitol and built a bridge from the Palatine to connect with it. A planned palace on the Capitol in association with the Temple of Jupiter is certainly not to be ruled out, since it would to some extent parallel Augustus' palace-temple complex on the Palatine. The bridge is a different matter. The distance to be spanned would be some 250m (825 ft), at its highest point some 30m (99 ft) above the ground, and the whole idea should perhaps be dismissed as fantasy, prompted possibly by a another jocular remark of Caligula. The idea is introduced by Suetonius not as part of Caligula's building programme but rather in the context of his insane conversations with the gods. At any rate, none of it has survived. The notion, though curious, does receive some support from Pliny's observation that the city had been ringed by Caligula's houses; the great Italian archaeologist, Lugli, at any rate, took the idea seriously, suggesting that the bridge might have been built of wood.[62]

Perhaps the most useful aspect of Suetonius' story about the bridge is that it provides the location of the Temple of Augustus, over which it is said to have passed. The archaeological remains are scanty but Lugli has been able to confirm Suetonius and show that the Temple did in fact stand in the depression between the Capitoline and the Palatine, immediately behind the Basilica Julia.[63] Building began under Tiberius and seems to have reached a fairly advanced stage by the time he died, enough for it to be completed and dedicated by Caligula by the end of August 37.[64] To mark the dedication Caligula issued a striking sestertius, whose reverse depicts a sacrifice taking place in front of a temple (fig. 18). In the foreground is a veiled figure in a toga, presumably Caligula himself, sacrificing at a garlanded altar, with a dish in his right hand. Behind him an attendant with an axe in his belt is leading a bull to the altar, while a second attendant holds a dish. The Temple is identified by the inscription DIVO AUG(USTO). It has six Ionic columns with festoons hanging across the front. There are various figures on the pediment; the central one holds a *patera* and possibly a sceptre, and may be Divus Augustus. On the left edge a figure variously identified as Mars or Romulus, and on the right a group consisting of Aeneas, Ascanius and Anchises. The temple was restored by Antoninus Pius in 158/9 and is depicted on his coins, showing that by this later date it now has a range of eight columns of the Corinthian order.[65]

One of the most notorious incidents of Caligula's reign, and perhaps the most striking example of wasteful extravagance, was the building of the bridge of boats across part of the Bay of Naples from Puteoli to the vicinity of Baiae. The occasion is impossible to date with certainty. Dio places it in 39, in the general context of events preceding Caligula's departure for Germany and Gaul. This is plausible but he does not relate the episode very closely to what is described before or after, and he may not have known when it occurred, but simply have inserted it at this point for convenience. A very vivid description of the whole episode is provided in Dio and Suetonius. Boats needed for the construction were built on the spot, but since they did not suffice others had to be brought in from other stations.[66] The boats were anchored in a double line, and earth was then heaped on them. In Dio's account the bridge was more than a mere passage but had resting places located along its course with fresh drinking water. On the first day Caligula donned what he claimed was the breastplate of Alexander, supposedly brought back from his sarcophagus in Alexandria, putting it over a purple cloak decorated with gold and gems.[67] Wearing an oak garland, and decked with sword and shield, he sacrificed to a number of gods, including Neptune and Envy, and entered the structure at the Baiae end, charging at full tilt with a train of infantry and cavalry, identified specifically as Praetorians by Suetonius. Suetonius also has him moving back and forth for two days, while Dio says that he waited in Puteoli until the second day, before returning in splendid style.

Both sources indicate that the real spectacle was reserved for the second day. On this occasion Caligula was pulled by a team of victorious race-horses followed by a train of 'spoils' and hostages, including Darius, son of Artabanus, King of Parthia. He had an enormous retinue, beginning with friends and associates in garlanded robes, followed by the Praetorians, then the general public, in whatever attire each individual might choose. Dio says that Caligula enjoyed calm seas, prompting him to suggest that Neptune was afraid of him. At the centre of the bridge he climbed onto a platform and harangued the crowd. He contrasted his great exploit with the famous crossings of Xerxes (Hellespont) and Darius (Bosphorus) and pointed to the fact that he had bridged a much wider expanse of water than they had done. He congratulated the troops, who had undergone great hardships and perils (they may have been involved in its construction), then distributed money and ordered a celebration which lasted the rest of the day and through the night, both on the bridge and on boats anchored nearby. The whole event was lit by torches on the structure and the surrounding mountains. As the party progressed it inevitably got out of hand. People were invited from the shore to join in, and during the drunken revelry some were thrown into the sea, and seem to have become caught up in mock sea-battles. A number of people were drowned, but the casualties were kept to a minimum because the sea was exceptionally calm during the whole period.

What were Caligula's motives in building the bridge? Josephus and Seneca cite it as an example of madness. Josephus says that he found it tedious to cross the bay in a trireme, and also that it was his privilege as lord of the water to ride across it in a chariot, while Seneca sees it as an imitation of Xerxes, for which Caligula squandered his resources although there was only seven days' food left in the city. Suetonius, who places the event among the acts of the 'princeps' rather than the 'monster', provides three theories: to outdo Xerxes, whose bridging of the Hellespont was such a celebrated event; to inspire fear among the Britons and Germans; or (the story that his grandfather picked up), to confound the predictions of the court astrologer Thrasyllus that Caligula had no more chance of becoming emperor than of riding over the gulf of Baiae. It has even been suggested that the bridge involved some kind of military defence or even a mole- we know that Caligula undertook a harbour near Rhegium and a canal through the Isthmus of Corinth, and he may have undertaken similar work in the Bay of Naples.[68] But rational explanations are hardly needed. Caligula would not have been the first autocratic ruler to prove his manhood by grandiose construction, witness Versailles, or the Summer Palace in Peking. Suetonius' grandfather may have come closest to the truth. After Baiae, no one could doubt who was in control at Rome!

Appendix
The Location of the Bridge

The ancient sources are in disagreement about the location of the bridge. Dio 59.17.1 says that it stretched from Puteoli to Bauli, Jos. *AJ*. 19.5 from Dicaearchia (Puteoli) to Misenum, Suet. *Cal*. 19.1 from Puteoli to Baiae. The Puteoli end seems secure enough. Bauli is described by Piny *NH* 9.172 as part of Baiae, although at another point (*NH* 3.61) he says that it was between Baiae and Puteoli. Tac. *Ann*. 14.4.3-4 identifies Bauli as the name of a villa between Misenum and Baianus lacus (Lucrine lake?). Bauli may be the modern Bacoli, between Miseno and Baiae. Josephus gives the length of the bridge as 30 stades (at *AJ* 18.249, however, he gives the grossly underestimated figure that Puteoli was 5 stades from Baiae). Suetonius gives the length as 3.6 Roman miles (4.8k), Dio as 26 stades and since he uses a system of 7.5 stades to the Roman mile this produces a distance of 3.46 Roman miles (4.6k). The actual distance from Puteoli to Bacoli is 2 $\frac{1}{4}$ (3.6k).

· 14 ·

FIT TO RULE?

BECAUSE OF THE distortions in the historical tradition, it is very difficult
to determine to what degree Caligula might be considered mentally and
physically fit for the task of being emperor. It does appear that in his
early years he suffered from delicate health. He was prone to epileptic
fits, and Augustus was concerned enough in AD 14 to appoint two doctors
to accompany him when he travelled north to join his parents. As he
grew older, his strength gradually improved, but fainting fits still at times
made it difficult for him walk or stay standing up.[1] There are signs that
he continued to be troubled by various ailments as an adult, such as his
serious illness in 38, and his stomach-ache on the day of his death, but
he was hearty enough to make the arduous journey north in 39, and to
amuse himself racing chariots in his own private race-course in Rome.

It is clear that Caligula was highly strung and nervous. This came out
whenever he spoke in public. His words and ideas would pour out, and
in delivering a speech he would become so excited that he had to keep
moving about. During theatrical perfomances he would get carried away,
and join in, adding his own words and gestures. It comes as no surprise
that he suffered from insomnia (to which Augustus also was prone).
Suetonius claims that he never managed more than three hours sleep in
any one night, and would wander through his apartments calling for the
dawn. Even when he did manage to fall into sleep, it was fitful and
disturbed by vivid nightmares. Consequently he would sometimes nod
off at dinner parties.[2] The more colourful accounts of his nervousness
must be treated with caution. During storms, Suetonius tells us, Caligula
became so frightened that he hid under the bed, and during an eruption
of Aetna he ran in panic from the city of Messana. The reliability of such
stories can be gauged by a third, patently absurd report that he was so
panic-stricken on news of a defeat in Germany that he fitted out a fleet
to escape from Rome and seek refuge in the provinces. Such anecdotes
were traditionally told about emperors. Augustus, for instance, supposedly
hid in an underground room during thunderstorms, and Tiberius was
said to be so terrified by storms that he wore a laurel wreath, in the
belief, fortunately never put to the test, that it offered protection

against lightning.[3]

During the nineteenth century the prevalent scholarly view of Caligula was that he was more than just nervous and excitable, and in fact a totally deranged madman, so depraved and cruel that his actions could not be judged by the norms of human behaviour. Possibly the most celebrated study of this type was that of L. Quidde, *Caligula. Eine Studie ber rémische Cäsarwahnsinn,* published in Leipzig in 1894, in which Caligula was used to attack the political excesses of the German emperor William II (the 'Kaiser'). The notion is, admittedly, reflected to some degree in the ancient sources, and there was clearly a tradition that explained Caligula's behaviour as resulting from madness caused by some external agent. Both Josephus and Suetonius report the belief, echoed in the poet Juvenal, that Caesonia sent him mad with an aphrodisiac. This claim can be discounted. It is certainly difficult to reconcile with other stories of his sexual prowess, and perhaps arose to explain Caesonia's strange hold over her husband. The poet Lucretius was similarly said to have been sent mad by a love philtre.[4] Suetonius suggests that Caligula was mentally unsound, but his story that he recognized his own mental infirmity and thought of retiring to purge his brain is probably an echo of one of Caligula's own jokes.[5] On the issue of his supposed madness we are fortunate to have two contemporary writers who had known him personally: Seneca and Philo. Since both are extremely hostile, Seneca largely for personal reasons, Philo because of his profound religious convictions, they would obviously miss no opportunity to describe any display of madness. Seneca goes out of his way to paint Caligula in the darkest possible colours, dwelling in particular on his savagery and brutality. Moreover he uses terms appropriate to the vocabulary of insanity, such as *dementia* and *furiosa inconstantia.* The difficulty is that in their contexts these expressions denote not so much madness as excessively arrogant or even foolish behaviour, as do similar expressions in Tacitus, and Seneca called even Alexander the Great *vesanus* (mad) and *furibundus* (wild).[6] Moreover, for all his deep antipathy towards Caligula, Seneca attributes to him not a single specific act that could be described as mad, in the full sense of the word. In fact, one incident, although described by Seneca as an act of *dementia,* provides an excellent check on the stories of his madness in the other sources. Suetonius claims that Caligula would hold conversations with the statue of Jupiter in the temple on the Capitoline, and would sometimes challenge the god with the line Ajax used in the famous wrestling match in Homer's *Iliad,* when, to break the deadlock with Odysseus, he called out 'Lift me, or I'll lift you!' Dio tells the same story in a different form, in the context of Caligula's thunder-machine, a device that echoed thunderclaps when it thundered and gave out flashes when it lightened. To the accompaniment of this, whenever a bolt fell, Caligula would hurl a javelin at a rock and shout out the very same challenge. Seneca, writing for an audience that may well have participated in the event, tells us what probably did happen. Caligula had been planning to put on a theatrical show of some sort (perhaps echoed in Dio's thunder-machine), and was looking forward to performing in it himself, when the whole set was suddenly washed out by a thunderstorm. His reaction was to yell out the familiar challenging words. Thus what is presented in the later sources as an instance of Caligula's craziness, turns out to be little more than a blasphemous outburst uttered in anger (or mock anger), a not uncommon human reaction when sudden bad weather ruins a special treat.[7]

To Philo, Caligula was a lunatic, but he was bound to appear as such to a devout Jew, given that he demanded recognition from his people as a god and even planned to expropriate the Temple of Jerusalem for his own worship. Philo is especially valuable because he is the only source who provides us with an eyewitness account of Caligula's behaviour as late as the autumn of 40, a short period before his death. At their meeting, Philo was convinced that he was dealing with a madman, but, viewed dispassionately, the scene he describes as a participant presents an almost engaging Caligula, with a sharp sense of humour, a penchant for engaging in clever verbal badinage, a man who knows that his audience is afraid of him and plays on this knowledge, disconcerting his company by making them follow him from room to room. Even Philo admits that by the time the audience was finished Caligula had adopted a milder tone (*pros to malakoteron*), asserting that the Jews were not criminals but mentally incompetent for not believing that he had a divine nature.[8] Even though the intention of Philo's account is to depict Caligula as unhinged, the final impression is not of a madman, but of a conceited, ill-mannered and rather irresponsible young ruler.

In this century the scholarly tendency has been to move away from the notion of simple madness (which has managed to remain firmly rooted in the popular mind). One approach has been to attempt a more sophisticated quasi-clinical diagnosis of his mental state. This process may be said to have originated in Hans Sachs, *Bubi. Die Liebensgheschichte des Caligula,* published in 1930, a fairly uncritical compendium of Suetonius and Dio, but dressed up in modern psychological garb. Among more recent studies, A. Esser has concluded that Caligula was schizophrenic, while J. Lucas insists that he was in fact schizoid, only veering towards schizophrenia, and that he suffered from psychopathy.[9] Their approach is surely a dubious one. Even in the best clinical conditions psychoanalyis is a complex and difficult procedure. It seems particularly unscientific to analyze a 'patient' through symptoms reported by hearsay, by writers who are in the main several generations separated from the object of study, and, most seriously of all, have an established record of recounting the titillating gossip that would encourage later analysts to assume mental instability. The sources for the career of Caligula provide difficulties enough for the traditional historian; they present even more serious problems for the would-be psychoanalyst.

One fatal obstacle to the attempt to psychoanalyse Caligula in any depth from such a remove is that much of what has been attributed to him seems to originate from his own ironical view of the world, not fully understood in his time, and much distorted in the tradition. He clearly had a highly developed sense of humour, a humour that was often cruel and sadistic and which made its effect essentially by cleverly scoring points. Helicon, it will be remembered, became one of Caligula's favourites because he was so clever with maliciously cruel jokes. Inevitably many of Caligula's jokes must have been much funnier at the time, and would have been helped by having an appreciative and captive audience. His humour seems invariably to have been in bad taste, and it is hardly surprising that it has been used to create such a negative impression of him. When a man thought rich, for example, was eliminated for his money, but turned out to own nothing, Caligula reputedly commented, 'He died in vain'. When selecting prisoners from a row to be slain he pointed to their line, with a bald man at either end, and said 'From the bald-headed one to the bald-headed one', an expression that seems to have become proverbial. Some of the jokes are a little more subtle, involving literary allusions or a clever use of language, such as his description of Livia as a 'Ulysses in petticoats', and his play on the name Frugi (literally 'frugal') when, at a banquet, he set out an expensive course and said that a man should either be 'Frugi' or 'Caesar'. The best description of Caligula in a joking mood is, again, provided by Philo's account of his meeting with the embassies in 40. His good humour was probably enhanced by the appreciative audience of hangers-on. Caligula was clearly at his most impish, and Philo's overall observation that *to pragma mimeia tis en* ('the affair was a kind of farce') must evoke some sympathy. The hearings were conducted as work was taking place on the palace and the delegations were obliged to rush from room to room, following the emperor as he moved briskly about, giving instructions to the decorators on the furnishings and fittings. The place, according to Philo, was something between a *theatron kai desmoterion* ('a theatre and a prison'). To the great amusement of the Greeks, Caligula greeted the Jews with the mock pedantic term *theomiseis* ('haters of the gods'), because they could not recognize his divinity. The Jews were no more capable of understanding Caligula's sense of humour than were the Romans. They protested that they had demonstrated their loyalty by making sacrifices. This provoked a piece of word-play, that the sacrifices had been *for* him but not *to* him, and *ti oun ophelos?* ('what use is that?'); the humour escaped them and the rejoinder reportedly terrified them. When he asked 'Why don't you eat pork?' everyone, apart from the Jews, burst into loud peals of laughter, and Philo admits that their amusement was at least in part genuine. The precise point of the joke, so well received, is lost to us, since we do not know what immediately preceded. But the Wildean character of his follow-up is readily apparent. When the Jews pointed out that in avoiding pork they were not exceptional, since other communities had dietary prohibitions against ordinary foods, such as lamb, 'Quite right, too', was his reply, 'It isn't nice!' When they finally came to the serious question at issue, the political rights of the Jews, Caligula pretended only to half-listen, absorbed more in the window arrangements of one room or the pictures to be hung in another. The Jews were in despair by the end of the meeting. They did not seem to appreciate that Caligula was essentially amusing himself at their expense, and did so right up to the close of the meeting, when he ended with the observation that they should be considered unfortunate lunatics rather than criminals, for not believing that he was a god. That was the last communication that the envoys received from the emperor, and the hearings ended without any decison. As patently happens in this account of Philo, Caligula's cruel and ironical squibs must have been turned against him by the hostile sources, and probably lie at the heart of many of the uncomplimentary anecdotes about him. His *bons mots* would be taken from their original contexts and repeated in whatever way would create the most prejudicial impression of him. His supposed plans to make his horse consul (or priest), to set up house next door to Jupiter, to flay Apelles (as a hybrid Greco–Latin word the name would mean 'skinless') to eliminate whole legions on the Rhine, probably have their roots in sardonic and sarcastic jests.[10]

Caligula's barbs of humour were directed at every available target, including himself (the suggestion that he would retire to purge his brain), and members of his own family. This latter group, in particular, have been much misunderstood, and casual references in Suetonius, not generally reflected in the other sources, have been inflated out of all proportion to their significance. Caligula's devotion to his family, to his parents, grandparents, brothers and sisters is well established in the sources. When in 40 he informed the senatorial embassy that none of his family was to receive honours his anger was clearly directed against his two surviving sisters, and perhaps his uncle Claudius, as a direct and specific response to the treachery he had exposed. To take it as an injunction against his ancestors, his wife Caesonia, his daughter, is surely perverse. Moreover, it is clearly dangerous to read any serious or profound intentions in isolated comments reported almost *en passant* by Suetonius.[11] Suetonius mentions that Caligula refused to be thought of as the grandson of Marcus Agrippa because of his humble origins and became angry if anyone spoke of him as his ancestor. To top this he supposedly claimed that his mother Agrippina (daughter of Agrippa) had been born as a result of incest between Augustus and his daughter Julia.[12] That this must have resulted from some casual joke in poor taste is indicated clearly by the numismatic and epigraphic record. On the funerary urn that contained the remains of Caligula's mother Agrippina in the Mausoleum of Augustus her relationship to Agrippa is clearly stated: *ossa Agrippinae M. Agrippae [f.] divi Aug. neptis...* ('the bones of Agrippina, daughter of Marcus Agrippa, granddaughter of Divus Augustus'). A statue base of the Caligulan period at Aphrodisias also identifies Agrippina as the daughter of Marcus Agrippa and mother of Caligula. At Mytilene, dedications to Agrippa and others were made under Caligula.[13] The 'Agrippa as', bearing the head of Agrippa on the obverse, is now recognized as having been minted throughout Caligula's reign, and is, in fact, his commonest coin (Fig. 24). It is imitated in the local issues of the colony of Caesaraugusta in Spain, and the same mint produced dupondii with the head of Agrippina, with the filiation *MF (Marci Filia)*, 'daughter of Marcus (Agrippa)' (p. 251). Moreover, the official sestertius series from the Rome mint, honouring Agrippina, undated but clearly belonging to Caligula's reign, (she is identified as 'Mother of Gaius Caesar') has the same filiation, *MF (Marci Filia)* (Fig. 19). One copper piece of Caligula, classed by Grant as a medallion, depicts Caligula's head on the obverse and is accompanied by the legend *C. Caesar Germanici F. M. Agrippae N.* (Gaius Caesar, son of Germanicus, grandson of Marcus Agrippa).[14]

Suetonius claims that Caligula similarly tried to cast a slur on the memory of Augustus by forbidding the celebration of the battle of Actium and Sicily. The notion that Caligula tried to distance himself from Augustus is absurd, and totally disproved by the great weight of the literary evidence, and by the emphasis that he constantly places on his descent from Augustus in his coins and inscriptions. Some scholars have read profound implications into the idea that Caligula decided to promote himself as the grandson of Antony rather than of Augustus, and accordingly punished the consuls for celebrating the victory at Actium. Garzetti and Momigliano, for instance, suggest that Caligula's dream of absolutism had been inspired by Antony's example, and Ceauçescu even sees his support of Antony as a propaganda tool to help effect a conciliation between the eastern and western parts of the empire.[15] Yet when the incident is considered more closely it appears far less significant. Dio reports that Caligula's posing as a descendant of Antony rather than of Augustus was simply a pretext. The emperor reputedly told his closest advisers that he was determined to find fault with the consuls, and that if they had *not* celebrated Actium he would have used that as an excuse to get rid of them. Dio's cynicism is borne out by the newly discovered fragment of the Arval record. It shows that in 38 Caligula in fact carried out sacrifices on 1 August at the Temple of Augustus, as part of the festival constituted in 30 BC to mark the final defeat of Antony. There is not a single scrap of numismatic or epigraphic evidence to show any special favour for Antony. Certainly, a few months after the incident of the dismissed consuls, Caligula does not seem to have shown much sentimentality about Antony's memory and sold at auction one of his possessions, seized as spoil by Augustus.[16] The Arval records show that the birthdays of Augustus, Livia, Tiberius and Antonia were all celebrated during Caligula's reign. Antony's birthday fell on 14 January. The Arval record for the early part of 38 has survived and shows unmistakably that Antony's birthday was not celebrated, at least in that year. Moreover Suetonius reports that his successor Claudius honoured Marc Antony, insisting that the birthday of Drusus, his father, be celebrated all the more vigorously because it fell on the same day as Antony's. This seems to be presented as a novelty, without any hint that Caligula had preceded Claudius in granting these honours.[17] Similarly, Suetonius' claim that Caligula treated Claudius only as a *ludibrium* ('laughing-stock') is disproved by the facts, given that under him Claudius for the first time received the consulship and entry into the senate, as well as a special place at the games. It is also difficult to know what to make of Suetonius' report that Caligula charged in a letter that Livia was of low birth, and that her grandfather, Aufidius Lurco, had been only a local official in Fundi. Suetonius responds that Lurco had actually held offices in Rome. But in fact inscriptions show that Suetonius is totally confused, and that Livia's grandfather was a Marcus Alfidius, probably from Marruvium.[18]

Another approach to the problems of Caligula's personality has been to see him as a man obsessed by oriental ideas and customs. This seems to be an area where the scholarly imagination has allowed itself free rein, and claims have been made that, for their outrageousness, could rival anything that Caligula could devise. The source of his supposed inspiration varies. Lugand, for instance, even argued that Caligula was a Mazdaean who prepared for his future travels with the sun with a rehearsal at Baiae. The Mazdaeans sacrificed to the sun, and Incitatus, the intended victim, was kept in much comfort to be prepared for his apotheosis.[19] The source of inspiration favoured by modern scholars, however, is Egypt, and some of the supposed manifestations of his mania for that country are richly imaginative. Gagé, for instance, observed that the first day of the Egyptian year was Thot, 30 August, just before Caligula's birthday, and asserts that the emperor must have gone through life conscious of this — perhaps the punishment of the consuls in 39 for the celebration of Actium in September was because the anniversary came close to Thot. Lambrechts has argued that Caligula's aversion to Homer may result from the poet's use of the traditional account of Helen, rather than the Egyptian version that she stayed in Egypt and never went to Troy. The fullest treatment of the theme, however, is that of Köberlein, who insists that the guiding principle for the whole of Caligula's reign is an adherence to the religious and political traditions of Egypt.[20] Thus the amnesty at the beginning of the rein is supposedly inspired by the example of the pharaohs, Caligula's departure from Rome is inspired by the departure of Isis after the death of Osiris, and the recovery of his mother's ashes is modelled on Isis' similar service for Osiris.

The most frequently cited example of his mania for things Egyptian is the story of his incest with Drusilla. This, it is claimed, was dicated by Pharaonic or Ptolemaic practices, which condoned marriage between the siblings of the royal dynasty in order to preserve the sacred bloodline.[21] Yet apart from the general scepticism that we should apply to stories of Caligula's supposed incest, two specific objections arise. The first is that Caligula's fling with Drusilla is originally said to have been discovered in the emperor's youth at the home of Antonia, well before there was any serious prospect of his becoming princeps. Also, an obsession with the purity of the bloodline is hard to reconcile with the two husbands of Drusilla and the four wives of Caligula. It is in fact worth noting that there is only a *single* explicit allusion in the sources to Caligula's supposed predilection for Egypt — the belief that he planned to move his capital to Alexandria. Even this example is not compelling. Philo reports it only as a rumour, while Suetonius is not sure whether he planned to move to Alexandria or the very Italian town of Antium. In any case, Alexandria was to the Romans the epitome of oriental corruption, and a charge that Caligula planned to move there was an easy way to discredit him. The very same accusation was levelled against Caesar and Marc Antony.[22]

A much repeated claim has been that Caligula was a devotee of the worship of Isis. The main evidence for this is Josephus' statement that he was initiated into some of the mysteries and that he enjoyed dressing up in women's clothing and wig, which is thought to denote his performing as a priest of Isis in long robe.[23] It is also suggested that he might have been responsible for building the Isaeum that had been erected on the Campus Martius by 65. There was an a Temple of Isis there by 65, to which the poet Lucan alludes, but its adscription to Caligula is founded on little more than the aversion to Egyptian cults displayed by Augustus and Tiberius.[24] The date of the Roman festival of Isis may provide a clue. The fourth century calendar of Philocalus records the festival of Isis as beginning in Rome on October 28; its Egyptian prototype began on Hathyr 17. Now Philocalus seems to have based his Roman date on the correlation of Hathyr 17 in the 'old' pre-Julian Egyptian calendar, which survived in Egypt alongside the reformed Julian version and whose dates, lacking a leap year, shift one day every four years relative to the Julian. Hathyr 17 happened to fall on October 28 in the years 40–43. Thus if the institution of the festival of Isis in Rome coincides with the building of the Isaeum (though this is far from certain), the chronological data would suit a Claudian just as well as a Caligulan foundation.[25] There is also a piece of spurious archaeological evidence. The supposed Isiac chapel (the 'Aula Isiaca'), incorporated into the substructures of the later Flavian palace on the Palatine, has been assumed by many scholars to have been commissioned originally by Caligula, because of his interest in Isis. It consists of a long apsidal room with wall paintings with symbolic Egyptian motifs, often thought to depict Isis or one of her priestesses.[26] Unfortunately for the theory, it is now known that the paintings preceded his reign by at least half a century, and in any case may not even have an Isiac theme.[27] They can have no bearing whatsoever on Caligula's attitude towards Isis or Egyptian civilization generally.

It would, of course, be foolish to deny that Caligula might have had an interest in the culture and civilization of Egypt. Certainly on the day of his death he was supposed to have been preparing a *pervigilium* in which mystery scenes from the underworld were represented, involving Egyptians and Ethiopians.[28] But Romans were generally fascinated with things Egyptian. From Augustus' time Roman art and architecture reflects this. The famous pyramid tomb of Gaius Cestius was built some time before 12 BC, and Egyptian obelisks were erected by Augustus himself in various places, most notably at the entrance to his own mausoleum and as part of his sundial in the Campus Martius. This fascination continued through the century. Pliny the Elder speaks of the passion for personal adornments from Egypt in his own day, reporting that 'now indeed even men are beginning to wear on their fingers Harpocrates and figures of Egyptian deities.'[29] There is no reason to think that Caligula could have been immune to these trends, but there is simply no evidence to show that any interest that he may or may not have had developed into a mania. Nor, of course, would Claudius have been immune, and we can not assume that Caligula's successor would have been averse to the revival of the worship of Isis, or to the building of the Isaeum in the Campus Martius. The famous Mensa Isiaca, a bronze tablet inlaid in silver with divine figures and pseudo- hieroglyphs was presumably made for a Roman sanctuary, and can be dated to Claudius, whose name was added in hieroglyphs in a cartouche.[30]

It has also been asserted that Caligula would have been especially vulnerable to oriental ideas of autocracy because of the time that he spent with his grandmother Antonia and with the client kings from the east that he met as a child.[31] No doubt Antonia did teach him something of the importance of the eastern client kingdoms in the overall imperial system, and this may have influenced him when he became emperor. But she was perhaps the most responsible and level-headed of the Julio-Claudians, and it seems inconceivable that she would have sought to fill Caligula's young head with dangerous ideas of oriental despotism. Claudius lived with Antonia much longer than did Caligula and was exposed to the same influences, but did not have his mind warped.

Caligula did not need oriental rulers to provide a precedent to transform the principate into a monarchy, as Suetonius puts it. Nor did he need Herod Agrippa and Antiochus as teachers of tyranny. The senate by conferring absolute authority on him in 37, had already given the inexperienced youth all the powers a despot might seek. No doubt as his reign progressed Caligula would have been influenced by his friends of the Hellenized east, and this could explain his interest in such things as his exotic clothing. The eastern client kings may well have suggested to him the *style* of absolutism. The main drive to attain it was entirely his own, nurtured by a cooperative senate.[32]

In fact, Caligula seems to have achieved some of his greatest successes in his dealings with the client-kings, and in his arrangements for the eastern part of the empire was able to display the most creative application of his autocratic powers. Caligula seems to have been concerned primarily with preserving stablility in this part of his empire, rather than with extending the Roman imperium (this would be sought in the north), and client rulers were an excellent means to this end. His appointments were very personal, but not familiar. Even his closest friend, Agrippa, the most prominent of these rulers, was careful to keep his place in his relations with the emperor. Suetonius tells an anecdote of visiting kings who attended a banquet with Caligula, and in the casual after dinner conversation gave the impression that they felt they were all fellow-monarchs, drawing fom Caligula a rebuke, in the form of a line of Homer: 'Let there be one master, let there be one King'.[33] Personal considerations apart, he generally chose rulers who served Rome loyally.[34] Among his arrangments an otherwise unknown Sohaemus was created ruler of Itauraea, perhaps related to the Sohaemus who succeeded to the throne of Emesa in the first year of Nero's reign. Mithridates, son of Gepaipyris, was confirmed in his position as ruler of the Bosporus, where he served Rome's interests well.[35] Antiochus of Commagene received back his father's old kingdom, earlier organized into a Roman province by Germanicus, as well as territory in Cilicia.[36] He also received 100 million sesterces for the taxes and other revenues from his kingdom that had accumulated during the twenty years that had elapsed since his father's death — by AD 69 he was reputed to be the richest of the client kings.[37] With Agrippa, Antiochus was associated in the minds of the Romans as Caligula's 'tutors in tyranny'. Unfortunately, the sources say nothing about his early relationship with Caligula, but it must have been friendly, since, along with Agrippa, he was one of the first rulers to receive benefits from the new emperor. His links with Agrippa and his presence in Gaul suggest that he might in fact have enjoyed Caligula's special friendship, and it was possibly in honour of the emperor that he founded a new city in Cetis, which he named Germanicopolis.[38]

The great importance of personal ties is well illustrated by the fortunes of the three sons of the late Cotys, the murdered King of Thrace, who had been sent to Rome on the death of their father and had become friends of Caligula, presumably in Antonia's house. Eighteen years later, a year after Caligula had come to power, the three young men were rewarded by the bestowal of client kingdoms that exceeded by far their simple Thracian inheritance. Their investiture took place in a splendid ceremony in the forum at Rome.[39] Rhoemetalces received the whole of his father's dominions in Thrace as sole ruler. Polemo II, grandson of Polemo I, was awarded his 'ancestral domain' of Pontus. Cotys was made ruler of Armenia minor, which had also once belonged to his grandfather Polemo II, and, Dio cryptically states, was later granted part of Arabia also. We have no details on their rule, but no crises are reported in their territories during Caligula's reign. Polemo, at any rate, proved to be one of the most loyal and endurable of the client kings, surviving until Nero's reign, when he provided help to Corbulo in the Parthian campaigns. He lost his kingdom in 64/5 when it was annexed by Nero.

The arrangements that Caligula made in the East in fact reflect the one talent that he clearly did seem to possess as an administrator, the ability to choose competent subordinates. The appointment of Roman legates like Petronius and Galba were outstanding. The eastern client kings, often personal friends of the emperor, and in most cases connected with their old kingdoms by a complex nexus of political marriages, are further examples. Certainly Claudius was generally willing to maintain the *status quo*, and to leave his predecessor's choices in place.

Caligula does seem to have taken a broad interest in the the empire outside the boundaries of Italy, although it is risky to draw firm conclusions from a reign as brief as his. His stay in Gaul marked the first visit of an emperor to one of the provinces in over half a century. In recruiting men to the equestrian order he made a point of bringing in candidates from throughout the empire. The large scale extension of citizenship to provincials, which began under Julius Casear, had come almost to a stop under Tiberius. It had resumed by the time of Claudius, but there are indications that the process may actually have been started again under Caligula, who certainly seems to have been concerned about the problem of bogus claims for citizenship.[40] Philo cites a supposed letter of Herod Agrippa, where the king notes that Caligula had bestowed the citizenship on the cities of some of his friends. These might have included Vienne, in Narbonese Gaul, the birthplace of the emperor's friend Valerius Asiaticus; this city had honoured Caligula with statues even before his accession. At some point before 48 was a change in its status, when it seems to have acquired the standing of a *colonia*, with the benefits of full citizenship. But while this development has been generally, and perhaps correctly, attributed to Caligula, it could very well be due to Claudius.[41] Certainly, there can be no doubting the awe in which Caligula was held by the Gauls, who were willing to pay as much as 200,000 sesterces for an invitation to dine with him. Willrich has also suggested that the closing of the Spanish mints, observable in Caligula's reign, might be part of a process to unify and centralize the empire, by replacing local coins with 'official' issues, at any rate in the west.[42]

It may have been under Caligula that certain military districts of the empire were organized as provinces. The Alpine district of Raetia had been left by Tiberius with one detachment of troops under a miltary prefect. It appears afterwards to have been joined with the Alpes Penninae under a civilian procurator. Quintus Septicius Pica seems to be the first, and to have served in that office under both Caligula and Claudius. The same arrangement has been suggested for Noricum, the mountainous area south of the Danube, where H.-G. Pflaum identifies Caligula's first procurator as Aulus Trebonius.[43]

In Rome itself any talent that Caligula might have possessed for administration would probably be most severely tested in his handling of financial affairs. It is very difficult, however, to evaluate the financial policies of any of the Julio–Claudian emperors, because of the uncertainty about the division between the income of the emperor as head of state, and of the emperor as private individual. By the late empire the emperor's fiscus ('chest') was a kind of imperial treasury. In the first two centuries it could imply state funds that were under imperial control, but it generally seems to have referred to the emperor's personal wealth.[44] Given the overlap between their personal and public finances it is hardly surprising that the emperors made little attempt at formal accounting. Augustus presented *rationes* (balance-sheets) on two occasions, each time when he feared that he was near death. The first occurred during his serious illness in 23 BC, and just before he died he gave another. Tiberius apparently gave only one report to the senate, in 33. The practice was revived by Caligula at the beginning of his reign, for which he won much praise, but there is no evidence that he repeated the process in later years.[45] This account in 37 revealed a considerable surplus, which Suetonius reports as 2, 700 million sesterces, Dio as 2,300 or 3,300 million.[46] Again, it is not clear what these figures actually represent, and the discrepancies may well result from confusion over the precise status of the imperial fiscus. On one point both sources are in agreement, that Caligula found no problem in spending this carefully accumulated surplus, an achievement apparently much admired by Nero.[47]

Some of his expenditures would have been due to his own extravagance. He clearly spent a vast fortune on his lavish way of life, even if we make allowance for the inevitable exaggeration of the sources. He engaged in a costly building programme, and constructed fine villas throughout Campania. It is claimed that he dined on one occasion at a cost of 10 million sesterces, reputedly equal to the annual revenues of three provinces.

He had a habit of giving money away irresponsibly. It was of course a time-honoured tradition for the emperor to be generous, but with discretion. As Fergus Millar notes, 'The maintenance of the emperor's rule demanded not only a constant outflow of gifts, but the giving of them in a magnanimous and dignified manner'. Some of his gifts were in this category. When a devastating fire destroyed much of the Aemiliana district in October 38 he not only assisted directly in putting it out but made up the losses of those who suffered. This was imperial behaviour at its traditional best. But often Caligula's manner was far from 'dignified'. He lavished gifts on friends, actors, gladiators and chariot-drivers. He reputedly gave the men who played ball with him 100,000 each. Lucius Caecilius, presented with only 50,000, is said to have queried, 'Do I play one-handed?' Few could have refused the money, and only one is recorded as having done so. When Caligula tried to give Demetrius the Cynic 200,000, the philosopher retorted that if the emperor wanted to bribe him he would have to offer him his whole kingdom.[48]

It is only fair to point out, that the healthy balance accrued by Tiberius was in part illusory. His frugality had left Caligula with certain obligations. The legacies of Livia had not been paid, and a number of building projects remained uncompleted. Thus it has to be recognized that the new reign did begin with a number of liabilities. In the settlement of Tiberius' will, the people received a bequest of 45 million. This was probably distributed to them in a *congiarium*, held on 1 June, when each was given 300 sesterces. A second *congiarium* followed on 19 July, when an extra 240 sesterces was presented to each to make up for the sum they had missed when Caligula assumed the toga virilis, and he added the accrued interest of 60 sesterces, for a similar total of 300.[49] Bequests were also paid to the Praetorians, urban cohorts (a kind of city police force), the Vigiles and the legionaries. There were also various minor bequests, such as to the Vestal Virgins, as well as a million to Claudius. Caligula did not stop here, however. Livia's will had not been executed by Tiberius, and the new emperor proceeded to honour it. The legacies apparently were substantial: the future emperor Galba, for instance, became a rich man through his inheritance from Livia.[50]

This massive injection of cash into the financial system would have given the Roman economy a tremendous boost. We perhaps have a glimpse of this in an unexpected source, the *Satyricon* of Petronius. One of Petronius' most memorable characters, Trimalchio, took the first step in building up his considerable fortune when he managed to buy five old barges and fill them with wine, which he sold in Rome for a massive profit, as wine was 'worth its weight in gold' at the time. Trimalchio is, of course, a fictitious character, but he operates within a historical setting, and the best dramatic date for his early business career is the late 30's. A boom in the price of wine suggests an excess of cash in the economy, and a run on luxury items, which best suits the first few months of Caligula's reign, and would certainly have contributed to the general feeling of well-being.[51] The economy would have received yet another boost by the abolition, in 38, of the sales tax. Until 284, during the reign of Diocletian, direct taxes were levied exclusively in the provinces, inhabitants of Italy paying only indirect taxes. The most important during the Augustan period was the 1 per cent sales tax (*centesima rerum venalium*), intended to finance the military treasury (*Aerarium Militare*) Tiberius had faced much pressure to remove it, and with the revenues accruing from Cappadocia after its incorporation into the empire in 17, he was able to reduce the tax to .5 per cent, but bowed to financial necessity and restored it to its original rate of 1 per cent in 31. Under the year 38 Dio reports that Caligula was able to abolish the tax altogether.[52]

Heavy spending, combined with a reduction in taxes, was bound, sooner or later, to place unbearable strains on the treasury. Dio suggests that Caligula had used up his vast surplus by his second year, and the raising of two new legions in 39 would have involved massive extra expenditure. We unfortunately do not have a clear understanding of the precise relationship between the minting of money and 'economic policy' in the ancient world. Precious metal coinage is relatively scarce during the reign of Caligula but, to judge from dated issues, is most plentiful in this first year, suggesting perhaps heavy mintage to pay for the legacies of Tiberius and Livia. For reasons that are not clear there is no dated official coinage for the second year of his reign (excepting the quinarius, or half-aureus) in either precious metal or aes issues. Their minting resumes in 39/40. Certainly, Caligula found that before his reign was over he was in the position of trying desperately to raise revenues.[53] Some of his reputed schemes are distinctly bizarre. Pliny claims that he found a way of producing gold from orpimentum (sulphur of arsenic), but in too small quantities to be economically viable. It is said that he opened a brothel in his Palatine residence staffed by the children and wives of noble families, and sent touts into the city to drum up business among young and old alike. Shortage of ready cash was no problem, as he was willing to extend credit. Dio reluctantly admits that this was not an unpopular measure.[54] He seized every opportunity to raise cash in auction sales. He auctioned off gladiators from the shows, using agents to push up the bidding. Aponius Saturninus once had the misfortune to nod off during the proceedings and woke to find that he had bought thirteen gladiators for nine million. In Gaul he sold off the possessions of his sisters, and on the rostrum played the role of auctioneer with gusto, rebuking his audience for their stinginess, joshing them for being richer than himself, and expressing mock regret that ordinary men could possess such fine princely possessions. He would boost the quality of the items, dwelling on their splendid pedigrees (they were family heirlooms). The descriptions of these antics are intended to make Caligula look ridiculous, but they sound like standard auctioneering tactics, and it is worth noting that the later emperor Trajan was actually praised for selling off goods at auction to help make the books balance.[55]

Some of his schemes were less unusual, and possibly more effective. At the simplest level he seems to have revived the Augustan custom of accepting New Year's gifts of money from individuals. During his absence in Gaul they were even deposited by his vacant throne on the Capitol. When he was in Rome he collected the money at the entrance to the palace in the folds of his toga, then went home, according to Suetonius, and rolled in it. He was also an inveterate legacy hunter, for which he is subjected to considerable criticism, although by the 30's it is claimed that nearly everyone was leaving something to his predecessor Tiberius, who was accepting everything left to him. As the sources portray it, Caligula greatly extended the practice. They speak of his being left bequests on a massive scale, mainly as a result of intimidation. Suetonius suggests that to hurry matters on he would actually send people poisoned cakes, and if anyone had a change of thought about leaving something to him the whole will was declared null and void.[56] In fact, only two specific legacies are known. Suetonius says that Caligula obtained the estate of Domitius Ahenobarbus, husband of his sister, although only named co-heir with his nephew Nero. The latter supposedly received a third at the time, although the full amount was restored by Claudius.[57] He was also heir to the estate of his distant relative Sextus Pompeius, a wealthy man with lands in Campania, Sicily and Macedonia, and a house in Rome near the Forum.[58] According to Seneca Caligula deprived Pompeius of his house and invited him to stay at the palace where he starved him to death, although afterwards arranging a state funeral. It would, in fact, have been appropriate for Pompeius to bequeath property to the emperor, since he was his relative, and he had been on close terms with Germanicus. He may have been very elderly at this time, and his entertainment and state funeral are hard to reconcile with Seneca's account of enforced starvation.[59] The sources also speak at length of Caligula inheriting the legacies of those who had been condemned (*bona caduca*).[60] There were Augustan and Tiberian precedents, and Caligula's action would not have been unusual.[61] Indeed, the general accusation seems to be contradicted by what Philo says of the specific case of Flaccus, the condemned governor of Egypt. Flaccus' collection of *objets d'art*, his furnishings, cups, carpets and his household slaves were of very high quality and attracted the emperor's attention. Philo claims that this was the only instance where Caligula confiscated the condemned person's goods, though he allowed a small amount to go into the *aerarium* to comply with the law.[62]

Some of Caligula's methods of acquiring inheritances do not, however, have clear precedents. According to Dio, a senatorial decree stipulated that whoever had bequeathed money to Tiberius and then survived him would be obliged to leave it to Caligula.[63] This is important in the symbolic development of the concept of the princeps, in that estates left to him would be seen as left not to an individual but to him as the holder of the principate, and this measure would become a constitution under Antoninus Pius.[64] A somewhat similar development is suggested by the declaration that if any senior centurion since the beginning of Tiberius' reign did not name Tiberius or Caligula as heirs the wills would be set aside on the grounds of ingratitude. One of the principles of inheritance law under the Julio-Claudians was the *officium pietatis*, essentially the obligation of the legator to members of his family. A will that did not observe these obligations could be challenged through a *querela inofficiosi testamenti*. It seems that Caligula regarded the emperor as someone who had undertaken obligations for the state as a whole, and could expect legacies on the grounds of *pietas*.[65] The regulations concerning legacies may or may not have had major financial implications, but they were significant for the evolving concept of the principate.

Perhaps Caligula's most innovative measure was to institute a number of direct taxes previously unknown in Rome. Suetonius and Dio (under 40), report the imposition of what they considered shameful ways of raising revenue. Caligula placed taxes on taverns, artisans, slaves and the hiring of slaves. There was a fixed tax on all edibles sold in the city, a *quadrigesima* (2.5 per cent) on the sum involved in legal actions, an *octava* (12.5 per cent) on the daily wages of *geruli* (porters?) and a tax on prostitutes equivalent to the income from a single transaction (possibly in a month); to prevent evasion of this last measure a tax was placed on pimps and on prostitutes who married. Josephus claims that the revenues from these measures did not prove sufficient, and towards the end of his life Caligula was obliged to double them.[66] Italians had long been in a sense sheltered from financial reality, and their exemption from direct taxes had given them a distinctly unfair advantage over other parts of the empire. Caligula's policies would have helped to redress the balance somewhat. They were not, however, likely to be popular, and perhaps represent the only measures of Caligula that caused serious resentment among the ordinary people, to the extent that there were outbreaks of unrest at public games when petitions for annulment of the new taxes were presented.

The sources depict Caligula as an irresponsible spendthrift, who brought the state to the verge of financial ruin and sought to impose outrageous taxes to salvage the situation. The reality seems to have been quite different. For all his predecessor's supposed extravagances, Claudius must have found the treasury in a fairly healthy state. He gradually abolished most of the taxes, and refunded some of the money collected, even though he was able to engage in such expensive ventures as the building of the harbour at Ostia. Nor could the new taxes have been so outrageous. At least one of them stayed in force for centuries. Severus Alexander apparently used the proceeds of the tax on prostitution for the construction of buildings in Rome.[67]

It is perhaps easiest to judge Caligula's fitness to rule by considering him in relation to those he ruled over. As he returned to Rome from his northern campaign in early 40, he is said to have issued a proclamation that he would be returning only to those who wanted him back, the equestrians and the ordinary people, since he could no longer consider himself either fellow-citizen or princeps to the senators. This is a remarkable statement, since it not only displays Caligula's hostility towards the senate but it shows also where he hoped to find his allies. Whether or not he had formed a conscious and deliberate scheme to draw in the people and the equestrians as allies in his struggle with the senate is a much more difficult issue.[68]

Caligula began his reign as the darling of the masses — Suetonius speaks of the *immensus civium amor* ('the massive affection of his fellow-citizens'). It also seems clear that he stayed popular with the ordinary people right up to the end, and indeed their reaction to the news of his death seems to have caused the sources some embarrassment. There was none of the jubilation that followed the passing of Tiberius, and Suetonius offers the unconvincing explanation that no-one believed that he was really dead, and thought that the report had been spread by Caligula himself, just to test people. Josephus is perhaps more honest, when he admits that the people in the theatre were upset at the news of his assassination. He dismisses their concern, however, with the observation that many of them were silly women, children and slaves, who knew no better. But he does not have a ready explanation for the anger of those citizens who assembled in the Forum and demanded a proper investigation of the murder. Yavetz has argued that the populace saw Caligula as an ally in a sort of class war, and that his humiliation of the nobility would have been a source of popularity. This does not seem to be warranted by the evidence. At the most Josephus concedes that the people saw the emperor as a curb on the senatorial class in its efforts to regain its old privileges.[69]

While Caligula's behaviour seems to have caused distress among the sober members of the nobility, it did not meet with general disapproval, and according to Dio the people actually enjoyed his licentiousness. No doubt it provided a great sense of release after the austerity of the Tiberian years. Also, a number of his measures seem to have been designed intentionally to court popularity. The celebration of the Saturnalia, previously a three day event, was extended by Caligula with a festival called the Juvenalis. He apparently added two days, although for some reason the final one was later removed, only to be restored by Claudius in 45. Seats at the games were provided free of charge.[70] Another highly popular act was the drastic reduction of the size of the traditional Saturnalia gift, from recipients of the corn dole, for the manufacture of statues. The number of people involved is uncertain, but the *Res Gestae* indicates that there were 200,000 recipients in 2 BC.[71] He reintroduced clubs (*collegia*) that had previously been banned.[72] *Collegia* were often made up of men from the same trade or calling, but their purposes tended to be social rather than professional. In the republic they had become involved in political activities, and many of them were suppressed by Caesar. The Lex Julia of AD 7 laid down that every club had to receive the sanction of the emperor, and Tiberius would have enforced this rule vigorously. Its relaxation by Caligula would have added to the general atmosphere of release that characterized his reign at the outset.

The story of the Gallic cobbler who supposedly made fun of Caligula but did not suffer because of his humble status suggests that he was prepared to be generally tolerant towards the lower classes, and Dio admits that he was not offended by the frankness of ordinary people. There is a suggestion that he bore a grudge against the masses because of their lack of enthusiasm at the *spectacula* and their applause for performers of whom he did not approve, but this seems to indicate passing irritation rather than deep antipathy. Almost inevitably, there are stories of his supposed acts of brutality against the ordinary people, but it is difficult to assess their accuracy, and they may belong to a tradition that the 'bad' emperors like Caligula and Nero were hated by all classes.[73] One reported incident, however, may well be based on fact. Under 40 Dio and Josephus report that there was dissatisfaction with the numerous new taxes Caligula had introduced, and that the people made their protest in the circus. There had been a tradition from Augustus' time for the Romans to make requests to the emperor at places of public entertainment. Tiberius on occasion yielded to public pressure. In 32, however, when there were loud protests about the high price of corn and demands for reductions were made in the theatre, he prevailed on the senate and the consuls to check such demonstrations. Caligula seems to have been prepared to revive the tradition of petitions, but it is claimed that on the occasion of the protest over the taxes he behaved savagely, rounding up people and executing them, and Dio and Josephus report that he had large numbers arrested and put to death.[74] The disturbances may well have got out of hand, and have been suppressed with some brutality, but the stories of mass executions can almost certainly be dismissed as standard exaggerations.

Caligula did attempt one measure of symbolic importance. He restored to the people a consitutional right that the senate had acquired from them, the nominal control of elections. In the republic, magistrates had been elected by the *comitia* (popular assemblies). Julius Caesar as dictator had limited their power, stipulating that half the positions be elected by them and half nominated by himself. Only the consulships were excluded from this arrangement. Augustus restored the traditional system in 27 BC, but in fact controlled the process to such an extent that the privileges of the assemblies were more apparent than real. Tiberius introduced an important innovation, when the elections were transferred to the senate, and the assemblies merely ratified the selection of candidates already made, the latter measure presumably being a gesture towards tradition.[75] The withdrawal of this privilege caused no serious popular protest, and the senate was happy with the change, because it relieved them of the necessity of undignified canvassing and expense. The precise character of Tiberius' reform has been the object of much scholarly debate, but in general terms there would have been two provisos in the scheme, that all candidates would have the general approval of the emperor, and also that he might actively support certain candidates whose election would therby be secured. In addition, he would decide how many vacancies there would be each year for the consulship and praetorship.

Suetonius and Dio (under 38) report that Caligula put the elections back into the hands of the people, rescinding the arrangements that Tiberius had made. The gesture was, of course, largely symbolic, since his powers of *commendatio* and *nominatio* would still be retained. Only one consul, Domitius Afer, is specifically identified as having been elected under the new system, in early September 39, and as Dio comments 'the people chose Domitius consul in theory but he [sc. Caligula] chose the consul in fact.' In the end, even this essentially symbolic reform failed. Dio comments that the people had for too long grown unused to performing the 'duties of free men'. Usually only sufficient candidates presented themselves to match the number of vacancies, or, if there were more candidates, they arranged the offices amongst themselves beforehand. In the end Caligula was obliged to restore the elections once again to the senate, and things reverted essentially to what they had been under Tiberius. Yavetz has commented that the people would have shown little interest in holding on to what was a purely notional power that had no real significance in the overall scheme of things. There may be an element of truth in this, but the real reason for the reform's failure is surely the hostility of the senate, since as a body they alone could have manipulated the number of candidates to fit the number of vacancies or agreed beforehand about the outcome.[76]

At a loftier level on the social scale than the ordinary people stood the equites. The precise nature of Caligula's dealings with this class is difficult to determine because of our uncertainty over precisely how equestrian status was acquired. It is generally agreed that a census rating of 400,000 sesterces, and free birth, were prerequisites for entry into the order, and also that the honorific distinction of the *equus publicus* ('public horse') was granted, and if necessary removed, at the pleasure of the emperor. What is not resolved is whether the financial prerequisites alone qualified a man automatically for equestrian rank or whether this also had to be bestowed by the emperor; the literary sources are not explicit and the inscriptional evidence seems contradictory.[77] The equestrians were an important element in the Augustan system, and to ensure that the order retained its integrity Augustus had used his quasi-censorial powers to hold *recognitiones*, to appoint new holders of the *equus publicus* or to dismiss those who had fallen from grace. The poet Ovid is an example of someone who underwent the emperor's scrutiny and survived the test.[78] Augustus also fixed at four the number of *decuriae* (panels) of judges, who were of equestrian rank.

The sources do speak of Caligula's mistreatment of Roman knights. In a confused passage Dio says that Caligula put to death twenty-six equestrians; Suetonius, however, describes a fracas in the course of which over twenty knights (and a number of women) were crushed to death. Clearly one and the same occasion is involved, and the deaths seem to have been accidental. The most vivid story of cruelty towards a member of the order involves a knight who was thrown to the beasts and had his tongue cut out, a story that is almost certainly bogus (p. ix). Many of the other stories of friction with the knights seem to be decidedly trivial. It is claimed that Caligula scattered free tickets for the theatre beforehand to let the urban mob seize the seats reserved for the equestrians. He supposedly interrupted a gambling session to go out and confiscate the property of two knights he saw passing by, then returned to his game commenting on his lucky streak. When a knight created a disturbance in the theatre he was reputedly sent to Mauretania on a fool's errand, and when one made a noise during Mnester's dance Caligula is said to have flogged him personally. Similar stories are told of Tiberius, who is said to have condemned to the treadmill one of the equestrians charged with handling the funeral of Livia.[79]

In fact Caligula seems to have gone out of his way to show respect for the order. At the outset of his reign the knights were allowed into the chamber when he made his first address to the senate; they were assigned to carry the remains of Agrippina and Nero to the Mausoleum of Augustus, and were invited to come and listen to Caligula when he gave his speeches in senatorial trials.[80] Dio notes that the size of the equestrians order had declined during the final years of Tiberius' reign and that Caligula did his best to make up the numbers, enrolling wealthy men from the whole of the empire.[81] He held a *recognitio*, revising the lists carefully but fairly, removing those who had been guilty of wicked or scandalous behaviour (*probra* or *ignimonia*), but making allowance for trivial misdemeanours.[82] It may have been this scrupulous examination that prompted Josephus to make the exaggerated claim that he launched a full-scale attack on the equites, depriving them of their honours; it is certainly the best context for criticisms that Caligula is said to have made of the knights, as devotees of the stage and the arena.[83] A *senatus consultum* of AD 19 regulated the conduct of the upper classes and prohibited them from taking part in the spectacula. This ruling seems to have been disregarded under Caligula. Both Dio and Suetonius suggest that he compelled knights to perform as gladiators, and Dio cites the case of one who was forced to fight in single combat on the grounds of insulting the emperor's mother, Agrippina. In view of Caligula's criticisms, it is likely that these appearances were voluntary. This is also suggested by Claudius' actions later. He applied the law in its full force, obliging equestrians who had appeared on the stage under Caligula to appear once more, not because he enjoyed watching them, but to make them feel embarrassed about their behaviour. This would not make sense if the original participation had been compulsory. Caligula's failure in this area may have been that he was too lax in implementing the senatorial decrees.[84]

Enrolment of equites in the panel of judges, or *decuriae*, seems to have been neglected by Tiberius after his departure for Capri. The number of panels had been established by Augustus at four, and Caligula added a fifth, encountering no shortage of candidates to fill them. He also encouraged equestrians who had ambitions for a senatorial career, and, according to Dio, permitted some to wear the *latus clavus*, the broad-striped toga, symbolic of the senatorial order, before they had reached the office (quaestorship) that granted normal access to the senate, in other words, that he elevated to the senatorial order those knights who intended to pursue a senatorial career. Suetonius observes that Augustus had allowed the sons of senators to assume the *latus clavus* immediately after the toga virilis, but says nothing of similar privileges for the equestrians, and Dio goes on to comment that *it seems* that before Caligula only the sons of senators had been permitted to wear the senatorial toga.[85] Caligula's measure seems very progressive and Dio comments that it proved to be popular. Its precise signficance, however, is disputed. Scholars have pointed out the uncertainty of Dio on Augustus' practice ('it seems'), and claim that Suetonius' neglect to mention the equestrians in the discussion of that emperor's policy does not mean that Augustus necessarily excluded them from wearing the *latus clavus* as a preliminary to a senatorial career. Certainly it seems that Vespasian, an equestrian, was granted the *latus clavus* from Tiberius before his quaestorship.[86] It may be that under Tiberius the careers of ambitious equestrians had stagnated and that the *latus clavus* had been bestowed on very few. But whether Caligula's measure was an innovation, or simply the full implementation of a practice that had fallen into general abeyance, it shows, in any case, a sympathy for the equestrians as an order. After his time it seems that it became regular for equestrians to receive the *latus clavus* from the emperor before actually seeking senatorial office.

The reign of Caligula is often seen as a battle between the emperor and the senate. This was certainly not the case at the outset. At first Caligula seems to have gone out of his way to be accommodating. In his first speech to the senators he promised full partnership and cooperation in the Augustan manner. He showed senators consideration even in trivial matters, allowing them to sit on cushions instead of bare boards at shows, and to wear hats to protect their heads from the sun. Since the senators faced a physical problem in getting to the senate house quickly for important sessions (their houses were scattered all through Rome), Caligula seems to have given them in advance a written outline of the items he would like to see discussed at each session. He attended their debates on several occasions.[87] He showed a responsible interest in their proceedings, such as the question of order of precedence. Augustus had essentially used a system that operated under the Republic, by which senators of consular rank were called upon at random, and others below that by seniority. Under Tiberius the consular Marcus Junius Silanus, Caligula's father in law, was invariably called upon first, not because of seniority but because of his personal eminence. Caligula arranged that henceforth the consulars, like other members, should be called on in order of seniority.[88] The important consequence of this was, of course, that he personally would be left to near the end, thus discouraging senators who might be inclined simply to take their lead from him. His uncle Claudius would also appear near the end of the list, thus explaining Suetonius' charge that Caligula made a point of always calling on him last.[89] At the outset Caligula seems to have limited the appeal to the emperor against the verdicts of magistrates. This process seems to have begun with Augustus, since in a confused passage Dio refers to the right to entertain appeals among the powers granted to him in 30 BC, and Suetonius notes that he delegated his authority to hear appeals to the *praetor urbanus* or, for the provinces, to men of consular rank. While Caligula seems to have given up the right of appeal, at some point he must have resumed it, since we learn that the the senate did not have the final authority in criminal cases, and that many appeals were in fact made to the emperor.[90]

The basically congenial relationship between emperor and senate did not last beyond the first few months. Already by the end of 37, Silanus, one of the most respected members, had been forced to commit suicide, and his removal could be regarded in a sense as the first provocation. A small number of senators, like Julius Graecinus, apparently refused to be party to the proceedings against Silanus. But they were in a distinct minority. Caligula seems to have encountered little opposition, and even to have enjoyed their collaboration. Philo suggests that he was congratulated for what he did: 'almost the whole inhabited earth, though they deplored what was going on, flattered Gaius all the same, glorifying him unduly and thus increasing his vanity'. In 37 his problems seem to have been of an essentially internal nature, involving intrigue within the court during his illness. In 39 he faced a quite different situation, with opposition not only from within his own family but also, apparently, from disaffected army commanders and unhappy senators. His policy for handling the threat of conspiracy was to isolate his enemies, to make every senator fear for himself and to ensure that each would see it to be in his self-interest to make his loyalty to the emperor patent. In the short term it was effective. Dio speaks of the great number of trials that occurred when Caligula was away in the North, trials before the senate, where he evidently must have been able to count on considerable support. In the last few months of Caligula's life there were still senators prepared to betray those few of their numbers principled enough to stand up to autocracy. The fate of Proculus, hacked to death by fellow-members, shows how little confidence could be placed in his colleagues, who added insult to injury by voting special festivals in honour of Caligula afterwards. Caligula's response to those who plotted against him was ruthless. The sources claim, however, that it was also indiscriminate, Dio making the observation that it was 'nothing but slaughter'.[91] But it is difficult to accept that the executions occurred on a wide scale. The list of the named victims is a very short one, and in almost every case there seems to be good reason to suspect guilt.

The historian will legitimately look for patterns in Caligula's treatment of individual senators. When he destroyed the papers that related to the trials of his relatives he claimed that his purpose was to show that he bore no grudge against those involved in the cases. These would, of course, have been, by and large, adherents of Sejanus, and in his denunciation of the senators in 39, his general term of abuse was 'clients of Sejanus'. It would, then, seem a reasonable assumption that from 39 on Caligula was determined to be rid of those whose names were linked with that of the hated Prefect.[92] Yet the evidence does not bear this out. Granted, Gaetulicus, the treacherous commander in Germany, was certainly an old Sejanian, and Calvisius Sabinus, governor of Pannonia, was one of the five men accused of *maiestas* in 32 after the fall of Sejanus and generally assumed to have been among his adherents. Their executions in 39 might well seem at first sight to be some kind of final reckoning. Yet two men from that group of five survived, and prospered, under Caligula. Vinicianus became a close friend of Lepidus (and possibly of the emperor) and was coopted into the Arvals in 38, the only man from a non-traditional Arval family to be so honoured during Caligula's reign. A second member of the group was Gaius Appius Silanus, consul of 28, He was magister of the Arvals in 39, and became governor of Hispania

Citerior probably in about 40. Moreover, Caligula's partner in the consulship for 39 was Lucius Apronius Caesianus, brother-in-law of Gaetulicus the conspirator. Yet Apronius was not only granted the consulship, but allowed to complete his whole term when Caligula stepped down after thirty days. Publius Pomponius Secundus, who had been imprisoned because of his association with Sejanus, was freed on Caligula's accession. Cassius Longinus, possibly brother of the accuser of Drusus, Caligula's brother, was made proconsul of Asia in 40/1.

In fact, Caligula seems to have been remarkably free of malice towards the relatives and associates of those who had opposed either himself or his family. Lucius Arruntius Camillus, for instance, was appointed governor of Dalmatia in about 40. Yet he is the adopted son of the Arruntius accused of *maiestas* under Tiberius and who committed suicide rather than serve under Caligula. Lucius Piso, the son of Germanicus' arch foe, was Praefectus Urbi at Caligula's accession and remained in that post, probably until his appointment as proconsul of Africa. Publius Dolabella, either the consul of AD 10, and thus co-accuser of Agrippina's friend Quintilius Varus, or the son of the accuser, was one of the group coopted into the Salii in 37.

Moreover, many eminent senators seem to have been more than happy to collaborate with the emperor. It is noticeable that a large number of individuals seem to have prospered under Caligula but anxiously sought later to create the impression that they would have suffered from his arbitrary cruelty had it not been for lucky circumstances, or their own ingenuity. Lucius Vitellius, for instance, is supposed to have been summoned from Parthia to be punished. But in a brilliant move he supposedly performed *proskynesis* and worshipped Caligula as a god. Reputedly, when asked if he could see the moon in the emperor's presence Vitellius had the swiftness of mind to reply promptly that 'only the gods were permitted to see one-another'. His timely flattery is said to have won him a reprieve. Yet Petronius, who replaced him in Syria, was hardly from the opposing camp. He was the son-in-law of a Vitellia, and his own daughter was married to Vitellius' son Aulus, the future emperor. In fact, Vitellius probably had little to fear when he left his province, and his recall was probably routine. Certainly he felt sufficiently relaxed to give thought to collecting together exotic species of figs to bring back from Syria to his Alban estate. He also went on to prosper, holding the consulship under Claudius, and earning the sneers of Tacitus and Dio.[93] Seneca was supposedly marked for execution but saved because the emperor was persuaded that he was in an advanced state of consumption and near death in any case. He went on to flatter Claudius, the next emperor, while alive, and then to ridicule him, after his death. Domitius Afer was charged, apparently with *maiestas*, and prosecuted by Caligula personally. He supposedly had the brainwave of expressing astonishment at the emperor's eloquence, and thereby gained not only a reprieve but even, remarkably enough, a consulship. Vinicianus, coopted into the Arvals in 38 and on Caligula's death one of the most prominent senators in Rome, claimed that he lived under threat of constant reprisal because of his friendship with Lepidus. Some survived purely by lucky chance. Memmius Regulus, Cassius Longinus, Publius Petronius were all slated for execution, and won eleventh-hour reprieves with Caligula's death. Some Romans, apparently, decided that instead of trying to rewrite history, they would simply be reticent. Ummidius Quadratus, it will be recalled, had loyally administered the oath to Caligula in Lusitania, in 37, and was probably awarded a consulship in 40. But on an inscription from Casinum in Italy, covering his career, he describes himself as a legate of Tiberius in Lusitania then as legate of Claudius in Illyricum, dropping any reference to his service under Caligula.[94]

The hostility between Caligula and the senate was no doubt highly exaggerated in those senatorial sources that dealt with the topic after Caligula's death. The senators had to face the embarrassing fact that not only did the majority of them survive unscathed, but many collaborated against the principled few who had taken a strand, and as a body they were prepared, time after time, not only to condone but even to applaud some of Caligula's outrageous actions. They saw fit later to pretend that they had lived under autocratic repression. Yet they may in fact have enjoyed considerable political independence right to the end. For the election of Domitius in late 39 the comitial system was still in operation. It failed, as Dio points out, because the senate refused to cooperate and took measures to sabotage it. This notice is of some importance since it indicates that the senate at this time was still able to act with much independence, and felt secure enough from personal reprisals to oppose the emperor in a purely political arena.

Certainly, by 39 Caligula's general hostility towards the senate as an institution was undisguised, and this does manifest itself in his treatment of certain individual senators, particularly those from ancient and distinguished families, who presumably might have been seen to pose a threat, if not to his life, then to his status. But his favoured punishment seems not to have been execution but humiliation. One of his known victims was Gnaeus Pompeius Magnus, the son of Marcus Crassus Frugi and Scribonia, who had named the boy after Scribonia's distinguished ancestor. He clearly for a time enjoyed Caligula's favour and was inducted into the Salii as late as 40. But he seems to have been an arrogant young man, and the Imperial favours may have gone to his head. The grandiloquent name given to Pompeius by his parents would have been provocative at the best of times, and at some point Caligula became so irritated by him that he is said to have stripped him of the title of Magnus. Pompeius may well have had excessive political ambitions. He was important enough for Claudius not only to restore his title, but also to give him his daughter Antonia in marriage. He was put to death in 46/7 without trial, presumably for political reasons.[95] Other senators who took a particular pride in their lineage were marked for similar degradation. This was the fate of Decimus Junius Torquatus, son of Marcus Silanus and Aemilia Lepida, the grand-daughter of Augustus. He also enjoyed Caligula's favour at the outset, and was one of the men inducted into the Salii in 37. He seems, however, to have taken an excessive pride in his family connections, and would boast of his descent from Augustus. He was deprived of his distiguished *cognomen* 'Torquatus'. His fortunes did revive under Claudius, and he attained the consulship in 53, but was forced under Nero to commit suicide in 64. A similar humiliation seems to have been inflicted by Caligula on an otherwise unknown (Quinctius) Cincinnatus.[96]

It has been suggested already that apart from the small number of senators engaged actively in attempts to remove Caligula, the great majority had no reason to fear for their lives from the arbitrary exercise of his power, despite the impression that they tried desperately to create later. But senators had a right to more from their emperor than a reasonable expectation that if they did not plot against him they would not be eliminated. They would rightly have resented deeply his refusal to show them the basic deference to which they were entitled, a deference that had been shown by Augustus and even by Tiberius. The position of the Roman senator was a curious one. Outside of Italy, in either the 'senatorial' provinces, or in the more direct service of the princeps, they could perform useful service in positions of great power and prestige, commanding armies or governing small nations. Back in Rome they found themselves bereft of any real power and obliged to give way to a princeps whose ability and experience was much inferior to theirs but whose power was almost unlimited. They had invested this young man with the powers of a monarch, yet they expected him as a Roman to behave only as a first citizen, with the old Augustan virtue of *civilitas*. Caligula was incapable of respect to anyone, and Seneca comments on his inability to deal with people without insulting them. Since Caligula had so little regard for the senate, it is natural that he would be sensitive to any perceived slight from them. 'Who dares teach me?' is one of the most revealing phrases attributed to him by Philo. Thus senators, for example, who tried to ingratiate themselves with him by calling him a 'young Augustus', found that it had the very opposite effect — he took it as a criticism that he was reigning despite being so young. To some extent this might explain his success with the ordinary people, and the equestrians. He was able, as Dio comments, to accept the frank comments of the common man, who would be lacking the pretensions that might be seen as a challenge, and who would simply not expect to be treated with tact and deference.[97]

On close examination the senate does not, as a body, distinguish itself under Caligula. They perhaps had little choice at the outset in confirming him as princeps, given the swift preemptive arrangements that Macro made with the legionary commanders and the Praetorian guard. Yet they must bear responsibility for the massive grant of powers they made to the young, inexperienced and almost totally unknown Caligula, and for their own reluctance to try to curb or restrain him. Nor does the fact that their response to each humiliation with even more fulsome honours command respect. Nor their willingness to expend vast sums to entertain the emperor, driving themselves to bankruptcy in their desire to please. They in fact behaved with the same docility that had often excited the contempt of Tiberius.[98] The autocracy that caused such resentment was an autocracy that they themselves had helped to create, and continued to foster. Despite the senate's failings, however, it must be acknowledged that Augustus and Tiberius had managed to work with the body tolerably well, as would Claudius later, and Talbert's recent study has shown that as an institution the senate could make an enormous positive contribution to the orderly government of Rome. Their shortcomings in no way excuse Caligula for his much greater failings.

Caligula had, at the outset, conducted himself as an *exoptatissimus princeps*, 'good, generous, fair and community spirited', as Philo calls him.[99] By the end he was an arrogant despot. It is significant that the sources cannot agree on when the dramatic deterioration took place. Philo places the change immediately after his illness. Josephus states precisely that he ruled the state nobly for two years, presumably until driven mad by Caesonia's aphrodisiacs. Josephus is inconsistent, however, since at one point he says that Caligula began administering the empire in a highminded fashion and exercised moderation until he was corrupted by power; yet he also describes him as bloodthirsty and perverse by nature, and a sinister character even before coming to power. Dio emphasises the contradictions in his personality, that he expressed liberalism, practised tyranny, preached moderation and indulged in excess, forgave criminals but executed the innocent, and he places the beginning of the indiscriminate political murders early in 38. Plutarch says ambiguously that he ruled *epiphanos* ('splendidly') for a short time, the 'short time' presumably referring to the initial period of the reign, rather than to the reign as a brief whole. Suetonius divides his *Life of Caligula* into two sections, the first of which he devotes to the 'princeps', who 'fulfilled the hopes of the Roman world if not of mankind', the second and longer one to the *monstrum*. He gives no precise chronological information, but a number of the acts that he attributes to the 'princeps' occurred fairly late in the reign. The bridge at Baiae probably belongs to the summer of 39, the oratorical contest at Lyons to the winter of 39/40, while the award of money to Quintilia the torture-victim belongs at the earliest to the autumn of 40, only a few months before the emperor's death.[100]

In fact we see that Caligula was able, when the occasion and his inclination demanded, to behave sensibly in every phase of his reign. The fire in the Aemilian district, when his assistance was commended by Dio, is fixed by the Fasti in October 38. The excellent appointments that he made in 39, of men like Galba and Petronius, men who were responsible for the relative success of his reign in the provinces, show that he was still then capable of making sound judgement. Right to the very end of his reign he seems to have been willing to accept good advice. He changed his mind about his plan for returning the elections to the popular *comitia* when faced with the implacable opposition of the senate, and reversed his position on the Temple in Jersualem at the urging of Agrippa. At all periods he seems to have sought to govern with a remarkable degree of openness. The most striking examples, of course, are his publication of the financial accounts and the lifting of censorship in 37. Dio also comments that he went to considerable trouble to have Tiberius' will annulled, even though he could simply have suppressed it. But his openness was not confined to the early cooperative period of the reign. When he reintroduced the *lex maiestatis* in 39 he ordered that its terms should be inscribed on a bronze tablet. He published the names of those condemned by *in camera* trials. Divorces were recorded in the *Acta Diurna*. He even published the names of clients at his brothel on the Palatine.[101]

Caligula was clearly capable of acting right to the end in a rational manner. Why then does he seem so often to have behaved otherwise? What emerges clearly from the sources is that while he was not clinically mad he was so obsessed with a sense of his own importance as to be practically devoid of any sense of moral responsibility. This attitude might well have resulted from the experience of his early youth, when any moral indignation over the deaths of his mother and brothers needed to be suppressed if he was to survive. It might have resulted from the heady experience of being catapulted from sequestred obscurity to the central position of authority over a world empire. This is speculative. But what is clear is that once in power he manifested a totally self-centred view of the world. This had unfortunate results. While we are not able to assess the validity of the constant charges of sadistic cruelty in the sources, we can not ignore what Caligula indirectly reveals about himself. As has been pointed out earlier, many of the hostile anecdotes about him may arise from his grimly ironical sense of humour. But the very fact that his witticisms come from a cruel and sadistic background tells us very much about his view of the world. He would deplore the state of the times because there had been no great disasters, to match the massacre of the legions in Germany under Augustus, or the collapse of the amphitheatre at Fidenae. He advocated killing a person slowly so that he would know that he was dying. He laughed out loud in the presence of the consuls, and when asked why said that with a single nod he could have had their throats cut on the spot. He spoke of eliminating whole legions, or the whole of the senate, or the legal profession, wished that the Roman populace had a single neck so that he could break it with one blow, threatened to torture his wife Caesonia, commented when kissing the neck of a mistress or wife that he could cut if off at a simple order. None of these or similar comments would have been meant to be taken as seriously intended (even though the sources persist in so taking them), but Caligula's disturbing obsession with the dark humour of destructive power suggests that he was a man who would see the principate as an expression of his right to exercise unchecked powers. The executions of Caligula's reign do not seem to have been indiscriminate. But principled Romans would have recognized something sinister in a man who was so lacking in moral scruples that sending fellow humans to their deaths was looked upon not as a cruel yet inevitable necessity of governing, but as a matter of almost total indifference. If Caligula was mad, he was not the potty eccentric typified by a Ludwig of Bavaria, but a much more frightening Stalinesque figure, capable of rational decisions, capable of statesmanlike acts (when it suited him), but morally neutral, determined to sweep all before him in the pursuit of his own personal ends, and ultimately indifferent to the consequences of his actions on others.[102]

There is no great mystery to why the relationship between Caligula and the senate should have turned sour. As long as an adoring Rome paid homage to him there was no reason why the dark and perverse side of his personality should show itself. Dio claims that in 37 the senators could not believe that anyone so young would be capable of deceit. But it is probably unlikely that Caligula tried deliberately to deceive. The 'honeymoon period', at the outset of a new regime, is not a phenomenon that is restricted to the ancient world. The austerity of Tiberius' reign, the magic of Germanicus' name, and a healthy surplus in the treasury would assure him of an initial period of euphoria, a euphoria in which he could participate — *optimus est post malum principem dies primus*, as Tacitus observed.[103] But when the inevitable problems arose he saw any criticisms or suggestions as a challenge to his prestige and authority, to be met by confrontation, not by compromise. Ultimately he could not seriously alienate the senatorial class. At the outset the Roman army had effectively placed Caligula in power, yet the authority of the senate was needed to sanction his investiture. Similarly, the Praetorians did not need the physical assistance of the senate to remove Caligula, but it was the backing of the senate, or at least of its prominent members, that gave them the moral authority to carry out the deed.

APPENDIX I
NAMED VICTIMS OF CALIGULA

Some of the dates are tentative.

37

Atanius Secundus equestrian	humiliated?	Suet. *Cal.* 14.2, 27.2; Dio 59.8.3
P. Afranius Potitus, plebeian	executed or humiliated?	
Gemellus, adopted son	suicide	Philo *Leg.* 23.; Suet. *Cal.* 23.3.; Dio 59.8.1
M. Junius Silanus, distinguished senator, father-in-law	suicide	Philo *Leg.* 65; Suet. *Cal.* 23.3; Dio 59.8.4

38

Macro and Ennia, Praetorian Prefect and wife	suicide	Philo *Flacc.* 16, *Leg.* 62; Suet. *Cal.* 26. 1; Dio 59.10.6
Children of Macro and Ennia	[executed?]	Philo *Flacc.* 14

39

Suffect consul	suicide	Dio 59.20.3
Titius Rufus, probably senator	suicide	Dio 59.18.5
Junius Priscus,	suicide	Dio 59.18.5
Carrinas Secundus	banished then suicide	Dio 59.20.6
Calvisius Sabinus, Legate of Pannonia	suicide	Dio 59.18.4
Cornelia, wife wife of Sabinus	suicide	' '
Gaetulicus, Legate of Upper Germany	executed	AFA xlix.6-8; Dio 59. 22.5
Lepidus, friend of Caligula	executed	Sen. *Ep.* 4.7; Dio 59.22.6-7
Agrippina and Livilla	banished	Suet. *Cal.* 29.2; Dio 59.22.

Avillius Flaccus, prefect of Egypt	banished then executed	Philo *Flacc.* 185–91
Anteius	banished then executed	Jos. *AJ* 19. 125
Tigellinus Ophonius friend of imperial family	banished	Dio 59.23.9
Lucilius Junior, friend of Seneca	tortured	Sen. *QN* 4 praef. 15
Julius Sacerdos wealthy Gallic notable	executed	Dio 59.22.4

40

Sextus Papinius	executed	Sen. *Ira* 3.18.3; Dio 59.25.5b
Betilienus Bassus, quaestor and his son Capito, procurator	executed	Sen. *Ira* 3.18.3; Suet. *Cal.* 26.3; Dio 59.25. 6–8
Julius Canus, Stoic philosopher	executed	Sen. *Tranq.* 14.4–10
Rectus, friend of Canus	executed?	Plut. *Frag.*211
Julius Graecinus, father of Agricola	executed	Sen. *Ben.* 2.21.5; Tac. *Ag.* 4.1
Quintilia, actress, friend of Pomponius	tortured	Jos. *AJ* 19.34; Suet *Cal.* 16.4; Dio 59.26.4
Scribonius Proculus, senator	hacked to death	Suet. *Cal.* 28; Dio 59. 26. 1–2

Undated:

Son of Pastor, distinguished knight	executed	Sen.*Ira* 2.33.3–7
Sextus Pompeius, relative of Caligula	starved to death	Sen. *Tranq.* 11.10
Aesius Proculus, son of Centurion	publicly executed	Suet. *Cal.* 35.2
Columbus, gladiator	poisoned	Suet. *Cal.* 55.2

APPENDIX II
COINS, INSCRIPTIONS AND SCULPTURE

COINAGE:

Coinage is clearly of great importance as a historical tool, especially in the case of an emperor like Caligula, for whom the literary sources are often scarce and unreliable. Apart from being a unit of currency, a coin is a useful vehicle for propaganda in the broadest sense. By the choice of type the issuing authority can ensure that certain images are constantly before the public eye, to remind the user of its achievements or to give a visual authority to its policies. The historical significance of some of Caligula's coin issues has already been discussed in the text, and what follows is a brief general summary for non-numismatists of a topic that in iself provides material for a whole monograph.

Unfortunately, there exists no account in any ancient authority about either the theory or practice of Roman coin minting, and our views on the 'policies' of coin production are, by necessity, largely conjectural. It appears that from the third century BC the minting of bronze and precious metal coinage was under the charge of a board of three men (from time to time afterwards increased to four). They would have been responsible for the practical operation of the mint, but not for overall monetary policy, which would have rested with the senate. After 5 BC the names of the moneyers were dropped from the coins and thereafter we have no idea of the size of the board. Nor can we be sure how much freedom of action its members had under the empire. B. Levick has argued that in one sense at least the freedom was considerable, in that imperial coin types were selected not by the emperor but by the moneyers.[1] For practical purposes, of course, it perhaps makes little difference, since the moneyers would at the very least have been sensitive to what the princeps would have considered appropriate.

In the chaos of the final century of the republic the powerful generals decentralized the supply of coinage by minting it in their own provinces, and after the death of Caesar the supply of metal for the Roman mint soon ceased. With the division of territory during the triumvirate, the minting of state coinage, often bearing the portraits of individual triumvirs, was similarly divided. The regular operation of the Roman mint could not be revived until some time after the battle of Actium. Along with this central operation, however, Augustus maintained the mints that had developed during the civil wars, with locations identified after 27 BC in Spain, Gaul, Greece, Asia and Syria. Tiberius appears to have limited the range of official mints outside of Rome to Lyons and Caesarea in Cappadocia (and briefly Commagene). This was the situation at Caligula's accession. It should be added that the precise location of the mint in Rome itself during the Julio-Claudian period is unknown. The first mint was set up originally in the temple of Juno Moneta on the Capitoline and may still have been there in Caligula's time, but certainty is impossible. Inscriptions show that by the reign of Trajan it was located on the Caelian Hill.[2]

The general view of Augustan coinage, evolving from the original theory of Mommsen, is that Augustus maintained for himself the right to mint gold and silver by virtue either of his *imperium maius*, or his consular authority, while he left bronze coinage to the senate, whose authority was indicated by the letters SC. There is no explicit evidence for senatorial authority, and in practice any arrangement would in any case be guided by the will of the emperor. It is by no means certain even that the letters SC need imply senatorial authority. K. Kraft, for instance, has claimed they indicated not senatorial sanction for the coins but senatorial participation in the honours for Augustus depicted on them; Wallace-Haddrill suggests that the SC was used to distinguish official base metal coins from purely local issues and to give them greater authority and circulation. Sutherland argues that it marked the right of the senate to draw aes coinage from the treasury.[3]

In using Imperial coins to obtain an insight into the policy and aims of the emperor, we must rely primarily on the 'official' imperial mints, where coins were struck by the central authority for circulation in a wide area of the empire. There were numerous other mints of cities throughout the empire that seem to have operated under a local authority, probably without specific directions from Rome.[4] These mints are of considerable interest in showing how the emperor was perceived in the provinces, but their distribution areas are so limited and they are physically so far removed from Rome that only in the most remote and indirect way could they be seen as reflecting imperial propaganda. At the least, however, it can be assumed that they would avoid producing types that might give offence. Caligula appears to have adopted a highly restrictive policy towards local mints. In particular, he seems to have closed the wide range of city mints in Spain, causing a shortage of aes issues that resulted later in a number of local imitations of Claudian issues.[5] M. Grant has argued that the Spanish mints had become so closely associated with types honouring Caligula's family that when the emperor turned against them in 39 he withdrew the right to mint coins. But it seems unlikely that Caligula would have been so vindictive against such a remote target; in any case the Spanish mints were not reopened by Claudius. Willrich on the other hand has suggested a far-sighted policy- that the closure of the local western mints was an attempt to unify the western part of the empire through the use of a single official coinage. Unfortunately, much of the economic 'policy' of the Roman empire is a closed book to us, and the ending of the local Spanish coinage might have been prompted by financial considerations of which we are totally unaware.

In his official coinage Caligula followed essentially the practice of his predecessors. Augustus' gold and silver issues had been patterned essentially on the coins of the republic. Augustus did, however, make innovations in low-value coinage. Using the model suggested by Julius Caesar he minted sestertii and dupondii of orichalcum (brass) and asses and quadrantes of copper, both latter groups conventionally grouped under the term 'aes'.

The following were the official issues from the Rome mint under Caligula. The weight peaks (ie. the ranges where the highest concentration of weights occur), are taken from RIC[2]:

> aureus (gold, = 25 denarii) 7.8-7.65 grams
> quinarius (gold, = half-aureus) 3.9-3.8 grams
> denarius (silver, = 4 sestertii) 3.85-3.6 grams
> sestertius (orichalcum, = 2 dupondii) 28.25-27.75 grams
> dupondius (orichalcum, = 2 asses) 16 grams
> as (copper, = 4 quadrantes) 11.75-10.75 grams
> quadrans (copper) 3.50-3.10 grams

There are no significant differences in weight from the coins of his predecessor. His precious metal issues are slightly lighter; of his aes issues the sestertii are somewhat heavier, his dupondii more so, while his asses are more or less at the Augustan/Tiberian norm. Die axes are adjusted for aes coinage (the obverse image is oriented to the reverse image) and unadjusted for gold and silver. It is generally observable from dated coins that the minting seems to have been heaviest in the first year of Caligula's reign and, after a virtual hiatus in the second year and possibly the third,reduced considerably in the fourth. The reason for this pattern eludes us.

The most debated numismatic question of the reign of Caligula is the location of the mint for his gold and silver issues. Strabo, writing in about AD 18, states quite explicitly that imperial gold and silver were minted at Lyons, and his assertion receives some support from inscriptions, which indicate the presence of individuals connected with the mint at

Lyons in the early principate.[6] By the Trajanic period the minting of gold and silver at Rome is attested on inscriptions, and the homogeneity of precious metal and aes issues has been traced back to the time of Vespasian. Thus the minting of gold and silver coinage was transferred to Rome at some point between Tiberius and Vespasian; many would narrow the limit for the change to the currency reform of Nero in 64, and certainly Otho could not have had access to the Lyons mint for his precious metal issues. Since Mattingly's time it has been regularly argued that the transfer of the mint to Rome is to be dated to early in Caligula's reign.[7] Mattingly's thesis rests essentially on a basic feature of Caligula's early coins. Issues dated between March 37 and March 38 have an obverse *bare* head. Some issues in this period, and all issues in later years, have an obverse *laureate* head, indicating a change in the choice of type during Caligula's first year, one that is accompanied by slight changes in the style of the letter forms. This development is seen as an appropriate point for the change of mint. Sutherland has pointed to other differences in the style of the heads and reinforced Mattingly's theory, although he does concede that changes could be explained by the appointment of new staff from Rome.[8]

Recently, however, the weight of scholarly opinion seems to have moved against the notion of a change of mint under Caligula. In particular J.-B. Giard has drawn attention to the discovery at Paray-le-Mondial (Saone-et-Loire) in Gaul of two dies for precious metal coins of Caligula, each with laureate head, and has associated one with coins minted as late as 40. He believes that these dies represent the remains of the mint of Lyons and that the equipment was looted and scattered all around the town. Moreover H.B. Matttingly has recently observed that the dies on Caligula's gold and silver (unlike his aes) remain unadjusted throughout his reign. They started to become adjusted after Nero's currency reform in 64.[9]

TYPES

Caligula's first gold and silver issues have conventional obverses. The reverses are more innovative. In one of the bare head issues, the reverse depicts, with no legend, the radiate head of an emperor, with two stars to the left and right of the head (*BMC* 1; fig. 9). It is interesting that some of these specimens bear a head with the features of Tiberius, although Augustan depictions seem much commoner, and some scholars find it hard to believe that the resemblance to Tiberius is accidental. Mattingly suggests that at the outset the head of Tiberius was used with two stars to suggest his divinity, but that when the plans for apotheosis fell through, the Tiberius head was dropped for that of Augustus. The two stars, he suggests, represent Augustus and Tiberius.[10] Given that the plan for Tiberius' apotheosis was abandoned at the very beginning of his reign when Caligula was in his 'constitutional' phase, and went out of his way to avoid acting without senatorial approval, it is highly unlikely that he would have transmitted instructions to the mint on his own initiative. It may be rash to read too much into the discrepancies in the portraits, given that the engravers would have been in the habit of cutting heads of Tiberius. Images on the small precious metal coins are often inconsistent, in any case, and R. Brilliant has observed that even the obverses of Caligula on this issue hardly seem to be of the same person, while the reverse portraits (whether of Augustus or Tiberius) in some instances resemble those on the obverses![11] A variant of the type depicts the radiate head of Augustus and the legend, *Divus Augustus Pater Patriae* (*BMC* 10; fig. 10). These types owe their basic inspiration to Tiberian models (Tiberius *BMC* 28,29), but in their details they are strikingly different.

More original is another series in gold and silver emphasizing the importance of family. They bear on the reverses the heads of both Agrippina and Germanicus (*BMC* 7,13; figs. 11, 12), identified in the legends as Caligula's mother and father respectively. These types appear with both the 'bare' and 'laureate' obverses. With the 'laureate' only is a scarce issue beginning in his first year with the standard reverse of SPQR/P(ATER) P(ATRIAE)/ OB C(IVES) S(ERVATOS), perhaps in association with his assumption of the title of Pater Patriae (*BMC* p.396.20; fig. 13) The quinarius issue continues the conventional reverses of Tiberius, the seated Victory (*BMC* 6; fig. 14).

It is interesting that with the exception of the gold quinarii, there are no precious issues that can be dated between April 38 and January 40.

AES:
The general standard of workmanship is much higher on the aes than on the precious metal mainly because of the larger field that these coins, especially the sestertii, offered. The aes issues mark a major break with the practices of Tiberius, and A. Savio sees in them a revolutionary content, aimed at the ordinary Roman people.[12]

Dated Coins
In Caligula's first year four sestertii types were produced: Three obverses have the head of Caligula bare or laureate; the reverses are

(a) the three sisters (*BMC* 37; fig. 15). The local mint of Apamea imitates this type with the addition of Diva to Drusilla's name (Trillmich, 108-110; Mionnet no. 23; fig. 30)

(b) the *corona civica* (*BMC* 38; fig. 16)

(c) *adlocutio cohortis* (lacking SC) (*BMC* 33; fig. 17) This type is strikingly original, the first depiction on coinage of an imperial speech to the army. It probably marks Caligula's donative to the Praetorians on his accession. Sutherland suggests that while most of the donative would have consisted of denarii, part of it might have consisted of aes. The coin was reissued in 39-41. H.W. Ritter believes that its reissue was connected with the episode of the Bridge at Baiae, at which Praetorians were present.[13]

(d) The fourth sestertius issue has the obverse of a seated pietas, with the dedication of the Temple of Augustus on the reverse (*BMC* 41; fig. 18)

There is one dated dupondius, with Nero and Drusus as riders on the obverse, and Caligula's legend around SC as the reverse (*BMC* 44; fig. 20). The obverse is imitated by Herod Agrippa (Meshorer no. 1), although depicting only a single figure, with similar flowing cloak and raised arm, identified as Agrippa's son.[14]

There are two dated asses:

(a) obverse of Caligula's head and reverse of Vesta (*BMC* 59; fig. 22).

(b) obverse of Germanicus' head and reverse identical to the obverse of dated dupondius (*BMC* 49; fig. 23)

Beginning in the latter part of 39 Caligula's quadrans issue appears, with obverse of pileus (cap of liberty) between SC, and reverse of Caligula's legend around RCC (*BMC* 57; fig. 25). This is perhaps the most puzzling of his issues. In 1796 J. Eckhel claimed that the letters stood for *rei censitae conservator* (based on an obscure inscription no longer extant) but they are now universally taken to stand for *remissa ducentessima*, a reference to a removal of the .5 per cent sales tax.[15] There are some serious objections to this idea. In the first place the literary evidence strongly favours the notion that the sales tax when removed by Caligula stood at 1 per cent, not .5 per cent. Also Dio places the removal of the tax in 38, while the coins do not appear until late enough in 39 for Caligula to be designate consul for the following year.[16] Eckel also argued that the cap of liberty was meant to refer to the restoration of the elections to the comitia. But this is open to the same objections, since the elections were restored to the people in 38, a year before the coin was issued. A.U. Stylow has recently claimed that the cap has nothing to do with the elections but, like the reverse, echoes the theme of the tax reduction, as a stage in the development of the concept of *libertas* as the concern and provision of the emperor for his people. By the third century, he argues, there is little distinction between *libertas Augusti* and *liberalitas Augusti*.[17] In fact, there is no way of knowing whether the issue has anything at all to do with the sales tax or what the letters RCC might stand for (the combination is otherwise unknown). The types on quadrantes tend to have a commercial theme- their small field makes them generally unsuitable for grandiose propaganda purposes. But Caligula was innovative in his use of coin types. The curious coincidence of the cap of liberty and the issue date of late 39 (when events were dominated by the conspiracy of Lepidus) at least raises the possibility that they have some assocation with the suppression of the conspiracy.

All of these denominations continue to appear after Caligula's first year, with the exception of the the 'three sisters' type which was suspended after the disgrace of Caligula's two surviving sisters. As with the precious issues, there is a gap in the dated aes issues after April 38, until April 39 at the earliest. With the exception of the quadrantes they do not show consular years and it is not possible to tell if the gap of the main aes series parallels that of the precious issues, continuing up to January 40. The quadrantes, at any rate, reappear in late 39.

Undated Coins

Sestertius, with obverse bust and legend of Agrippina, and a *carpentum* ('carriage') on the reverse (*BMC* 85; fig. 19). Caligula decreed games in the circus in honour of his mother, with a *carpentum* to carry her image.[18] This issue has tended to be dated to the opening of Caligula's reign, but Trillmich has argued on stylistic and numismatic grounds that it is spread throughout the reign, and makes a common group with the Divus Augustus dupondius and the Agrippa asses (see below), all emphasizing Caligula's blood-relationship with Augustus.

Dupondius, with obverse radiate head and legend of the Divine Augustus (*BMC* 88; fig. 21) Reverse: Enthroned figure holding an orb in the left hand and a branch in the other and the legend consensu *senat et eq. orn, p.q.r.* ('with the consent of the senate and equestrian order and Roman People). The attribution of this coin to Caligula is by no means certain. This seated figure is generally recognized as Augustus; H.M. von Kaenel argues that it represents Caligula, on (dubious) iconographical grounds and because the theme suits Caligula's accession. But the *consensus* motif is essentially Augustan, used on Caligula's accession in a deliberate attempt to associate himself with his predecessor. Recently, B. Levy has detected traces of a radiate crown on the head of the seated figure, hardly appropriate of Caligula in a coin that stresses his constitutionality. The Augustan identification seems most likely.[19]

One undated dupondius has an obverse of Germanicus standing in a quadriga holding a sceptre, with an advancing figure of victory on the chariot, and a reverse of a standing Germanicus and the legends SIGNIS RECEPT(IS) and DEVICTIS GERM(ANIS) (*BMC* 93). It was imitated in bronze issues of Agrippa.[20] The dupondius is generally assumed to be Caligulan, although some ascribe it to Tiberius.[21]

The commonest of the issues of Caligula is the so-called Agrippa as

(*BMC* (Tiberius) 161; fig. 24). It depicts on its obverse a bust of Agrippa, facing left, with rostral crown and the legend M. AGRIPPA L F COS III. On the reverse is a Neptune holding a dolphin in his right hand and trident in his left, and the letters *SC*. It is found most commonly near the Rhine frontier. Scholars have generally accepted that this coin was minted under Caligula, but it has been argued by some that it appeared first under Tiberius. Opinion has differed over whether it was produced at a number of different mints, in the provinces as well as in Rome.[22] J. Nicols, however, has pointed out that the adjusted die axis of these asses, with 'upside-down'reverse, is not compatible with that of Tiberian coins. In the mid-Tiberian reign the adjusted axis with upright reverse is always found on at least some of his aes. By the end of his reign it predominates. There are no Agrippa asses found with this arrangement, which is foreign also to Caligulan issues. Nicols argues that Caligula issued this coin in conjunction with other family types, to be continued under Claudius although in reduced numbers. She suggests that the coins originate in the issues of the colony of Nimes (Nemausus), bearing the portraits of Agrippa and Augustus, back to back, which were often neatly halved to keep the heads intact. The Agrippa as represents the continuity of this tradition.[23] The Agrippa as was imitated in issues of Caesaraugusta, the richest of the local mints of Spain. As shown by the names of the moneyers the colony produced three coin issues, dated by Trillmich to the first three years of Caligula's reign. The Agrippa imitations appear in the second and third issues.[24]

A mint existed in Syria at Antioch from Augustus to Valerian with coins of a type and quality that suggest an official mint. There are apparently no official issues of Caligula from Antioch but there are tetradrachms of the city which seem to have sufficed for the silver needs of the province.[25] Also Augustan and Tiberian issues were countermarked for each year of his reign at Antioch.[26] One of the foremost of the eastern mints was at Caearea in Cappadocia. Latin-inscribed silver coins can be compared in style and fabric to Greek-inscribed issues apparently intended for local use (with the type of Mount Argaeus) and this confirms the mint-location of the Latin coins. Coins were produced here by all the emperors from Tiberius to Nero, the mint activity being closely connected with the degree of Roman military activity in the East. It might not have been felt wise to entrust the minting of large amounts of silver coinage to the already powerful governor of Syria.

(a) Didrachm (*BMC* 104; fig. 26)
obverse: head of Germanicus
reverse: type of Germanicus standing at right holding a spear in his left and placing a tiara on the head of Zeno Artaxias, both identified by the legends Artaxias and Germanicus, possibly to celebrate the

twentieth anniversary of the event. We can not be certain that these two coins were not minted in AD 18, at the time of the event, but it seems unlikely that they would have promoted Germanicus to such a degree without the head of the reigning emperor during the former's lifetime.

(b) Drachm (*BMC* 102; fig. 27), probably from Caligula's first year, as suggested by legend TRPOT without further enumeration: obverse: bare head of Caligula. reverse: priestly implements of the pontifex maximus.

(c) Drachm (*BMC* 105; fig. 28): obverse bare head of Germanicus, with legend IM in legend presumably standing for IMP, not Pontifex Maximus, but note that the letters are separated by dots. reverse: radiate head of Augustus

INSCRIPTIONS

Inscriptions are of enormous potential value as a historical tool. In practice their use for the reign of Caligula is somewhat limited. Since, unlike coins, they were not issued in enormous multiples their survival rate is much lower, and in absolute terms few are known for this period. Also, most inscriptions are of provincial origin, where honorifics and titles do not always conform to the official imperial practice, and where dates may be confused or mistaken. There are two important exceptions. The Fasti, known from least the fourth century BC, were technically calendars. They marked the *dies fasti* and *nefasti* for the conduct of business, and eventually embraced a wide range of information, recording magistrates, festivals, triumphs and important state events. For the reign of Caligula the Fasti of Ostia, though surviving only for 37/8 within our period, provide an invaluable sequence of events. They reveal the delay between the arrival of Tiberius' body into the city and his funeral (showing that it was not hasty), the dates of Caligula's *congiaria*, of Antonia's and Drusilla's death, and of the fire in the Aemiliana.

Probably the most important epigraphic material for our specific purposes are the surviving inscriptions of the Arval brotherhood.[27] Most of the information on this priestly college must be extrapolated from its own record, since there are scant literary references. Its cult centre lay some four miles to the west of Rome on the Via Campana outside the city limits, at the shrine of the goddess Dea Dia, although rites took place also in the city. It was made up of twelve men in addition to the emperor. At the head stood the magister, selected from the brotherhood on an annual rotating basis. Although its roots probably go back to the early days of the republic the Arval brotherhood began to flourish with the establishment of the principate. Most importantly for the historian the college started then to keep a record of its rituals inscribed on stone, which has survived from 21 BC to AD 304. One of the most noticeable features of these inscriptions is the prominence of the imperial family, indicated by the annual vows and sacrifices performed for the emperor and, where appropriate, members of his family. Also there are rites carried out on birthdays and on the anniversaries of important events in the imperial family calendar. For Caligula's reign the Arval record is useful at the most basic level for showing often when Caligula and other prominent individuals were in the vicinity of Rome, as well as providing information on such items as the date of his acclamation as Imperator. The most important epigraphic development for the reign of Caligula in recent years has been the discovery of a large fragment of the record for 38, enabling us, among other things, to date the assumption of the title of Pater Patriae firmly to September 37 (it was usually placed in the spring of 38).

Inscriptions must be evaluated judiciously, since a contemporary record is not necessarily an accurate one. In particular the Tabulae Ceratae, wax tablets, found especially in Pompeii, whose information tends often to be of a private and ephemeral nature, are to be treated with caution. One example, dated to 5 January, 41, showing Caligula no longer consul is highly suspect, since Suetonius, who tends to be fairly reliable on such details, claims that he did not hand down the office until 7 January. Another, dated to 8 June, 37, has Caligula and Claudius consuls by that time, even though the Fasti and the literary sources indicate that they did not enter the consulship until 1 July. The most curious example of all is dated to April of an unspecified year, showing Caligula consul with Marcus Cocceius Nerva, which contradicts all the epigraphic and literary evidence. In no year was Caligula consul in April, and he was never the colleague of Nerva.[28]

SCULPTURE

When a deputation representing the league of several Greek states arrived in Rome on Caligula's accession to offer him various honours, he recommended that they save themselves some expense by limiting the number of statues erected to him, and by restricting the locations to the sites of the great games: Olympia, Nemea, Delphi and the Isthmus. Dio even goes so far as to suggest that he forbade the manufacture of his own statues, presumably a specific injunction applied to a specific request, and misrepresented by Dio as general policy. In fact, for most of his reign statues of Caligula seem to have been produced in some quantity, as suggested by the literary evidence and the statue bases found throughout the empire.[29] In Alexandria the Greeks supposedly provoked the Jews by setting up a statue of Caligula in a refurbished triumphal chariot that had once housed Cleopatra but had fallen into rusty decay. In Rome statues of Caligula and Claudius were set on the Capitoline to mark their entry into the consulship in 37. In 39 Domitius Afer dedicated one to the emperor in Rome. Probably in the same year Caligula's golden image was set up in the Temple of Jupiter on the Capitoline, and he may similarly have placed his statue in the Temple of Castor and Pollux. These seem to have been the targets of malicious vanadalism, and the senate arranged for an armed guard to watch over them. Ultimately this was to be no protection. Some of the statues seem to have suffered during the confusion of the assassination, and although there was no formal *damnatio memoriae*, Claudius discreetly arranged for the remaining ones to be destroyed.[30]

None of the surviving sculpted heads that have been attributed to Caligula have been found in association with their inscribed bases, and the identifications are founded, essentially, on the resemblances to coin portaits. It is clearly a far from exact process, and while it may be possible to assign a sculpted head to its general historical period with some certainty, it is rarely possible to assign it with any degree of confidence to a particular individual. In the final analysis such identifications will be largely subjective. In the attributed sculpture, we do note the deeply-set eyes. The forehead is long and almost vertical. The nose is slightly bulbous. The mouth is small, and the lower lip tends to retract. There is only a hint of baldness in the high hairline in some of the examples, and we also see attempts to comb the hair forward at the temples to conceal a receding hairline. On many of the sculpted heads the locks of the hair fork near the centre of the forehead and then curl back to the left and the right. This last feature is common also on portraits of Tiberius. Hair grows down to the nape of the neck.

Useful lists of attributed pieces can be found in:

D. Boschung, *Die Bildnisse des Caligula* (*Das römische Herrscherbild* 1.4: Berlin, 1988)

R. Brilliant, 'An early Imperial Portrait of Caligula', *AAAH* 4 (1969), 13-17.

V. Poulsen, 'Portraits of Caligula', *AArch* 29 (1958), 175-190

L. Fabbrini, 'Caligola': il rittrato dell'adolescenza e il ritratto dell' apoteosi', *MDAI(R)* 73-4 (1966-7), 134-146

J. C. Faur, 'Un nouveau visage de Caligula', *AArch* 42 (1971), 35–42

H. Jucker, 'Caligula', *Arts in Virginia* 13 (1973) 17-25

F. S. Johanson, 'The Sculpted Portraits of Caligula', *Ancient Portraits in the J. Paul Getty Museum*. Vol. 1 (1987) 89-106; see also 'Antike Porträts von Caligula in der Ny Carlsberg Glyptothek', *WZBerl* 31 (1982), 223-4

J. Pollini, 'A Pre-Principate Portrait of Gaius (Caligula)', *JWAG* 40 (1982), 1-12 offers an excellent discussion of the criteria for identifying a Caligulan piece.

NOTES
AND REFERENCES

1 Family background (*pages 1–16*)

1 See C.M. Wells, *The German Policy of Augustus* (Oxford, 1972), 238-40; J.C. Mann, 'The Frontiers of the Principate', *ANRW* II 1 (1974), 518-9

2 For 16: B. Levick, 'Drusus Caesar and the Adoptions of A.D.4', *Latomus* 25 (1966), 227-55; for 15: G.V. Sumner, 'Germanicus and Drusus Caesar', *Latomus* 26 (1967), 413-23

3 Dio 55.13.2. Suet. *Tib.* 16.1 gives a figure of 5

4 Levick (1976), 57-60 suggests that the charges about his character were a front to explain his disgrace following some political intrigue

5 Tac. *Ann.* 1.33.3, 2.73.2-3, 82.3; Suet. *Cal.* 3.1; see also, Dio 57, 18.6-8

6 Tac. *Ann.* 1.33.6, 2.72.1, 4.12.7, 52-54, 6.25.3; Suet. *Aug.* 86.3; Dio 57.6.3

7 Tac. *Ann.* 2.54 places Livilla's birth in early 18 in Lesbos, in error, according to Mommsen, 'Die Familie des Germanicus', *GS* 4. 271-90, who argues for a date of late 17. The dates of 15 and 16 respectively for Agrippina and Drusilla are generally accepted by scholars (but see J. Humphrey, 'The Three Daughters of Agrippina Maior', *AJAH* 4 (1979), 125-43, who believes that Drusilla was the oldest sister). Suet. *Cal.* 7 states that the girls were born *continuo triennio*, which, Humphrey points out (see also P. Herz, 'Die Arvalakten des Jahres 38 n. Chr. Eine Quelle zur Geschichte Kaiser Caligulas', *Historia* 30 [1981], 103), may mean 'in a three year period' rather than 'in three years in succession'. The child carried by Agrippina in the autumn of 14 (Tac. *Ann.* 1.44.2) is generally considered to have been stillborn

8 Suet. *Cal.* 1.1; Dio 55.31.1, 56.25.2. Germanicus' return some time before the end of 11 is indicated by the birth of Caligula in August of the following year

9 Suet. *Cal.*8.1; *Fasti Vallenses* and *Fasti Pighiani*; cf Dio 59.6.1

10 For recent discussions, see B. Baldwin, *Suetonius* (Amsterdam, 1983),

158, and A. Wallace-Hadrill, *Suetonius* (London, 1983), 89

11 A.Taylor, 'An Allusion to a Riddle in Suetonius', *AJP* 66 (1945), 408-10, suggests that the triple element of the epigram indicates the standard formula of a riddle

12 On the *Acta Diurna*, see B. Baldwin, 'The *Acta Diurna*', *Chiron* 9 (1979), 189-203; F.Schultz, 'Roman Registers of Births and Birth Certificates', *JRS* 32 (1942), 78-91, 33 (1943), 55-64, suggests a reference to registry of birth, probably preserved in the Aerarium Saturni, which would sometimes have mentioned the birthplace

13 Tac. *Ann.* 1.41.3

14 Suet. *Cal.* 8.4

15 Sen. *Cons.* 18.4 Tac. *Ann.* 1.41.3;69.5; Suet. *Cal.* 9.1; Dio 57.5.6; Aur. Vict. *Caes.* 3.4, *Epit.* 3.2; Eutrop. 7.12.1; Suda sv. *Kaligolas.* Suet. *Cal.* 52 notes that as an adult he wore a variety of footwear, including guardsmen's boots '*caliga speculatoria*'. The name Caligula does not appear in inscriptions, with the exception of a forgery from Gallipoli (*CIL* III. 28★). Seneca notes that the use of the name 'Gaius' also offended him

16 Tac. *Ann.* 1.69.5

17 On the succession: Vell. 2.124, Tac. *Ann.* 1.7-13: Suet. *Tib.* 22-24; Dio 57.2-3

18 E. Hohl, 'Wann hat Tiberius das Prinzipat übernommen?', *Hermes* 68 (1933), 106-115, D. Timpe (1962), 37, Seager, 53-54, Levick (1976), 76-70

19 Velleius 2.125; Tac. *Ann.*1.31-49; Suet. *Tib.* 25.2; Dio 57.5-6

20 Suet. *Cal.* 48.1; Dio 57.5.6

21 Tac. *Ann.* 1.41-44; Suet. *Cal.* 9; see, J. Burian, 'Caligula und die Militärrevolte am Rhein', *Mnema V. Groh* (Prague, 1964), 25-9

22 The concessions were later cancelled by Tiberius: Tac. *Ann.* 1.78.2; Dio 57.6.4

23 Tac. *Ann.* 1. 49.5- 51.9; Dio 57.6.1

24 Tac. *Ann.* 1.55.1 seems to indicate that the triumph was initially voted for   14. Timpe, *Der Triumph des Germanicus* (Bonn, 1968), 43, thinks that it was for 15

25 Tac. *Ann.* 2.26.6

26 Tac. *Ann.* 2. 43.7, 3. 56.5. The marriage of Drusus and Livilla must be placed very soon after AD 4, when Gaius Caesar, Livilla's first husband, died, as their daughter was old enough to be married herself by AD 20 (to Nero, brother of Caligula)

27 F.B. Marsh, 'Roman Parties in the Reign of Tiberius', *AHR* 31 (1926), (1931), 65-68; attacked by W. Allen, 'The Political Atmosphere of the Reign of Tiberius', *TAPA* 72 (1941), 1-25; 41f; see Talbert 276-7

28 Tac. *Ann.* 2.41.2-4

29 Tac. *Ann.* 2.42.2-6; Suet. *Tib.* 37.4; Dio 57.17.3-7. Tacitus and Dio both place his death in 17, but it may have occurred shortly before (see Magie 1349 n.1)
30 Tac. *Ann.* 2.42.7; Jos. *AJ* 18.53
31 For a good summary of the scholarship up to 1976, see H. Jucker, 'Der Grosse Pariser Kameo', *JDAI* 91 (1977), 211-50
32 Tac. *Ann.* 2.53.1. E. Koestermann, 'Die Mission des Germanicus im Orient', *Historia* 7 (1958), 339 sees Germanicus' visit to Nicopolis as a provocative act, perhaps implying that it marked him out as one who would inherit the world pacified by Augustus
33 *IGR* 4.251 (Smallwood 33)
34 Tac. *Ann.* 3.12.2. It should be noted that despite the senatorial approval, Syria was an 'imperial province'
35 Tac. *Ann.* 2.55
36 Armenia: Suet. *Cal.* 1.2 states that Germanicus defeated (*devicisset*) the King of Armenia, either a confused error or textual corruption in the manuscripts; Cappadocia: Dio 57.17.7; Tac. *Ann.* 1.78.2, 2.42; Commagene: Tac. *Ann.* 2.56.5
37 Tac. *Ann.* 2.57
38 Tac. *Ann.* 2.59.3-4
39 The date is given by the Fasti of Antium (EJ p.63). Tac. *Ann.* 2.83.3 says that he died in the suburb of Epidaphne, a confusion with Antioch epi Daphne, the name given to Antioch because of its most famous quarter. On the illness, see Tac. *Ann.* 2.69-72
40 Tac. *Ann.* 3.7.2. On this see Syme, 'Governors Dying in Syria', *Papers*, 1376-92
41 Pliny *NH* 11. 187; Suet. *Cal.* 1.2; Tac. *Ann.* 2.73 doubts that the body showed any signs of poisoning. The heart survived the cremation, a fact used in Piso's later trial to show that he had been poisoned. Piso was able to retort that the hearts of heart attack victims similarly did not burn; see F. D'Ercé, 'La Mort de Germanicus et les poisons de Caligula', *Janus* 56 (1969), 123-48
42 Tabula Hebana (*EJ* 94a); Tabula Siarensis (*ZPE* 55 [1984], 55-100)
43 Tac. *Ann.* 3.1-4; Suet. *Cal.* 5
44 Tac. *Ann.* 3.17.2-5

2 Struggle for the succession (*pages 17–41*)

1 Tac. *Ann.* 2.84.1. For Gemellus as nickname for Tiberius Julius Caesar, see Jos. *AJ* 18. 206. The baby princes were honoured in the provinces: *SEG* IV. 515; *IGR* III. 997, and their heads appeared on Imperial coinage (*BMC* Tiberius 95)
2 Tac. *Ann.*4.4.3. Marsh, 161 interprets Drusus' kindness to the sons as an indication that he recognized that the succession should pass eventually to them

3 Tac. *Ann.* 3.29.5 says that Nero was made pontifex but there is no inscriptional evidence for this, and there may be some confusion with his brother Drusus' pontificate (*ILS* 185). Suet. *Cal.* 12.1 mistakenly calls Drusus an augur. *EJ* 96 indicates that Nero was flamen Augustalis

4 Tac. *Ann.* 3.56.1

5 Tac. *Ann.* 4.2.1; Suet. *Tib.* 37.1; Dio 57.19.6

6 Tac. *Ann.* 4.2.4; Dio 57.19.7, cf. Dio 58.4.3

7 Suet. *Claud.* 27.1. His name was Claudius Drusus

8 Tac. *Ann.* 4.10; Dio 57.22.1-3

9 At the beginning of 23 the young Drusus, on assuming the toga virilis, had received the same honours as had been granted earlier to his brother Nero (Tac. *Ann.* 4.4.1; Suet. *Tib.* 54.1). Unlike Nero, Drusus was made pontifex, rather than flamen Augustalis

10 Tac. *Ann.* 4.8.6-8, 15.6

11 Tac. *Ann.* 4.12.5, 17.4

12 Tac. *Ann.* 14.39-40. The authenticity of the correspondence between Sejanus and Tiberius on this matter, and indeed the incident itself, is doubted by some

13 Tac. *Ann.* 4.52; Suet. *Tib.* 53.1

14 Tac. *Ann.* 4.53-4

15 At *Ann.* 6.20.1 Tacitus seems to suggest that Caligula went to Capri with Tiberius at the outset, which is clearly incorrect

16 Tac. *Ann.* 4.60.5-6

17 Tac. *Ann.* 4.66.1. On the betrothal, see Sen. *Contr.* 1.3.10

18 Among modern treatments: M.P. Charlesworth, 'The Banishment of the Elder Agrippina', *CPh* 17 (1922), 260-1, CAH 10. 635, V. Gardthausen, 'Nero Iulius Caesar', *RE* 10 (1918), 475, M. Gelzer 'T. Iulius Caesar Augustus', *RE* 10 (1918), 511, E. Köstermann, *Tacitus. Annalen* (Heidelberg 1963-68), II. 223, on *Ann,* V.3, Marsh 184-7, Syme, *Tacitus*, I. 404-5, R.S. Rogers, 'The Conspiracy of Agrippina', *TAPA* 62 (1931), 160, *Criminal Trials and Criminal Legislation under Tiberius* (Middletown, 1935), 101, *Studies in the Reign of Tiberius* (Baltimore, 1943), 57-9, J. Colin, 'Les Consuls du César-pharaon Caligula et l'héritage de Germanicus', *Latomus* 13 (1954), 389, L. Petersen 'C. (Iulius) Caesar', *PIR*² I 217, Meise, 240

19 Velleius 2.130.4-5; Pliny *NH* 8. 145; Tac. *Ann.* 5.3.1; Suet. *Cal.* 10.1

20 Sen. *Ira* 3.21.5; Tac. *Ann.* 4.67.6. The villa was later destroyed by Caligula. K. Scott, 'Notes on the Destruction of Two Roman Villas', *AJP* 60 (1939), 462 suggests that Agrippina was held at Herculaneum temporarily when moved between various places of exile

21 Tac. *Ann.* 4. 68-70; Dio 58.1.1-3

22 Suet. *Cal.* 16.3, 23.2

23 Tac. *Ann.* 5.1; Suet. *Cal.* 10.1. Rogers, *op. cit,* n 18, 98, puts the death of Livia towards the end of 29. Tac. *Ann.* 5.2.3, however, notes

that after Livia's death Tiberius criticised the consul Fufius for courting her favour. Fufius was consul ordinarius for 29 and was replaced almost certainly by the end of June. On this basis we can place both the attacks on Agrippina and Nero, and Caligula's subsequent move to Antonia in early rather than late 29; see Levick, (1976), 276 n.108

24 Tac. *Ann.* 1.33.6, 2.43.7, 4.12.5, 5.3-5

25 Philo *Flacc.* 9

26 See R.S. Rogers, 'The Conspiracy of Agrippina', *TAPA* 62 (1931), 141-168; A. Boddington, 'Sejanus. Whose Conspiracy?', *AJP* 84 (1963), 1-16

27 Tac. *Ann.* 5.1-6; Suet. *Cal.* 10.1. Gelzer, 382 argues that the delivery of Livia's funeral oration already marked him out as a successor. But such performances by young men were a tradition of the Julian house; see Maurer, ad loc.

28 Tac. *Ann.* 11.3.1; *IGR* 4. 145 (Smallwood 401)

29 See Marsh, 244. There have been suggestions that Gaetulicus and Sejanus were related, through Sejanus' grandfather Cn. Lentulus Maluginensis; C. Cichorius, 'Zur Familiengeschichte Sejans', *Hermes* 39 (1904), 469-70; Stewart, 73 n.21, disproved by Sealey, 103. H. Bird, 'L. Aelius Sejanus and his Political Influence', *Latomus* 28 (1969), 77, plays down the connections between Gaetulicus and Sejanus

30 Tac. *Ann.* 6.23.1-3; Dio 58.3.1-6, 23.6

31 Dio 58.3.8 notes that Tiberius eventually 'sent Drusus to Rome', and it is generally assumed that this must have been from Capri. It may be that Tacitus' comment (*Ann.* 6.20.1) that Caligula accompanied Tiberius to Capri at the outset resulted from confusion between the movements of Caligula and Drusus

32 Suet. *Tib.* 54.2, *Cal.* 7; Dio 58.3.8. Cassius may be the consul of that year C. Cassius Longinus or his brother L. Cassius Longinus (who married Drusus' sister, Drusilla, three years later). There may, of course, be a third, unknown Cassius

33 Dio 58.3.9 (epitome) must be mistaken in saying that it was to Livilla's daughter Julia that Sejanus was betrothed. See Seager, 213. n.6

34 Consulship: Suet. *Tib.* 65.1; *EJ* 50a, 358a; surrender of consulship: Suet. *Tib.* 26.2, EJ p.42; proconsular power: Dio 58.7.4

35 Jos. *AJ* 18.182; Suet. *Tib.* 65.1; the idea is reflected in Tac. *Ann.* 6.8; Val. Max. 9." *ext.*4; *EJ* 51, 52, 85

36 Jos. *AJ* 18.182; Dio 65.14.1-2; on the possible exaggeration of Antonia's role, see J. Nicols, 'Antonia and Sejanus', *Historia* 24 (1975), 48-59

37 Tac. *Ann.* 6.3.4

38 Suet. *Tib.*61.1. Sealey, 98 suggests that this autobiography may have been the source of the story about Antonia's letter

39 Suet. *Tib.* 54.2, 61.1; Dio 58.6.2-4.

40 Suet. *Tib*.54.1, *Cal.* 10.1; Dio 59.2.2. Levick (1976), 175 argues that Caligula was taken to Capri for his own protection

41 Willrich, 100. Levick (1976), 175 says that speed was needed because of the threat posed by Sejanus

42 Dio 58.23.1. Suet. *Tib.* 54.1 notes with reference to Drusus and Nero that he felt that honours should be conferred only on those with maturity and experience

43 Suet. *Cal.* 12.1; Dio 58.7.4. Drusus clearly held a pontificate (*ILS* 185), but there is no evidence that he was an augur and Suetonius may be in error in suggesting that Caligula was marked out to succeed him in that office. Caligula may have succeeded Nero, rather than Drusus, in his pontificate (Tac. *Ann.* 3.29.3). Caligula's priesthood is recorded in *ILS* 189 (one of a pair) from Vienna Alloborgum. He was an augur after his accession, but there is no evidence that he was so before then. He appears as augur on local coins of 37 (Cohen I. 238.12) with the symbols of the augur on the reverse. To keep them off their guard Sejanus and his son Strabo were elevated to priesthoods at the same time as Caligula

44 Dio 58.8.1-2; Dio adds that Sejanus was deterred from armed rebellion when he realized how popular the decision was

45 On Macro see F. De Visscher, 'L'amphithêatre d'Alba Fucens et son fondateur Q. Naevius Macro, préfet du prétoire de Tibère', *RAL* 12 (1957), 39-49, 'Macro, préfet des vigiles et ses cohortes contre la tyrannie de Séjan', *Mélange d'archéologie et d'histoire offerts à A. Piganiol* (Paris, 1966), 761-8, La Politique dynastique sous le régne de Tibére', *Synteleia V. Arangio-Ruiz* (Naples 1964), 54–65

46 Tac. *Ann.* 6.23.5; Dio 58.12, 13.1

47 Tac. *Ann.* 4.11.4; Dio 58.11.6-7

48 As suggested by Balsdon, 15

49 Philo *Leg.* 35-8

50 Tac. *Ann.* 6.3.4-4.1,5-6, 6.5-6, 9.2-5. Cotta had said that Caligula was a person of *incertae virilitatis*, perhaps an ambiguous joke on his late assumption of the toga virilis

51 Tac. *Ann.* 6.9.5-7, 14.2, 29.4-6; see, Stewart, 73, Levick (1976), 202-3

52 Jos. *AJ* 19.209 Willrich, 101 believes that Tiberius with his traditional Roman ideas would have seen his role as a counter-balance to the influence of Hellenism

53 Tac. *Ann.* 4.58.1; Suet. *Cal.* 10.2, cf. 70; on Curtius Rufus' literary links, see Ovid *ex P.* 2.11

54 Consular: Suet. *Tib.* 61.6. Syme, *Tacitus* 277 identifies him as Servilius Nonianus; Asinius Gallus: Dio 58.3.3; Galba: Tac. *Ann.* 6.20.3 Vitellius: Suet. *Vit.* 3.2

55 Tac. *Ann.* 6.20.2; Suet. *Cal.* 10.2 repeats the phrase without giving the author

56 Suet. *Cal.* 12.3

57 Philo *Leg.* 14; Suet. *Cal.* 11

58 Dio 58.23.1:'not among those who were first'. Levick (1976), 291, n.31 explains that this does not mean an inferior quaestorship, but that he was designated to hold office not in the following year but in the one after that; Sumner *op. cit.* I n.2, 425, suggests that he was designated suffect for AD 33

59 He held a duumvirate at Caesaraugusta in Spain (Cohen I. 199. no. 103) and Pompeii (*ILS* 6396, with *CIL* 10. 902, dated to 34), and was quinquennalis at Carthago Nova, also in Spain (Cohen I 245 no.1), and Pompeii (*ILS* 6397)

60 Tac. *Ann.* 6.23.4-6, 24; Suet. *Tib.* 54.2,61.1; Dio 58.22.4, 25.4

61 Tac. *Ann.* 5.10. Dio 58.25

62 Dio 58.22.4 implicates Tiberius. Suet. *Tib.* 53.2, however, says that Agrippina's death was suicide, and Tac. *Ann.* 6.25.1 accepts the suicide version after some hesitation

63 Tac. *Ann.* 6.20.1 provides the date; Dio 58.25.2 provides the location, Antium, and the presence of Tiberius, but dates the marriage to 35; Suet. *Cal.* 12.1 gives the bride's name as Junia Claudilla, and puts the marriage before Caligula's priesthood, in 31; see, Syme, *Papers* 4.228-9

64 Tac. *Ann.* 3.24, 57.2, 6.2.2; Dio 59.8.5-6; Syme, *Aristocracy*, 195, stemmata XII and XIII

65 Longinus: Tac. *Ann.* 6.15.1-2; Lucius: Sen. *Contr.* 10.4.25. Vinicius: Tac. *Ann.*6.15.1 calls him *mitis ingenio* ('gentle by nature'), echoed by Dio 60.27.4; Blandus: Tac. *Ann.* 6.27.1; Syme, *Papers* 4.177-98; on the marriages: Levick (1976), 208

66 Suet. *Cal.* 12.2; Dio 59.8.7 is clearly in error in stating that Caligula divorced Junia afer his accession

67 *PIR*² E65. Ennias's age is uncertain. It has been speculated since the time of C. Cichorius, *Römische Studien* (Leipzig, 1922), 391 that Ennia was the grand-daughter of the astrologer Thrasyllus. If this identification is correct she may have been born about 15; see H.H. Cramer, *Astrology in Roman Law and Politics* (Philadelphia, 1954) 107

68 Tac. *Ann.* 6.45.5; 58.28.4; Philo *Leg.* 39, 61 places the blame on Ennia, suggesting that she deceived Macro, who had no idea of the affair, while Suet. *Cal.* 12.2 blames Caligula, claiming that he seduced Ennia

69 Agrippa's nomen 'Julius' is given in IG III², 3449. There is no record of *his* praenomen, but we do know that his son was called Marcus : *SEG* 7, 216,217 (cf *IGR* 3. 1089), a name that he may have adopted from his father; see Smallwood, *Jews,* 187

70 Jos. *AJ* 18. 143, 147-50, 165, 168-204; Willrich, 101.

71 See, Timpe (1962), 60–61. As Gagé, 'Divus Augustus', *RA* 34 (1931), 11,pointed out, 'Une loi tacite… ait réguliérement dévolue l'empire au représentant le plus proche ou le plus qualifié du sang d'Auguste'

72 Meise, 50–5 argues that speculations about Tiberius's intentions arose from the claims put forward by the 'Gemellus Party' and the 'Caligula Party' in the period before Gemellus' death, with Josephus retailing the views of the former, Dio of the latter

73 Philo *Leg.* 24, 33-4, *Flacc.* 24; Jos. *AJ.* 18.215; Tac. *Ann.* 6.46.9; Suet. *Tib.* 55, *Cal.* 11, 19.3; Dio 58.23.3

74 Suet. *Tib.* 62.3; Dio 58.23.2

75 Suet. *Tib.* 76, *Cal.* 14.1. The notion of a dual principate does have its supporters, eg. E. Kornemann, *Doppelprinzipat und Reichsteilung im Imperium Romanum* (Lepizig– Berlin, 1930), 37, H. Gesche, 'Datierung und Deutung der CLEMENTIAE– MODERATIONI Dupondien des Tiberius', *JNG* 21 (1971), 55, 65, Levick (1976), 209–10

76 Dio 59.1.1; Philo *Leg.* 23, *Flacc.* 10

77 See n.59. Levick (1976), 209–10 explains this as due to Tiberius' formalism and the belief that he would live long enough for Gemellus to reach office in due course (Suet. *Tib.* 62.3; Dio 58.27.3). She suggests (p.209) that Gemellus held a pontificate, citing Espérandieu, 618. But the attribution of this inscription to Gemellus is far from certain, and in its original publication, F.-P. Thiers, 'Rapport sur les Fouilles de Castel-Roussilon en 1911,' *Bulletin Archéologique* (1912), 84 assigned it to Claudius

78 Philo *Leg.* 23, 30-31; Tac. *Ann.* 6.46.1 (he may have meant only that he had not yet not attained the toga virilis); Dio 58.23.2. Tac. *Ann.* 2.84 is quite specific about the date of Gemellus' birth and even notes that people saw the tragic irony of the happiness of one family coinciding with the loss of the other. O. Hirschfield, 'Zur annalistischen Anlage des Taciteischen Geschichtswerkes', *Hermes* 25 (1890) 363-73 argues that Tacitus is in error that the twins must have been born before AD 20

79 Philo *Flacc.* 9; Suet. *Cal.* 13

80 Balsdon, 16-18; see also Timpe (1962), 58

81 Tac. *Ann.* 1.13.1-2, 6.7, 45.5, 47.2-4, 48.3-5, *Hist.* 2.65.2; *Suet.* Tib 63.2; Dio 58.8.3; Dio 58.27.4 adds that Arruntius said that he could not in his old age become a slave of a new master

82 Tac. *Ann.* 6.50.6. P Ryl. II. 141 indicates that news of Caligula's accession had reached Egypt by no later than April 27

83 Tac. *Ann.* 6.50.9; Suet. *Tib.* 73.2, *Cal.* 12.2. The Seneca cited in Suet. *Tib.* 73.2 is presumably Seneca the Elder; Philo *Leg.*25 implies that he believed that Tiberius died naturally

3 Private pursuits (*pages 42–49*)

1 Sen. *Ira* 3.19.1, *Cons.* 18.1; Pliny *NH* 11.144; Suet. *Cal.* 3.1, 50.1
2 A. Banti & L. Simonetti, *Corpus Nummorum Romanorum* 13 (Florence, 1977), 141-50; M. Grant, *Aspects of the Principate of Tiberius* (New York, 1950) 35, 101 pl. 6.3; A. Vives, *La Moneda Hispanica* 4 (Madrid 1926), pl. 132.3-6
3 Suet. *Cal.* 29.1: the manuscripts actually read *adiatrephia*
4 Suet. *Cal.* 52. Suet. *Jul.* 45.3 records that Caesar also wore a long-sleeved tunic, an oriental custom, the traditional Greek and Roman tunic being without sleeves
5 Pliny *NH* 12.10; Suet. *Cal.* 37.1-2
6 Sen. *Con. Pol.* 17.4; Suet. *Cal.* 41.2; Dio 59.22.3
7 Suet. *Cal.* 37.1 stresses the exotic nature of his drinking rather than the quantity. Philo *Leg.* 14 speaks of heavy drinking, but only by contrast to his abstemious life before his accession. See T.E. Jerome, *Aspects of the Study of Roman History* (New York and London, 1923), 418-419
8 Sen. *Cons.* 18.2; Suet. *Cal.* 36.1-2; Dio 59.3.3, 22.6; Plut. *Galb.* 9
9 Suet. *Cal.* 16.1, 27.4. B. Baldwin, *Suetonius* (Amsterdam, 1983), 271 says that he banished the *sphintriae* because of what they might reveal about him
10 *Gell.* 5.14.5
11 Pliny 11. 144, 245; Suet. *Cal.* 30.3, 32.2, 38.4, 54.1, 55.2; Dio 54.2.3, 55.31.4, 59.14.1-3. On the *munera gladiatoria* presented by Caligula and his addiction to this form of entertainment, see Ville, 130-134, 169, 281, 443
12 Jos. *AJ* 19.257; Suet. *Aug.* 45.1, *Cal.* 19.3, 55.3, *Vit.* 4, 14.3, 17.2; Dio 59.14.6, 28.6
13 Suet. *Cal.* 15.2, 18.3; Dio 59.7.3, 13.8-9, 24.7, 60.27.2. The expense of these games may well have been a source of friction with the senate, examined by R.F. Newbold, 'The Spectacles as an Issue between Gaius and the Senate', *PCA* 13 (1975), 30-4
14 M. Rostovtzeff, *Römische Bleitesserae, Klio Beih.* III (1905), 72, proposed that these were special games set aside for the young men of the senatorial order
15 Philo *Leg.* 42; Tac. *Ann.* 4.14.4; Suet. *Tib.* 37.2, *Cal.* 18.2, 36.1, 54.2, 55.1; Dio 57.21.3, 59.2.5, 5.2, 5.5, 7.5, 21.2
16 On Germanicus' oratorical and literary skills: Ovid *Fast.* 1.21.22, Ex *Pont* 2.5.41-56, 4.8.67; Suet. *Cal.* 3. 1-2, see E.R. Parker, 'The Education of Heirs in the Julio-Claudian Family', *AJP* 67 (1946), 29-50
17 Liberal and rhetorical studies and *grammatici*: Suet. *Tib.* 56, 57, 70; knowledge of the law: Tac. *Ann.* 3.64.4, 70.4, 4.38.3; pedantic learning: Dio 57.17.1-3; Rhodes: Suet. *Tib.* 11.3; Dio 55.9.5-8. Tiberius' intellectual pursuits are well covered by Levick (1976),

15-17; see also F.R.D. Goodyear, 'Tiberius and Gaius: their Influence and Views on Literature', *ANRW* 2.32.1 (1984), 606

18 Jos. *AJ* 19.207-11; Tac. *Ann.*13.3.6; Suet. *Cal.* 20, 53.1-2; Dio 59.16.1-8, 19.1-7; the Suda is the only source for the book on oratory; see J.C. Faur, 'Un discours de l'empereur Caligula au Sénat (Dio, *Hist.rom.* LIX, 16)', *Klio* 40 (1978), 439-47

19 Suet. *Cal.* 34.2; Quint. 10.1.32; Donat. *Vit.Verg.* 43-6; Just. 38.3.11; Goodyear, *op.cit.* n.17, 603-10

20 *SHA Hadrian* 16.6; P.Lambrechts, 'Caligula dictateur littéraire', *Bull. Inst. Hist. Belge de Rome* 28 (1953), 219-32 claims that the antipathy arose because Vergil and Livy glorified Augustus, and because Homer downgraded the importance of Egypt in the treatment of Helen

21 H. Bardon, *Les Empereurs et les lettres latines d'Auguste à Hadrien* (Paris 1968), 122-3 thinks that *commissio* is a technical term applied to masonry (but not attested at this period). J. Stroux, 'Vier Zeugnisse zur römischen Literaturgeschichte des Kaiserzeit II. Caligula's Urteil ber den Stil Senecas', *Philologus* 86 (1931), 349-55 believes that the MS read *commissura-* the join between the stones in construction

22 Gell. 12.2.1; see, Goodyear, *op. cit.* n. 17

4 **The new emperor** (*pages 50–72*)
1 Jos. *AJ* 18.225-33; Suet. *Tib.* 75
2 Jos. *AJ* 18.234; Suet. *Tib.* 75.2
3 Dio 59.3.7. The request is so placed by Dio in his narrative that it seems to postdate Caligula's arrival (so dated by Balsdon, 28). But the reference to his absence is explicit and makes sense only if the request came from Misenum
4 Philo *Leg.* 23, *Flacc.* 10; Jos. *AJ* 18.234; Dio 59.1.1
5 *PIR²* A32; see W. Kunkel, *Herkunft und soziale Stellung der römischen Juristen* (1952), 128; R. Syme, 'Fiction about Roman Jurists,' *Papers,* 1414. H. Siber, 'Zur Entwicklung der römischen Prinzipatsverfassung', *ABAW* 42.3 (1933), 42 suggests that a formal senate commission was set up under the authority of the consuls
6 Suet. *Cal.* 16.3
7 Dio 59.15.1; this became a constitution under Antoninus Pius
8 With the possible exception of Pius; see Brunt, 'The 'Fiscus' and its Development', *JRS* (1966), 78
9 Tac. *Hist.* 1.80; Dio 64.10; see Brunt (1966), 79
10 H. Bellen, 'Verstaatlichung des Privatvermögens Römischer Kaiser', *ANRW* 3.1 (1972), 100-101 argues that Caligula could have inherited on the basis of the discretionary clause in his *lex imperii*. Gemellus may have retained property in Egypt. The tax-rolls of Philadelphia, according to A.E. Hanson, 'Caligulan Month Names at Philadelphia and Related Matters', *Atti xvii cong. intern. pap.* III. show property

held by the *Kaisares* in 37/38, which must surely be Caligula and Gemellus

11 Suet. *Cal.* 14.1 notes that on the occasion of the senate meeting that followed Caligula's arrival, no attention was given to the claims of Gemellus. This does not necessarily mean that the will was actually revoked at this second meeting, as argued by some scholars (eg. Balsdon 26, Levick, 220)

12 *AFA* xliii, 10 (Smallwood 3.10)

13 See Syme, *Papers,* 367-7, Crawford, 487-95; on the senate's rôle: Cic. *Phil.* 14.5.12; R. Combes, *Imperator* (Paris 1966) 76-7. Antony is the only imperator known to have been so acclaimed by the *comitia*

14 Dio 57.8.1

15 L. Pareti, *Storia di Roma* (Turin, 1952), 4.763-4

16 Philo *Leg.* 231; Jos. *AJ* 18.124. Vitellius was in Jerusalem for the Passover, which fell in 37 on April 20. The news had reached Egypt by April 27 (see III n. 82; n. 20 [below])

17 Tac. *Ann.* 1.7.3, 34.1; Dio 57.3.2. On the oaths, see, P. Hermann, *Der römische Kaisereid* (Göttingen, 1968); see also, A. von Premerstein, in H. Volkman, *Von Werden und Wesen des Principats* (Munich, 1937) II. 13-116

18 *IGR* 4.251 (Smallwood 33)

19 *ILS* 190 (Smallwood 32). The career of Quadratus is laid out in *ILS* 972

20 Timpe (1962), 65. There survives another oath from Sestinum in Umbria (*CIL* XI 5998a), very similar in content to the Aritium oath in its formulae and perhaps to be assigned to the Caligulan period (see Hermann, *op. cit.* n.17, p53). This title of 'Augustus' is similarly omitted from Caligula's name on PRyl II.141, an Egyptian papyrus dated to April 27, 37

21 M. Hammond, 'The Transmission of the Powers of the Roman Emperor', *MAAR* 24 (1956), 65; Timpe (1962) 68. C.Gatti, 'Un Compromesso Politico dell' Imperatore Gaio all' Inizio del suo Regno. Nota in Margine a Dione Cassio LIX 3.1-2', *Miscellanea di Studi Classici in Onore di Eugenio Manni* (Rome, 1980), 1055-64 claims that the senate voted some of his titles on March 18. A. Jakobson and H.M. Cotton, 'Caligula's Recusatio Imperii', *Historia* 34 (1985), 497-503, suggest that Caligula was offered the principate on March 18 and went through the motions of a formal refusal. But this is difficult to reconcile with Macro's immediate instructions to the provincial governors

22 See Levick (1976), 246

23 Suet. *Cal.* 13. On the image of the star as a symbol of accession, see S. MacCormick, *Art and Ceremony in Late Antiquity* (Berkely 1981), 45

24 Philo *Leg.* 10-13, 232, 356 *ILS* 8792 (Smallwood 361); *IGR* 4. 251 (Smallwood 33)

25 *AFA* xliii.15-17 (Smallwood 3.15-17). The fourth-century calendar of Philocalus (*CIL* I² 260, *Inscr. Ital* 3.2.243) lists the Initium Caiani under 28 March. Philocalus uses the phrase initium muneri to mark the beginning of the quaestorian games on 2 December and D. Fishwick, 'The Cannophori and the March Festival of Magna Mater', *TAPA* 97 (1966), 193 suggests that the Initium Caiani may be a relic of a celebration initiated by Caligula, who raced in the Gaianum on the Vatican Hill

26 Dio 59.3.1; the reference to his not writing to the senate would refer not to routine communications, but to formal *relationes*

27 Dio 53.18.4, 63.29.6, 78.16.2, 79.2.2-3; Plut. *Galb.* 11; see Talbert, 355

28 Suet. *Cal.* 41.1 *statim*. Opinion is divided on the date: Grenade (1961), 276, Gatti *op. cit.* n. 21, 1060 argue for 28 March, Timpe (1962), 16, H.W. Ritter, 'Adlocutio und Corona Civica unter Caligula und Tiberius', *JNG* 21 (971), 83, Brunt (1977), 98 for 29 March. Dio 59.6.1 gives Caligula's age as 25 years less 5 months and 4 days at the time of the senatorial meeting, which, by inclusive reckoning from 31, 12 August, would provide a date of 28 March

29 Suet. *Cal.* 14.1; Dio 59.6.1. Suetonius suggests that the people had forced their way in. But instances where non- members were prohibited from the curia seem to involve hostile outsiders (Tac. *Ann.* 3.14.6, 5.4.3); on the prohibition of equestrians, Statius *Silv.* 4.8.60-1

30 *RG* 34; see Grenade (1961) 277, L. Lesuisse,'La nomination de l'empereur et le titre d' 'imperator" *AC* 30 (1961), 420-21, A. Alföldi (1970), 79

31 Suet. *Cal.* 14.1; Dio 59.3.1-2. Grenade (1961), 289, Parsi, 84-6, 129; J. Bleicken, *ZSS* 81 (1964), 395 sees a reference to the exclusion of Gemellus from a share in power. Gatti, *op. cit.* n.21 argues that the final granting of *tribunicia potestas* did not occur until after his return from collecting the bones of his family

32 *ILS* 244; see Brunt (1977); Parsi (1963), 84-5; Mommsen, SR II. 909; Timpe (1962), 75; Bellen op. cit.

33 Philo *Leg.* 119, 190; Suet. *Cal.* 22.1; Dio 59.10.1-2; Parsi, 108-11

34 Syme, *Papers,* 362

35 L. Lesuisse, 'Le titre de Caesar et son évolution au cours de l'empire', *LEC* 29 (1961), 277 suggests that Claudius could have made a claim to the name 'Caesar' through Livia, who was adopted into the Julian family in Augustus' will (Tac. *Ann.* 1.8.2)

36 Suet. *Tib.* 26.2; Dio 57.2.1

37 *SEG* 2. 703, Perge (Pamphylia); *ILS* 8789; 8792 (Smallwood 361),

Mytilene; *CIL* III. 6664, from Jabrud,in Coele-Syria (dubious). On the praenomen imperatoris, see Syme, *Papers,* 370-7, D. McFayden, *The History of the Title Imperator under the Roman Empire* (Chicago 1920), esp 44-52, J. Deininger, 'Von der Republik zur Monarchie: Die Ursprünge der Herrschertitular des Prinzipats' *ANR W* 1.1. 982-997. The title imperator at the end of the name is similarly found only in the provinces:*ILS* 193 (Cordoba), *IGR* 4. 1379 (autokrator) Koula

38 *RG* 10 and Fasti. Dio 54.27.2 is in error in assigning the assumption to 13 BC

39 Willrich, 115, n.5

40 Dio 59.3.2

41 Suet. *Cal.* 22.1. On *IGR* 4. 1022 (Calymna) dated to Caligula's visit there with his father in AD 18, he is called *eusebes* (= *pius*); usage in the Greek east does not, however, signify official sanction. A patently bogus inscription from Cadiz (*CIL* 2. 150* Peutinger 527 f.53.v.2) reads: *C. Caesar Pius Castrorum* F *Pater Exercituum Opt. Max. Caesar,* forged by someone who knew his Suetonius, and even got the order right!

42 Dio 59.6.1

43 *AFA* Scheid 222 (38); *SEG* 30. 1633 (Paphos); *AE* 1980.638 (Gaul); *ILS* 189 (Vienne, pre-accession), *ILS* 8972 (Smallwood 361) all identify Caligula as Tiberius' grandson, and Dio 59.3.7 concedes that he used the same expression in his first letter to the senate. *AFA* xlviig. 5-7 (Smallwood 6.5-7), heavily restored, seems to indicate Arval offerings made on Tiberius' birthday, November 16, 38

44 Dio 59.4.2, 6.7

45 *Fasti Ostienses* (Smallwood 31. 19-20). Dio 59.3.7 says that the body was brought in at night

46 Jos. *AJ* 18.236; Suet. *Cal.* 15.1; Dio 59.3.8. No source explicitly places his remains in the Mausoleum. The inscription on his funerary urn (*CIL* 6.885), now lost, agrees in content, however, with others in the mausoleum. Sen. *Apoc.* 1.2 refers ironically to the Appian way as the route Tiberius took to heaven. E. Bickermann, 'Die römische Kaisarapotheose', *Archiv für Religionswissenschaft* 27 (1929), 16 suggests that this indicates that someone claimed to have seen Tiberius' apotheosis

47 Dio 60.10.2. Claudius ended the practice

48 Dio 59.9.1. The recent origins of this oath went back to the one taken in 45 BC by the new magistrate not to oppose Julius Caesar's *acta,* which became an annual oath thereafter (Appian *BC* 2.106; Dio 44.6.1). The privilege had been extended to Octavian in 29 BC, and by at least 24 BC the senators, as well as the magistrates, participated in the procedure (Dio 51.20.1, 53.28.1, 57.8.5)

49 Tac. *Ann.* 1. 72.2, 4.42.3; Dio 57.8.4-5, 58.17.2-3

50 Dio 59.2.1 (cf. 57.24.5) says that he paid the Praetorians *eythys* ('immediately'). On *BMC* 33, Eckel, *Doctrina Numorum Veterum* (Vienna 17 96), 6.221 expresses the suspicion that the coins were minted by Caligula to pay for this donative (see Gelzer 386). But this seems unlikely. The issue continued as late as 40/1 (*BMC* 67-8), and the Praetorians would probably have been paid in silver denarii rather than sestertii; Sutherland, 'Gaius and the Praetorians', (1987), 69-70, suggests that part of the payment may have been made in sestertii. Ritter, *op. cit.* n. IV n. 28, 82 suggests that the coin was reissued at the time of the crossing of the Bridge at Baiae, at which Praetorians were present

51 Suet. *Tib.* 54.2, *Cal.* 15.1; Dio 58.22.5; *ILS* 180, 183, 187 (Bergamo). Nero's inscription is known from copies. Dio 59.3.5 says that Caligula went to collect the remains of both brothers, mistakenly, as Suet. *Cal.* 15.1 indicates

52 Suet. *Claud.* 9.1; *BMC* 44

53 *AFA* Scheid 221.3, *AFA* xlix.1-4 (Smallwood 9.11-15); *BMC* 7, 11

54 Suet. *Cal.* 15, cf Suet. *Tib.* 26.2. Maurer ad loc., K. Scott, 'Greek and Roman Honorific Months', *YClS* 2 (1931), 230, Meise, 94, J.R. Rea, 'Calendar of Gaius', *Oxyrhynchus Papyri* 55 (1988), 10-14, Hanson *op. cit.* IV n. 10, C. Balconi, 'Su alcuni Nomi Onorifici di Mesi nel Calendario Egiziano', *ZPE* 59 (1985), 84-8. Of the month names introduced in Egypt under Caligula only 'Germanikeios' and 'Kaisareios' lasted beyond the early days of Claudius

55 Sen. *Ira* 3.21.5; *BMC* 81

56 Philo *Leg.* 41-51; Suet. *Cal.* 23.2

57 Tac. *Ann.* 4.16.6; Suet. *Aug.* 44.3, Cal. 15.2; Dio 59.3.4

58 *AFA* xliii. 7 (Smallwood 3.7). Suet. *Claud.* 11.2 (with Lipsius' emendation) has Claudius bestow the title; but see A. Brown West, *Corinth Latin Inscr.* 15 -17, no 17. Local bronze coins of Corinth and Thessalonica of Caligula's reign call her Augusta, the only mints to do so (Trillmich, 104-5, 142, 162-7)

59 Jos. *AJ* 18. 236; Suet. *Cal.* 29.1

60 *Fasti Ostienses* (Smallwood 31.22); Suet. *Cal.* 23.2, Dio 59.3.6. Suetonius adds, almost formulaically, that some claimed that he poisoned her

61 *AFA* xxxiii. 12; Suet. *Cal.* 15.3, *Tib.* 54.1; Dio 58.2.8, 59.3.5. The preamble to consular proposals is preserved by Suetonius: *Quod bonum felixque sit C. Caesari sororibusque eius* ('may this be good and propitious for C. Caesar and his sisters'). The standard formula was: *Quod bonum faustum felix fortunatumque sit populo Romano Quiritium* (see A. O'Brien Moore, *RE* Suppl 6 (1935), 711)

62 Suet. *Cal.* 15.3, Dio 59.3.4, 9.2. On Tiberius' accession Valerius

Messala had suggested that the oath of loyalty be taken annually; the scheme was not taken up. Hermann *op. cit.* IV n. 17, 109 has suggested that the annual oath might have been instituted under Tiberius in 32 after the suppression of the Sejanus conspiracy, in conjunction with the innovation of swearing to uphold Tiberius' *acta*, as well as those of Augustus (Dio 58.17.2) Suetonius preserves the text of the oath of loyalty: Neque me liberosque meos cariores habebo quam Gaium habebo et sorores eius ('I shall not consider myself or my children dearer than I consider Gaius and his sisters')

63 *BMC* 36-7

64 Jos. *AJ* 18. 102; Suet. *Cal.* 14.3, *Vit.* 2.4; Dio 59.27.3. Unlike Suetonius and Dio, Josephus places the meeting not in Caligula's but in Tiberius' reign, probably incorrectly since the important episode is not mentioned by Tacitus in his summary of Parthian events at the end of Tiberius' reign (*Ann.* 6.31-7); on this see A. Garzetti, 'La Data dell'Incontro all'Eufrate di Artabano III e L. Vitellio, Legato di Siria', *Studi in Onore di R. Paribeni- A. Calderini* (Milan 19 56), 1.211-29

65 Sen. *Tranq.* 11.12; Tac. *Ann.*11.8.1; Dio 60. 8.1

66 Tac. *Ann.* 11. 8-9; Dio 60.8.1; See, Willrich, 301; Balsdon, 199-200

67 Tac. *Ann.* 1.72.3-5; for a good summary of the question, see J.E. Allison, and J.D. Cloud, 'The Lex Julia Maiestatis', *Latomus* 21 (1962), 711-31

68 Suet. *Cal.* 15.4; Dio 59.4.3. Dio's comment under 37 (59.3.6) that he punished those who had plotted against his family must refer to a later period, when *maiestas* trials were revived

69 Suet. *Cal.* 15.4; Dio 59.4.3, 6.2-3, 60.40.2; see Meise, 117

70 Pliny *NH* 14.56; Pliny *Ep.* 7.17.11; (Tac.) *Dial.* 13.3; Tac. *Ann.* 11.13.1, 12.28; Quint. 10.1.98

71 Tac. *Ann.* 5.8.1; Pliny *NH* 14.56; Dio 59.6.2. Dio calls him Quintus, confusing him with his brother, and mistakenly says that he had been arrested after his consulship, which in Publius' case did not fall until 44. Quintus was consul in 41; see Syme, *Papers,* 811-2; Stewart (1953) suggests that Caligula was still under the influence of the old Sejanus party, knowing nothing as yet of the prefect's role against his mother

72 R.A. Bauman, *Impietas in Principem* (Munich, 1974), 19

73 Suet. Cal. 16.1 Augustus had been responsible for extending *maiestas* to cover slanderous writings, and Cassius Severus and Titus Labienus were the first to suffer, although there is disagreement about which came first: Sen. *Contr.* 10. pr.4-8 (Labienus); Tac. *Ann.* 1.72 (Severus); see also H. Volkmann, Zur Rechtsprechung im Principat des Agustus: historische Beiträge, *Münchner Beiträge zur Papyrusforschung und antiken Rechtsgeschichte* 21 (1935), 207 (Severus), F.H. Cramer,

'Bookburning and Censureship in Ancient Rome', *Journal of the History of Ideas* 6 (1945), 157-196, D. Hennig, 'T. Labienus und der erste Majestätsprozess de famosis libellis', *Chiron* 3 (1973), 245-63 (Labienus)

74 Sen. *Contr.* 3. pr.3-6; Tac. *Ann.* 1. 72.4-5; Dio 55.4.3, 56.27; Macrobius 2.4.9; Jerome *Chron.* (or AD 32)

75 Sen. *Marc.* 1.2-3, 22.4-7, Tac. *Ann.* 4.34.5; Suet. *Tib.* 61.3; Dio 57.24.2-4. Cremutius: Quintilian 10.1.104; Labienus: Quintilian 1.5.8, 4.1.11, 9.3.13; Cassius: Quintilian 10.1.116-7

76 Suet. *Cal.* 15.2, Dio 59.8.1. On the term, see Balsdon 'Gaius and the Grand Cameo', *JRS* 26 (1936), 152-60, Willrich, 113

77 Suetonius places the adoption firmly among Caligula's enlightened acts. Philo *Leg.* 25-8 places it after Caligula's illness, just before Gemellus' death. Dio is vague on chronology at this period and may not have known the precise sequence. Absolute certainty is impossible, but an early date seems most plausible. M.H. Prévost, *Les adoptions politiques à Rome sous la république et le Principat* (Paris, 1949), 43 observes that *patria potestas* would give Caligula the *ius vitae necisque* over Gemellus, and thus the power to eliminate him (see Meise, 117)

78 *AFA* Scheid 224. 26-32; *BMC* Tiberius 146; see Béranger 338-40, 331-52; Fishwick 1.1.180-3; M.P. Charlesworth 'Providentia and Aeternitas', *HThR* (1936), 107-32; R.T. Scott, 'Providentia Aug.', *Historia* 31 (1982), 436-59

79 *Fasti Ostienses* (Smallwood 31.14); *AFA* Scheid 224.33-7; Suet. *Cal.* 15.2, *Claud.* 7.1; Dio 59.6.5-6. A Tabula Cereata from Pompeii mistakenly has Caligula and Claudius consuls on June 8, 37 (*AE* 1969/70.100)

80 Dio 59.6.7 Dio claims that the speech involved personal invective against Tiberius

81 *ILS* 8792 (Smallwood 361)

82 *AFA* Scheid 224.38-42; the anniversary of the actual dedication in 9 BC fell on January 30, before Caligula's accession, and thus too early for 37, but it was similarly celebrated in the following year: *AFA* xlii.b 8-10 (Smallwood 2.8-10)

83 Dio 59.7.1-4; *BMC* 41 (fig. 18)

84 The *Fasti Ostienses* (Smallwood 31.15) indicate a consulship of exactly two months (confirming Suet. *Cal.* 17. 1 and *Claud.* 7. 1, in contrast to Dio's 2 months, 12 days. P.A. Gallivan, 'The Fasti for the Reign of Gaius', *Antichthon* 13 (1979), 66-9 notes that the new consuls, Aulus Caecina Paetus and Caius Caninius Rebilus, had probably been designated under Tiberius

85 *AFA* Scheid 225.57-8

86 Cicero: Cic. *Rab. perd.* 27, *Pis.* 6, *Sest.* 121; Plut. *Cic.* 23.3; Gellius 5.6.15; Caesar: Appian *BC* 2.106; 144. Crawford, 491

87 RG 35; Suet. *Aug.* 58.2; see also Dio 55.10.10, *Fasti Praenestini* (Feb. 5); *ILS* 8744a; *ILS* 96. That the title was far more than routine is shown by Tiberius' refusal to accept either it for himself or that of *mater patriae* for Livia (Tac. *Ann.* 1.72.2; Suet. *Tib.* 26.2, 50.3; Dio 57.8. 1, 58.12.8) It was applied to him in the provinces, and Dio says that on Livia's death the people, out of regard for Livia called her *mater patriae (EJ* 10 2.9; Dio 58.2.3)

88 Suet. *Cal.* 16.4

89 Suet. Cal. 19.2; Dio 59.17.3. A. Alföldi, 'Die Geburt des kaiserlichen-Bildsymbolik', *MH* 9 (1952), 239

90 Augustus: *BMC* 5, 6, 35, 134, 139, 147, 314, 317, 330, 376, 378, 381, 737 (cf. *AE* 1955. 265); Tiberius: *BMC* 109; see, Sutherland, 'Tiberius and the Corona Civica', [1987], 63-6; Caligula: *BMC* 32, 38, p. 396.20; see A. Alföldi, *Der Vater des Vaterlandes im römischen Denken* (Darmstadt, 1971), 74-5, Fishwick 107-12

91 Suet. *Tib.* 26.2, *Claud.* 17.3; see Alföldi, RM 50 (1935), 131

5 Signs of strain *(pages 73–90)*

1 On the illness: Philo *Leg.* 14-21; Suet. *Cal.* 14.2; Dio 59.8.1-2

2 Suet. *Cal.* 14.2, 27.2; Dio 59.8.3. On Augustus: Dio 53.20.2-4, who mentions that it was a Spanish custom. Cf. Val. Max. 2.6.11

3 Inter alios: Balsdon, 36, Smallwood, *Legatio* 164, H.C.V. Sutherland, *Coinage in Roman Imperial Policy 31 BC- AD 68* (London 1951), 115, A. Piganiol, *Histoire de Rome* (Paris 1954⁴), 248

4 A.T. Sandison, 'The Madness of the Emperor Caligula', *Medical History* 2 (1958), 202-9; R.S. Katz, 'The Illness of Caligula', *CW* 65 (1972), 223-5, 'Caligula's Illness Again', *CW* 70 (1977), 451; V. Massaro and I. Montgomery, 'Gaius- Mad, Bad, Ill or all Three', *Latomus* 37 (1978), 894-909; D.T. Benediktson, 'Caligula's Madness: Madness or Interictal Temporal Lobe Epilepsy', *CW* 82 (1989), 370-5, argues for a particular form of epilepsy

5 Among scholars who believe that the illness was the cause of Caligula's erratic behaviour, A. Passerini, *Caligola e Claudio* (Rome 1941), 10, Charlesworth *CAH* 10. 656; for criticism of the view, see M.G. Morgan, 'Caligula's Illness Again', *CW* 66 (1973), 327-9, 'Once Again Caligula's Illness', *CW* 70 (1977), 452-3

6 Vegetius 4.39

7 Scott, *op. cit.* IV n. 54, 249, 258; J. Tait, Greek Ostraka (London, 1930), 118; Balconi, *op. cit.* IV n. 54, 87-88; see also E.J. Bickerman, *Chronology of the Ancient World* (London, 1968), 50, A. Samuel, *Greek and Roman Chronology* (Munich, 1972), 177. 'Soter' must be distinguished from 'Soterios' (= Egyptian Payni). It was in use by at least October 20, 38 (BGU IV. 1078)

8 Philo *Leg.* 356

9 Suet. *Cal.* 27.2; Dio 59.8.3. R. Lugand 'Suétone et Caligula', REA 32 (1930),10 argues that the death of the gladiator was a human sacrifice, in traditional form, for the protection of the emperor; see, Ville 130-131

10 Philo *Flacc.* 16 *Leg.* 23, 65; Suet. *Cal.* 23.3; Dio 59.8.1, 4-6, 10.6; *AFA* Scheid 221.6

11 Philo *Leg.* 23-32; Suet. *Cal.* 23.3; Dio 59.8.2. Dio's explicit comment that no reference was made to the senate is reflected in Suetonius' use of *repente* and *inopinantem* to describe the circumstances of his death

12 *ILS* 172

13 Dio 59, 10. 8

14 Philo *Leg.* 68

15 We do not know Silanus' age at death. Balsdon, 38 feels that he must have been elderly; Scheid, 203 says he must have been 50 at the time of his consulship (AD 15); Syme, *Papers,* 1361 n.89 feels that he need not have been particularly old

16 Philo *Leg.* 62-5; Dio 59.8.5; cf. Sen. *Apoc.* 11.2. Dio is very confused in his treatment of Silanus, claiming that Caligula divorced his daughter Junia at this time, late 37, whereas she had died in 34 or thereabouts. He also claims that Caligula used to call Silanus his 'golden sheep', while this expression was in fact used of a different Marcus Junius Silanus, consul of 46 and proconsul in Asia in 54 (*PIR* I² 833; Tac. *Ann.* 13.1.1); see Gelzer, 390

17 Suet. *Cal.* 23.3

18 Tac. *Ag.* 4.1 The fact that Graecinus was still alive in 39/40 is a problem only if Tacitus means that his refusal led immediately to his death. A number of individuals, such as Avillius Flaccus, Prefect of Egypt, who offended Caligula were not executed immediately

19 P. Grimal, 'Les allusions la vie politique de l'empire dans les tragédies de Senèque', *CRAI* (1979), 205-20 believes that the character of Creon in Seneca's *Oedipus*, the man accused of masking ambitions, was inspired by Silanus

20 On the marriage: Suet. *Cal.* 25.1; Dio 59.8.7. Since Suetonius is the more likely to have used official records, he should be given the benefit of the doubt on the name. If she was called Livia, as he reports, Caligula's joke would have more force. M. Kajava, 'The Name of Cornelia Orestina/ Orestilla', *Arctos* 18 (1984) 23-30, cites the evidence for Orestina and Orestilla, both of which are attested. On Piso: PIR² C284 (Scheid 2 07-09); on Cornelia *PIR²* C1492. Piso's precise relationship to the other members of the family is uncertain. He was possibly the son of L. Calpurnius Piso 'Augur' (cos. 1 BC) or L. Cornelius Piso 'Pontifex' (cos. 15 BC)

21 Meise, 104, suggests that this could also explain why she was forbidden to cohabit with Calpurnius, who might have shown up Caligula by

producing a child

22 Dio 59.9.3

23 Philo *Flacc.* 13-16, *Leg.* 32-62; Suet. *Cal.* 26.1; Dio 59.10.6

24 Philo *Flacc.* 16; Dio 59.10.6; Willrich, 288, sees the appointment as a demotion. But it need not be so. Seius Strabo, father of Sejanus, held the Prefecture of Egypt after that of the Praetorian guard (Dio 57.19.6). A. Pelletier, *In Flaccum* (Paris 1967), 56. n.1, followed by Schwartz, 191, puts the death shortly after 31 January, 38

25 Dio 59.10.7

26 R.A. Bauman, *Impietas in Principem* (Munich, 1974), 176

27 *AE* 1957. 250. Philo *Flacc.* 14 is the only source to claim that their children died also, and his testimony is therefore suspect; for modern speculation about the real reasons for Macro's death: F. De Visscher, 'La politique dynastique sous le règne de Tibère', *Synteleia V. Arangio-Ruiz,* (Naples, 1964), 54-65; Meise, 252; Dabrowski argues that Macro (as well as Gemellus and Silanus) was put to death by Lepidus and Caligula's sisters

28 Smallwood 436 A.16-18, B. 14-17. There has been much debate about the dating of the trial; some argue that the fragment is to be dated to 41 and that it involves Agrippa I. The arguments for both dates are summarized by Musurillo, *The Acts of the Pagan Martyrs* (Oxford, 1954) 118-23, Smallwood, *Jews,* 253-5 (she tentatively prefers 41)

29 As restored by H.I. Bell, 'A New Fragment of the Acta Isidori', *APF* 10 (1932), 5-16. The reading has won general but not universal acceptance. F. Münzer hesitantly accepted the reading in 'Naevius', *RE* 16 (1933) 1568; A. Stein, 28, rejected it. Apart from the strangeness of Isidorus' involvement Stein is concerned that Macro would be called *eparchos* (prefect) many years afterwards, though he never took up the office. Bell, CR 2 (1952), 104 notes that the Acta are not verbatim accounts. Musurillo, *Acta Alexandrinorum* (Leipzig 1961) 12 and 14 , and (1954) 19 and 21 accepts the reading

30 Philo *Flacc.* 26; see Balsdon, 134; Dabrowski, 210

31 Suet. *Cal.* 56.1: *praefectorum praetori*, Dio 59.25.8: *tous hyparchous*. One of the prefects may have been M. Arrecinus Clemens who is said by Tac. *Hist.* 4.68.2 to have held office under Caligula

32 On this, see J.A. Crook, *Consilium Principis* (Cambridge, 1955)

33 Philo *Leg.* 26; Dio 59.5.5, 20.2

34 Vitellius: Suet. *Vit.* 4; 17.2; Asinius: Pliny *NH* 9.67. Groag *PIR*² A1225 mistakenly states that he bought it from Caligula

35 Dio 59.11.1, 22.6-7; we do not know when the remarriage took place. Groag *PIR*² A371 places it at the beginning of the reign

36 Suet. *Cal.* 24.1. Mommsen, *SR* II, 1135.5 accepts the notion of Drusilla's being bequeathed the principate

37 See Syme, *Aristocracy,* 179

38 Tac. *Ann.* 1. 13. 2; Syme, 'Marcus Lepidus, Capax Imperii', *JRS* 45 (1955), 22 shows that the Lepidus involved in the incident is Marcus not Manius, as often previously assumed

39 Syme, *Papers*, 820; Groag PIR^2 A371; von Rohden, 'Aemilius', *RE* I (1893) I. 5 61-3; Meise, 108; Bergener 119, Stewart 74, L. Hayne, 'The Last of the Aemilii Lepidi', *AC* 42 (1973), 501. J. Lipsius, *Ad Annales Liber Commentarius* (Leyden, 1585), 238 on Tac. *Ann.* 14.22 (followed by Balsdon, 42; Nony, 359) argued that Lepidus was the son of Julia, grand daughter of Augustus and her husband Aemilius Paullus (and thus the cousin of Caligula and his sisters), mainly on the grounds that the poet Namatianus 1. 306 called the affair between Lepidus and Agrippina an *incestum adulterium. Incestum,* however, means 'foul, disgusting' not necessarily 'incestuous', and is an appropriate general epithet for adultery, especially since Agrippina was the sister of Lepidus' late wife

40 Faur (1973), 15 assumes from his accelerated career that Lepidus can have been only 22/3 when he was given his advancement. But we can not be sure that the intended office was the quaestorship

41 *SEG* 30. 1251; discussed by J.M. Reynolds, 'The Origins and Beginning of Imperial Cult at Aphrodisias', *PCPhS* 26 (1980), 70-84

42 Philo *Leg.* 203-6

43 Gelzer 409; against this see Willrich, 466

44 Thus Caligula probably acquired an Aphrodisius, whom he owned before his accession, from his parents' household (*CIL* 6.2.4119); his daughter Elate became a freedwoman of Julia, daughter of Drusus

45 Sen. *Ep. Mor.* 47.9; Jos. *AJ* 19.64-9; Pliny *NH* 36.60; Plut. *Galb.* 9.1

46 PIR^2 C763. Stat. *Silv.* 3.3; Martial 6.83, 7.40; see P.R.C. Weaver, 'The Father of Claudius Etruscus: Staius, Silvae 3.3', *CQ* 15 (1965), 145. His son, Claudius Etruscus, attained considerable wealth and was the patron of Martial and Statius

47 Philo *Leg.* 166-77, 181, 203, 206 (an interpolation in the original text, perhaps added by Philo himself)

48 Jos. 19.204; Suet. *Cal.*24.1; Dio 59.22.6; Eutropius 7.12.3; Vict. *Caes.* 3.10 *epit.* 3,4; Hieron ap Eus. 178 (Helm); Scholiast on Juvenal 4.81, Orosius 7.5.9

49 Tac. *Ann.* 14.2.4

50 Willrich, 292

51 Scholiast on Juvenal 4. 81, where he confuses Passienus Crispus with another Vibius Crispus, courtier of Domitian. The passage came originally from Suetonius, *De Oratoribus* (now lost)

52 Suet. *Cal.* 24.3

53 *Fasti Ostienses:* III *Idus Iun. Drusilla excessi[t]* (Smallwood 31.30). Köberlein, 52 n. 14 conjectures that Drusilla died in childbirth

54 Suet. *Cal.* 24.2; Dio 59.11. Herz, (1981), 324-36

55 Sen. *Polyb.* 17.4; Suet. *Cal.* 20, 24.2
56 Gaius or Lucius Caesar: *CIL* 6.895; Augustus: Tac. *Ann.* 1.16.2, 1.50.1; Germanicus: Tac. *Ann.* 2.82.4-5; Drusus: Suet. Tib. 52.1; Drusilla: Philo, *Flacc.* 56
57 *AFA* Scheid 224-5
58 Dio 59.11.2 uses the term *epsephisthe* which suggests a senatorial decree. A *Lex Valeria Cornelia* of 5 AD regulated the cult honours to be paid to Gaius and Lucius Caesar, and Dio's language at 56.42.3 and 43.1 suggests that the funeral honours paid to Augustus were also made by a senatorial decree
59 c. *Ann.* 5.2.1; Dio 58.2.2-3
60 Livia: Suet. *Claud.* 11.2; Claudia: Tac. *Ann.* 15.23.4; Poppaea: Tac. *Ann.* 16.21.2
61 Based on the restoration by Henzen of *AFA* xlvi e. 5-12 (Smallwood 5.5-12), where Drusilla is mentioned in some capacity. H. Temporini, *Die Frauen am Hofe* (Berlin, 1978) 72 dates the consecration before September 23
62 Suet. *Aug.* 100.4; Dio 56.46.2. Dio gives the name as 'Geminius'. Sen. *Apoc.* 1.2 says that the individual who saw Drusilla ascend was the *curator* of the Appian Way (and thus of Praetorian rank)
63 Cyzicus: *IGR* 4.145 (Smallwood 401.12); Mytilene: *IGR* 4. 78b (Smallwood 128b); Magnesia: O. Kern, *Die Inschriften von Magnesia am Maeander* (Berlin 1900) 156
64 Suet. *Cal.* 24.2; Dio 60.5.2
65 Taeger, 283, n. 163 says that the word used by Dio, *sekos*, is ambiguous but is generally applied to a temple. Sen. *Con. Pol.* 17.5 says that he set up *templa* and *pulvinaria* to her
66 Velleius 2.75.3; Dio 56.41.1; Ritter, *Chiron* 2 (1972) 313-338
67 *CIL* 8. 26222. P. Lambrechts, 'Caligula dictateur littéraire', *Bull. Inst. Hist. Belge de Rome* 28 (1953),227 claims that Panthea was chosen as a common cult name of Isis
68 Diva: Caere: *CIL* XI. 3598; Veleia; *CIL* XI. 1168; Tibur:*ILS* 196 (Smallwood 128a); Caburro: CIL V 7345; Bourges: ILS 197; Apamea: Cohen 1 248; M. Grant, *Roman Imperial Money* (Edinburgh, 1954), 146 (Fig. 30); Thea: Priene: F. Hiller von Gärtringen, *Inschriften von Priene* (Berlin, 1906), no.228; Epidaurus: *IG* IV 1400; Delphi: J. Jannoray, 'A popos de Deux Dedicaces Delphiques', *BCH* 60 (1936), 382; Mytilene: *SEG* 34. 180; Nea Charis ('New Grace'): Samos: *IGR* IV 1721; Homonoia ('Concord'): Halsarnae: *IGR* IV 1098; Pythia: Delphi: *AE* 1923.53; Persephone: Smyrna: *BMC*, Ionia etc, 269, no. 272 (Smallwood 222)
69 See Scott, *op. cit.* IV n. 54, 249-51; Rea, *op. cit. ibid.* 11, 13; A.E. Boak, 'Men Drousilleos', *JEA* 13 (1927), 185-6; The name appears in a register for 39/40 (P. Mich. Inv. 876 [recto]) but compiled after

mid-40. Its last known entry seems to be on December 42 (P. Mich. V. 321.19)

70 *CIL* I, p.235; *Inscr. Ital.* XIII 2.435-7; Ovid *Fast.* 4.353-4 reports that the Megalesia was a time of hospitality. It is to be distinguished from the more orgiastic March festival of Cybele; see D. Fishwick, 'The Cannophoroi and the March Festival of Magna Mater', *TAPA* 97 (1966), 193-202

71 *RG* 19; Val.Max. 1.8.11; Ovid *Fast.*4.347-8. On a cameo in Vienna, Livia, as Cybele, holds a radiate bust of Augustus. (A. Furtwängler, *Die Antike Gemmen* (1900: reprinted Amsterdam, 1964-65) 3.318

72 *ILS* 112 (*EJ* 100), Dio 54.8.5, 26.2, 55.6.6

73 Dio 59.13.8. Dio's account seems to place it relatively early in the year, but we may not be justified in pressing his chronology too hard on this point (see Humphrey *op. cit.* I n.7, 128-9)

74 Caesar: Dio 43.45.2; Germanicus: Tac. *Ann.* 2. 83.2; Britannicus: Suet. *Tit.* 2

75 See H. Scullard, *The Elephant in the Greek and Roman World* (London, 1974) 124, 254

76 *BMC* Tiberius: 102, 108, 125; Nero: 7; Suet. *Claud.* 11.2; Philip of Thessalonika records an elephant, pulling the chariot of divine Caesar, in an epigram (AP 9. 285) ascribed by C. Cichorius, *Römische Studien* (1922, reprinted Darmstadt, 1961), 344-6, and O. Weinreich, *Studien zu Martial* (Stuttgart 1928) 78 to Caligula's time

77 *AFA* xxxvi.5 (restored); Suet. *Tib.* 26.1; Dio 58.12.8

78 Pliny *NH* 9.117; Suet. *Cal.* 25.2 (he calls her husband C. Memmius); Dio 59.12.1

79 Tac. *Ann.* 5.11.1, 14.47.1; Dio 58.9.3; Schneider, Senat n.61, 388,519; Scheid, 213-218; see, Vogel-Weidemann no. 47

80 Some scholars see in Dio's term (*enguesai*) a reference to the Athenian procedure of *engyesis,* whereby in order for a woman's marriage to be valid she had to be pledged by her *kurios* ('guardian'), which in the case of a married woman would, of course, be the husband; see, Brasloff in E. Groag 'Memmius', *RE* 15. 633); J.H. Oliver, 'Lollia Paulina, Memmius Regulus and Caligula', *Hesperia* 35 (1966), 150-3 (for a somewhat different interpretation, questioned by J. & L. Robert, *Bull.Ep.* 1967, no.195). But elsewhere Dio uses the term loosely for simple marriage (Dio 48.38.3, 48,54.4).On the term see A.R.W. Harrison, *The Law of Athens. The Family and Property* (Oxford, 1968), 3-9. M.B. Flory, 'Caligula's *Inverecundia*: A Note on Dio Cassius 59.12.1,' *Hermes* 114 (1986), 365-71, suggests a Caligulan quip inspired by the circumstances of Octavian's marriage with Livia, which was arranged in haste and according to some sources carried out in the presence of her former husband

81 *AFA* xlvie 10 (Smallwood 5.10). Henzen explained his presence in

Rome by his need to be there for the co-option of May 38 (*AFA* xliv. 34 [Smallwood 3. 34]); but Memmius' past services could well have merited him entry into the Arvals under Tiberius much earlier than 38 (Scheid, 214; Espérandieu, 633). Scheid, *AFA* 229, favours C. Caecina Largus as candidate for May 24

82 Tac. *Ann.* 14. 47.1; Syme, *Tacitus* 787; Groag *RE* 15.626

83 Jos. *Ant.* 19.8.10; Dio 59. 28.3-4

84 Philo *Flacc.* 108-115; see P.A. Brunt 'Charges of Provincial Administration,' *Historia* 10 (1961) 209

85 Philo *Flacc.* 125-6; P.J. Sijpstein, 'The Legationes ad Gaium', *Journ. Jew Stud.* 15 (1964), 94 n.24 argues that Isidorus and Lampon in accusing Flaccus were not motivated by personal grudges but were trying to divert the blame away from the Alexandrian Greeks and attributing it to Flaccus

6 Conspiracy (*pages 91–113*)

1 Tac. *Ann.* 1.72.1, 4.73.1; Dio 58.19.1-2

2 Tac. *Ann.* 6.4.4; Suet. *Cal.* 17.1; Dio 59.13.1-2. Tacitus reports that Sanquinius came to the defence of Regulus in the senate (see Colin [1954], 405-9)

3 Dio 59.16.1-7. Dio 59.13.3 implausibly speaks of a major rift with the ordinary populace, supposedly over lack of enthusiasm for the *spectacula*

4 Charlesworth *CAH* 10. 657; Stewart, 77: Balsdon, 48-9

5 Faur (1978), 446 suggests that the speech immediately preceded Caligula's departure for Germany. He notes that after it the emperor hurried to the *proasteion* ('suburb') (Dio 5 9.16.8) and is similarly reported to have gone to *proasteion ti* ('a certain suburb') before setting out for Germany (Dio 59.21.2). The difficulty is that the two events are separated in Dio's narrative, and the historian makes no attempt to connect them

6 Suet. *Cal.* 30.2; Dio 59.4.3, 16.3; Balsdon, 50

7 Suet. Cal. 30.1 observes that he was fond of the line, and claims (*Tib.* 59.2) that Tiberius was given to using the variant *oderint dum probent*. P. Grimal, 'Les Allusions la vie politique de l'empire dans les tragédies de Sénèque', *CRAI* (1979), 205-20, thinks that the speech was the inspiration for a speech of Oedipus in Seneca's *Oedipus,* where the same idea is expressed (lines 703-4)

8 R.A. Bauman, *Impietas in Principem* (Munich, 1974), 209

9 Dio 59.16.10. Dio calls the image an *eikon,* presumably in the tradition of the republican *imagines,* not a statue (*agalma*), which would be worshipped

10 Caesar: Plut. *Caes.* 57.3; App. *BC* 2.106; Dio 44.6.4; Crawford, 480.21); Tiberius: *BMC* 85; Tac. *Ann.* 4.74.3

11 Dio 59.16.11 states that the senate granted him an ovation, which may be a confusion with the ovation offered by the senatorial deputation sent north to Caligula in Gaul later in the year (Dio 59.23.2)

12 Suet. *Cal.* 25.2 ; Dio 59.12.1

13 Dio 59. 23. 7; Hülsen *CIL* VI. 32347 places the marriage later than October 39. Carcopino (1943), 195 n.4 suggests that they were married in Lyons; Gelzer, 404, Garzetti, 99 and Nony, 338 believe the same. On the inscription, see p. 133

14 Persius 6.47; Jos. *AJ* 19.11; Suet. *Cal.* 25.4; Dio 59.28.7

15 Balsdon, 48; Meise, 119; E.J. Phillips, 'The Emperor Gaius' Abortive Invasion of Britain', *Historia* 19 (1970), 371

16 See E. W. Gray, *JRS* 38 (1948), 121. Humphrey, 235 suggests that sections 23.7-9 somehow had been dislocated from an earlier part of the narrative (possibly after 20.5) and misplaced

17 Tac. *Ann.* 12.2.2; Dio 59.23.7

18 Suet. *Cal.* 25.2; Meise, 104. S. Eitrem, 'Zur Apotheose', *SO* (1932), 22 explains the prohibition on the grounds of personal divinity, that the wife of a god is taboo for other men

19 Jos. *AJ* 19, 193; Tac. *Ann.* 2.85.1-4; Pliny *NH* 7.39; Suet. *Cal.* 25.3-4, 33; Dio 59.23.7, 28.7

20 Through her mother's previous marriages four of Caesonia's half-brothers reached consular rank: Quintus Pomponius Secundus, suffect in 41, Publius Pomponius Secundus (who had enjoyed the benefits of Caligula's amnesty in 37), suffect in 44 (from the second), Publius Suillius Rufus possibly suffect in 45 (from the fourth) and Cn. Domitius Corbulo, possibly suffect 39 (from the fifth); listed in Syme, *Papers,* 811-12, also see C. Cichorius, *op. cit.* II n. 67, 429-32

21 See Syme, *Aristocracy,* 175. According to Tac. *Ann.* 13.19.2 Agrippina Minor tried to prevent the marriage of Junia Silana with a young nobleman on the grounds that she was vergentem annis ('getting on'). It is interesting that Nero was similarly at least six years younger than Poppaea Sabina

22 See A. Burnett, 'The Coinage of King Agrippas I of Judaea and a New Coin of King Herod of Chalcis', *Mélanges Pierre Bastien* (Wetteren, 1987) nos. 3, 5 & 6, the popular identification of Caesonia on a coin of Carthago Nova (whose mint had almost certainly closed by 39) is erroneous; see R. Sear, *Roman Coins and their Values* (London, 1981³), no. 524

23 Jos. *AJ* 19. 193; Seut. *Cal.* 50. 2; Juv. 6. 615-7, 624

24 Suet. *Aug.* 94.8. *ILS* 197 (Bourges) records a dedication to Minerva and Drusilla (sister) for the Salus of Caligula and the Roman people. See H.P. L'Orange, 'Das Geburtsritual der Pharaonen am römischen Kaiserhof', *SO* 21 (1941), 105-16, and Köberlein, 58-61 for the

supposed Egyptian connection

25 Suet. *Cal.* 25.4

26 Suet. *Cal.* 23.1, 26.3; Dio 59.20.1. The Victory games (see *Fasti Amiterni* (*EJ* 51) are to be distinguished from the Actian games, celebrated near Actium itself every four years (Strabo 7.7.6; Jos. *BJ* 1.398; Suet. *Aug.* 18.2; Dio 51.1.2). Dio himself confuses them at 53.1.4-5

27 A view widely held: Balsdon, 72; Bergener, 121, Faur (1973), 25

28 Dio 59.15.5: *tote men hypateusen*. On this question, see J.W. Humphrey and P.M. Swan, 'Cassius Dio on the Suffect Consuls of A.D. 39', *Phoenix* 37 (1983), 324-7; G. Townend, 'Traces in Dio Cassius of Cluvius, Aufidius and Pliny', *Hermes* 89 (1961), 235 (before the recent epigraphic evidence)

29 Stein 'Domitius' *RE* 5 (1903) no 49; Colin, 409-10, Groag *PIR*² D141

30 Tac. *Ann.* 3.31.3; Pliny *NH* 7.39; Dio 59.15.3-5

31 Syme, *Papers,* 810, Townend op.cit. n.28)

32 Suet. *Cal.* 26.3; Dio 59.20.1. Dio 59.20.3 (unless the text is corrupt) mistakenly says that Afer was appointed as colleague to Caligula

33 *AE* 1973. 138, Gallivan, 67

34 Quintilian 6.3.42

35 William C. McDermott, 'Saint Jerome and Domitius Afer', *VC* 34 (1980), 19-23, suggests that a witticism of Domitius is preserved in Saint Jerome, Letter 52.7: *Scitum illud est oratoris Domitii: 'ego te', inquit, 'habeam ut principem, cum tu me non habeas ut senatorem.'* ('I would consider you as a princeps, even though you might not consider me a senator.)'. But there is no certainty that the orator in question is Domtius Afer

36 Dio 59.19. 1-7

37 Front. *De Aq.* 102

38 R.H. Rodgers, 'Curatores Aquarum', *HSCP* 86 (1982), 174-5 argues plausibly that there was a gap in Frontinus' text between Cato and Didius and that Didius was not appointed curator until the mid-40's. Certainly the text is corrupt at this point

39 The *ad hoc* arrangement of his election in 39 speaks against the suggestion of L. Vidman, 'Ad Frontinum, De aq. 102', *LF* 96 (1973), 16-9, that Didius was already consul designate in late 38

40 Quintilian 6.3.68. For a good summary of Didius' career, see A.R. Birley, *The Fasti of Roman Britain* (Oxford, 1981), 44-9

41 Dio 59.18.1-4, 23.8

42 Dio 59.18.5; *PIR*² I 801, T 201

43 Dio 59.20.6; Juvenal 7.203-6; *PIR*² C449; Charlesworth *CAH* 10.664. The Carrinas Secundus sent to scour Greece and Asia for masterpieces for Nero may well have been his son (Tac. *Ann.* 15.45.3; *PIR*² C 450)

44 Philo *Leg.* 259

45 *CIL* III. 8472, 9864a; Pliny *NH* 7.62; Tac. *Ann.* 13.30.4; Suet. *Claud.* 13.2; Dio 60.15.1-2; see J.J. Wilkes, *Dalmatia* (London, 1969) App. II, 442-3

46 Gallivan, 69. n. 19. Quadratus' predecessor, Fulcinius Trio, attested in Lusitania in 31 January (*AE* 1953.88) assumed the consulship on 1 July of that year

47 PIR² I.822; cf. Bergener 149, D. McAlindon, 'Senatorial Opposition to Claudius and Nero', *AJP* 77 (1956), 117. Alföldi, *Fasti Hispanienses* (Wiesbaden, 1969), 15, 193 tentatively puts Silanus in Spain in 40

48 On the date, see Smallwood *Leg.* 116. John Malal. 10.244 says that in the third year of Caligula's reign the governor of Syria was 'Pronios'

49 Tac. *Ann.* 3.49.2, 6.32.5-7; Suet. *Vit.* 2.5; Dio 59.27. 4-6

50 A. Dobo, Die Verwaltung der Römischen Provinz Pannonien von Augustus bis Diocletianus (*Amsterdam,* 1968), 26; T. Nagy, 'Die Regierungsjahre des C. Caesar mit besonderer Rücksicht auf Illyricum', *AAntHung* 29 (1981), 344-5

51 Tac. *Ann.* 6.9.5-6; Dio 59.18.4; His difficulties in 39 are not mentioned by Suetonius

52 Tac. *Hist.* 1.48.2-3; Plut. *Galb.* 12.1

53 Simpson (1980), 358 suggests that the crime may have been limited to lowering the morale of the Pannorian legions and allowing discipline to grow lax

54 See Dobo, *op. cit.* n. 50, 26-7

55 Groag *PIR²* C 1391, 1479, Garzetti, 91, Stewart, 72

56 Velleius 2.116.2 cf Dio 55.28.4, Florus 2.40

57 Pliny *Ep.* 5.3.5; Martial *Praef.* See also Sidonius Apollinaris, *carm* 9.259; ep. 2. 10. Nine epigrams appear in the Greek anthology under the authorship of a Gaetulicus, but their attribution to Lentulus Gaetulicus is far from certain; see H. Malcoveti, 'De Gaetulico Graecorum epigrammatum scriptore', *Athenaeum* 1 (1923) 32; D.L. Page, *Further Greek Epigrams* (Oxford, 1981)

58 Praetor: *CIL* I² p.71; Consul: *EJ* p.42; Tac. *Ann.* 4.46.1. As consul designate in the previous year Gaetulicus was noted for pressing for lesser penalties in the conviction of Aquila for adultery with Varius Ligus (Tac. *Ann.* 4.42.3)

59 The date is provided by Dio 59.22.5 who reports that by 39 Gaetulicus had held the legateship for 10 years. Thus he must have been appointed in 29 or 30; Stein, 'Cornelius', *RE* 4 (1900) 1385, argues for 29, Groag *PIR²* C 1390 for 30, as does Sealey, 102. In any case he had held the command long enough by 39 to have won the affection of his troops (Tac. *Ann.* 6.30.3)

60 Tac. *Ann.* 6.30.3; Groag *PIR²* C 1381, 1390

61 Tac. *Ann.* 6.30; Dio 58.19.1 reports that Tiberius ignored an insult to himself from L. Apronius Caesianus, a friend of Sejanus and son of L. Apronius, commander of lower Germany

62 Suet. *Cal.* 8.2. O. Jahn, *Persius* (Berlin, 1893) cxlii, n.1, believes that the poem dealt with a projected campaign of Germanicus. H. Peter, *Die Geschichtliche Literatur ber die Römische Kaiserzeit bis Theodosius* (Leipzig 1897), I. 419 believes on the other hand that Gaetulicus' comments must have appeared in a prose work

63 Most editors emend *tantum* ('only') of l.2 to read *Tauri* ('of the bull')

64 Tac. *Ann.* 4. 72, 6.30; Suet. *Tib.* 41, *Galb.* 6.3

65 Suet. *Cal.* 43; Dio 59.21.2-3; Willrich, 307

66 Suet. *Cal.* 43.Germanicus: Tac. *Ann.* 2.16.5; Claudius: *CIL* XI. 395

67 Schol. on Juv. IV. 14: see Simpson (1980), 360; Syme, *Aristocracy,* 180

68 *AFA* xlix. 6-8 (Smallwood 9. 18-20). Elsewhere Gaetulicus' name might have been erased from the record, as on an inscription from Vindonissa (*CIL* 13.11513); see H. Lieb, in R. Fellmann, *Die Principia des Legioslagers Vindonissa* (Brugg, 1958), 70-2

69 Suet. *Cal.* 8.2, *Galb.* 6.2; Dio 59.21.4, 22.5

70 As suggested by Faur, 32-5, developing the idea of G. Teuber, *Beiträge zur Geschichte der Eroberung Britanniens durch die Römer* (Breslau, 1909), 1-15, 82-6

71 Stein, 'Cornelius', *RE* 4 (1900), 1385. no.220; Simpson (1980), 362; see also Willrich, 307; Linnert, 81; Bergener, 120

72 Meise, 114-5; Bergener (1965), 119; Stewart; Faur (1973), 19

73 Bergener, 121. Faur, 23 speculates that the investigation into Sabinus and Cornelia might have revealed Gaetulicus' participation in a plot

74 Sen. *Ep.* 4.7; Suet. *Cal.* 24.3, 29.2, Dio 59.22.6-8; Orosius 7.5.9; Suet. *Vesp.* 2.3 reports that Vespasian moved that the conspirators be cast out unburied

75 Suet. *Claud.* 9.1, *Cal.* 24.3, 39.1; Dio 59.22.8

76 Against this, see Willrich, 307; Gelzer, 402

77 Dio 59.23.8; Simpson (1980), 252-3 suggests that Lepidus' crime may have been limited to his affair with the two sisters; see also Auguet, 166. Nero: Tac. *Ann.* 15.74.2

78 Bergener, 120

79 Jos. *AJ* 19. 20, 49, 52. Since Vinicianus was a candidate for the principate in 41 it seems a fair assumption that he must have held the consulship before that date (see Degrassi 12); yet it is difficult to see why he should have been described as especially noble, since the Annii had no republican consul in the family (Schneider, 166)

80 *PIR²* I A677, P. v. Rohden 'Annius', *RE¹* (1894), 2277. no 72; Bergener, 133; B. Borghesi, *Oeuvres Complètes* (Paris, 1862-97), 4.477-88, suggested that Annius Pollio married a sister of M. Vinicius

cos. AD 30; Scheid, 198 n.4 says that she was the daughter of M. Vinicius (cos. 19 BC), and he may have derived the agnomen Vinicianus from her rather than by adoption (see Br. Boer, *Die Römische Namengebung* (Stuttgart, 1937) 96, 100–107)

81 See Groag *PIR*² I 701; R. Hanslik, 'Vinicius', *RE* 9A (1961), 111, 118, 120 no. 11; Rohden *op. cit.* n. 00, no. 72; Scheid, 198–203

82 The other Arval appointments are: M. Furius Camillus, Ap. Iunius Silanus, C. Calpurnius Piso and C. Caecina Largus (if Sheid is correct about his cooption in May 38)

83 *AFA* l.10–18 (Smallwood 10.10–18). Unfortunately the list of members at the 27 October session is lost, but Domitius' absence from Rome on 1 June, 40, as indicated by the Arval record of that date, is taken by Griffin (Nero), 27 to indicate that he left Rome with his son on receiving news of his wife's disgrace. Domitius died towards the end of the year in Pyrgi of dropsy (see R.M. Geer, 'Notes on the Early Life of Nero', *TAPA* 62 (1931), 59–61). The claim in Suet. *Nero* 6.3 that Agrippina was banished *after* the death of her husband seems to be in error

84 Vogel-Weidemann (1982), 306 tentatively suggested that Vinicius was proconsul of Asia, 39–40 (but see 'Miscellanea zu den Proconsules von Africa und Asia', *ZPE* 46 (1982), 289–91

85 Linnert, 81, Willrich, 297, Faur, 16, Meise, 101–22

86 Apart from Claudius the possible claimants for the succession would have been: Rubellius Plautus, son of Julia (daughter of Drusus) and Rubellius Blandus, or the three sons of Aemilia Lepida (great-granddaughter of Augustus) and M. Silanus Torquatus, M. Junius Silanus, D. Iunius Silanus Torquatus and L. Junius Silanus

87 Tac. *Ann.* 14.2.4

88 Suet. *Nero* 6.2. see Willrich, 291; Balsdon, 42

89 Bergener, 122. Stewart, 76 suggests that Livilla's involvement was through Vinicius

90 Philo *Flacc.* 185–191

91 Jos. *AJ* 19. 125; Tac. *Ann.* 2.6.2; Orosius 7.5.9; P.v.Rhoden, 'Anteius', *RE* 1.2349; Groag, *PIR*² A727,8. An Anteius was among those given the task by Germanicus of constructing a fleet in AD 16

92 Suet. *Claud.* 9.1

93 Linnert, 61–82; Willrich 308; Meise 110–11, 119; Faur, 19

94 Dio 59.23.9; scholiast on Juv. *Sat.* 1.55

95 Tac. *Ann.* 14.63.2; Suet. *Claud.* 29.1; Dio 59.19.7–8, 60.8.5, 61.12.1; C. Marchesi, *Seneca* (Milan 1934), 11 n.18, I. Lana, *Lucio Anneo Seneca* (Turin 1955), 106–10, 15; G.W. Clarke, 'Seneca the Younger under Caligula', *Latomus* 24 (1965), 62–69, argues that Dio's source may have been friendly to Seneca (eg. Fabius Rusticus) and that Agrippina was not mentioned because of her later feud with him; see

Griffin (1976), 55

96 Sen. *Ad Marc.* 22.4-5, *Ep.* 55.3, *QN* 1.1.3. The *Ad Marciam* is not earlier than the republication of Cremutius Cordus' works. K. Abel, *Gnomon* 30 (1958), 610 & *Bauformen in Senecas Dialogen* (Heidelberg, 1967), 159 argues for a date before Seneca's exile in 41, and suggests 37. E. Albertini, La *composition dans les oeuvrages philosophiques de Sénèque* (Paris, 1932), 14-5, and Griffin (1957), 397, argue for a date after 39 on the basis of complimentary references to Tiberius. C.E. Manning, *On Seneca's 'Ad Marciam'* (Leiden, 1981) concludes that 40 is the most likely date

97 Sen. *QN* 4. *praef.* 15; *Ep.* 31.9

98 W. Kroll 'Lucilius Junior', *RE* 13 (1927), 1645; Faur, 36-7; O. Hirschfeld, *CIL* XII p.xiii and Die Kaiserlichen Vervaltungsbeamte bis auf Diokletian (Berlin, 1905²), 436 n.3; E.Stein, Die *Kaiserlichen Beamten und Truppenkörper im römischen Deutschland unter dem Principat* (Vienna, 1932), 19 n.95: Walser 174, n. 42; H.G. Pflaum, *Les Carrières Procuratoriennes Équestres* (Paris 1960) 70-73, III 761-2, *PIR²* L388 argues that the relevant passage of Seneca is a rhetorical exaggeration, and does not prove an Alpine procuratorship for Lucilius.

7 North Africa (*pages 114 -123*)

1 See D. Fishwick & B.D. Shaw, 'The Formation of Africa Proconsularis', *Hermes* 105 (1977), 369-80, also St Gsell, *Histoire ancienne de l'Afrique du Nord* (Paris, 1928), 196, M. Benabou, 'Proconsul et légat en Afrique. Le témoignage de Tacite', *AntAfr* 6 (1972), 129-30

2 Pliny *NH* 18.35

3 Sall. *BJ* 18.1-2, Dio 53.26.2

4 For some good observations on Tacfarinas, see B.D. Shaw, 'Fear and Loathing: the Nomad Menace and Roman Africa', in C.M. Wells, *L'Afrique Romaine* (Ottawa 1982), 42-4

5 *IG* III. 555, 612; *OGIS 197,* 198; possibly *EJ* 164

6 Tac. *Ann.* 4.23.1, 26.4; *Mazard,* 440-450

7 Dio 59. 25.1. The last coins of Ptolemy are minted in the twentieth year of his rein (he had been joint ruler with his father since 21) and the era of Mauretania as a province begins in 40: Mazard, 143, no. 496, *CIL* 8.8630

8 Sen. *Tranq.* 11.12; *Suet.* Cal. 35.1. St Gsell, *op. cit.* n. 1, 8.285 places the execution in September, when Caligula was in Campania

9 J. Carcopino, *Le Maroc Antique* (Paris 1934) 197 placed Ptolemy's death in Lyons and argued that the incident of the purple cloak happened in the federal amphitheatre there, where Caligula was celebrating games in 39/40. Ptolemy would have had to be received in Rome in 39 and imprisoned in the city to be seen by Seneca, then

summoned to Gaul from Rome, not Mauretania, in early 40 (see D. Fishwick, 'The Annexation of Mauretania', *Historia* 20 [1970], 470)

10 Dio 59.21.3

11 Dio 59.25.1

12 M. Hofmann, 'Ptolemais von Mauretanien', *RE* 23 (1959), 1780. On the dating of the Isaeum in the Campus Martius, see p. 220

13 Jos. *AJ* 18.191,195; Suet. *Aug.* 60; Dio 57.13.5

14 D. Fishwick & B.Shaw, 'Ptolemy of Mauretania and the Conspiracy of Gaetulicus', *Historia* 25 (1976), 493 suggest that Gaetulicus might have been taken to Mauretania by his father and have met Ptolemy; J.C. Faur, 'Caligula et Maurétanie: La Fin de Ptolémée', *Klio* 55 (1973), 249-71, argues that Ptolemy was planning to seize independence

15 Pliny *NH* 5. 11. Pliny states that this happened under Claudius, but the passage in question is too vague for precise chronological evidence. T. Kotula, 'Encore sur la mort de Ptolémée de Maurétanie', *Archeologia* 15 (1964),   83 argues that there might have been friction between Ptolemy's freedmen and those in the imperial house

16 Balsdon 193-4, Hofman, *op. cit.* n. 12, 1777; P. Romanelli, 258; M. Rachet, *Rome et les Berbères: un problème militaire d'Auguste à Diocletian* (Brussels 1970), 128; Fishwick *op.cit.* n.9, (1971), 474-5 has argued that it might have been much much more limited than traditionally thought

17 Lixus: M. Euzennat, 'L'Archéologie Marocaine, 1958-60', *BAM* 4 (1960), 543-4; M. Tarradell, *Marruecos Punico,* 158-9. Tamuda: Tarradell, 117. Volubilis: M. Euzennat, Le temple C de Volubilis et les originine de la site *BAM* 2 (1957) 51; Tarradell, 184

18 *ILA* 634 (Smallwood 407b)

19 Pliny *NH* 5.2; Dio 60.9.5. Dio seems to put the commands of both Geta and Paulinus into one year, which is hardly possible. It is likely that Paulinus took his command in 41 and Geta in 42

20 *ILM* 56 Volubilis (Smallwood 407a). Strictly speaking, the inscription belongs to Claudius' fourth tribunician year, up to the end of January 45

21 Tac. *Hist.* 4.48; Dio 59.20.7

22 Pflaum, 1234

23 *IL Alg.*I. p.ix

24 Suet. *Galb.* 7.1

25 *CIL* 8. 2532, 18042. On the role of these soldiers see Domaszewski A.V. *Die Rangordnung des römischen Heeres* (Cologne,1967), 63

26 R. Cagnat, L'armée romaine d'Afrique (Paris, 1892) 211-5)

27 *CIL* 8.6987, 19492 (*ILA* II.550)

8 Britain and Germany *(pages 124-139)*

1 Suet. *Cal.* 19.2,52; Dio 59.7.1,17.3

2 Tac. *Ag.* 13.4; *Germ.* 37.5; Suet. *Cal.* 43.1, *Galb.* 6.3; Dio 59.21.1-2

3 Tac. *Hist.* 1. 55; Ritterling, 1759, 1800

4 Ritterling, 1758, 1797; see also Balsdon (1934), 13-16, Syme *CAH* 10. 788-9

5 *CIL* 10. 4723

6 *CIL* 13.11853-6; H. Klumbach, *Germania* 29 (1951), 165-6; D. Baatz, *Mogontiacum* (Berlin, 1962), Wells, 146

7 Suet. *Galb.* 6.3. Ritterling, 1508, 1551, 1798, also suggests, on epigraphic grounds, that elements of IV Macedonica from Spain, and III Cyrenaica and XXII Deiotaurana from Egypt may well have been concentrated on the Rhine in 39

8 For surveys of this period, see D. F. Allen, 'The Belgic Dynasties of Britain and their Coins', *Archaeologia* 90 (1944), 1-46 (outdated but still very useful); S.S. Frere, *Britannia* (London 1987³), 55-77; P. Salway, *Roman Britain* (Oxford, 1981) 40-61

9 Strabo 2.5.8, 4.5.3

10 Tac. *Ann.* 2.24.5. Only one of these coins of Caratacus, found at Guildford was known to Allen. Since then several others have come to light; see, G. Boon, "A Coin of Caratacus in the National Museum of Wales', *University of Wales. Bulletin of the Board of Celtic Studies* 25 (1974), 243-5, 26 (1974), 95-5; C. Haselgrove, *Iron Age Coinage in South-East England* (British Archaeological Reports, Oxford 1987), 245

11 G.M. White, *AntJourn* 14 (1934), 49, fig.5, no. 14

12 Philo *Leg.* 356; Suet. *Cal.* 19.3; Dio 59.21.1-2

13 Claudius would later assert, for similar strategic reasons, that his father Drusus had been able to launch his expedition against Germany because he was secure in the protection that a settled Gaul offered in his rear. (*ILS* 212 [Smallwood 369])

14 Suet. *Galb.* 6, 7.1; Dio 60.8.7

15 Tac. *Ann.* 4. 72-4; Suet. *Tib.* 41

16 Tac. *Ann.* 6.30.3

17 R. Nierhaus, 'Das Swebische Gräberfeld von Diersheim', *Römisch-germanische Forschungen* 28 (1966) 182-198, 230-34

18 Suet. *Cal.* 44.1, *Galb.* 6.2-3. Some of these measures are attributed by Suetonius to Caligula himself, which is at variance with his claim that Galba had perfected the troops' discipline before Caligula arrived. Dio 55.23.1 shows that the normal discharge fee was 12,000 sesterces

19 Suet. *Galb.* 6.3; Dio 59.22.2; Balsdon, 79-81

20 Suet. *Galb.* 6.3; Dio 59.21.3 (naming Caligula personally as going beyond the Rhine); Eutropius 7.12.2

21 Ritterling, *Annalen für nassauische Altertumskunde und Geschichtsforschung, Wiesbaden* 14 (1912), 1416; H. Schönberger, 'The Roman Frontier in Germany: An Archaeological Survey', *JRS* 59 (1969), 152-3; for a plan of the 'Caligulan' fort, see C.-M. Ternes, 'Die Provincia

Germania Superior', *ANRW* II 5.2 (1976), 865

22 W. Will, 'Römische 'Klientel- Randstaaten' am Rhein', *BJ* 187
(1987), 56–7 (see also, E. Fabricius, 'Limes', *RE* 13 (1926), 584 and
J.Klose, *Klientel-Randstaaten am Rhein und an der Donau* (Breslau,
1934), 55; K. Schumacher, *Siedlungs- und Kulturgeschichte der
Rheinlande* (1923), II. 42; O. Brogan, 'The Roman Limes in
Germany', *AntJourn* 92 (1935), 4

23 Tac. *Hist.* 4.15.2; H.-G. Kolbe, *BJ* 161 (1961), 104; D. Wortmann,
Rheinisches Ausgrabungen 3 (1968), 323–9

24 Suet. *Cal.* 43; Willrich, 306–7 notes that the sprinkling might have
been done for the sake of speed

25 Suet. Cal. 20. Jullian, *Histoire de la Gaule* (Paris, 1921), IV. 163 claims
that the punishment was a revival of Gallic tradition. 'Speaking at
Lyons' became a proverb for finding oneself in an uncomfortable
position (Juv. 1.44). D. Fishwick, 'Claudius *Submersus*', *AJAH* 3
(1987), 76–77 suggests that the fate of the bad orators might reflect a
local Celtic burial ritual

26 Dio 59.22.4. Suetonius in an unspecified context (*Cal.* 30.1) speaks of
a man who died instead of someone else because of confusion over
his name, perhaps this same Sacerdos; see, Faur, 38

27 Suet. *Cal.* 39.2; Dio 59.21.5–6

28 Dio 59.24.1,8

29 Dio 59.23.2; Suet. *Aug.* 22; Gell. 5.6.21

30 Suet. *Claud.* 9.1; Dio 59.23.1–5, *AE* 1980.638. The inscription is dated
to his third tribunician year, thus between April 39 and April 40. The
female figure is recorded as: ——]a [——] f. ('the daughter of [name
missing])

31 Suet. *Cal.* 17.1; Dio 59.24. The new consuls were C. Laecanius Bassus
and Q. Terentius Culleo; see Gallivan, 67

32 Suet. *Galb.* 6.3

33 *AE* 1977. 808

34 D. Boschung, 'Römische Glasphalerae mit Porträtbusten', *BJ* 187
(1987), Nos. 2 7, 27

35 See Campbell, 40–41

36 Dio 59.22.2; 60.21.4; Suet. *Cal.* 45.1–2, 51.2–3. Campbell, 124, appears
to accept the acclamations

37 Livy 5.28.13; Tac. *Ag.* 18.6; Persius 6.43–4; Suet. *Cal.* 45.3; Vesp.
3.3.; *ILS* 8791

38 Suet. *Cal.* 44–7; Dio 59. 21.3

39 Suet. *Cal.* 46; Dio 59.25.1–3

40 Gelzer, 405–6; Balsdon, 92, essentially followed by, for instance, E.J.
Phillips, 'The Emperor Gaius' Abortive Invasion of Britain', *Historia*
19 (1970), 369–74. Balsdon's alternative suggestion for the shells is
that the musculi are in fact the sappers' huts (Vegetius 4.16), which

the troops would have been instructed to collect before departure

41 Verg. *Aen.* 1. 207; Suet. *Cal.* 45.2

42 Dio 60.8.7

43 *Caes.* BG 5.8; see H. Dessau, *Geschichte der römischen Kaiserzeit* (Berlin 1924-30), 2.1.125

44 Suet. *Cal.* 49.1; Vegetius 4.39. The restriction on winter travel was sometimes ignored, see E. de Saint-Denis, 'Mare Clausum', *REL* 25 (1947), 196-215 and J. Rougé, 'La navigation hivernale sous l'empire romain', *REA* 54 (1952), 316-19, but only during emergencies

45 Suet. *Cal.* 54.2

46 Suet. Cal. 46

47 R.W. Davies, 'The Abortive Invasion of Britain by Gaius', *Historia* 16 (1966), 124-8; P. Bicknell, 'The Emperor Gaius' Military Activities in AD 40', *Historia* 17 (1968), 496-505

48 Suet. *Cal.* 44.2. D.F. Allen, 'Did Adminius Strike Coins?' Britannia 7 (1976), 96-100; D. Nash, 'Adminius did Strike Coins', *OJA* 1 (1982), 111-14. Nash points out the close affinity of some types of Cunobelinus with those of Amminus, and suggests that the style on the two rulers' coins is so close as to suggest the work of the same engraver. M. Henig and D. Nash, 'Amminus and the Kingdom of Verica', *OJA* 1 (1982), 243-6 established the correct spelling of the name, which is found also on an inscription from Chichester (*RIB* 90)

49 Orosius 7.5.5. H.H. Scullard, *From the Gracchi to Nero* (London 1979⁵), 286 associated the two incidents

50 Tac. *Ag.* 13.4. Moreover, in the imaginary speech that Dio 62.4.1 places in the mouth of Boudicca some twenty years later, Caligula's scheme of invading Britain is placed in the same category as that of Augustus, abandoned because of fear

51 Suet. *Cal.* 46; Dio 59. 25.3. This is the first record of the amount paid to troops on campaign (see Campbell, 166)

52 Dio 59.25.2 speaks of a single trireme, Suet. *Cal.* 47 refers to them in the plural, and says that they were taken partly overland

53 Suet. *Aug.* 29.2; *Cal.* 44.2

54 Pers. *Sat.* 6.4-7; Suet. *Cal.* 47, 48.2

55 See, for example, Gelzer, 406, Willrich, 313, Balsdon 88, J.G.C. Anderson- H. Furneaux, *De Vita Agricolae* (Oxford 1922), xiv, n.3, Gelzer 406, P. Bicknell, 'Gaius and the Sea Shells', *AClass* 5 (1962), 73, M. Todd, *Roman Britain* (Glasgow 1981), 61

56 Dio 59.25.5a uses the term *cheiro*, which presumably translated the Latin *subigo*. The word has a *double- entendre*, as in the bawdy song about Julius Caesar recorded in Suet. *Jul.* 49.4, which begins 'Caesar 'possessed' Gaul, Nicomedes 'possessed' Caesar...' (Suet. *Jul.* 49.4)

57 Suet. *Cal.* 48.1-2

58 An inscription (*ILS* 192) from Praeneste of uncertain date records a dedication to Fortuna Primigenia *pro salut(e) C. Caesaris Aug(usti) Germ(anici) et reditu,* perhaps with reference to the northen expedition

59 Sen. *Ira* 3.19.2; Suet. *Cal.* 49.1-2; Dio 59.23.7 25.5

9 Divine honours (*pages 140-153*)

1 Cic. *Sen grat.* 8, *Orat.* 1.106: Verg. *Ec.* 1.41; Scrib. *Praef.* C60,C.163

2 L.Ross Taylor (1931), 35-8; Weinstock 289; Fishwick 46-51; S.R.F. Price, *Rituals and Power. The Roman Imperial Cult in Asia Minor* (Cambridge, 1984), 40-47

3 Cic. *Q.Fr.* 1.1.26

4 Tac. *Ann.* 4.37.1; Suet. *Aug.* 52; Dio 51.20.6

5 Tac. *Ann.* 4.37-8; *SEG* 11. 922 (*EJ* 102)

6 *EJ* 320b

7 The evidence is collected in Taylor, 'The Worship of Augustus in Italy', *TAPA* 51 (1920), 116-33, (1931), 214-223, who suggests that only the emperor's genius was worshipped in Italy; see also, Taeger, 142-5; on this, see Fishwick, 91 n.55

8 M. Ward 'The Association of Augustus with Jupiter', *SMSR* 9 (1933), 203-12

9 Tac. *Ann.* 15.74.3-4; Dio 51.20.8, 53.27.3

10 Dio 51.19.7; see Hor. *Ode* 4.5.31

11 *CIL* VI. 454; Ovid *Fast.* 5.143-6; Suet. *Aug.* 30.1; Dio 55.8.6-7; Taylor (1931), 182-94; L.Cerfaux- J. Tondriau, *Le Culte des Souverains* (Tournai 1956), 318; Fishwick 84-85; M. Hano, 'A l'origine du culte impérial: les autels des Lares Augusti', *ANRW* 2.16.3 (1986), 2333-81

12 See D. Fishwick, 'Genius and Numen', *HThR* 62 (1969), 356-67 on the difference between the two concepts

13 The event is based on the restoration of the Fasti Praenestini; see A. Degrassi, *Inscr. Ital.* XIII.2.115; on the date, see A. Alföldi, 'Die zwei Lorbeerbäume des Augustus', in A. Wlosok, *Römischer Kaiserkult* (Darmstadt, 1978), 403-22

14 *ILS* 112. Public dedications for the delivery of Rome from the conspiracy of Sejanus, one from Interamna, the other from Crete, were made to Tiberius' *numen* (*ILS* 157, 158)

15 *IGR* 4.145.3 (Smallwood 401); *SIG*[3] 799.9; his father was similarly called the 'new god' at Mytilene (*IGR* 4.75)

16 G.J.D. Aalders, 'Helios Gaios', *Mnemosyne* 13 (1960), 242-3 assumed that Caligula adopted the cult name of Helios

17 C.Simpson, 'The Cult of the Emperor Gaius', *Latomus* 90 (1981), 489-511, suggests that since the temple was not actually dedicated, Philo may have done no more than speculate about the name

18 Taylor (1931), 270-77, Weinstock, 304, Taeger, 186, Ward *op. cit.* n. 8, 203-4

19 Suet. *Aug.* 60; *Cal.* 21; Dio 59.28.1
20 Herod. 6.19.3; Strabo 14.634
21 Vitr.7 (*praef*)16; Strabo 14.1.5; Paus. 7.2.6. A brief description of the site is provided by G. Bean, Aegean Turkey (London 1966), 231-42
22 B.M. Ionia etc. no. 143. Robert, Humphrey ad loc., S.R.F. Price, *op. cit.* n.2, 257 (hesitantly), cf B. Hausoulier, 'Caligula et le temple d'Apollon Didyméen', *RPh* 23 (1899), 161
23 *AE* 1912.134 (Smallwood 127); the inscription refers to a temple at Miletus, presumably with reference to the city and territory within the province of Asia
24 Capito was prefect of Egypt by early 49 (*IGR* 1.1262 [Smallwood 382])
25 Livy 31.50.7; Plut. *Quaest. Rom.* 44; Gell. 10.15.6; Suet. *Cal.* 35.3; Dio 59.13.1. A. Bernardi, 'L'interesse di Caligola per la successione del rex Nemorensis e l'arcaica regalità nel Lazio,' Athenaeum 31 (1953), 279 sees Caligula reviving old religious practices on the Augustan model
26 *ILS* 9339; see Th. Mommsen, 'Bruchstücke der Saliarischen Priesterliste', *Hermes* 38 (1903), 125-9. Groag, *PIR*² C1346, distinguishes the Dolabella in the list from the Dolabella who was partner of Afer in the prosecution of Quinctilius Varus (Tac. *Ann.* 4.66.2)
27 Dio 59.4.4. A.D. Nock, 'Synnaos Theos' *HSCP* 41 (1930), 3, claims that an *eikon*, while intended to honour an individual was not the object of a cult
28 Suet. *Cal.* 22; Dio 59.4.4; Aur. Vict. *Caes.* 39.4
29 Dio 59.25.5
30 Gods: Philo *Leg.* 75-114 Dio 59.26.6; Alexander: Dio 59.17.3; triumphator: Suet. *Cal.* 52; woman: Jos. *AJ* 19.30; Dio 59.26.8; Sudas
31 Suet. *Aug.* 70; *Cal.* 52; Dio 59.26.5
32 Suet. *Cal.* 33; Dio 59.26.9: *mega paralerema*. The noun is unparalleled, but the verb *paralero* is found in Arist. *Fr.* 594, *Kn.* 531 where it seems to mean 'to talk drivel'
33 Suet. *Cal.* 22.3, *Claud.* 9.2; Dio 59.28.5. Suetonius puts Claudius' payment at 8 million
34 Mommsen, RS, 352; Talbert, 60; R. Duncan-Jones, *The Economy of the Roman Empire* (Cambridge, 1982²) 150
35 Suet. *Cal.* 22.4; Dio 59.28.2-4
36 Pliny *NH* 12.94; Suet. *Aug.* 5.1; Dio 56.46.3. Gelzer, 410; Willrich, 445; Balsdon, 163 argue for the Palatine; S. Eitrem, 'Zur Apotheose', *SO* 10 (1932), 5 4, J. Gagé, *'Basiléia.' Les Césars, les rois d'Orient et les 'Mages'*, (Paris, 1968), 73 n.110 for the Capitol
37 Jos. *AJ* 19.8; Suet. *Cal.* 22.2-3, 57.1; Dio 59.28.3-4
38 Suet. *Cal.* 22.2; Dio 59.28.5. Jos. *AJ* 19.4 says that Caligula called Jupiter Capitolinus his brother. Aur. Vict. *Caes.* 3.10 reports that

Caligula supported his claim to be Jupiter on the basis of his incestuous birth

39 Cic. *ad Att.* 12.45.3; Suet. *Tib.* 26; Jos. *BJ* 2.194; Tac. *Ann.* 13.8.1; Fishwick, 78, T. Pekary, 'Zu Tacitus *Annalen* 13.8.1', *Hermes* 108 (1980), 125-8; H.G. Niemeyer, *Studie zur statuarische Darstellung der romischen Kaiser* (Berlin, 1968), 36

40 Cic. *Dom.* 92. C. Gatti, 'Considerazioni sul Culto Imperiale nel Quadro della politica di Gaio', *CISA* 7 (1980), 172-3, associates his supposed plan to move his capital to the Latin town of Antium with his supposed worship as Jupiter Latiaris

41 Suet. *Cal.* 22.1. Quint. 1.7.21 says that there is a tradition that *optimus maximus* appears in an inscription of Caligula for the first time with the new spelling of 'i' for 'u'. See Weinstock, 287, Eitrem, *op. cit.* n. VI n.18

42 R. Frei- Stolba, 'Inoffizielle Kaisertitulaturen im 1. und 2. Jahrhundert n. Chr.', *MH* 26 (1969), 28

43 Sen. *Clem.* 1.19.9

44 Bourges: *ILS* 4675; Santiago: *CIL* II.6233-4, see *AE* 1952. 112; Coimbra: *CIL* II. 4639

45 Espérandieu, 88, 89

46 *AFA* lvii.8.24 (Smallwood 14.8,24)

47 *IG* 12.1392-4 (Thera) Zeus Boulaios. It might be added that a number of inscriptions even in the east, dated to 40/1, do not include divine attributes: *IGR* 1.1086 (Alexandria), end of 40; *IGR* 1.1248 (Foakhir Valley, Egypt), 40/1; *IGR* 4.1615 (Philadelphia, Asia), September 40. Dio 59.28.8 claims that Caligula was called 'Zeus/Jupiter' in documents but does not elaborate either on their character or their source

48 The recent discovery of a radiate crown on a throned figure on a dupondius usually assigned to Caligula is not relevant, since the figure almost certainly represents Augustus (p. 21); on this, and Caligula's radiate coin in local coinage, see B.E. Levy, 'Caligula's Radiate Crown', SM 152 (1988), 101-107

49 See Head, *Historia Numorum,* 766, 853

50 *BMC* Tiberius 102, 108, 125, 141; Caligula 1-5, 10, 16, 24-25; Claudius 2 24

51 *BMC* Nero 52-60, 68, between 191 and 257, between 335 and 359. For a summary of the other supposed divine attributes on Nero's coinage, see R. Fears, *Princeps a Diis Electus* (American Academy in Rome, 1977), 325-8

52 Sen. *Tranq.* 14.9; see Lipsius, L. *Annaei Senecae Philosophi Opera quae Exstant Omnia* (Antwerp 1605), 165, 282. Scholars generally agree with Lipsius, eg. Willrich 447, Balsdon, 172, K. Latte, *Römische Religionsgeschichte* (Munich, 1960), 316 n.1. D.M. Pippidi, *Recherches sur le culte impérial* (Paris, 1939), 79-86, however, insists that

no irony was intended, and G. Herzog-Hauser, 'Kaiserkult' *RE Suppl.* 4 (1924), 834 even suggests on the basis of Seneca's text that Caligula's cult name was *Caesar Deus Noster*

53 J.B. Pritchard, *Ancient Near Eastern Texts relating to the Old Testament* (1955²), 275; Alföldi, 64

54 Tac. *Ann.* 1.13.7; Suet. *Jul.* 20.4

55 Suet. *Vit.* 2.5; Dio 59.27.4-6

56 Dio 59.27.1. Alföldi (1934), 39 points out that Dio is obviously thinking of senators

57 Dio 59.19.5, 28.28 (Patricius' epitome). Sen. *Ben.* 2.12.1-2 reflects a rare favourable tradition about Caligula, that in exending his foot he was not trying to be insolent but showing off his pearl- studded slippers

58 Jos. *AJ* 19. 234; Philo *Leg.* 352; Dio 60.5.4. The distinction is between *proskynein* and *prospiptein* (*see Gatti, op. cit.* n. 40) 165

59 Dio 44.6.3; 58.4.4; 59.24.4

60 Serv. on *Aen.* 1.276

61 R. Fears, 'The Cult of Jupiter and Roman Imperial Ideology', *ANR W* II.17.1 (1981), 72-4

62 This is the sense that it seems to have at Suet. *Cal.* 24.2; see, M.A. Levi, *L'Impero Romano* (Turin 1936), 119-20; A. Aiardi, 'Optimus Maximus Caesar: Considerazioni sull' Interesse di Caligola per il Culto di Giove', *AIV* 136 (1978), 100

63 Pers. 6. 48

64 Dio 59.25.5, 26.5

65 *Inst.* 2.23.1; *EJ* 114 ; *ILS* 157; Dio 60.5.6

66 Dio 59.14.7; Weinstock, 172-3

67 Dio 59.26.3. An inscription from Gaul (*CIL* VI.811) binds the Genius of Caligula with Salus, Pax and Victoria; see also *ILS* 197

68 Fishwick, 91 n.55

69 Suet. *Cal.* 27.3. In the Satyricon Trimalchio says that the slave Mithridates was crucified *'quia Gai nostri genio male dixerat'* (Pet. *Sat.* 53)

70 Dio 59.24.7, 27.2

10 **Assassination** (*pages 154–171*)

1 The evidence for his presence in the area of Rome in May appears in a fragment of the Arval record, *AFA* li (Smallwood 10), now lost and known only from an anonymous sixteenth-century copy in Florence (Appendix 1).

2 See Smallwood, *Leg.* 254

3 Philo *Leg.* 181; Suet. *Cal.* 22.1

4 Jos. *AJ* 18. 247-55. The possibility that Antipas made the journey to Campania in 39 can not be ruled out

5 *Tib.* 1.7, 64-5; Pliny *NH* 37.13; Suet. *Cal.* 49.2

6 Dio 59.20.4: presumably the elections were restored to the senate for the contests of 41

7 Jos. *AJ* 19.71; Suet. *Cal.* 37.1; Dio 59.25.5. Josephus reports that the donative was made from the *basilike* ('palace'); Suetonius presumably misread his source in claiming that it was made from the Basilica Julia (accepted by Gelzer, 407)

8 That there were two separate conspiracies: Charlesworth *CAH* 10. 664; Balsdon, 101; Gelzer, 412-14

9 The sources are vague about the number of conspiracies against Caligula. Suet. *Cal.* 56.1 comments that before the final plot there were 'one or two' others, and that the Prefects of the guard were implicated *in quadam coniuratione* ('in some conspiracy or other'); Jos. *AJ* 19.14 says that conspiracies were 'commonly' formed against him

10 Jos.*AJ* 19. 60-62 (claiming that equestrians also were privy to the plot), 133; Tac. *Hist.* 3. 68.1; Dio 59. 29. 1. Timpe (1962), 80-1, claims that the conspiracy was much wider-known than it needed to be, since it was necessary for Vinicianus, whom he sees as its leader, to build up a political following

11 Sen. *Ira* 3.18.3-19; Suet. *Aug.* 13.2; *Cal.* 27.4, Suetonius claims that Caligula would even send litters to convey fathers too ill to attend the executions

12 Sen. *Ira* 2.33.3-7

13 Dio 59.25.5b (epitome). Note that Zonaras and the Vatican epitome of John Patricius summarize somewhat differently. The latter states simply that Cerialis said nothing (thus only implying that Papinius did)

14 Sen. *Ira* 3.18.3

15 Tac. *Ann.* 15.74.3, 16.17.8

16 I.E. Grady, 'Dio LIX. 25.5b, a note', *RhM* 124 (1981), 261-7, suggests a textual corruption, and that Dio's account originally mentioned Anicius Cerialis and his son *and* Papinius. Sextus Papinius was in all probability the son of Sextus Papinius Allenius, consul in 36 (*CIL* 5.2823; Tac. *Ann.* 40.1). Another of Allenius' sons committed suicide shortly before Caligula's accession, by hurling himself from a window (Tac. *Ann.* 6.49.1)

17 Sen. *Ira* 3.18.3; Dio 59.25.6-7 (the name is given as Betilinus). Suet. *Cal.* 26.3 also speaks of the scourging (but not the execution) of a quaestor (almost certainly Bassus) who had been charged with conspiracy

18 Sen. *Tranq.* 14.4-10

19 Sen. *Ep.* 73.1, 103.5; P. A. Brunt, 'Stoicism and the Principate', *PBSR* 43 (1975), 9

20 Tac. *Ann.* 3. 51.3 (as amended). Boethius *Con. Phil.* 1.4.94 seems to reflect a tradition in which Canus was actually involved in a plot: *cum [sc Canus] a Gaio Caesare Germanici filio conscius contra se factae coniurationis fuisse diceretur*

21 *Chronographia* 1. 625 (Plutarch *fr,* 211). The information is attributed to Plutarch

22 Stein *PIR*² A742 (followed by Nony, 381) claims, without evidence, that Antiochus was also executed by Caligula. It is unlikely; Antiochus was still alive some time later, since Syncellus adds that Canus appeared to him in his sleep, to reassure him that his soul had passed to a higher place

23 Sen. *Ep.* 29.6, *Ben.* 2.21.5; Tac. *Ag.* 4.1. Balsdon, 98

24 Sen. *Ben.* 2.12.1; Jos. *AJ* 19. 32–36; Suet. *Cal.* 16. 4; Dio 59. 26. 4. Suetonius relates the incident without giving names. The names of Timidius and Quintilia are provided by Josephus, who calls the accused Pompedius (Roman names in Josephus are invariably transliterated wrongly). Dio gives his name as Pomponius. Seneca speaks of the acquittal of a Pompeius Pennus. The identification of Pompeius Pennus with Pomponius/ Pompedius is far from certain (A. Stein 'Timidius' *RE* 6a (1938), 1256 doubts it). Dessau *PIR* 3. 450 identifies Seneca's Pompeius with Sextus Pompeius, consul of AD 14 (PIR¹ 3.64.450). R. Hanslik 'Sex. Pompeius', *RE* 21 (1952) 2267 and Syme, 'Personal Names in Annals i–vi', *JRS* 39 (1949), 9 accept the identification, but Syme 'Obituaries in Tacitus', *AJP* 79 (1958), 21, n. 1 doubts it. This Sextus Pompeius seems to have been very wealthy, to judge from Ovid *Pont.* 4.15. He would have been at least in his 70's in 40/1; his father, the famous Sextus Pompeius, married to the neice of Scribonia, was defeated at sea in 36 BC and his son could not have been born after 35 BC at the very latest. Pompeius Pennus/ Pomponius may have been related to another Pompeius described by Seneca as a kinsman of Caligula and owner of great estates

25 Suet. *Cal.* 28; Dio 59. 26. 1–2; Orosius 7. 5. 10. Protogenes is mentioned by Juvenal (3. 120) among the famous delatores. He was executed in the first year of Claudius' reign (Dio 60.4.5) and the books were destroyed

26 Dio 59.26.3. The arrangement did not continue after his death, and Claudius sat on the consul's tribunal or on the tribune's bench in the body of the house

27 Tac. *Ann.* 6.15.5; Suet. *Aug.* 35.2, *Tib.* 65.1; Dio 54.12.3, 58.18.5, 59.26.3

28 See Willrich, 306; M. Durry, 'Praetoriae Cohortes', *RE* 22 (1954), 1613

29 Suet. *Aug.* 49. 1, *Cal.* 43. 1; Dio 55. 24. 8, 56. 23. 4. Keune, 'Custos', *RE* 4 (1901), 1902 says he filled out the numbers from prisoners of

war. The standard modern work on the subject is H. Bellen, 'Die Germanische Leibwache der römischen Kaiser des Julisch- Claudischen Hauses (Wiesbaden, 1981). There seems to be no parallel for the publicly appointed guard for the statues (see CIL 8. 9052 for a private guard). T. Pekary, Das Römische Kaiserbildnis in Staat, Kult und Gesellschaft (Berlin, 1985), 114, 140 thinks that it may have been honorary

30 Dio 59.25.7 (epitome)

31 Jos. AJ 19. 64-69; Tac. Ann. 11. 29. 1, 12. 1. 3; Suet. Cal. 56. 1; Dio 59. 29. 1,

32 Suet. Cal. 56.1. Dio on another occasion speaks of only a single eparchos being involved (59.29.1), but refers to both prefects in the context of Capito's charges (59.25.7). This may be the result of his using two different sources

33 Jos. AJ 19. 37-47; Tac. Hist. 4. 68.2; Suet. Titus 4

34 Jos. AJ 19.45; see Bergener, 124

35 Tac. Ann. 1. 32.5 calls him an adulescens (up to about 30 years old) at the time of the mutinies in 14; at the time of the assassination he is called a senior by Suet. Cal. 56.2

36 Even the fourth-century poet Ausonius writes of Chaerea mollis ('effeminate Chaerea') (De Caes. 4. 4)

37 Sen. Cons. 18. 3; Jos. AJ 19. 20-21; Suet. Cal. 56. 2; Dio 59. 29. 2

38 Jos. AJ 19. 46; Suet. Cal. 58. 2; Dio 59. 29. 1

39 Jos. AJ 19. 17, 19. The name 'Regulus' is reconstructed from a corrupt manuscript reading. Willrich, 456 proposed instead 'Rectus', who could be the friend of the philosopher Canus

40 Jos. AJ 19.20, 49, 52; Tac. Ann. 6. 9.5-7; Dio 60. 15. 1. The manuscripts of Josephus create difficulties since, throughout, the name 'Minucianus' is used where Vinicianus is clearly meant

41 Timpe (1962), 89, Bergener, 125, Scheid, 200-201, Gelzer, 414

42 Sen. Cons. 18. 2; Jos. AJ 19. 159; Tac. Ann. 11. 1-3

43 CIL 10. 1233; Suet. Cal. 57.1; Suet. Nero 37. 1; Jos. AJ 20. 1; Tac. Ann. 12. 11. 4, 12.12, 1, 16. 7. 3, 9. 1.22.9; Dio 59. 29. 3

44 Dio 59.9.1. A L. Nonius Asprenas was consul in 29, but the precise relationship with the Nonius, consul in 38 (son of 'Marcus'), is not clear

45 Jos. AJ 19.123. Josephus actually calls him Barbaros Norbanos. Two Norbani brothers held consulships. L. Norbanus Flaccus in 19, and L. Norbanus Balbus in 15, either of whom might have been the father of the Norbanus who died in 38. Neither is noted for the distinction of his ancestors, although the former had a reputation as an excellent trumpeter. It is possible that Norbanus was the grandson of Lucius Cornelius Balbus, who as proconsul in Africa defeated the Garamantes and others in 19 BC and was awarded a triumph (Dio 57.18.3), see

Groag, 'Norbanus' 8 *RE* 17 (1937), 931

46 Jos. *AJ* 19. 80-83; Philo *Leg.* 250, 338. The time of the year makes such a project unlikely; Philo claims that he planned to follow the coast, going ashore each day

47 Suet. *Cal.* 57. 1, 3; Dio 59. 29. 3. reports Pompey's failure to recognize a warning about Cassius, which turned out to be the name of the mountain at whose foot he was slain

48 Suet. *Cal.* 57. 3; Dio 59. 29. 4. The birthplace of the famous seer was Tyana, not Egypt. In 96 Apollonius spoke of Domitian's assassination at the moment it was carried out in Rome (Dio 67. 18. 1; Philostratus *VA* 8. 26)

49 Jos. *AJ* 19.94-5; Suet. *Cal.* 57. 4; Apollod. 52. 14. On that occasion Philip was celebrating the marriage of his daughter Cleopatra to Alexander of Epirus, an event that took place, in fact, in the autumn

50 Jos. *AJ* 19.87, on Asprenas; Suet. *Cal.* 57.4 on Caligula

51 Jos. *AJ* 19. 86, 93; Dio 59. 29. 5

52 Jos. *AJ* 19. 91-2. Cluvius (or Josephus) slightly misquotes Homer Iliad 14. 90-91 omitting 'this' (*touton*) before 'report'

53 Jos. 19. 96-103; Suet. *Cal.* 56.2, 58. 1, Claud. 10. 1. Josephus says that Caligula left at the ninth hour, as opposed to Suetonius' seventh

54 Jos. *AJ* 19. 102-5; Suet. *Cal.* 58. 1; Dio 59. 29. Josephus is the only one to mention the short cut. Dio adds that some of the youths came from Greece

55 Suet. *Cal.* 58. 2-3

56 Sen. *Cons.* 18. 3; Jos. *AJ* 19. 105-13; Suet. *Cal.* 58. 2-3; Dio 59. 29. 7, 30. 1

57 Jos. *AJ* 19. 153-6

58 Jos. *AJ* 19. 122; Suet. *Cal.* 55. 2, 58, 3. Sabinus was later rescued from death in a gladiatorial combat by Messalina, whose lover he was (Dio 60. 28. 2)

59 Jos. *AJ* 19. 123-6; Suet. *Cal.* 58. 3; Dio 59. 30. 1b

60 Josephus offers no explanation for Nonius Asprenas' presence by the body. Dabrowski, 255-6 suggests that he may have been killed simply as a bystander and his role elevated by later tradition

61 Anteius was perhaps the brother of Publius Anteius, legate in Dalmatia in 51/2, who committed suicide in 66

62 Jos. *AJ* 19.157

63 Jos. *AJ* 19. 190-200; Suet. *Cal.* 59. Suetonius calls the murderer a 'centurion' of the Praetorian guard

64 Jos. *AJ* 19. 237; Suet. *Cal.* 59.1, *Nero* 50, *Dom* 17.3

11 **Aftermath** (*pages 172–80*)
1 Herodian 2.12.4 was still able to say of the time when Didius Julianus was dethroned in 193 that the consuls took over business whenever

there was a succession crisis

2 Suet. *Cal.* 60; Dio 59.30.3, 60.1.1

3 Jos. *AJ* 19.160; Suet. *Cal.* 60. Dio 60.1.1 claims that at this first meeting a variety of opinions was expressed, some for the republic, some for the principate, but he has telescoped into a brief section a whole series of events following the assassination, and it is likely, as suggested by Josephus and Suetonius, that at this initial meeting the senators showed a unanimous intention of restoring the republic

4 Jos. *AJ* 19. 228

5 In describing the incident both Jos. AJ 19. 159–60 and Tac. *Ann.* 11.1.2 use the expressions appropriate of a formal assembly, but it is more likely to have been a spontaneous gathering.

6 Jos. *AJ* 19. 216–26

7 Roullet, 48

8 Jos. *AJ* 19.221–3; Suet. *Claud.* 10.2. Josephus calls the area *demosion* a term which elsewhere (*AJ* 13. 265–6, 16. 164) is used for 'treasury', but here seems to distinguish the private palace from the public area, as suggested to me by Peter Wiseman. In a highly corrupt text, Josephus seems to suggest that the bystanders saw and pitied Claudius inside the palace, which seems most implausible

9 Suet. *Claud.* 10; Dio 60.1

10 Jos. *AJ* 19.166–87, *BJ* 2.205

11 On Saturninus' speech, see Timpe (1960) 481–9. Josephus claims, without elaboration, that there were equestrians present

12 Jos. *AJ* 19. 236–45; Dio 60. 8.2. Agrippa's involvement is described briefly in *BJ* 2.206–208, where he plays a much more passive role, as little more than a go–between. It may be that Josephus used in the *AJ* a source that inflated Agrippa's part, but it is to be noted that the version there receives some confirmation from Dio, who claims that Agrippa helped Claudius become emperor. Timpe (1960) 502 says that *BJ* used a Jewish source, the later *AJ* a Roman source not yet available before 75 (the earliest possible date for the *BJ*)

13 Dio 60.1.4. Jos. *AJ* 19.234–5, 245, perhaps conflating two separate sources, seems to speak of two separate embassies

14 Jos. *AJ* 19. 186–7. On 'Libertas' in this context, see, M. Hammond, '*Res Olim Dissociabiles: Principatus ac Libertas*', HSCP 67 (1963), 98

15 Bergener, 133, Timpe (1962), 89

16 For a useful discussion of this passage, M. Swan, 'Josephus *AJ* XIX,251–252. Opposition to Gaius and Claudius', *AJP* 91 (1970), 149–64

17 Suet. *Galb.* 7.1; see C.L. Murison, 'Galba in Germany, AD 43', *Historia* 34 (1985), 254–6

18 Jos. *AJ* 19. 247 gives the sum as 5000 drachmae (= 20,000 sesterces), Suet. *Claud.* 10. 4 gives 15,000 sesterces. Suetonius claims that the donative was only promised on this occasion

19 Rufrius Pollio: Jos. AJ. 19. 267. Catonius Iustus was prefect in 43 at any rate, when he was put to death through Messalina (Sen. Ap. 13.5; Dio 60.18.3)

20 Jos. AJ 19. 264-66; Dio 60.1.4. In Jos. BJ 2. 209 the senate rejects Claudius' initial offer and Claudius sends back Agrippa with a declaration of war, at which point the soldiers abandon the senate, whose resistance crumbles. On Pomponius' role, see Timpe (1960), 490-1; Bergener, 131

21 Jos. AJ 19. 268-73; Suet. Claud. 11. 1; Dio 60. 3. 4-5

22 Tac. Ann. 11.29.1; Pliny NH 33.134; 36.60

23 On the possible role of Claudius in the assassination, see H. Jung, 'Die Thronerhebung des Claudius' Chiron 2 (1972), 367-86; Campbell, 81

24 Suet. Claud. 11.3; Dio 60.4.5-6. In the Lex de Imperio Vespasiani he is omitted from those emperors providing precedents- presumably he was simply allowed to drop out. As the Tabula Banasitana shows (CRAI [1971], 468-90), he did remain in the official list of the emperors who made grants of Roman citizenship; such grants clearly remained valid

25 Suet. Claud. 11.3; Dio 60.3.4, 4.5. On damnatio memoriae F. Vittinghoff, Der Staatsfeind in der römischen Kaiserzeit (Berlin, 1936), 102; J. Bleicken, Senatsgericht und Kaisergericht, AbhGöttingen 3 F 53 (1962) 104-5; J.P. Rollin, Untersuchungen zu Rechtsfragen römischer Bildnisse (1979) 165

26 Sen. Apoc. 11.2 depicts him as harrying Caligula even after death; see E.S. Ramage, 'Denigration of a Predecessor under Claudius, Galba and Vespasian', Historia 32 (1983), 202-206

27 ILS 205 (Smallwood 308b); Dio 60.8.6

28 Caligula: Dio 59.4.5; Agrippina: Dio 61.16.2a; Poppaea: Tac. Ann. 14.61.1. Dio 59.30.1a (epitome) speaks of the statues and images of Caligula being dragged down from their pedestals during the assassination, but this presumably refers to limited and spontaneous action on the part of the conspirators

29 See J. Ternbach, 'Further Comments on 'Caligula'', Arts in Virginia 14 (1974), 29-32. That the head originally belonged to the body has been established by scientific analysis of the marble

30 H. Jucker, 'Caligula', Arts in Virginia 13 (1973), 20, fig. 9; 'Die Bildnisstrafen gegen den toten Caligula' Festschrift U. Hausmann, 112, pl.14

31 Milan: ILS 194; Bologna: ILS 5674; Pompeii: ILS 6396; Dalmatia: 5948: Thugga (Africa), see L..Poinsott, Inscriptions de Thugga (1913) 45 n.35; Samos: IGR 4.1721; Alexandria (Egypt): IGR 1. 1057; Cyzicus: IGR 4.146

32 Dio 60.22.3

33 D. Nony, 'Quelques as d'imitation de Caligula trouvés à Bordeaux',

Trésors monétaires 3. 15-16

34 Scholarly opinion is divided: For recent discussions: Jucker *op. cit.* n.30, A. Burnett, 'The Authority to Coin in the Late Republic and Early Empire', *NC* 137 (1977), 55-6; D.W. Macdowall, 'The PNR Type of Claudius', *GNS* 18 (1968), 81; C.J. Howgego, Greek Imperial Countermarks (London, 1985), 6; G. Boon, *AntJourn* 67 (1987), 412, Sutherland, (1987), 79-80

35 Stat. *Silv.* 4.9. 23

36 See MacDowell, 81-2; Mattingly *BMC* I clviii however suggests that the better pieces of Caligula are the ones that escaped the melting, and that the majority as minted were underweight

37 J.-P. Callu & F. Rosati, Le Dépot monétaire du Pozarello', *MEFR* (1964), 51-90

38 R.A.G. Carson, 'The Bredgar Treasure of Roman Coins', *NC* (1959) 17-22. Carson cites 17 Tiberian aurei; two more are now known

39 J. Touratsoglou, 'The 1976 Patras Hoard of Aurei from the Early Empire', *NumChron* V-VI (1978), 41-52

40 See G.F. Hill, 'Roman Aurei from Pudukota, South India', *NC* 18 (1898), 304-320

41 I. Richmond, *Hod Hill II* (London, 1968)

42 R. Martini, 'Osservazioni su Contromarche ed Erosioni su Assi di Caligola', *RIN* 82 (1980), 52-83; D.W. MacDowall, 'The Economic Context of the Roman Imperial Countermark NCAPR', *Acta Numismatica* I (1971), 87; see J.-B. Giard, 'Pouvoir central et libertés locales: le monnayage en bronze de Claude avant 50 apres J.-C.', *RN* 12 (1970), 56-60 for a list

43 T. Pekary, Zur Datierung der Divus Augustus Pater-Providentia Prägungen. Ein Münzfund in Vidy bei Lausanne', *GNS* 15 (1965), 128-30; C.M. Kraay, *Die Münzfunde von Vindonissa* (1962) 107 no. 4237

44 Giard *op. cit.* App.2 n.9; J. Schwartz, 'Note sur le monnayage sénatorial entre 37 et 42 P.C.', *RN* 13 (1951), 37-41

45 Jucker *op. cit.* n. 30, E. Jonas, 'A Damnatio memoriae alkalmazása egyik duponiusán Caligula,' *Numizm Közlöny* 36-37 (1937-38), 89-91; *BJ* 166 (1966), 580

46 Dio 64.6.1

12 **Caligula and the Jews** (*pages 181–191*)

1 Luke 3.1; Jos. *AJ* 18. 237; Smallwood, *Jews* 150

2 Jos. *AJ* 18.36; Luke 13.32

3 Josephus *AJ* 18. 109-112, see Smallwood, *Jews,* 185

4 Jos. *AJ* 18.113. The territory in question was probably Gabala. The manuscripts read 'Gamala', which would indicate a region that belonged to Philip's former tetrarchy and could not have been the

subject of a dispute between Aretas and Antipas; see A. Negev, 'The Nabataeans and the Provincia Arabia', *ANRW* II 8 (1977), 567-9. On the conflict, see H.P. Roschinski, 'Geschichte der Nabatäer', *BJ* 180 (1980), 150-4

5 Jos *AJ* 18. 120-6

6 II *Cor.* 11.32, *Acts.* 9.23-5

7 J.-P. Rey-Coquais, 'Syrie romaine, de Pompée à Diocletien', *JRS* 68 (1978), 50-51 suggests that the ethnarch was there only as consul of Aretas and that Damascus remained part of the empire through this period

8 There is some uncertainty over the date of their visit to Italy; Jos, *AJ* 19.351 shows that Agrippa acquired Antipas' tetrarchy in his fourth year as king (40-41). The latest coins of Antipas date to his 43d year, 39-40 (*BMC* Palestine 230)

9 Jos. *AJ* 18.240-255, *BJ* 181-3

10 Jos. *AJ* 18.252 states that he went to Lugdunum in Gaul, which should mean Lyons, but at *BJ* 2. 183 says he was exiled to Spain, where he died. Antipas may have gone first to Lyons, then to Spain, or he might have been sent to Lugdunum Convenarum, a town in Gaul on the Spanish frontier (discussed by Braund, 177. n.76)

11 Jos. *Ap.* 2.63

12 Phil. *Leg.* 159-61, cf. *Flacc.* 1; Jos. *AJ* 18.81-4; Tac. *Ann.* 2.85.5; Suet. *Tib.* 36.1

13 Smallwood, *Jews,* 202-8. Note that Tacitus dates the expulsion of the Jews to 19, before Sejanus would have been in a position to do serious damage

14 Strabo 17.13 called Alexandria the commercial centre of the world, and Orosius *Pag.* 6.19.19 says that at the time of Actium it was by far the greatest and wealthiest of all cities

15 'Antisemitism in Alexandria', *JRS* 31 (1941), 1-18

16 *AJ* 14.188. The Caesar responsible for the stele must be Augustus, and not, as Josephus mistakenly assumes, Julius Caesar

17 Phil. *Flacc.* 9.11,58

18 The date is provided by Philo *Flacc.* 56, which indicates that the creation of the ghetto followed not long after the death of Drusilla, 10 June, 38

19 Phil. *Flacc.* 55-62, 94, *Legat.* 121

20 Phil. *Flacc.* 116 shows that the Jews were celebrating the Feast of the Tabernacles at the time of Flaccus' arrest. C. Vitrasius Pollio is known (*BGU* IV 1078 = Wilcken *Chrest.* 59) to have arrived in Egypt on the 23rd day of Soter, 20 October (see V n.7); see Stein (1950), 29; J. Schwartz, 'Préfets d'Egypte sous Tibère et Caligula', *ZPE* 48 (1982), 190

21 Philo, *Leg.* 370 gives the total number of Jews as five. Apart from

Philo we do not know the other delegates, but Philo's brother was in Rome at some point and was imprisoned by Caligula (*AJ* 19.276); he may have been part of the jewish team. Apion's presence on the Greek side is indicated by *AJ* 18.257-60

22 Each date presents a problem. The delegates sailed during the winter (Phil. *Leg.* 190). We know that they saw Caligula on two separate occasions, the second taking place no earlier than August 40, after his entry into the city and the decision to erect the statue in Jerusalem. The first must have taken place earlier in 40, after his return to Italy, or before his departure for Gaul in 39. The arrival of the envoys in 38/9 would necessitate their presence in Rome for a year; their arrival in 39/40 would mean a delay in their departure for over a year after the deposition of Flaccus. 38/9 is preferred by, *inter alios* Willrich, 387-470, Gelzer, 397, P.J. Sijpstein, 'The Legationes ad Gaium', *Journ. Jew St.* 15 (1964), 87-96; 39/40 by Balsdon (1934), 21-4, Smallwood, *Legatio*, 47-50, (1981). On balance this latter date seems preferable, with a period of grace allowed, after Flaccus' arrest, for his successor Pollio to initiate an investigation and if possible to sort out the problems locally. The apparent urgency of the Jewish departure could indicate no more than a desire to move earlier than the Greek delegation

23 Set out in detail in her 1957 article, criticised by P. Bilde, 'The Roman Emperor Gaius (Caligula)'s Attempt to Erect his Statue in the Temple of Jerusalem', *STh* 32 (1978), 67-93, who considers Josephus more reliable.

24 Tac. *Hist.* 5.9

25 S.J. De Laet, 'Le Successeur de Ponce Pilate', AC (1939), 418-19 argues that Marullus (*AJ* 18.237) is the same as the Marcellus appointed by Vitellius as Pilate's successor. This claim however has no support in the manuscripts and runs counter to Josephus' statement that Caligula 'sent out' *ekpempei* Marullus

26 Jos. *AJ* 18. 261. The date of Petronius' appointment to Syria is very controversial. Malalas places the appointment in 39, accepted, *inter alios*, by Smallwood, but not universally accepted; some have argued for an appointment in 40 (see Dabrowski, 415-6). Some scholars have maintained that New Testament texts such as Mark 13.14-20 refer to Caligula's plan for the Temple; see J.W. Swain, 'Gamaliel's Speech and Caligula's Statue', *HThR* 35 (1944), 341-9: S.G.F. Brandon, Jesus and the Zealots (Manchester, 1967), 88-92, 230, but the evidence is far from clear.

27 Malalas Chron. 10.315. Malalas' story is accepted by Downey, 193, G.I. Bratianu, 'Empire et 'démocratie' Byzance', *BZ* 37 (1937), 96-7 and by implication, R. Browning, 'The Riot of AD 387 in Antioch: the Role of the Theatrical Claques in the Later Roman Empire', *JRS*

42 (1952), 18. C.H. Kraeling, *JBL* 51 (1932), 148-9 notes that the story is unsubstantiated and argues that the theatre locale is implausible, but accepts that a serious disturbance of some kind probably did take place

28 Jos. *AJ* 18. 262-9, *BJ* 2. 187, *Leg.* 225-42, 245-6

29 Jos. *AJ* 18. 269-83; *BJ* 2. 192-201. Phil. *Leg.* 248, 254 says nothing of his visit to Tiberias and has Petronius write from Ptolemais

30 Phil. *Leg.* 248-54, Jos. *AJ* 18. 272, 274-5, *BJ* 2. 200-202. The date of the harvest is the key to the chronological problems. Philo dates the demonstrations, which he locates only in Ptolemais, to the time of the grain harvest (April-June). Jos. *AJ* 18. 272-4, *BJ* 2. 193, puts the demonstrations, in Tiberias, to the seed time (late autumn). Balsdon (1934), 23 tries to reconcile the two versions by suggesting that Philo's reference to the grain harvest refers to spring-sown cereals harvested in the autumn. News of Caligula's intentions concerning the temple reached the Alexandrian embassy in Rome before August 31, 40 (Caligula's entry into the city)

31 P.W.Barnett, 'Under Tiberius all was Quiet', *NTS* 21 (1975), 569 observes that if Jewish nationalism had been at its height at this period a war of liberation would have occurred.

32 Tac. *Hist.* 5.9. The incident is not mentioned by Suetonius

33 The bribe is accepted as possible by Bilde, *op.cit.* n.23, 85-6, Balsdon 138, Willrich 417

34 Bilde, *op. cit.* n. 23, 89 suggests that there was collaboration between Agrippa and Petronius for the latter to hold things up long enough for Agrippa to work on Caligula

35 Phil. *Leg.* 330-34; Jos. *AJ* 18.289-301. S. Zeitlin, 'Did Agrippa write a letter to Gaius?', *JQR* 56 (1965-66), 22-31 disputes the authenticity of the letter, basically on the grounds that its terms would have been unacceptable to an emperor suffering from insane megalomania.

36 Phil. *Leg.* 333-4

37 Phil. *Leg.* 337; Jos. *AJ.* 18.305, *BJ* 2. 203; see P. Winter, Simeon der Gerechte und Caius Caligula, *Judaica* 12 (1956), 129-32, Bilde *op. cit.* 68, H. Lichtenstein, *Hebrew Union College Annual* 8/9 (1931-2), 300. The Jewish Megillat Ta'anit, at the end of February, was recorded as a day of joy because the work the 'enemy' had ordered to be placed in the temple 'was stopped'

38 Jos. *AJ* 19.278-9; the presence of Jews from Egypt and Syria is inferred from the later proscription in *P.Lond.* 1912.96-98 (Smallwood 370) against bringing in such outsiders

39 Jos. *AJ* 19.279-285. The presence of the Greek deputation is inferred from a comment in the later edict *P. Lond.* 1912. 88 (Smallwood 370), 'after listening to both sides'

40 Jos. *AJ* 19.279, 286-91. Since Claudius is consul-designate the edict

must date to after the elections in 42

13 Caligula the Builder (pages 192–212)

1 Suet. *Aug.* 28.3
2 Jos. *AJ* 19.7-8; Pliny *NH* 35.18; Suet. *Cal.* 22.2,57.1; Dio 59.28.3
3 Pausanias 9.27.3; F. Millar, *Emperor,* 145-6
4 Philo *Leg.* 349-67
5 Suet. *Cal.* 37.3; Jos. *AJ* 19.205 on the other hand asserted that the harbour at Rhegium was his only major construction
6 Tac. *Ann.* 3.31.7; Suet.*Aug.*37; Dio 54.8.4, 59.15.3
7 Dio 59.15.4 combines these apparently separate issues into a single charge. Rogers (1935), 57-8 says that those who had a balance remaining at the end of the year would have been found guilty under the *Lex Iulia de Residuis*
8 Dio 59.15.3-5, 60.17.2
9 Suet. *Cal.* 21; Pliny *NH* 4.10
10 See F. d' Ercé, La Tour de Caligula à Boulogne- sur- Mer', *RA* 1 (1966), 89-96. The towers's name of 'The Old Man' in the Middle Ages is a corruption of the Celtic Alt Maen ('High Stone'). M. Reddé, *Mare Nostrum* (*BEFAR* 250. Rome, 1986), 274 doubts that the familiar Boulogne tower is the one originally constructed under Caligula/Claudius
11 Suet. *Cal.* 21, 37.3. See Willrich, 301; E. Howald and E. Meyer, *Die römische Schweiz* (Zurich, 1940), 196-7, no.377; F. Stähelin, Die Schweiz im römischer Zeit (Basle, 1948), 163-4; G. Walser, 'Die Strassenbau-Tätigkeit von Kaiser Claudius,' *Historia* 19 (1980), 443. n.25
12 Suet. *Vesp.* 5.3; Dio 59.12.3; R.F. Rossi, 'Tracce di lotta politica nel Senato di Caligola', *RFIC* 99 (1971), 164-71. Spain: *CIL* II. 4716, 4639, 6233-4
13 Front. *Aq.* 1.13; Pliny *NH* 36.122. Suet. *Cal.* 21 refers to only one, in the region near Tibur (the Aqua Claudia)
14 Tac. *Ann.* 11.13.2. *ILS* 218 (Porta Praenestina) records breakdowns in the Aqua Claudia in 71 and 81
15 Sen. *Brev.* 20.3; Seneca calls him 'Sextus'; Tac. *Ann.* 1.7.3, 11.31.1
16 Tac. *Ann.* 6.13.1-2; Sen. *Brev.* 18.5; Suet. *Cal.* 26.5, 39.1; Dio 59.17.2. The story is reflected also in Aur. Vic. *Caes.* 4.3
17 Dio 60.11.3; see P. Garnsey, *Famine and Food Supply in the Graeco-Roman World* (Cambridge, 1988), 222-3; G. Rickman, *The Corn Supply of Ancient Rome* (Oxford, 1980), 74
18 Jos. *AJ* 19.205; Willrich's suggestion (p.420) that it was intended for emergencies is difficult to reconcile with the scale of the project
19 Bologna: *ILS* 5674; Antioch: Malalas 10.313-4
20 Degrassi 11, Gallivan, 68-9. Their term may possibly belong to July/

August 41, but the construction would almost certainly have begun under Caligula in any case. Illustrated, E. Nash, *Pictorial Dictionary of Ancient Rome* (New York), I. 206-7

21 Tac. *Ann.* 3.72.2; Suet. *Cal.* 21; Dio 60.6.8-9. Balsdon, 175 mistakenly states that Caligula dedicated the theatre and left off Tiberius' name

22 Suet. *Cal.* 21; Dio 59.10.5; *ILS* 205 (Smallwood 308b)

23 Philo *Leg.* 181; Sen. *Ira* 3.18.4: *CIL* VI. 4346

24 Suet. *Cal.* 54.1, who appears to says that he 'drove chariots in a circus constructed in various places' (*extructo plurifariam circo*); Dio 59.14.6. Humphrey, *Circuses*, 550 seems to believe that the *Circus Vaticanus* and the *Gaianum* are one and the same. In the Regionary Catalogue of the Fourth Century the *Gaianum* is recorded some 300m north-west of the Mausoleum of Hadrian. The large stone structure identified there, some 100m by 300 + m is possibly not a race track but a *naumachia*, possibly built by Trajan; see Toynbee- Warde-Perkins 5, F. Coarelli, *Roma* (Rome, 1985), 360-65; Humphrey, *Circuses*, 683 n.42

25 Pliny *NH* 16. 201, 36.74; Tac. *Ann.* 15.44.7; Suet. *Claud.* 21

26 Pliny *NH* 36.74

27 *CIL* VI.882 The letters are partially erased; E. Iversen, 'The date of the so-called inscription of Caligula on the Vatican obelisk', *JEA* 51 (1965), 149-154 claims that this erasure was the work of Caligula, and that the inscriptions predate him

28 Toynbee- Warde-Perkins, n.30

29 *AE.* 1945. 136

30 G. Townend, 'The Circus of Nero and the Vatican Excavations', *AJA* 62 (1958), 216-8 (see also Iversen). On Claudius: Suet. *Claud.* 21.3; Nero: Tac. *Ann.* 14.14.4; Suet. *Nero* 22.2. On the basis of the position of the inscriptions, C. d'Onofrio, *Gli Obelischi di Roma* (Rome, 1965), 43 assumes a north south orientation of the circus, which, in view of the local topography, seems impossible. On the garden hippodromes: Pliny, *Ep.* 5.6.19,33; see P. Grimal, *Les Jardins Romains* 265-9

31 F. Castagnoli, 'Il circo di Nerone in Vaticano', *RPAA* 32 (1960), 97-121

32 Humphrey, *Circuses*, 124, 552

33 Tac. *Ann.* 14.14.4, 15.44.7; Suet. *Claud.* 21.3, *Nero* 22.2; *SHA* Eleg.23.1

34 L. Casson, *Ships and Seamanship in the Ancient World* (Princeton 1971), 189 calculates that 800-900 tons of lentils would have been needed

35 Suet. *Claud.* 20.3; Pliny *NH* 36.70; see, O. Testaguzza, 'Port of Rome,' *Archaeology* 17 (1964), 173-9, *Portus* (Rome 1970), 109,116-119 Precise dimensions are impossible because of the uncertainty over

the identification of the stern and starboard side (see Casson, *loc.* cit.)
36 Suet. *Cal.* 21; Willrich, 421. Inscriptions from Samos (*IGR* 4.981, 1721), refer to Caligula
37 Suet. *Cal.* 35.3, 37.2
38 The main account is G. Uccelli, *Le Navi di Nemi* (Rome 1950²); see also H. Denham, 'Caligula's Galleys', *Mariner's Mirror* 15 (1929), 347-50; Blake, 23; A. Boethius- J.Warde-Perkins, 49; G.S. Speziale, 'The Roman Galleys in the Lake of Nemi', *Mariner's Mirror* 15 (1929), 333-46 (on attempts to recover the ships)
39 Pipes: *ILS* 8676; Uccelli, 343-4; there is also evidence that at least one brick stamp bore Caligula's name (Uccelli, 344); On the mosaics: V.M. Strocka, 'Ein Missverstandener Terminus des Vierten Stils. Die Casa del Sacello iliaco in Pompeji', *MDAI(R)* 91 (1984), 135 n.4; F. Sear, *Roman Wall and Vault Mosaics* (Heidelberg, 1977) 25,73
40 D. Manacorda, *Un' officina lapidaria sulla Via Appia* (Rome, 1980), nos.28, 29 illustrates dated plaques of the Caligula period with imitation spiral fluted columns, presupposing architectural archetypes
41 Pliny *NH* 36.111; Vatican: Suet. *Cal.* 23.2
42 Horti Lamiani: *CIL* VI 8668; Suet. *Cal.* 59; Horti Maecenatis: Hor. *Sat.* 1.8.14; Dio 55.7.6. On the remains of the supposed throne, see, M. Cimma and E. La Rocca, *Le Tranquille Dimore degli Dei* (Venice, 1986)
43 Varro *LL.* 5.54; see Castagnoli (1964), 186 n.1
44 For the location of these houses, see Tamm, 28-45, F. Coarelli, *Il Foro Romano* (Rome, 1983), II. 25 and 31; on Marc Antony see Tamm, 47, n.23
45 Suet. *Aug.* 29.3, 57.2; Dio 49.15.5, 55.12.4
46 G.F. Caretonni, *Das Haus des Augustus auf dem Palatin* (Mainz, 1983). See also, 'The House of Augustus', *Illustrated London News,* September 1969
47 P. Zanker, 'Der Apollontempel auf dem Palatin', *Città e Architettura nella Roma Imperiale* (Odense, 1983), 24
48 Ovid, *Met.* 1.175-6
49 Velleius 2.81.3; Dio 49.15.5
50 Ovid *AA* 1.73-4; Propertius 2.31; Jos. *AJ* 17. 301 (Josephus loosely says that the crowd was 'in' the temple); see Zanker 26-30
51 Jos. *AJ* 19.117; Tac. *Hist.* 1.27.2
52 Cic. *Cael.* 7. 17, *Har. Resp.* 15.33; Tac. *Ann.* 12.69.1; Suet. *Nero* 8; *AFA* Scheid, 222. On the architectural concept of the Domus Tiberiana, see, Krause; on the Claudian *insula,* Tamm, 30-31
53 Suet. *Cal.* 41.1, 54.2; Dio 59.28.9
54 Suet. *Cal.* 22.2,4; Krause, 17-18; Domus Gelotiana: Suet. *Cal.* 18.3; *CIL* VI.8663
55 Suet. *Cal.* 22.2; Dio 59.28.5

56 Boni in Vagleri BC (1903), 201, Jordan-Hülsen I.3.85, R. Delbrück, 'Der Sydostbau am Forum', *JDAI* 36 (1921), 29; E. Van Deman, 'House of Caligula', *AJA* 28 (1924), 368-98, Lugli, *Roma Antica* (Rome, 1946), 481, 484, Blake II.20

57 See, H. Hurst, G. Morganti, F. Scoppola, 'Area di S. Maria Antiqua, '*BC*91 (1986), 470-81; H. Hurst, 'Nuovi scavi nell'area di Santa Maria Antiqua', *Quaderni del Centro di Studio per l'Archeologia Etrusco-Italica* (1987), forthcoming

58 Sen. *Polyb.* 16.5 seems to suggest that some houses were entered through temples, although his allusion could be to the house of Augustus, linked to the Temple of Apollo. See A. Boethius, *The Golden House of Nero* (Ann Arbor), 63

59 Tamm, 70-71 and 'Ist der Castortempel das vestibulum zu dem Palast des Caligula gewesen', *Eranos* 62 (1964), 146-69

60 T.P. Wiseman, 'Reading the City: History, Poetry, and the Topography of Rome', *JACT* 2(1987), 4, and 'Conspicui postes tectaque digna deo: the Public Image of Aristocratic and Imperial Houses in the late Republic and early Empire', in *L'Urbs. Espace Urbain et Histoire* (Ecole Francaise de Rome, Rome, 1987), 406-9

61 Dio 60.6.8

62 Suet. *Cal.* 22.4; cf. Dio 59.28.2; Lugli (1946), 187; see also Tamm, 66, 71, who suggests that the project was abandoned

63 To be distinguished from the shrine of Augustus on the Palatine: Suet. *Aug.* 5.1; Pliny *NH* 12.94; Dio 56.46.3. Lugli (1941) 29, 58, (1946), 185

64 The sources disagree on who actually finished the Temple. Tac. *Ann.* 6.45.2 says that Tiberius completed the construction but did not get round to the actual dedication; Suet. *Tib.* 47, *Cal.* 21 says explicitly that it was unfinished under Tiberius; Dio 57.10.2 is ambiguous

65 *BMC* 41 (Fig. 18). O.L. Richmond, 'The Temples of Apollo and Divus Augustus on Coins', in *Essays and Studies Presented to William Ridgeway* (1913), 198-212, argues that the sestertius depicts the Temple of Apollo on the Palatine. His view is generally dismissed but is treated with respect by Warde-Perkins, on the grounds that the Ionic order better suits the experimental architecture of Augustus' early reign than the conservatism of Tiberius; Antoninus: *BMC* 916, 924, 938, 2098. P.V. Hill, 'Buildings and Monuments of Rome on Flavian Coins', *NAC* 8 (1979), 207 argues that the temple on Antoninus' coins represents a Domitianic restoration, after the fire of 80; on the temple, see H. Hänlein-Schäfer, *Veneratio Augusti* (*Archaeologia* 39: Rome, 1985)

66 Sen. *Brev.Vit.* 18.5; Jos. *AJ* 19.5-6; Suet. *Cal.* 19, 32.1 Dio 59.17; Aur. Vict. *Epit.* 3.9

67 Alexander served as the obvious model for successful generals of the

late republic and early empire, such as Pompey, Julius Caesar, Antony, Augustus and Germanicus (see Balsdon, *JRS* 26 (1936) 159.160. Weinstock 38, 335 says that a similar story about Pompey, that he wore the purple cloak of Alexander in the triumph of 61 BC, was fabricated by his enemies to discredit him

68 L.H. Savile, *Antiquity* 15 (1941), 228, A. Franciscis *Archaeology* 20 (1967), 215

14 Fit to rule? (*pages 213–241*)

1 Suet. *Cal.* 8.4; 50.2

2 Philo *Leg.* 42; Suet. *Aug.* 78.1; *Cal.* 50.2, 53.2, 54.1

3 Suet. *Aug.* 90; *Tib.* 69, *Cal* 51.

4 Jos. *AJ* 19. 193; Juv. *Sat.* 6.614-7; Suet. *Cal.* 50.2; Jerome, on 94 BC. The story of the aphrodisiac may have originated from a quip of Caligula (Suet. *Cal.* 33) that he would torture Caesonia to discover why he loved her so passionately (see Benediktson, *op. cit.* V n. 5)

5 Suet. *Cal.* 50.2

6 Sen. *Clem.* 1.25.1, *Ben.* 2.16.1, *Ira* 1.20.9; *Tran.* 14.5; *Cons. Pol.* 17.5, Tac. *Ann.* 11.3, 13.3 6, *Hist.* 4.48, Ag. 13

7 Sen. *Ira* 1.20.8; Suet. *Cal.* 22.4; Dio 59.28.8

8 Philo *Leg.* 349-68

9 A. Esser, *Cäsar und die Julisch Claudischen Kaiser im biologisch-ärztlichen Blickfeld* (Leyden, 1958), 139; J. Lucas, Un empereur psychopathe: contribution à la psychologie du Caligula de Suétone', *AC* 36 (1967), 159-189

10 Philo *Leg.* 349-68; Suet. *Cal.* 27.1, 22.3, 23.2, 37.1; Dio 59.18.5, 22.3, 23.2, 37.1

11 M. Grant, 'The Decline and Fall of City Coinage in Spain', *NC* 9 (1949), 93-106, for instance, argues that the Spanish mints were closed because they frequently depicted members of his family

12 Suet. *Cal.* 23.1

13 *ILS* 180 (Rome); *AE* 1980.874 (Aphrodisias); *IGR* 4.79-80 (Mytilene)

14 M. Grant, *Roman Imperial Money* (Edinburgh, 1954), 106; listed as *BMC* p.397.108 (Smallwood 82a)

15 Suet. *Cal.* 23.1; Momigliano, *Personalità*, 212; Garzetti, 85; Ceauçescu, 'Caligula et le legs d'Auguste', *Historia* 22 (1973), 269-83

16 Dio 59.21.6; *AFA* Scheid 224

17 Suet. *Claud.* 11.3; *AFA* xlii (Smallwood 3); on Antony's birthday, see W. Suerbaum, 'Merkwürdige Geburtstage', *Chiron* 10 (1980), 332-4

18 Suet. *Cal.* 23.2; *CIL* 2.1667, 9.3661; *IGR* 4.983. Pliny *NH* 10.45 and Varro *RR* 3.6.1 show that Aufidius Lurco was a completely different person. See P. Wiseman, 'The Mother of Livia Augusta', *Historia* 14 (1965), 333-4

19 R. Lugand, 'Suétone et Caligula', *REA* 32 (1930), 11-12

20 J. Gagé, "Basiléia'. Les Césars, les rois d'Orient et les Mages', (Paris, 1968), 54; P. Lambrechts, 'Caligula dictateur littéraire', *Bull. Inst. Hist. Belge de Rome* 28 (1953), 219-32; E. Köberlein, *Caligula und die ägyptischen Kult* (Meisenheim 1962)

21 This notion has a surprising number of adherents: J. Colin, 'Les Consuls du César-pharaon Caligula et l'héritage de Germanicus', *Latomus* 13 (1954), 408, E. Kornemann, Doppelprinzipat und Reichsteilung im Imperium Romanum (Leipzig-Berlin), 51-3, *Die Stellung der Frau in der vorgriechischen Mittelmeerkutlur, Orient und Antike* Heft 4 (1927), 15, 44, Lambrechts, *op. cit.* 226 n.2, D.M. Pippidi, *Recherches sur le culte impérial* (Paris 1939), 105, H.P. L'Orange, 'Das Geburtsritual der Pharaonen am römishcen Kaiserhof', *SO* 21 (1941), 115

22 Caesar: Nic. Dam. *Caes.* 20 [*F GrHist* 90, F130.20]; Suet *Jul.* 79.3; Antony: Dio 50.4.1; Caligula: Philo *Leg.* 250; Suet. *Cal.* 8.5, 49.2. Josephus mentions only his plan to make a visit the city

23 Jos. *AJ* 19.30, 104; see also, Suet. *Cal.* 52 Sudas. sv *Kaligola*

24 Lucan *Bell. Civ.* 8.831; Jos. *AJ* 18.65-80; Dio 53.2.4, 54.6.

25 See, M. Malaise, La Condition de Pénétration et de Diffusion des Cultes Egyptiens en Italie (Leiden 1972), 226-7, updating Mommsen, CIL 1² p.333, who argued for a correlation in 36-39, followed by G. Wissowa, *Religion und Kultus der Römer* (Munich, 1912), 353; K. Latte, *Römische Religionesgeschichte* (Munich, 1960); Köberlein, 12

26 G.E. Rizzo and A. Bartoli, *Monumenti della pittura antica scoperti in Italia*. III. La *pittura elenistico-Romana, Roma* 2: *Le pitture dell'aula isiaca di Caligola (Palatino)* (Rome 1938), 213; Cumont, *Rev Hist Rel* 114 (1936), 126-9, Boethius- Warde-Perkins 206, Köberlein 24-5

27 H.G. Beyen, 'Les Domini de la Villa de la Farnésine', *Studia Vollgraf* (Amsterdam 1948), 11; K. Schefold, 'Helena im Schutz der Isis', *Studies presented to D. M. Robinson* (St. Louis 1957), II. 1096-1102; R.A..G. Carettoni, 'Roma (Palatino)', *NSA* 25 (1971),323-6; M. Malaise, *Inventaire Préliminaire des Documents Découverts en Italie* (Leiden 1972) 215-9; Roullet, 43-9

28 Jos. *AJ* 19. 104; Suet. *Cal.* 57.4

29 Pliny *NH* 33.41; Roullet, 69,81,83,94

30 Roullet, 324. Tiberius Claudius Callistus, possibly a freedman of Claudius is recorded as *aedituus templi Serapei* (*AE* 1977.28)

31 H. Jeanmaire, La Politique religieuse d'Antoine et de Cleopatre', *Rev Arch* 19 (1924), 258-9, *Le Messianisme de Virgile* (Paris 1930), 152-3

32 That the Romans might not in any case have been impressed by

Hellensistic client monarchs is argued by E. Rawson, 'Caesar's Heritage: Hellenistic Kings and their Roman Equals', JRS 65 (1975), 148-59

33 Suet. *Cal.* 22.1; Hom. *Il.* 2.204. This quotation from Homer seems to be the source of Aurelius Victor's claim that Caligula commanded that he be addressed as *dominus* (*Epit.* 3.8, cf. *Caes.* 39.4)

34 Reports in the sources that at some point he deprived some client-kings, such as Antiochus, Lysanias and Mithridates of the Bosporus, of their kingdoms, possibly arose over confusion caused by revocation of Caligula's *acta* at the beginning of Claudius' reign, after which the kings would have to be reconfirmed in their position by the new emperor (Jos. *AJ* 19.275, *BJ* 2.215; Dio 59.8.2, 60.8.1)

35 Sohaemus: Jos. *AJ.* 20. 158; Dio 59.12.2; see A.A. Barrett, 'Sohaemus, King of Emesa and Sophene', *AJP* 98 (1977), 154. A.H.M. Jones, *op. cit.* n. 38, 456 n.45, identifies his kingdom as Arca, at the northern end of the Lebanon range; Mithridates: Barrett, 'Gaius' Policy in the Bosporus', *TAPA* 107 (1977), 1-9

36 Dio 59.8.2, 24.1; *BM Galatia etc.*, xlvi and 106f; *Sylloge Numorum Graecorum: Levante- Cilicia.* Switzerland I (1986), passim. Coins inscribed Lykaonon also indicate that he received a certain amount of territory north of the Taurus in southern Lycaonia, which may have belonged originally to Archelaus I of Cappadocia (Tac. *Ann.* 6.41; D. Magie, *Roman Rule in Asia Minor* (Princeton 1950), 1338 n.24, 1368 n. 49

37 Suet. *Cal.* 16.3; Tac. *Hist.* 2.81.1

38 Dio 59.24.1; Braund, 108, A.H.M. Jones, The *Cities of the Eastern Roman Provinces* (Oxford 1971²) 211; The name may, however, have honoured Claudius or Nero

39 Dio 59.12.2. See R. Sullivan, 'Thrace in the Eastern Dynastic Network', *ANRW* II. 7.1 (1979), 207-11. Dio's date of 38 is borne out by numismatic evidence, which places the beginning of Polemo II's reign in 38/39; see A.A. Barrett, 'Polemo II of Pontus and M. Antonius Polemo ' *Historia* 27 (1978) 437. n.3. However, an inscription on an altar base dedicated to Poseidon at Cyzicus (*IGR* 4.147) gives the title of king to Rhoemetalces and Polemo, but not to Cotys, suggesting that his confimation as king might have been delayed. Later in 38 Antonia Tryphaena appears to have celebrated the consecration of Drusilla as the New Aphrodite, with games in Cyzicus in which Polemo and Rhoemetalces (but not Cotys) took part (*IGR* 4. 145 cf 144)

40 Suet. *Cal.* 38.1; Dio 60.17.7

41 Philo *Leg.* 285; Dio 59.9.5; Vienne:*ILS* 189, *ILS* 212 (Smallwood 369); Tac. *Ann.* 11.1.2; P. Fabia, *La Table Claudienne de Lyon* (Lyons, 1919), 108-18; A.N. Sherwin-White, The *Roman Citizenship* (Oxford

1973), 237-50, 352 n.1

42 Suet. *Cal.* 39.2 Willrich, 422; Similar restrictions seem to have been imposed on the African mints; see Grant, *op. cit.* XIV n.11, and *Aspects of the Principate of Tiberius* (New York, 1950), 36

43 Pica: *ILS* 1348, where he is called *Procurator Augustorum et pro Legato Raetiae et Vindeliciae et Vallis Poeninae*. See H.-G. Pflaum, *Procurateurs Equestres sous le Haut-Empire Romain* (Paris, 1950), 35, id., *Abrégé des Procurateurs Équestres* (Paris, 1974), 11, G. Walser, 'Zur römischen Verwaltung des Vallis Poeninae', *MH* 31 (1974), 171-2; Trebonius: *ILS* 4864. G. Winkler, 'Noricum und Rom', *ANRW* II 6 (1977), 203 believes that Noricum became a province under Claudius

44 For divergent views, see P.A. Brunt, 'The 'Fiscus' and its Development', *JRS* 56 (1966), 75-91, Fergus Millar, 'The Fiscus in the First Two Centuries', *JRS* 53 (1963), 29-42

45 Tac. *Ann.* 4.4.5-6; Suet. *Aug.* 28.1, 101.4, *Cal.* 16.1; Dio 53.20.1, 56.33.1-2, 59.9.4

46 Suet. *Cal.* 37.3; Dio 59.2.6; the figures presumably come from Caligula himself since Tiberius did not give regular accounts. Philo *Leg.* 9 describes the surplus in general terms as a 'fortune'

47 Suet. *Nero* 30.1 Suetonius says he spent the money in one year, Dio in two

48 Dinner: Sen. *Helv.* 10.4; Fire: Fasti Ostienses (Smallwood 31.30); Suet. *Cal.* 16.3; Dio 59.9.4. For similar action by Tiberius: Tac. *Ann.* 4.64.1 (AD 27), 6.45.1 (AD 36); Gifts: Dio 59.2.5; Ballplayers: Macr. *Sat.* 2.6.5; Demetrius: Sen. *Ben* 7.11.1-2; see, Fergus Millar, *Emperor*, 136

49 *Fasti Ostienses* (Smallwood 31); Suet. *Cal.* 17.2; Dio 59.2.2. Dio's narrative is ambiguous, and it is possible that the *congiaria* were over and above the original award

50 Suet. *Tib.* 76, *Cal.* 16.3, *Claud.* 6.2, *Galb.* 5.2, Dio 59.2.3

51 See G. Bagnagni, 'Trimalchio', Phoenix 8 (1954), 88-9

52 Augustus: Tac. *Ann.* 1.78; Dio 55.25; Tiberius: Tac. *Ann.* 2.42.6; Dio 58.16.2; Caligula: Dio 59.9.6. Suet. *Cal.* 16.3 speaks of his reduction of the *ducesima* (0.5 per cent). If Suetonius' figure is correct Tiberius or Caligula would have had to reduce it once before, unnoticed by the sources

53 On completion of their service the pension of certain legionaries was reduced by Caligula from 12,000 sesterces, the figure established by Augustus, to 6000. This is reported as a punishment for specific units that had been lax, and there is no justification for applying it to the whole Roman army; Suet. *Cal.* 44.1; Dio 55.23.1, see, Willrich, 424

54 Gold: Pliny *NH* 33.79; F. D'Ercé, La mort de Germanicus et les poison de Caligula', *Janus* 56 (1969), 123-48, believes that the process

involved the making of poison; brothel: Suet. *Cal.* 41.1; Dio 59.28.9-10.

55 Pliny *Pan.* 50; Suet. *Cal.* 38.4- 39.2; Dio 59.21.5-6. On the confused account of the selling of gladiators, see Ville, 162 n. 50

56 Suet. *Cal.* 38.3,42; Dio 59.15.1 claims that since he had neither wife nor children, he ordered a decree to be passed through the senate to make it easier for him to inherit. The *Lex Julia de Maritandis Ordinibus* imposed restrictions on the ability of the unmarried to inherit, although the widowed were allowed a grace period of three and later five years; see, Fergus-Millar, Emperor, 145-5

57 Suet. Ner. 6.3. R.S. Rogers, 'The Roman Emperors as Heirs and Legatees', *TAPA* 78 (1947), 146 attributes Nero's exclusion to the fact that his mother had just been exiled

58 Sen. *Tranq.*11.10; Ovid *Pont.* 4.15.5, 5.9

59 We also know that a slave that belonged to Pylaemenes, son of King Amyntas of Galatia, came into Caligula's possession, but it is unclear whether it was by bequest rather than by confiscation: *CIL* 6. 5188

60 Suet. *Cal.* 38.1; Dio 59.10.7, 18.1

61 Augustus: Jos. *BJ* 2.111, *AJ* 17.355; Dio 53.23.7; Tiberius: Tac. *Ann.* 4.20, 6.2.1,19.1; see Fergus Millar, Emperor, 161-3

62 Philo *Flacc.* 148-150

63 Dio 59.15.1

64 Gaius *Dig.* 31.56: *quod principi relictum est, qui antequam dies legati cedat ab hominibus ereptus est, ex constitutione divi Antonini successori eius debetur*

65 Suet. *Cal.* 38.2; Dio 59.15.2. Dio says 'any centurion since the Triumph of Germanicus'. See, J. Gaudemet, "Testamenta Ingrata et pietas Augusti": contribution à l'étude du sentiment impérial', *Studi in onore di Vincenzo Arangio-Ruiz* III (Naples, 1953), 131

66 Jos. *AJ* 19.28, Suet. *Cal.* 40; Dio 59.28.8. Willrich, 425 suggests that the prostitute tax was paid once a month

67 Dio 60.4.1; *CIL* III. 13750 shows soldiers in the Crimea in the reign of Commodus collecting a tax on prostitution; SHA Sev. Alex. 24.3: *lenonum vectigal et meretricum et exsoletorum in sacrum aerarium inferri vetuit, sed sumptibus publicis ad instaurationem theatri, Circi, Amphitheatri Stadii deputavit*

68 Suet. *Cal.* 49.1; Momigliano, *Personalità*, 214

69 Jos. *AJ* 19.129, 159, 228; Suet. *Cal.* 14.3, 60; Z. Yavetz, *Plebs and Princeps* (Oxford, 1969), 114-5

70 Dio 59.6.4, 28.10, 60.25.8. Julius Caesar extended the Saturnalia to three days, where it remained under Augustus (Macr. *Sat.* 1.10.23). Dio says that Caligula created a festival of five days, Suet. *Cal.* 17.2 says that he added one day, perhaps in confusion over the day later abolished. Free seats: Suet. *Cal.* 26.6; Dio 59.13.8; see, Ville 431

71 *Res Gestae* 15.4. Dio 59.6.4 gives the amounts as a drachma (= one Roman denarius), reduced to an obol (= 1/6 of a drachma). If approximate equivalence is intended, this would mean a reduction to a sestertius (1/4 of a denarius). Obol, however, may stand merely for the smallest coin, which in Roman terms would be an as. At all events the money raised would have been enormous, and the donation must, as Pekary points out (*op. cit.* X n.27, 114) have been intended for the manufacture of *gold* statues (against E. Cary, *Dio's Roman History* [Loeb Classical Library. London and New York, 1924], *ad loc.*)

72 Dio 60.6.6

73 Dio 59.13.3, 28.10; on Nero, Suet. *Nero* 45.2

74 Tac. *Ann.* 6. 13.1; Jos. *AJ* 19.24-7; Dio 59.28.11

75 Tac. *Ann.* 1.15.1-2; Suet. *Jul.* 41.2, *Aug.* 40.2

76 Suet. *Cal.* 16.3; Dio 59.9.6, 20.3; Z. Yavetz, *Plebs and Princeps* (Oxford, 1969) 104; H. Siber, 'Die Wahlreform des Tiberius', *Festschrift Paul Koschaker I* (1939), 171-217

77 See T.P. Wiseman, 'The Definition of 'Eques Romanus' in the late Republic and Early Empire', *Historia* 19 (1970), 67-83; Saller, 51-2

78 Ovid *Tr.* 2.89-92, 541-2; on equestrian service in the principate, see P.A. Brunt, 'Principes and Equites', *JRS* 73 (1983), 42-75

79 Suet. *Tib.* 51.2; *Cal.* 26.4, 41.2, 55.1. On *damnatio ad bestias*, see P. Garnsey, *Social Status and Legal Privilege in the Roman Empire* (Oxford, 1970), 129-31; Ville, 236 n. 21

80 Suet. *Cal.* 15.1, 53.2; Dio 59.6.1

81 Dio 59.9.5, alluding presumably, to the additional honorific of the *equus publicus*, unless, in fact, as noted earlier, imperial permission was required even for entry into the order. The reference may even be to enrolment in the decuries; see, Fergus Millar, *Emperor,* 280, n.10

82 Suet. *Cal.* 16.2; Claudius and Vespasian performed *recognitiones* during their censorships (Suet. *Claud.* 16.1, *Vesp.* 9.2). Caligula does not seem to have held a census (but see Wiseman, *op. cit.* n.77, 70 n.21

83 Jos. *AJ* 19.3; Suet. *Cal.* 30.2. B. Levick, 'The senatus consultum from Larinum', *JRS* 73 (1983), 97-115

84 Suet. *Cal.* 26.5; Dio 59.10.1-4, 60.70.1. Only one knight who fought in the arena is named, Atanius Secundus, who had offered to do so in return for Caligula's recovery from illness (Suet. *Cal.* 14.2, 27.2; Dio 59.8.3). Dio 59.10.2 asserts that he sought dispensation from the senate to allow the upper classes to take part in performances. Ville, 233-4 considers the possibility that Caligula instituted *damnatio ad ludum*

85 Suet. *Aug.* 38.2; *Cal.* 16.2; Pliny *NH* 33.33; Dio 59.9.5

86 Suet. Vesp. 2.2; Dio's position is supported by A. Chastgnol, "Latus Clavus" et "adlectio", *RD* 53 (1975), 375-94 and Talbert, 513; it is opposed by M. Griffin, *Seneca* (Oxford, 1984), 50-1, R.P. Saller, *Patronage under the Early Empire* (Cambridge 1982) 51

87 Dio 59.6.1&7, 7.7, 24.8 (see Talbert, 188)

88 Dio 59.8.6; Suet. *Aug.* 35.4 says that Augustus would sometimes abandon this custom altogether and call on all members at random to keep them awake

89 Suet. *Claud.* 9.2. In a similar way Tiberius used to try to delay giving his own opinions before the senators had spoken

90 Suet. *Aug.* 33.3. *Cal.* 16.2; Dio 51.19.6-7, 59.18.2 (see Fergus Millar, *Emperor* 509-10)

91 Dio 59.13.2; Suet. *Cal.* 26.2

92 See, Z.P. Stewart, 'Seianus, Gaetulicus and Seneca', *AJP* 74 (1963), 70-85

93 Tac. *Ann.* 3.49.2, 6.32.6.-7; Suet. *Vit.* 2.5; Pliny *NH* 15.83; Dio 59.27.2-6

94 *ILS* 972; see also Afranius Burrus *ILS* 1321

95 Sen. *Apoc.* 11; Suet. *Cal.* 35.1; Dio 60.5.9, 31.7; see Syme, 'Piso Frugi and Crassus Frugi', *Papers,* 506; McLindon, 126. Caligula supposedly also thought of killing him, but we must exercise the usual caution over claims of what he intended, rather than actually did

96 Tac. *Ann.* 15.25.1; Suet. *Cal.* 35.1; Gelzer, 421-3. On Cincinnatus, *PIR*¹ 3.121.3

97 Sen. *Cons.* 18.1; Dio 59.13.6, 26.9

98 Philo *Leg.* 344; Tac. *Ann.* 3.65.3

99 Philo *Leg.*67; Suet. *Cal.* 13

100 Jos. *AJ* 18. 255-6, 19.201; Suet. *Cal.* 22.1; Plut. *Ant.* 87.4; Dio 59.4

101 Fire: Dio 59.9.4; *Fasti Ostienses* (Smallwood 31.30); will: Dio 59.1.5; *maiestas:* Dio 59.16.8; condemned: Dio 59.18.2; divorces: Suet. *Cal.* 36.2; brothel: Suet. *Cal.* 41.1

102 Sen. *Ira* 3.19.2; Suet. *Cal.* 29, 30.1, 48.1; Dio 59.25.5, 30.1c. It is difficult to know how to evaluate a fragment of the Acts of the Alexandrian Martyrs (P. Giss. 46) that seems to indicate that shortly after his accession Caligula ordered an Egyptian accuser of the Alexandrians to be burned (or branded); see Musurillo, op. cit. V n. 28, 105-116 (and *ZPE* 15 (1974), 1-7)

103 Tac. *Ann.* 6.48

Appendix 2 *(pages 244–254)*

1 B. Levick, 'Propaganda and the Imperial Coinage', *Antichthon* 16 (1982), 104-116; for a discussion see A.H.M. Jones, 'Numismatics and History', *Essays in Roman Coinage presented to Harold*

Mattingly (Oxford 1956), 13-33, M.H. Crawford, 'Roman Imperial Coin Types and the Formation of Public Opinion', *Studies in Numismatic Method presented to P. Grierson* (1983) 47-64; H.V. Sutherland, 'Compliment or Complement. Dr. Levick on Imperial Coin Types', *NC* 146 (1986), 84-93

2 Livy 6.20.13; Sutherland (1976), 62; R.A.G. Carson, 'System and Product in the Roman Mint', *Essays in Roman Coinage presented to Harold Mattingly* (Oxford, 1956), 227-239

3 Mommsen, *RS* 2. 1026-8; K. Kraft, 'S(enatus) C(onsulto)', *JNG* 12 (1962), 7-49; A. Wallace-Hadrill, 'Image and Authority in the Coinage of Augustus', *JRS* 76 (1986), 66-87; Sutherland (1976), 5-21, 'The Formula SC on Augustus' Aes Coinage' (1987), 35-8; for a good basic summary of the problem, see Talbert, 379-83

4 On the distinction see M. Grant, 'The Pattern of Official Coinage in the Early Principate', in *Essays in Roman Coinage presented to Harold Mattingly* (Oxford, 1956), 96-112; but see Trillmich, who argues that the types of local issues were determined at Rome as part of a coherent programme of official propaganda

5 M. Grant, *From Imperium to Auctoritas* (Cambridge 1946), 443-6; *id.* 'The Colonial Mints of Gaius', *NC* 8 (1949), 113-130; M. Campo, 'El problema de las monedas de imitacion de Claudio I en Hispania', *ANum* 4 (1974), 155-63; J. Vogt, *Die Alexandrinischen Münzen* (Stuttgart 1924), 22-3 identified certain coins of Alexandria as Caligulan; they were later rejected by J.G. Milne, *Catalogue of Alexandrian Coins in the Ashmolean Museum* (Oxford 1933), who argued that the mint of Alexandria was closed down also. Recent scholarly opinion is to accept that they might be Caligulan (correspondence: A. Burnett) see, A. Savio, *La Coerenza di Caligola nella Gestione della Monete* (Florence 1988), 1-51

6 Strabo 4.3.2; *CIL* xiii, 1820, 1499. Sutherland (1976), 46-8 reviews the evidence

7 Mattingly, *BMC* cxlii-iii

8 Sutherland (1976),64; *id.* 'The Mints of Lugdunum and Rome under Caligula: an Unsolved Problem', *NAC* 10 (1981), 297-9; *RIC*² 103 n.1

9 J.-B., Giard, 'Les émissions d'or et d'argent de Caligula dans l'atelier de Lyon' *RN* (1976), 69-81. There is a danger that these were forgers' dies. See also H.-m von Kaenel, 'Die Organisation der Münzprägung Caligulas', *SNR* 66 (1987), 42-3; A.M. Burnett, 'The Authority to Coin', *NC* 137 (1977), 62, Trillmich, 80-86, H.B. Mattingly, *NC* 145 (1985), 256, Savio, *op. cit.* n.5, 73

10 Mattingly, 'Some Historical Roman Coins of the First Century', *JRS* 10 (1920) 37-38; G.G. Belloni, 'Significati storico-politici delle figurazioni e delle scritte dell Monete a Augusto a Traiano', *ANRW*

(1974), 2.1.1043–44); Sutherland, 'Gaius and the Deification of Tiberius' (1987), 65–8

11 R. Brilliant, 'An Early Imperial Portrait of Caligula', *AAAH* 4 (1969), 13–7

12 A. Savio, 'Note su alcune monete di Gaio-Caligula', *NAC* 2 (1973), 107–119

13 H.W. Ritter, 'Adlocutio und Corona Civica unter Caligula und Tiberius', *JNG* 21 (1971), 81–96; Sutherland 'Gaius and the Praetorians' (1987), 70; cf. A. Robertson, 'Two Groups of Roman Asses from North Britain', *NC* 8 (1968), 63

14 For the identification of a gilded bronze equestrian group as Nero and Drusus, see F. Nicosia, *Bronzi Dorati da Cartoceto* (Florence 1987).

15 J. Eckhel, *Doctrina Numorum Veterum* (Vienna, 1796), 6.224

16 There is, unfortunately, no consistency in the dates by which the *designatio* was determined, but G. Elmer, 'Die Kleinkupferprägung von Augustus bis Nero', *NZ* 67 (1934), 24 argued that on the basis of frequency the 39 quadrans issue must have appeared late in the year

17 A.U. Stylow 'Die Quadranten des Caligula als Propaganda Münzen', *Chiron* 1 (1971), 285–90

18 Suet. *Cal.* 15.1

19 H.M. von Kaenel, 'Augustus, Caligula oder Claudius', *GNS* 28 (1978), 39–44; B.E. Levy, 'Caligula's Radiate Crown', *SM* 38 (1988), 101–107; H. Küthmann 'Claudius, Germanicus und Divus Augustus', *JNG* 10 (1959/60), 47–60 claims that the seated figure is Claudius

20 Y. Meshorer, *Ancient Jewish Coinage* (New York, 1982)[2] II. 53

21 *RIC*[2] 1.107; K. Christ, *Gymnasium* 64 (1957), 516 n.79; but D. Mannsperger, 'ROM. ET AUG. Die Selbstdarstellung des Kaisertums in der römische Reichspragung', *ANRW* II. 1 (1974) 948 no. 74 assigns BMC 93–100 to Tiberius (see also Trillmich 48. n.106)); Küthmann op. cit. and H.M. von Kaenel, 'Die Fundmünzen aus Avenches', *SNR* 51 (1972), 86 nr.536 believe it was issued by Claudius

22 See recently Küthmann, Die Prägzeit der Agrippa Asse', *SMzB* 4 (1954), 73 (Tiberius); H. Chantraine, *Novaesium III* (*Limes Forschungenen* Bd. 8, Berlin 1969) (Caligula); C.M. Kraay, *Die Münzfunde von Vindonissa* (Basel 1962), 35 (Tiberius to Nero), S. Jameson, 'The Date of the Asses of M. Agrippa', *NC* (1966), 95–124 (Tiberius to Claudius)

23 J. Nicols, 'The Chronology and Significance of the M. Agrippa asses', *ANSMusN* 19 (1974), 65–86. Aes for a donative seems unlikely, but see *BMC* 33ff and M. Crawford 'Money and Currency in the Roman World', *JRS* (1970), 45,47–8; there is no evidence that Caligula actually visited Vindonissa

24 A. Vives, *La Moneda Hispanica* (Madrid, 1926), 4.84. nos 66–77; W. Trillmich, 'Zur Münzprägung des Caligula von Caesaraugusta', *MDAI (M)* 14 (1973), 151–73; Küthmann, *op. cit.*, n.22 dates all the moneyers to Caligula's first year
25 Trillmich, 113
26 C.J. Howgego, *Greek Imperial Countermarks* (London 1985), nos 521–4
27 For a recent survey of the Arval Brotherhood, see M. Beard, 'Writing and Ritual', *PBSR* 53 (1985), 114–62
28 37: *AE* 1969/70.100; *Fasti Ostienses* (Smallwood 31.15); Suet. *Cal.* 17.1; Dio 59.6.5; 41: *AE* 1978.137; Nerva: *AE* 1982.200
29 A partial list of Caligulan statue bases appears in M. Stuart, 'How were Imperial Portraits distributed throughout the Roman Empire?' *AJA* 43 (1939), 601–17
30 Phil. *Leg.* 134–6; Suet. *Cal.* 22.3; Dio 59.4.4, 19.2, 26.3, 28.3, 30.1a, 60.4.5; *ILS* 8972 (Smallwood 361)

BIBLIOGRAPHY

Abbreviations

Standard abbreviations are used for Classical journals and Collections

AFA	Henzen, W., *Acta Fratrum Arvalium* (Berlin, 1874)
AFA Scheid	Scheid, J., & Broise, H., 'Deux nouveaux fragments des Actes des Frères Arvales de l'année 38 ap. J.-C.', *MEFR* 92 (1980), 215-48
Alföldi	Alföldi, A., *Die monarchische Repräsentation im römischen Kaiserreiche* (Darmstadt, 1970) = *MDAI(R)* 49 (1934), 1-118 & 50 (1935), 1-171
Balsdon	Balsdon, J.P.V.D., *The Emperor Gaius* (Oxford, 1934)
Balsdon (1934)	Balsdon, J.P.V.D., 'Notes concerning the principate of Gaius,' *JRS* 24 (1934), 13-24
Béranger	Béranger, J. 'La 'prévoyance' (providentia) impériale et Tacite, Annales, I, 8', in *Principatus. Etudes de notions et d'histoire politiques dans l'Antiquité gréco-romaine* (Geneva, 1973) 331-52 [= *Hermes* 88 (1960) 475-92]
Bergener	Bergener, A., *Die Führende Senatorenschicht im Frühen Prinzipat 14-68 n.Ch.* (Bonn, 1965)
Blake	Blake, M.E., *Roman Construction in Italy from Tiberius through the Flavians* (Washington, 1959)
BMC	Mattingly, H., *A Catalogue of the Roman Coins in the British Museum* (London, 1923)
Braund	Braund, D.C., *Rome and the Friendly Kings* (New York, 1984)
Brunt	Brunt, P.A., 'Lex de Imperio Vespasiani', *JRS* 67 (1977) 95-116
Campbell	Campbell, J. B., *The Emperor and the Roman Army* (Oxford, 1984)
Crawford	Crawford, M.H., *Roman Republican Coinage* (Cambridge, 1955)
Dabrowski	Dabrowski, A.M., *Problems in the tradition about*

the principate of Gaius (Diss. Toronto, 1972)

Degrassi — Degrassi, A., *I fasti consolari dell'impero romano dal 30 avanti Cristo al 613 dopo Cristo* (Rome, 1952)

EJ — Ehrenberg, V., and Jones, A.H.M., *Documents Illustrating the Reigns of Augustus and Tiberius* (Oxford, 1955[2])

Espérandieu — Espérandieu, E., *Inscriptions Latines de Gaule* (Paris, 1929)

Faur — Faur, J.C., 'La Première Conspiration contre Caligula', *RBPh* 51 (1973), 13-50

Fergus Millar, Emperor — Fergus Millar, *The Emperor in the Roman World* (Ithaca, 1977)

Fishwick — Fishwick, D., *The Imperial Cult in the Latin West* (Leiden, 1987)

Gallivan — Gallivan, P.A., 'The fasti for the reign of Gaius', *Antichthon* 13 (1979), 66-9

Garzetti — Garzetti, A., *From Tiberius to the Antonines*, tr. J.R.Foster (London, 1974)

Gascou — Gascou, J., 'M. Licinius Crassus Frugi, légat de Claude en Maurétanie, *Mélange P. Boyancé*, (Paris, 1974) 299-310

Gelzer — Gelzer, M., 'Iulius Caligula' *RE* 10 (1918), 381-423

Grenade — Grenade, P., *Essai sur les origines du principat. Investiture et renouvellement des pouvoirs impériaux* (Paris, 1961)

Herz — Herz, P., 'Diva Drusilla. Ägyptisches und Römisches im Herscherkult zur Zeit Caligulas', *Historia* 30 (1981), 324-36

Humphrey, Circuses — Humphrey, John H., *Roman Circuses. Arenas for Chariot Racing* (London, 1983)

Humphrey — Humphrey, John W., *An Historial Commentary on Cassius Dio's Roman History, Book 59 (Gaius Caligula)* (Diss. University of British Columbia, 1976)

Köberlein — Köberlein, E., *Caligula und die ägyptischen Kulte* (Meisenheim, 1962)

Krause — Krause, C. et al., *Domus Tiberiana: Nuove Richerche, Studi di Restauro* (Zurich, 1985)

Levick (1976) — Levick, B., *Tiberius the Politician* (London, 1976)

Linnert — Linnert, U., *Beiträge zur Geschichte Caligulas* (Diss. Jena, 1908).

Magi — Magi, F., 'In Circo Vaticano in base alli più Recente Scoperte', *RPAA* 45 (1972-3), 37-73

Magie — Magie, D. *Roman Rule in Asia Minor* (Princeton, 1950)

Marsh — Marsh, F.B., *The Reign of Tiberius* (Oxford, 1931)

317

Maurer	Maurer, J.A., *A commentary on C. Suetoni Tranquilli, Vita C. Caligulae Caesaris, Chapters I-XXI* (Philadelphia, 1949)
Meise	Meise, E., *Untersuchungen zur Geschichte der Julisch-Claudischen Dynastie* (Munich, 1969)
Momigliano, *Personalità*	Momigliano, A., 'La personalità di Caligola', *Annali della R. Scuola Normale Superiore di Pisa. Lettere, Storia e Filosophia* NS 1 (1932),205-28
Momigliano, *Osservazioni*	Momigliano, A., 'Osservazioni sulle fonte di Caligola, Claudio, Nerone', *RAL* 8 (1932) 293-336
Mommsen *GS*	Mommsen, Th. *Gesammelte Schriften* (Berlin, 1904, reprinted Berlin, 1965)
Mommsen *RS*	Mommsen, Th., *Römisches Staatsrecht* (Lepizig, 1887³, reprinted Graz, 1963)
Nony	Nony, D., *Caligula* (Paris, 1986)
Parsi	Parsi, B., *Designation et Investiture de l'Empereur Romain* (Paris, 1963)
Ritterling	Ritterling, E., 'Legio', *RE* 12 (1924-5) 1186-1829
Roullet	Roullet, A., *The Egyptian and Egyptianizing Monuments of Imperial Rome* (Leiden, 1972)
Romanelli	Romanelli, P., *Storia dele Province Romane del' Africa* (Rome, 1959)
Scheid	Scheid, J., *Les Frères Arvales. Recruitement et origine sociale sous les empereurs julio-claudiens* (Paris, 1975)
Seager	Seager, R., *Tiberius* (London, 1972).
Sealey	Sealey, R., 'The political attachments of L. Aelius Seianus', *Phoenix* 15 (1961), 97-114
Simpson (1980)	Simpson, C.J., 'The "Conspiracy" of A.D. 39', *Studies in Latin Literature and Roman History* II (Collection Latomus 168, 1980), 347-66
Smallwood, *Jews*	Smallwood, E.M., *The Jews under Roman Rule* (Leyden 1976, rep. 1981)
Smallwood, *Legatio*	Smallwood, E.M., *Philonis Alexandrini. Legatio ad Gaium* (Leyden 1970²)
Stein	Stein, A., *Die präfekten von Ägypten in der römischen Kaiserzeit* (Bern, 1950)
Stewart	Stewart, Z., 'Seianus, Gaetulicus and Seneca', *AJP* 74 (1953), 70-85
Sutherland (1976)	Sutherland, H.C.V., *The Emperor and the Coinage* (London 1976)
Sutherland (1987)	Sutherland, H.C.V., *Roman History and Coinage, 44 BC-AD 69* (Oxford, 1987)
Syme, *Tacitus*	Syme, R., *Tacitus* (Oxford, 1958)
Syme, *Papers*	Syme, R., *Roman Papers* (Oxford, 1979-87) vol. 1-3, unless otherwise noted
Syme, *Aristocracy*	Syme R., *The Augustan Aristocracy* (Oxford, 1986)

Taeger	Taeger, F., *Charisma. Studien zur Geschichte des antiken Herrscherkultes* Vol. 2 (Stuttgart, 1960)
Talbert	Talbert, R.J.A., *The Senate of Imperial Rome* (Princeton, 1984)
Tamm	Tamm, B., *Auditorium und Palatium* (Stockholm Studies in Classical Archaeology 2, Stockholm, 1963)
Thomasson	Thomasson, B.E., *Die Statthalter der römischen Provinzen Nordafrikas von Augustus bis Diocletianus* (Lund, 1960)
Timpe (1960)	Timpe, D., 'Römische Geschichte bei Flavius Josephus', *Historia* 9 (1960), 474-502
Timpe (1962)	Timpe, D., *Untersuchungen zur Kontinuät des frühen Prinzipats* (Historia Einzelschrift 5, Wiesbaden, 1962).
Toynbee-Ward Perkins	Toynbee, J.M.C. and Ward Perkins, J.B., *The Shrine of St Peter and the Vatican Excavations* (New York, 1957)
Trillmich	Trillmich, W., 'Familienpropaganda der Kaiser Caligula und Claudius. Agrippina Maior und Antonia Augusta auf Münzen', Antike Münzen & geschnittene Steine, Band 8 (Berlin, 1978)
Ucelli	Ucelli, G. *Le Navi di Nemi* (Rome, 1950²)
Ville	Ville, G., *La gladiature en Occident des origines à la mort de Domitien* (*BEFAR* 245: Rome, 1981)
Weinstock	Weinstock S., *Divus Julius* (Oxford, 1971)
Willrich	Willrich, H., 'Caligula', *Klio* 3 (1903), 85-118; 288-317; 397-470

Select Bibliography of Works relating to Caligula
(other than works listed under Abbreviations)

Aalders, G.J.D., *Caligula, zoon van Germanicus* (Assen, 1959)

Aalders, G.J.D., 'Helios Gaios', *Mnemosyne* 13 (1960), 242-243

Aiardi, A., 'Optimus Maximus Caesar: Considerazioni sull' Interesse di Caligula per il Culto di Giove', *AIV* 136 (1978), 99-108

Alföldi, A., *Der Vater des Vaterlandes im römischen Denken* (Darmstadt, 1971)

Allen, W., 'The political atmosphere of the reign of Tiberius', *TAPA* 72 (1941), 1-25

Allison, J.E. and Cloud, J.D., 'The Lex Julia Maiestatis', *Latomus* 21 (1962), 711-31

Auguet, R., *Caligula ou le pouvoir à vingt ans* (Paris, 1975)

Baldwin, B., Suetonius (Amsterdam, 1983)

Balsdon, J.P.V.D., 'The principates of Tiberius and Gaius', *ANR W* II 2

(1975), 86-94

Bauman, R.A., *Impietas in Principem* (Munich, 1974)

Bellen, H., *Beitrage zur Rechtsprechung der stadtrömischen Gerichte-unter dem Prinzipat des Gaius und Claudius* (Diss. Köln, 1955)

Bellen, H., 'Verstaatlichung des Privatvermögens Römischer Kaiser', *ANRW* 2.1 (1972), 94-102

Bellen, H., *Die Germanische Leibwache der römischen Kaiser des Julisch-Claudischen Hauses* (Wiesbaden, 1981)

Bell, H.I., 'A New Fragment of the Acta Isidori', *APF 10* (1932), 5-16

Benediktson, D.T., 'Caligula's Madness: Madness or Interictal Temporal Lobe Epilepsy', *CW* 82 (1989), 370-5

Béranger, J., L'hérédité du Principat', *REL* 17 (1939), 171-87

Bernardi, A., 'L'interesse di Caligola per la successione del rex Nemorensis e l'arcaica regalitá nel Lazio,' *Athenaeum 31* (1953), 273-87

Beyen, H.G., 'Les domini de la villa de la Farnesine', *Studia Vollgraf* (Amsterdam, 1948), 3-21

Bicknel, P., 'Gaius and the sea-shells', *AClass* 5 (1962), 72-74

Bicknell, P., 'The Emperor Gaius' Military Activities in A.D. 40,' *Historia* 17 (1968), 496-505

Bilde, P., 'The Roman Emperor Gaius (Caligula)'s Attempt to Erect his Statue in the Temple of Jerusalem,' *STh 32* (1978), 67-93

Blazquez, J.M., 'Propaganda dinástica y culto imperial en las anuñaciones de Hispania', *Numisma* 23-24 (1973-74), 311-29

Bourne, F.C., *The Public Works of the Julio-Claudians and Flavians* (Diss. Princeton, 1946)

Braun, E., 'Zum carcer Romanus (Sueton. *Calig.* 27.2)', *JOEAI* 37 (1948), 175-177

Brilliant, R., 'An Early Imperial Portrait of Caligula', *AAAH* 4 (1969) 13-17

Burian, J., 'Caligula und die Militärrevolte am Rhein', *Mnema V. Groh* (Prague 1964, 25-9

Campo, M., 'El problema de las monedas de imitación de Claudio I en Hispania', *A. Num.* 4 (1974), 155-163

Carcopino, J., 'La mort de Ptolémée roi de Mauretanie', *Le Maroc Antique* (Paris, 1943⁵) 191-9

Carettoni, G., 'Roma (Palatino)' *NSA* 25 (1971), 323-6

G.F. Carter et al. 'Chemical compositions of copper-based Roman coins. Imitations of Caligula, Claudius and Nero,' *RN* 20 (1978), 69-88

Castaglioni, F., 'Il circo di Nerone in Vaticano', *RPAA* 32 (1959-60), 97-121

Castagnoli, F., 'Note sulla topographia del Palatino e del Foro Romano', *Arch Class* 16 (1964), 173-99

Ceausescu, P., 'Caligula et le legs d'Auguste', *Historia* 22 (1973), 269-83

Ceausescu, P., 'ALTERA ROMA- Histoire d'une folie politique', *Historia*

25 (1976), 79-107

Cerfaux L. and Tondriau J., *Le Culte des Souverains* (Tournai, 1956)

Charlesworth, M.P., 'The tradition about Caligula', *Cambridge Historical Journal* 4 (1933), 105-19

Charlesworth, M.P. 'Some Observations on Ruler Cult, Especially in Rome', *HThR* 28 (1935), 5-44

Chastagnol, A., 'Latus clavus et Adlectio. L'accès des hommes nouveaux au Sénat romain sous le haut empire', *RD* 53 (1975), 375-94

Chastagnol, A. 'La naissance de l'*ordo senatorius*', *MEFR* 85 (1973), 583-607

Clarke, G.W., 'Seneca the Younger under Caligula', *Latomus* 24 (1965), 62-69

Colin, J., 'Les consuls du César-pharaon Caligula et l'héritage de Germanicus, *Latomus* 13 (1954), 394-416

Curry, M.R., 'The aes quadrans of Caligula', *NAJN* 7 (1968), 9-11

Davies, R.W., 'The abortive invasion of Britain by Gaius,' *Historia* 15 (1966) 124-28

Delbrueck, R., 'Der Sydostbau am Forum Romanum' *JDAI* 36 (1921), 8-33

Deman, E. van, 'House of Caligula', *AJA* (1924), 368

D'Ercé, F., 'La tour de Caligula à Boulogne-sur-mer,' *Rev. Arch.* NS 1 (1966), 89-96

D'Ercé, F., 'La mort de Germanicus et les poisons de Caligula', *Janus* 56 (1969), 123-48

Dessau, H., *Geschichte der römischen Kaiserzeit II.* 1 (Berlin 1924-1926)

Downey, A *History of Antioch in Syria from Seleucus to the Arab Conquest* (Princeton, 1961)

Dumont, C., *C. César, empereur epileptique. Quelques aspects d'une personanalité.* (Thesis Liège, 1964)

Eitrem, S., 'Zur Apotheose', *SO* 10 (1932), 31-56

Enking, R., 'Minerva Mater', *JDAI* 59-60 (1944-45), 111-24

Enrile, D., *Seneca, Caio Cesare, Claudio* (Palermo, 1946)

Esser, A., *Cäsar und die Julisch-Claudischen Kaiser im biologisch-ärztlichen Blickfeld* (Leyden, 1958)

Euzennat, M., 'L'histoire municipale de Tigzirt', *Mélanges d'Archéologie et d'histoire* 67 (1955), 127-48

Euzennat, M., 'Le temple C de Volubilis et les origines de la cité', *BAM* 2 (1957), 51

Fabbrini, L. 'Caligola: il ritratto dell' adolescenza e il ritratto dell' apoteosi', *MDAI(R)* 73/4 (1966/67), 134-46

Faur, J.C., 'Un nouveau visage de Caligula', *A. Arch.* 42 (1971), 35-42

Faur, J.C., 'Un discours de l'empereur Caligula au Sénat (Dio, *Hist. rom.* LIX, 16)', *Klio* 40 (1978), 439-47

Faur, J.C., 'Caligula et la Maurétanie: La Fin de Ptolémée', *Klio* 55

(1973), 249–71

Feldman, L.H., 'The Sources of Josephus' 'Antiquities,' Book 19', *Latomus* 21 (1962), 320–33

Fishwick, D., 'The Annexation of Mauretania', *Historia* 20 (1971), 467–87

Fishwick D., and Shaw, B.D., 'Ptolemy of Mauretania and the Conspiracy of Gaetulicus', *Historia* 25 (1976), 491–4

Fittschen, K., Die Bildnisse der mauretanischen Könige und ihre stadtrömischen Vorbilder', *MDAI(M)* 15 (1974), 156–73

Fraccaro, 'C. Herennius Capito di Teate, procurator di Livia, di Tiberio e di Gaio', *Athenaeum* 28 (1940), 141–44

Frei-Stolba, R., Inoffizielle Kaisertitulaturen im 1. und 2.Jahrhundert n. Chr.', *MH* 26 (1969), 8–39

Fuhrmann, H., 'C. Herennius Capito', *Epigraphica* 2 (1940), 25–9

Gagé, J., Un manifeste dynastique de Caligula', *REA* 37 (1935), 165–84

Gagé, J. *'Basiléia'. Les Cesars, les rois d'Orient et les "Mages"* (Paris, 1968)

Gagé, J., 'L'étendard d' Eutychus. Sur un mot de Cassius Chaeréa, le meurtrier de Caligula', *Hommages M. Renard* II. 275–83

Garnsey, P., *Social Status and Legal Privilege in the Roman Empire* (Oxford, 1970)

Gatti, C., 'Considerazioni sul culto imperiale nel quadro della politica di Gaio', *CISA* 7 (1980), 161–73

Gatti, C., 'Un compromesso politico dell' imperatore Gaio all' inizio del suo regno. Nota in margine a Dione Cassio LIX. 3.1-2', *Miscellanea di Studi Classici in onore di Eugenio Manni* (Rome, 1980) III 1055–64

Gaudemet, J., ' "Testamenta Ingrata et pietas Augusti" ': contribution à l'étude du sentiment impérial', *Studi in onore di Vincenzo Arangio-Ruiz III* (Naples, 1953), 115–37

Ghetti, A., et al., *Esplorazioni sotto la confessione di San Pietro in Vaticano eseguite negli anni* 1940-49 (Vatican City, 1951)

Giacchero, Marta, 'Le reminiscenze erodotee in Seneca e la condanna di Caligola', *Sandalion* 3 (1980), 175–189

Giard, J.-B., 'Pouvoir central et libertés locales: le monnayage en bronze de Claude avant 50 apres J.-C.', *RN* 12 (1970), 33–60

Giard, J.-B., 'Les émissions d'or et d'argent de Caligula dans l'atelier de Lyons', *RN* 18 (1976), 69–81

Goodyear, F.R.D., 'Tiberius and Gaius: their Influence and Views on Literature,' *ANRW* 2. 32. 1 (1984) 603–10

Grady, I.E., 'Dio LIX.25.5b, a note', *RhM* 124 (1981), 261–67

Grant, M., 'The colonial mints of Gaius', *NC* (1948), 113–30

Grant, M., 'The Decline and Fall of City-Coinage in Spain', *NC* 9 (1949), 93–106

Grant, M., *Roman Imperial Money* (Edinburgh, 1954)

Grenade, P. 'Problemes que pose l'avènement de Caligula', *REL* 33 (1955), 53-5

Grimal, P., 'L'"exil" du roi Ptolémée et la date du De Tranquillitate animi', *REL* 50 (1972), 211-23

Grimal, P., 'Les allusions à la vie politique de l'empire dans les tragedies de Sénèque', *CRAI* (1979), 205-20

Gross, W.H., 'Caligula oder zulässige und unzulässige Interpretationen eines römischen Herrscherbildes', *WZ Berl* 31 (1982), 205-7

Guey, J., 'Les bains d'or de Caligula, Suétone, Cal. 42.3', *BSFN* 31 (1976), 50

Guey, J., 'Les bains d'or de Caligula, immensi aureorum acervi. Suétone, Cal. 42.3', *MEFR* 89 (1977), 443-6

Hammond, M., *The Augustan Principate* (Cambridge Mass., 1933)

Hammond, M., 'The Tribunician Day during the Early Empire', *MAAR* 15 (1938), 23-61

Hammond, M., 'Imperial Elements in the Formula of the Roman Emperors during the First Two and a Half Centuries of the Empire', *MAAR* 25 (1957), 19-64

Hanson, A.E., 'Evidence for a reduction in laographia at Philadelphia in Gaius' second year', *Proc. XVIth Int. Congr. Pap.*, 345-55

Hanson, A.E., 'Caligulan Month Names at Philadelphia and Related Matters', *Atti XVII cong. intern. pap. III*, 1287-95

Haussoullier, B., 'Caligula et le temple d'Appolon Didyméen', *RPh* 23 (1899), 147-64

Hayne, L., 'The last of the Aemilii Lepidi', *AC* 42 (1973), 497-507

Hermann, P., *Der römische Kaisereid* (Göttingen, 1968)

Herouville P.d', 'Le cheval de Caligula', *MB* 32 (1928), 45-7

Hertel, D., 'Caligula-Bilnisse vom Typus Fasanerie in Spanien. Ein archäologischer Beitrag zur Geschichte des Kaisers Caius', *MDAI* (M) 23 (1982), 258-95

Herz, P., 'Die Arvalakten des Jahres 38 n. Chr. Eine Quelle zur Geschichte Kaiser Caligulas', *BJ* 181 (1981), 89-110

Hill, P.V., 'Buildings and Monuments of Rome as Coin Types,' *NC* 143 (1983), 81-94

Hofman, M., 'Ptolemaios von Mauretanien', *RE* 17 (1959), 1768-87

Homo, L., *Le Haut-Empire* (Paris, 1933), 236-46

Humphrey, John W., 'The Three Daughters of Agrippina Major', *AJAH* 4 (1979), 125-143

Humphrey, John W. and Swan, P.M., 'Cassius Dio on the Suffect Consuls of A.D. 39', *Phoenix* 37 (1983), 324-7

Hurst, H, Morganti, G., Scoppola, F., 'Area di S. Maria Antiqua', *BC* 91 (1986), 470-81

Hurst, H., 'Nuovi scavi nell'area di Santa Maria Antiqua', *Quaderni del Centro di Studio per l'Archeologia Etrusco-Italica* (1987), forthcoming

Iversen, E., 'The date of the so-called inscription of Caligula on the Vatican obelisk', *JEA* 51 (1965), 149-54

Jakobson, A. & Cotton, H.M., 'Caligula's Recusatio Imperii', *Historia* 34 (1985), 497-503

Jerome, T.S., *Aspects of the Study of Roman History* (New York & London, 1923)

Johansen, F.S., 'Antike Porträts von Caligula in der Ny Carslberg Glyptothek', *WZ Berl* 31 (1982), 223-24

Johansen, F.S., 'The Sculpted Portraits of Caligula', *Ancient Portraits in the J. Paul Getty Museum*, Vol I 1987, 86-107

Jonas, E., 'A Damnatio memoriae alkalmazåsa egyik dupondiusån Caligula', *Numizm. Közlöny* 36-37 (1937-38), 89-91

Jordan H., *Topographie des Stadt Rom im Altertum*. vol 1 (part 3) revised Ch. Huelsen (Berlin, 1907)

Jucker, H., 'Die Bildnisstrafen gegen den toten Caligula', *Festchr. U. Hausmann*, 110-18

Jucker, H., 'Caligula', *Arts in Virginia* 13 (1973), 17-25

Jucker, H., 'Der Grosse Pariser Kameo', *JDAI* 91 (1977), 211-50

Jung, H., 'Die Thronerhebung des Claudius', *Chiron* 2 (1972), 367-86

Kaenel, H.-M. von, 'Augustus, Caligula oder Claudius?', *GNS* 28 (1978), 39-44

Kajava, M., 'The Name of Cornelia Orestina/Orestilla', *Arctos* 18 (1984), 23-30

Katz, R.S., 'The Illness of Caligula', *CW* 65 (1972), 223-5

Katz, R.S., 'Caligula's illness again', *CW* 70 (1977), 451

Kneissl, P., *Die Siegestitulatur der römischen Kaiser. Hypomnemata* 23 (Göttingen, 1969)

Koll, R.A., *The Ruler Cult under Caligula* (Diss., Case Western Reserve, 1932)

Kornemann, E. *Doppelprinzipat und Reichsteilung im Imperium Romanum* (Leipzig-Berlin, 1930)

Kotula, T., 'Encore sur la mort de Ptolémée, roi de Maurétanie', *Archeologia* 15 (1964), 76-94

Kretschmer, M., 'A portrait in marble', *CJ* 37 (1942), 210-12

Kunisch, N., 'Neue römische Porträts der Charelottenburger Antikenabteilung', *AA* 82 (1967), 611-15 = *Burlington Magazine* 109 (1967), 329

Kyrieleis, H., 'Zu einem Kameo in Wien', *AA* 85 (1970), 492-98

Laffranchi, L., 'La monetazione imperatoria e senatoria di Claudio I, durante il quadriennio 41-44 d.C.', *RIN* 51 (1949), 41-51

Lambrechts, P., 'Caligula dictateur littéraire', *Bull. Inst. Hist. Belge de Rome* 28 (1953), 219-32

Laser, S., 'Zur Ikonographie des Caligula', *AA* 69 (1954), 241-51

Lanciani, *The Ruins and Excavations of Rome* (London, 1897)

Lesuisse, L., 'La nomination de l'empereur et le titre d' "imperator", *AC* 30 (1961), 415-28

Lesuisse, L., Le titre de Caesar et son évolution au cours de l'histoire de l'empire', *LEC* 29 (1961), 271-87

Lesuisse, L., 'L'aspect héréditaire de la succession impériale sous les Julio-Claudiens', *LEC* 30 (1962), 32-50

Levy, B.E., 'Caligula's Radiate Crown', *SM* 152 (1988), 101-107

L'Orange, H.P., 'Das Geburtsritual der Pharaonen am romischen Kaiser-hof', *SO* 21 (1941), 105-16

Lucas, J., 'Un empereur psychopathe. Contribution à la psychologie du Caligula de Suétone', *AC* 36 (1967), 159-89

Lugand, R. 'Suétone et Caligula', *REA* 32 (1930), 9-13

Lugli, G., 'Aedes Caesarum in Palatio e Templum Novum divi Augusti *BCAC* 69 (1941), 29-58

Lugli, G., *Roma Antica* (Rome, 1946)

MacDowall, D.W., 'The PNR type of Claudius', *GNS* 18 (1968), 80-6

MacDowall, D.W., 'CAC, a Claudian countermark from lower Germany', *GNS* 20 (1970), 37-41

Magi, F., 'Le iscrizioni recentemente scoperte sull' obelisco Vaticano', *Stud Rom* 11 (1963), 50-56

Maj, B.M. Felletti, *Caligola. Enc. d'Arte antica* II. (Rome, 1959), 273-5.

Martini, R., 'Osservazioni su contromarche ed erosioni su assi di Caligola', *RIN* 82 (1980), 53-83

Massaro, V. & Montgomery, I., 'Gaius- Mad, Bad, Ill or All Three?' *Latomus* 37 (1978), 894-909

Massaro, V. & Montogmery, I., 'Gaius (Caligula) doth murder sleep', *Latomus* 38 (1979), 699-700

McDermott, W.C., 'Saint Jerome and Domitius Afer', *VChr* 34 (1980), 19-23

Morgan, M.G., 'Caligula's illness again', *CW* 66 (1973), 327-29

Morgan, M.G. 'Once again Caligula's illness', *CW* 70 (1977), 452-3

Moss, G.C., 'The Mentality and Personality of the Julio-Claudian Emperors', *Medical History* 7 (1963), 165-75

Musurillo, H., *The Acts of the Pagan Martyrs* (Oxford 1954)

Nagy, T., 'Die Regierungsjahre des C. Caesar mit besonderer Rücksicht auf Illyricum', *AAntHung* 29 (1981), 337-62

Newbold, R.F., 'The Spectacles as an issue between Gaius and the senate', *PACA* 13 (1975), 30-5

Nicols, J., 'The chronology and significance of the M. Agrippa asses', *ANSMusN* 19 (1974), 65-86

Nikliborc, A., 'Temat Kaliguli w Teatrze Francuskim', *Meander* 26 (1971), 66-76

Nony, D., 'Quelques as d'imitation de Caligula trouvés à Bordeaux', *Trésors monétaires 3, 15-16*

Nottbohm, G., 'Caligula oder Saloninus', Festschrift Bernhard Schweitzer (Stuttgart, 1954), 364-66

Onofrio, Cesare d', Gli Obelischi di Roma (Rome, 1965)

Parker, E.R., 'The education of heirs in the Julio-Claudian family', AJP 67 (1946), 29-50

Passerini, A., Caligola e Claudio (Rome 1941)

Pflaum, H.G., A propos de la date de création de la province de Numidie', Libyca 5 (1957), 61-75

Pflaum, H.G., 'Légats impériaux à l'intérieur de provinces sénatoriales', Hommages à Albert Grenier (Coll. Latomus 58) (Brussels,1962) 1232-42

Phillips, E.J., 'The emperor Gaius' abortive invasion of Britain', Historia 19 (1970), 369-74

Pollini, J., 'A pre-principate portrait of Gaius (Caligula)', JWAG 40 (1982), 1-12

Poulsen, V., 'Portraits of Caligula', AArch 29 (1958), 175-90

Quidde, L., Caligula, Eine Studie der römische Casarenwahnsinn (Leipzig, 1894³)

Rea, J.R., 'Calendar of Gaius', Oxyrynchus Papyri 55 (1988), 10-14

Richard, J.C., 'Un aureus de Caligula découvert à Saint-Columban- des-Villards (Savoie)', CahNum 19 (1982), 155-7

Richard, J.C., 'A propos de l'aureus de Caligula découvert à Saint-Columban-des Villards (Savoie)', CahNum 19 (1982), 188-9

Richmond, O.L., 'The Temples of Apollo and Divus Augustus on Coins': Essays and Studies Presented to William Ridgeway (Cambridge, 1913), 198-212

Ritter, H.W., 'Adlocutio und corona civica unter Caligula und Tiberius', JNG 21 (1971), 81-96

Rizzo, G.E. & Bartoli A., Monumenti della pittura antica scoperti in Italia. III. La pittura elenistico-romana, Roma 2: Le pitture dell'aula isiaca di Caligola (Palatino) (Rome, 1938)

Robert, L., 'Le culte de Caligula à Milet et la province d'Asie', Hellenica 7 (1949), 206-38

Rogers, R.S., 'The Roman Emperors as Heirs and Legatees', TAPA 78 (1947), 140-58

Romanelli, P., Storia delle province romane dell' Africa (Rome, 1959)

Rosborough, R.R., An Epigraphic Commentary on Suetonius' Life of Gaius Caligula (Philadelphia, 1920)

Rossi, L., 'Le insegne militari nella monetazione imperiale romana da Augusto a Commodo', RIN 67 (1965), 41-81

Rossi, L., 'La guardia pretoriana e germanica nella monetazione giulio-claudia. Elementi storici ed archeologici per una nuova interpretazione', RIN 69 (1967), 15-38

Rossi, R.F., 'Tracce di lotta politica nel Senato di Caligola', RFIC 99 (1971), 164-171

Roullet, A., *The Egyptian and Egyptianizing Monuments of Imperial Rome* (Leiden, 1972)

Sachs, H., *Caligula* (Berlin 1930). Trans. H. Singer (London, 1931)

Saletti, C., 'Tre ritratti imperiali da Luni. Tiberio, Livia, Caligola', *Athenaeum* 51 (1973), 34-48

Sandison, A.T., 'The Madness of the Emperor Caligula', *Medical History* 2 (1958), 202-209

Savio, A., 'Note su alcune monete di Gaio-Caligula', *NAC* (1973), 107-19

Schäfer, E., 'Der Mythos von den Cesaren, z.B. Caligula', *AU* 23.6 (1980), 72-89

Scheid, J., *Les Frères Arvales. Recruitement et origine sociale sous les empereurs julio-claudiens* (Paris, 1975)

Scheider, K. Th. *Zusammensetzung des römischen Senates von Tiberius bis Nero* (Diss. Zurich, 1942)

Schwartz, J., 'Note sur le monnayage sénatorial entre 37 et 42 P.C.', *RN* (1951), 37-41

Schwartz, J., 'Préfets d'Égypte sous Tibère et Caligula', *ZPE* 48 (1982), 189-192

Scott, K., 'Notes on the Destruction of Two Roman Villas', *AJP* 60 (1939), 459-62

Scott, K., Greek and Roman Honorific Months, *YClS* 2 (1931), 201-78

Siber, H., 'Die Wahlreform des Tiberius', *Festschrift Paul Koschaker* I (1939), 171-217

Sijpesteijn, P.J., 'The Legationes ad Gaium', *Journ. Jew St.* 15 (1964), 87-96

Simpson, C.J., 'The cult of the emperor Gaius', *Latomus* 90 (1981), 489-511

Smallwood, E.M., 'The chronology of Gaius' attempt to desecrate the temple', *Latomus* 16 (1957), 3-17

Speidel, M.P., 'Germani corporis custodes', *Germania* 62 (1984), 31-45

Steidle, W., *Sueton und die Antike Biographie* (Munich, 1951: Zetemata 1)

Stroux, J., 'Vier Zeugnisse zur romischen Literaturgeschichte der Kaiserzeit. II. Caligulas Urteil uber den Stil Senecas', *Philologus* 86 (1931), 338-68

Stuart, M. , 'How were Imperial Portraits Distributed throughout the Empire?', *AJA* 43 (1939), 601-17

Stylow, A.U., 'Die Quadranten des Caligula als Propaganda Munzen', *Chiron* 1 (1971), 285-90

Sutherland, H.C.V. *Coinage in Roman Imperial Policy 31 B.C.–A.D. 68* (London, 1951)

Sutherland, H.C.V., 'The mints of Lugdunum and Rome under Gaius: an unsolved problem', *NAC* 10 (1981), 297-9

Swain, J.W., 'Gamaliel's speech and Caligula's statue', *HThR* 37 (1944), 341-9

Swan, M., 'Josephus *AJ* XIX, 251-252. Opposition to Gaius and Claudius', *AJP* 91 (1970), 149-64

Szaivert, W., *Die Münzprägung der Kaiser Tiberius und Caius* (Caligula) 14/41 (Vienna, 1984)

Tamm, B., 'Ist der Castortempel das vestibulum zu dem Palast des Caligula gewesen' *Eranos* 62 (1964), 146-69

Tarradell, M., 'Nuevos datos sobre la guerra de los Romanos contra Aedemon', *I Congreso Arqueologico del Marruecos Espan ol* (Tetuan, 1954)

Tarradell, M., *Marruecos Punico* (Tetuan, 1960)

Taylor, A., 'An Allusion to a Riddle in Suetonius', *AJP* 66 (1945), 408-10

Testaguzza, O., 'Port of Rome', *Archaeology* 17 (1964). 173-9

Testaguzza, O., *Portus* (Rome, 1970)

Thiers, F.-P., 'Rapport sur les Fouilles de Castel-Roussillon en 1911', *Bulletin Archéologique* (1912), 76-86

Townend, G.B., 'The Circus of Nero and the Vatican Excavations' *AJA* 62 (1958), 216-8

Townend, G.B., 'Traces in Dio Cassius of Cluvius, Aufidius, and Pliny', *Hermes* 89 (1961), 227-48

Townend, G..B., The Sources of the Greek in Suetonius', *Hermes* 88 (1980), 98-120

Toynbee, J.M.C., 'The Shrine of St. Peter and its Setting', *JRS* 43 (1953), 8-12

Trillmich, W. Zur Münzprägung des Caligula von Caesaraugusta (Zaragoza)', *MDAI (M)* 14 (1973), 151-73

Venturini, L., *Caligola* (Milan, 1906)

Visscher, F. De, 'L'amphithéâtre d'Alba Fucens et son fondateur Q. Naevius Macro, préfet du prétoire de Tibère', *RAL* Ser. 8, 12 (1957), 39-49

Visscher, F. De, 'La politique dynastique sous le règne de Tibère', *Synteleia V. Arangio-Ruiz* (Naples, 1964), 54-65

Visscher, F. De, 'Macro, préfet des vigiles et ses cohortes contre la tyrannie de Séjan', *Mélanges d'archéologie et d'histoire offerts à A. Piganiol* (Paris, 1966) 761-68.

Vogel-Weidemann U., *Die Statthalter von Africa und Asia in den Jahren 14-68 n.* Chr. (Bonn, 1982)

Winter, P., 'Simeon der Gerechte und Caius Caligula', *Judaica* 12 (1956), 129-32

Wirszubski, C., *Libertas as a Political Idea at Rome during the Late Republic and Early Principate* (Cambridge, 1950)

Wiseman, T.P., 'Reading the City: History, Poetry, and the Topography of Rome', *JACT* 2 (1987), 3-6

INDEX

Proper names are abbreviated where possible, and their alphabetical order is based on common usage; unfamiliar names are arranged by *nomen*. Buildings and sites are listed geographically. Items in the footnotes already indexed through the text are not listed separately; reference to independent footnote material is by chapter and note, not page. Unamplified citations of literary sources are not indexed.

Accius 93
Acta Alexandrinorum 79
Actium, Battle of; 96, 218, 219; VI.26
Adminius 137-8
Aedemon 118, 120
Aelius Gallus 26, 66
Aemilia Lepida (dr. of Julia) 82
Aemilia Lepida (wife of Drusus) 26, 84;
    V.38
Aemlius Regulus 161
Afer, Domitius 20, 21, 48, 84, 97-8, 150,
    231, 236-7, 253
Afranius Potitus 73
Agrippa, 'Herod' 34-7, 50, 63, 78,
    79-80, 95, 117, 133, 154, 174, 182-3,
    190-1, 222, 223, 240, 248
Agrippa, Marcus 2, 4, 141, 192, 217, 218,
    250
Agrippa Postumus 4, 5
Agrippina (mother of Caligula) 2,
    4-24, 26, 29, 31-2, 39, 46, 58, 60-1, 80,
    85, 97, 167, 185, 217, 232, 233, 248,
    250
Agrippina (sister of Caligula) 6, 24, 33,
    62-3, 85, 88, 106-7, 109-10, 226; V.27
Alcyon 165
Alexandria 7, 14, 36, 52, 55, 74, 80,
    84-6, 141, 154, 163, 184-7, 189, 191-2,
    220
Alfidius, M. 219
Amminus *see* Adminius
Adrocles 44
Anicius Cerialis 156-7
Annius Pollio 108; VI.80
Anteius 111, 166

Antiochus III 12, 14
Antiochus IV 63, 117, 133, 222
Antiochus of Seleucia 157
Antipas, Herod 154, 182-3, 189
Antium 7, 32
Antonia 2, 24, 26, 29, 34, 36-7, 50,
    61-2, 85, 88, 162, 203, 221, 219
Antonia (dr. of Claudius) 121, 237
Anthony, Marc 1-3, 24, 33, 116, 118,
    159, 205, 217-18, 220; IV.13
Apelles 46, 84, 146, 189, 217
Aphrodisius V.44
Apion 187
Apollonius of Tyana 163, X.38
Aponius Saturninus 226
Appius Silanus, C. 29, 100, 108, 167, 235
Apronius, L. 24, 30, 91, 101, 129-30
Apronius, Caesianus L. 91, 105, 236
Aquila 165
Archelaus of Cappedocia 12, 14; XIV.36
Aretas 14, 183
Armenia 12, 14
Arruntius, L. 40-41, 58, 82, 99
Arruntius Camillus, L. 236
Arruntius, Paulus 164
Artabanus 63, 64, 154, 211
Arval Record 53, 61, 68, 69-71, 86, 87,
    89, 90, 104, 108-9, 111, 148, 167, 218,
    252; X.1
Asiaticus, Valerius 24, 44, 81, 162, 164,
    174-5, 223
Asinius Celer 81
Asinius Gallus 20, 26, 32, 81
Asinius Pollio 29, 66
Assos 13, 47, 54-5, 62, 72

Atanius Secundus 73; XIV.84
Atellan farce 67
Atrebates 127
Aufidius Lurco 219
Augustus 6-7, 8, 11, 40, 45, 51, 54, 55-6,
    65, 67, 69, 76-7, 87, 89, 91, 115-16,
    118, 126, 127, 133, 138, 140, 141, 147,
    169, 172, 175, 205, 213, 218-20, 230-
    33, 238, 245, 247, 251, II.71
Aurelius Victor IX.38; XIII.33
Ausonius X.35

Betilienus Bassus 157
Betilienus Capito 160
Bocchus of Mauretania 115
Boethius X.20
Boudicca VIII.50
Boulogne: Lighthouse 193

Caecilius, L. 225
Caesar Julius 45, 46, 53, 61, 72, 94, 115,
    126-7, 129, 141, 147, 150, 155, 174,
    201, 220, 231, 246; VIII.56; XIV.70
Caesonia 44, 94-5, 109-10, 133, 138, 146,
    160, 166-7, 214, 239-40; VI.22
Caligula:
    accession 8, 71
    African command 119-23
    Agrippa, Herod 34-7, 63, 80, 167, 189,
        190
    Agrippa, M. 217-218
    Antonia 24, 61-2, 221
    Antony, Marc 218-19
    appearance 42-3
    arrogance 43, 240–41
    Augustus 52, 54, 56, 68, 69-70, 87,
        210, 218, 238
    birth 6; I.8
    birthday 69, 96, 154, 187
    Britain 102-3, 105, 117, 125-9, 135-9
    citizenship 223
    Claudius 68, 219
    client kings 37, 63, 154, 183, 221-3
    communications 193-5, 200-1
    consulships 68-9, 74, 86, 91, 253
    cruelty viii-ix, 92, 99, 156-7, 230, 232,
        235, 239-41
    damnatio memoriae 177-80
    divinity 145-53
    dress 43; IX.57
    drink 44
    Egypt and Orient 96, 219-21
    elections 230-31

Ennia 79
freedmen 84-5, 98, 160, 176-7, 188
Gaetulicus 105-6
gambling 43, 132, 232
Gemellus 39, 67, 74-5
genius 145, 151-2, 155
Germanicus legend 15, 27, 29, 39, 52,
    55, 64, 241
German guard 103, 159, 166, 171
Germany 102-5, 125, 129-35, 137, 159,
    213
gladiators 44-5
grain and water supply 193-4, 212
health 213
horse-racing 45, 81
humour 77, 99, 214-16, 240-41
illness 71, 73-4
intellectual and literary skills 13, 24,
    30, 47-9
Isis 117-18
Jews 143, 147, 150, 154, 183-91, 193,
    216
Jupiter 96, 146-9, 214
Lepidus 81-2, 105, 107-11
Livia 24, 47, 219
Lyons 132-3, 139
madness 214-15
Macro 34, 39-41, 50-55, 58, 61,
    78-80
maiestas 64-7, 93, 240
minor offices 27, 31
mother and brothers 30-31, 60, 61
names and titles 7, 56-8, 70, 86, 134,
    138, 145
nervous disposition 213
philosophers 149-50, 157-8, 225
plots viii, 65, 74-6, 76, 78-80, 90, 92,
    94, 99-101, 104-7, 109-113, 118,
    132, 155-67, 235, 249
popularity in provinces 13, 54-5, 59,
    143, 223-4
powers 56, 62
Praetorians 52-3, 60, 159-60, 177
provincial governors 64, 89-90,
    99-100, 101-3, 109-11, 119-23, 150,
    161, 183, 189-90, 223, 236-6
Ptolemy 117-118
Roman religion 145
Sejanus 93
senate 50, 52, 54-8, 60, 72, 91-2, 94,
    139, 155, 158-9, 229, 234-41
senators (*see also* provincial governors
    76, 81, 91, 97-8, 108, 112-13, 150,

156-9, 161-2, 235-8
sex 31, 44, 85
sisters 24, 44, 62-3, 81-2, 85-9,
    105-10, 226
stage 31, 46
statues 70, 145, 158, 178, 253-4
succession 38-41, 51-2
Temple at Jerusalem 85, 188, 215, 240
Temple at Rome 145
Temple at Miletus 143-4
Tiberius 29-31, 37-41, 51, 59, 61,
    68-9, 89, 93
triumph 138, 154
wives 44, 77, 89, 94-5, 133, 166-7, 214
youth (Germany) 7-9, 43
youth (East) 12-16
youth (Rome) 7, 12, 16, 21-2
youth (Capri) 27, 30-41, 47, 81
Callistus 44, 84, 98, 150, 157, 160,
    176-7
Canus, Julius 149, 157-8
Canninefates 130, 136
Caratacus 128
Carrinas Secundus 99
Cassius Chaerea 9, 158, 161, 164-5, 174,
    176, 192
Cassius Longinus, C. 162-3, 236, 237
Cassius Longinus, L. 33-4, 81, 162
Cassius Severus 67
Catonius Iustus 176
Catulus, Q. 96
Catuvellauni 127-9
Cicero 48, 70, 72, 140-41, 147, 205; IV.13
Cincinnatus 238
Claudia Pulchra 20-21, 97
Claudia (dr. of Nero) 87
Claudius 2, 16, 36-7, 52, 54, 60, 64-5, 68,
    75, 79, 85, 87, 95, 99, 103, 107, 111,
    112, 119-20, 126, 129, 133-4, 139, 146,
    148, 151, 160, 164, 172-80, 190, 195,
    199, 217, 218, 221, 223, 227-8, 234,
    236, 237; IV.35
Claudius Etruscus 104; V.46
Claudius Nero, Ti. 2
Claudius, Ti. (freedman) 84
Clemens 161, 166, V.31
Clementia 32, 93
Cleopatra Selene 116, 118
Cluvius Rufus 164, 168-9
Cocceius Nerva 30, 196
Collegia 230
Corbulo (father) 97, 193
Corbulo (son) 97

Cornelia Orestina see Livia Orestilla
Corinth (Isthmus) 193, 212
Corona Civica 70-71, 248
Cotys 223
Cremutius Cordus 66-7
Cunobelinus 128, 137; VIII.48

Damnatio memoriae 172, 177
Demetrius the Cynic 225
Dexter 106-7
Didius Gallus 97-8
Dio 9, 26-7, 34, 38-9, 41, 43, 46, 51-2, 55,
    59, 62, 65, 68, 70, 73, 74-9, 81, 86, 91-
    101, 104-7, 112, 117,
    119-22, 124, 129-35, 138, 141, 143,
    146-50, 153, 155, 157, 160-63, 169,
    173, 193, 196, 202, 207, 211-12, 215,
    218, 226, 228, 230-34, 237; II.44, 62,
    66; IV.28, 38, 45, 50-51, 71, 77; V.58,
    62, 73; VI.3, 11, 61; VIII.18; X.24, 32;
    XI.3; XIV.47, 56, 70, 71
Domitian 167
Domitius Ahenobarbus 33, 82, 108, 111,
    227
Drusilla 6, 24, 33, 43, 46, 62-3, 81, 85, 87-
    9, 94, 109-10, 162, 220; XIV.39
Drusilla (daughter) 96, 166
Drusus (brother of Caligula) 6, 17-18, 21,
    26-7, 29, 31-2, 61-2, 81; V.38
Drusus (father of Germanicus) 2-3, 125
Drusus (son of Tiberius) 5, 8, 11-13, 16,
    18, 36

Elate V.44
engyesis V.80
Ennia 34, 44, 79
Etnosus 148
Eutropius 131
Eutychus 37

Fadius Celer 119
Flaccus 23, 39, 66, 78, 80, 90, 92, 109,
    110, 111, 185-7, 191, 227; V.18

Gabinius Secundus 129
Gaetulicus 6, 26, 30, 101-6, 111, 118, 130-
    33, 155
Gaius Caesar 4-5, 17, 67, 91; VI.58
Galba 68, 104-5, 120, 126, 129-31, 135,
    137, 168, 175, 206, 223, 240
Gemellus 17, 26, 37-9, 51-2, 66, 67,
    74-8, 81, 105; II.72; IV.31
Genius 142-3, 151-2, 155

German Guard 103, 159, 166
Germanicus 2-3, 5-6, 8, 10, 17, 47, 55, 58, 61, 125, 141, 184, 241, 248, 249, 251
Germany 3, 7-11, 125, 129-35, 137, 159
Graecinus Laco 28
Graecinus, Julius 76, 158, 235
Grand Camée 12-13
Gratus 173

Helicon 84, 189, 216
Herennius Capito 36, 189
Herod the Great 24, 34, 182
Herodias 154, 183; XI.I
Homer 48, 164, 168, 214, 219, 222
Homilos 85
Hosidius Geta 119, 121

Incitatus 45, 217, 219
Isidorus 79, 90, 185-7
Isis 117-8, 184, 220-1

Jamnia 143, 188, 191
Josephus 26, 36, 38, 47, 50, 59, 62, 64, 98, 111, 155-6, 160-62, 164-6, 168-76, 184, 188, 190, 206, 212, 214, 228-30, 239; IV.64; X.7, 9, 24; XI.5, 8, 12, 18
Juba I 115
Juba II 24, 116
Julia the Elder 2, 4, 5
Julia the Younger 4, 5, 82; V.39
Julia (daughter of Drusus) 17, 34
Julius Rusticus 23
Julius Sacerdos 132
Junia Claudia 32, 34
Junius Priscus 99
Jupiter Latiaris 147
Juvenal 214

Labienus, T. 66-7
Laecanius Bassus, C. VIII.31
Lampon 79, 90, 187
Lepidus, Marcus 44, 81-2, 85-6, 90, 106-111, 155, 235, 237, 249
Liburnian galleys 201
Licinius Frugi, M 120
Livia 2, 6, 8, 19, 21-3, 36, 47, 60, 86-8, 141, 169, 216, 219, 225-6, V.71
Livia Orestilla 77
Livilla (sister of Caligula) 6, 13, 21, 24, 26, 33, 62-3, 85, 88, 106, 109-10, 112, 118, 226, 248; V.27
Livilla (sister of Germanicus) 2, 11, 18, 19, 29, 38

Livius Geminus 87
Livy 48
Lollia Paulina 89, 94-5
Lucanius Latiaris 22
Lucilius 112-13
Lucius Caesar 4, 5, 67, 91; V.58
Lupus 166-7
Lyons 94, 104, 132-3, 139, 141, 183, 247; VI.13
Licinius 63

Machaon 77
Macro 28-9, 34, 37-41, 50-55, 58, 61, 74, 78, 80, 90, 92, 155, 185-6, 239
Maenius Bassus 122-3
maiestas 64-5, 86, 93
Malalas, John 189, 195; XII.26-7
Mamercus Scaurus 29, 66, 108
Marcellus, procurator 188
Marcia 67
Marius 41, 70
Marcius Barea, Q. 120
Marsyas 50
Martial 101
Memmius Regulus 28, 89-90, 92, 105, 163, 168, 237
Messalinus, M. Cotta 29, 31, 44
Mevania 103-5, 107
Miletus (Temple of Caligula) 143-4
Mithridates of Armenia 64, 117
Mithridates of Bosporus 222
Mnester 44, 46, 163, 232

Namatianus 109
Naples (Bridge over Bay) 98, 129, 145, 195, 211-12, 248
Nemi (ships) 43, 201-2
Nemi (shrine of Diana) 145, 201
Nero (brother of Caligula) 6, 17-8, 20-3, 27, 32, 60-62, 232; II.43
Nero, emperor 6-7, 52, 54, 68, 85, 108-110, 147-9, 157, 167-8, 177-9, 196, 199, 223-4, 227; VI.21
Nonius Asprenas 162, 164, 166
Nonius Quintilianus 81
Noricum 224
Norbanus Balbus 162, 166
numen 142
Nymphidia 44, 83

Octavian see Augustus
Olympia, status of Jupiter 163
Orosius 137

Ostia (harbour) 195, 201
ovation *see* triumph
Ovid 232

Paconianus, Sextius 27, 29
Papinius, Sex. 156, 161
Papinius, tribune 161
Parthia 12, 63, 72
Passienus Crispus 31, 85
Pastor 156
pater patriae 70, 248
Persius 134, 138, 151
Petronius 100, 189-90, 223, 236-7, 240;
   XII.26
Philo 29, 31, 36, 38-9, 41, 51, 57, 61, 67,
   73-80, 84-5, 99, 109-11, 143, 145, 149,
   154, 184-8, 190, 193, 196,
   214-16, 227, 234, 239; II.68; III.7;
   V.27; XII.21, 30; XIV.46
Philopator II 12, 14
Piso, C. Calpurnius 77
Piso, Cn. Calpurnius 13-6
Piso, L. Calpurnius 50, 119, 121-2, 236
Plancina 14, 16
Pliny the Elder 6, 22, 42-3, 66, 73, 89, 95,
   97, 101, 119, 199, 201, 212, 221, 226
Pliny the Younger 199
Plato 48
Plautius, Aulus 101
Plutarch 239
Polemo I 24
Polemo II 24, 223
Pontius Pilate 188
Pompeius, kinsman X.24
Pompeius Magnus, Cn. 121, 237-8
Pompeius Pennus 150, 158; X.24
Pomponius, conspirator 158
Pomponius Secundus, P. 66, 164, 236
Pomponius Secundus, Q. 176, IV.71;
   X.24
Popilius Heracla 198
Praetorians 17, 28, 52, 103, 105, 159, 167,
   172, 175-7, 241
Proculus, Acerronius 51
Proculus, victim 235
proskynesis 150
Protogenes 85, 158, 176
providentia 68
Ptolemy 46, 116-18, 121, 135
Pylaemenes XIV.59

Quinctilius Varus 97
Quintilia 158, 239

Quintilian IX.41

radiate crown 149, 250
Raetia 224
Rectus 157; X.39
Rhoemetacles 24, 223
Rhegium (harbour) 212
Rome:
   Aqueducts 178, 194
   Ara Pacis 69
   Aula Isiaca 173, 221
   Bridge to Capitoline 209
   Capitoline Residence 147, 210
   Esquiline estate 193, 203
   Gaianum 45, 196; IV.25
   Golden House of Nero 202
   Horrea Agrippina 208-9
   Saepta 196
   Temple of Apollo 171, 205; XIII.65
   Temple of Augustus 46, 69, 210-11,
     218
   Temple of Castor 207, 209-10
   Theatre of Pompey 178, 196
   Tullianum 195
   Vatican circus 196-201
   Vatican gardens 188, 196, 203
   Vatican obelisk 198-201
Romulus 77
Rubellius Blandus 34, 122
Rufrius Pollio 176

Sabinus, T. 21, 22, 29
Sabinus, Calvisius 100-101, 105, 108
Sabinus, Praetorian 162, 165, 176
Sabinius, German guard 166
Salii 145, 237-8
Salus 46, 152; VI.24; IX.67
Sanquinius Maximus 92, 105
Samos, Palace of Polycrates 201
Saturninus 174
Scribonianus, Camillus 99
Scribonius Largus 140
Scribonius Proculus 152, 158
Sejanus 3, 17-24, 26, 28-30, 38, 40, 62, 78,
   89-91, 93, 97, 105, 108, 112, 151, 154,
   184, 235; IX.14
Seneca Elder vii, 41; II.17
Seneca (as source) 42-3, 67, 85, 117, 148-
   9, 156-8, 162, 196, 212, 214, 227, 236,
   238; IV.46; V.19, 62; VI.7; IX.57;
   X.24
Seneca (as courtier) 49, 112-3
Septicius Pica 224

Servilius Nonianus 169, 170
Sextus Pompeius 227
Saturnalia 229-30
Silenus, D. Junius Torquatus 145, 238
Silanus, M. Junius (father in law) 32, 74, 76, 78, 234
Silanus, M. Junius governor of Africa 119, 122
Silanus, M. Junius consul 46; V.16
Sohaemus 222
sphintriae 31, 44
Suetonius 5-7, 15, 21, 26-7, 30, 34, 38, 41-3, 46, 56, 59, 62, 64, 70-1, 73-5, 79, 81-2, 93-7, 104, 107, 111, 118, 124, 133-8, 146-8, 158, 160, 162-3, 165, 169-70, 173, 175, 184, 193, 207, 211, 212-14, 217, 227-9, 231, 233-4, 239; I.7, 36; II.32, 62-3; III.7; IV.28, 61-2, 77; V.20; VI.51; VIII.18; X.7, 9, 17, 24, 35, 63; XI.18; XIV.47, 52, 55, 88
Suetonius Paulinus 119, 121
Syracuse, city walls 195

Tacfarinas 116, 118
Tacitus 5-7, 10-11, 13-14, 19, 21-3, 31-2, 34, 38-9, 41, 48, 66, 85, 90, 95, 97, 101, 109, 123, 125, 130, 132, 137, 155, 158, 160, 168, 176, 184, 188, 190, 206, 214; I.24; II.3, 15, 62-3; IV.64; V.31; X.35; XI.5; XII.13
Tasciovanus 127-8
Terentius Culleo, Q. VIII.31
Theophilus 134
Thespiae, Cupid of 192
Tiberius 2, 4-6, 8-11, 16-17, 19-23, 26-31, 36-41, 46-7, 50, 53, 56, 58, 60, 65, 68, 76, 84, 89, 94, 102, 105, 118, 126, 141-2, 145, 150-1, 172, 175, 177,

179, 206, 219-20, 226-7, 229, 231, 233, 238-9, 247; VI.7
Tigellinus 112
Timidius 158
Titius Rufus 99
Togodumnus 128
Trebellius Maximus 174
Trebonius, A. 224
Trimalchio 225; IX.69
triumph 133, 138, 154; VI.2
Turannius, C. 194

Ummidius Quadratus 54, 100, 237

Valerius Catullus 44
Valerius Severus, M. 118-9
Vegetius 74, 136
Velleius Paterculus 21, 34, 101
Vergil 48, 102, 151
Vergilius Capito 144
Verica 128, 137
Vespasian 106, 120, 134, 233; VI.73
Vibius Rufus 196
vigiles 28
Vinicianus 29, 66, 108, 111, 161-2, 164, 168, 174-5, 235, 237; X.10
Vinicius 33, 82, 108-10, 112, 164, 174-5; VI.80
Vinius, T. 101
Vistilius, Sex. 29, 31, 44
Vitellius, A. emperor 24, 30, 45, 81, 100, 168, 180, 237
Vitellius, L. 24, 53, 63-4, 100, 150, 153, 183, 188, 236
Vitrasius Pollio 187; XII.20
Volusius Saturninus 99

Zeno of Armenia 14